Economic Doctrines of

KNUT WICKSELL

PUBLICATIONS OF THE INSTITUTE OF BUSINESS AND
ECONOMIC RESEARCH UNIVERSITY OF CALIFORNIA

Economic Doctrines of

KNUT WICKSELL

by CARL G. UHR

UNIVERSITY OF CALIFORNIA PRESS

BERKELEY and LOS ANGELES · 1962

UNIVERSITY OF CALIFORNIA PRESS
BERKELEY AND LOS ANGELES, CALIFORNIA
CAMBRIDGE UNIVERSITY PRESS, LONDON, ENGLAND
© 1960 BY THE REGENTS OF THE UNIVERSITY OF CALIFORNIA
SECOND PRINTING, 1962
LIBRARY OF CONGRESS CATALOG CARD NUMBER: 60-13019
MANUFACTURED IN THE UNITED STATES OF AMERICA

To the memory of
PROFESSOR LEO ROGIN,
inspiring teacher and friend

PREFACE

Although Knut Wicksell's work has received increasing attention in economic literature in recent years, thus far no systematic account and evaluation of his scientific contributions as a whole has appeared. This study is intended to fill that gap. It was written with the conviction that there is still much to be learned from the way he formulated and struggled with fundamental economic problems. His major works, all of which have now been translated into English, speak for themselves. Still they do not reveal the background and context of doctrinal history from which they sprang. Neither do they show the further development in several branches of economic theory which Wicksell's ideas stimulated in the minds of his followers in Sweden and, not least, among British and Austrian economists who had no direct contact with him. It is therefore hoped that the present study will prove helpful to students of the history of economic thought, monetary theory, capital theory, and public finance.

This book is an outgrowth of a doctoral dissertation begun at the suggestion of the late Professor Leo Rogin (1893-1947) and completed under the guidance of Professor William J. Fellner in 1950. Since then it has been completely rewritten and revised to incorporate new materials which have appeared in the interim, to achieve more effective organization of its contents, and to make changes in the exposition which suggested themselves on further reflection.

In writing the present work I have had generous assistance and advice from several persons. The late Professor Emil Sommarin, Lund University, Sweden, supplied me with valuable biographic information concerning Wicksell's life and career as well as with many of his tracts, which had long since disappeared from print. The late Professor Erik Lindahl, University of Uppsala, gave me further help along these lines, and read my dissertation in its final form. He also suggested the main lines of its revision, which I have carried out here.

During my stay in Sweden in the spring and summer of 1958, considerable portions of the present manuscript were read by Professor

Erik Lundberg, Stockholm University, and Professor Karl-Gustav Landgren, University of Uppsala, both of whom gave me helpful comments and criticisms.

Professor Frank L. Kidner's encouragement and support are in a very material sense responsible for my having been able to complete the present study. As director of the Bureau (now Institute) of Business and Economic Research, University of California, Berkeley, he not only extended me secretarial aid over a long period of time to get the present manuscript completed, but, through the resources available to this Bureau, he also arranged financial assistance for the publication of this study. Professor Robert A. Gordon, University of California, Berkeley, made suggestions which proved invaluable in reducing this work to a manageable size.

To my wife, Miriam, I owe a considerable debt of gratitude. She has read several versions of the manuscript and has invariably suggested improvements in its exposition.

My thanks are expressed also to a number of persons and publishers for permission to quote copyrighted materials, as follows: to George Allen and Unwin, Ltd., publishers of *Studies in the Theory of Money and Capital* (London, 1939; New York: Rinehart and Company, Inc., 1939), by E. Lindahl, also of *Value, Capital and Rent* (London, 1954; New York: Rinehart and Company, Inc., 1954), by Knut Wicksell; to G. K. Eastham, editor of *Economic Essays in Commemoration of the Dundee School of Economics* (Dundee, Scotland, 1955), and Duncan Black, author of "Wicksell's Principle in the Distribution of Taxation" in that volume; to William Hodge and Company, Ltd., publishers of *Monetary Equilibrium* (London, 1939), by Gunnar Myrdal; to R. F. Kahn, translator, and Macmillan and Company, Ltd., publishers on behalf of the Royal Economic Society of *Interest and Prices* (London, 1936), by Knut Wicksell; to the late E. Lindahl, author of *Die Gerechtigkeit der Besteuerung* (Lund, Sweden, 1919); to Macmillan and Company, Ltd., publishers of *A Treatise on Money*, Vol. I (London, 1930; New York: Harcourt, Brace and Company, 1930), by J. M. Keynes; to The Macmillan Company, publishers of *Lectures on Political Economy*, Vol. II (New York, 1935; London: Routledge and Kegan Paul, Ltd., 1935), by Knut Wicksell; to Routledge and Kegan Paul, Ltd., publishers of *Lectures on Political Economy*, Vol. I (London, 1936), by Knut Wicksell, also of *The Pure Theory of Capital* (London, 1941; Chicago: University of Chicago Press, 1941), by F. A. von Hayek; and to Yale University Press, publishers of *The Theory of Money and Credit* (New Haven, 1953), by L. von Mises.

Riverside, California   CARL G. UHR

NOTE ON TRANSLATION

Knut Wicksell's major works, five books, were originally published in German, as were also some of his articles. His several tracts and pamphlets as well as most of his scientific articles, numbering over 150 items, were published in Swedish only.

By now all of his books have been translated into English. Wherever possible in quoting passages or making references in the text to these works, I have made use of the available English translations.

All quotations from the writings of Wicksell and other authors available only in Swedish have been translated by me. The same holds for quotations from sources available only in German or in French, including quotations from Wicksell's *Finanztheoretische Untersuchungen*.

The titles of references, as distinct from quotations, published in German or French have not been translated. However, the titles of all references to Swedish sources have been translated. The practice followed both in the text and in the bibliography has been first to state the title and source in Swedish, which is then followed immediately by an English translation of the title alone, stated in parenthesis.

In several places in the text I have found it necessary to present some of Wicksell's mathematical proofs for a number of theories. I have done this with one change in the notation used in his works. In this I have followed the precedent established by G. J. Stigler in his *Production and Distribution Theories*, New York, 1941. In his chapter on Wicksell in that work, Stigler changed the symbol "l" used by Wicksell to represent "wages" in all his books, to "w." This symbol is easier for English-speaking readers to associate with what it represents. I have applied the same change throughout.

C. G. U.

CONTENTS

of the demonstrated effect; Technical issues raised by the
Wicksell effect; Wicksell's structural theory of capital formation and his approach to the problem of business cycles; Åkerman's and von Hayek's development of Wicksell's capital
structure analysis; The Wicksell effect versus "Forced Saving"
or versus von Hayek's "Ricardo effect"; Eclipse of capital structure analysis and capital shortage hypotheses of business cycles

FIGURES

TABLES

CHAPTER I

Sketch of Wicksell's Life

Knut Wicksell's significance as one of the foremost economic theoreticians of his generation has only recently begun to be appreciated in the English-speaking world, and then mainly on the basis of his monetary writings. Yet the latter comprise but one part, although a large part, of his scientific activity. They reveal him only in his main role as an ingenious academician. They do not show that he was also an indefatigable social reformer who influenced many phases of social and economic development in Sweden during the first quarter of the twentieth century. In addition he was a philosophical rationalist and a political radical who engaged in politics entirely as an individual in complete independence of existing political parties and organizations.

As one might expect, Wicksell's nonacademic interests and activities cost him dearly at various junctures in his life. With his gifts of extraordinary intellect, persuasiveness, witty manner of speech and writing, and his uncompromising habit of speaking the truth as he saw it regardless of personal consequences and of the offense it might give, it was inevitable that he frequently came into conflict with those elements in his society which control power and mold public opinion. This in turn retarded his professional career and jeopardized its continuation after its belated start.

Career until Middle Age

Johan Gustav Knut Wicksell was born on December 20, 1851, in Stockholm, as the fifth and youngest child of a Swedish middle-class family. He was a contemporary of Böhm-Bawerk, Pareto, and von Wieser; he was only slightly younger than Léon Walras. When he died in his seventy-fifth year on May 3, 1926, he had survived Walras by sixteen years, Böhm-Bawerk by twelve, Pareto by three, and von Wieser by about three months. It was not without significance that his life span as an economist coincided with theirs. He was influenced by the doctrines of these distinguished contemporaries both during his years of study and as a mature theoretician.

At the age of eighteen, after completing the customary classical secondary schooling, Wicksell enrolled at the University of Uppsala, in 1869, to embark on an unusually long career of study, research, and writing, which lasted thirty years before he received his first meager academic appointment. In the course of these many "years of study" he earned advanced degrees in three different fields (mathematics and physics, economics, and law); he pursued advanced studies of economics abroad for a number of years; he was married and had two children; and he published the first three of the five books he wrote in economics. The main events in his career during these three decades are given below.

At first he made unusually rapid progress in his studies, earning a *fil. kand.* (B.A.) degree in mathematics, Latin language and literature, Scandinavian languages, and theoretic philosophy, in 1872 after only five semesters of study. Some years later he was elected chairman of Uppsala University Student Corps (the equivalent of student-body president). In this capacity he became increasingly active in the philosophical, political, and literary debates and activities of student circles. He lectured and pamphleteered on a broad range of social questions such as the population problem, birth control, emigration, alcoholism and its causes, prostitution, the future of marriage, the right to universal suffrage, and the need for direct progressive taxes on incomes.[1] As will be shown later, it was his advocacy of limiting the population by the application of birth control which almost cost him his career and which accounts for his eventual change-over from mathematics to economics as his major interest. Meanwhile his progress on advanced studies of physics and mathematics was retarded considerably.

[1] This biographical sketch has been written to afford the reader an appreciation of the social milieu in, and often against which, Wicksell was working. It is also intended to serve as a background for obtaining a better understanding of Wicksell's economic policy and social reform proposals, which are dealt with especially in chapter xii, and in various sections of chapters viii, and xi, in this study.

For reasons of space it will not be feasible to discuss, beyond passing mention, all the vicissitudes of Wicksell's career and their causes. Neither should this be necessary now that T. Gårdlund's *The Life of Knut Wicksell* (Stockholm, 1958), a definitive and excellent biography, is available. For a shorter, yet quite adequate, treatment of the same subject, see the introductory essay by E. Lindahl, "Wicksell's Life and Work," in K. Wicksell, *Selected Papers on Economic Theory* (London, 1958), pp. 9-48.

He earned an advanced degree, *fil. lic.,* in mechanics, mathematics, and physics, as late as 1885.[2]

During the period 1885-1890, Wicksell went abroad to study economics at universities in England, France, Germany, and Austria. One reason for this was that at that time Sweden had no well-developed economics faculties. Economics was then taught only as an elective subject within the country's faculties of law. At first, 1885-1886, he went on his own resources, and later, 1887-1890, as a Lorén Foundation scholar.

In 1889, Wicksell married a Norwegian lady, Anna Bugge, in Paris. Shortly after their return to Sweden in 1890 their first son, Sven Dag (1890-1939), who later became a professor of statistics at Lund University, was born. A second son, their last, Finn Hjalmar, was born in 1893. During his early student years he perished in an accident in 1913.

It was the consequences of a lecture Wicksell delivered to a temperance group in Stockholm, 1880, on the causes and remedies of alcoholism, which accounts for his change, five years later, from a career in mathematics and physics to one in economics. Among the causes of excessive drinking Wicksell pointed to the abject poverty and dreariness of home life for the majority of urban workers, a poverty reinforced by the arrival of more and more children. As a remedy he suggested that the medical profession perfect simple, safe methods of contraception to arrest excessive procreation, and disseminate the knowledge and application of such methods. If the substance of his lecture had not been reported in the daily press, Wicksell might calmly have returned to his mathematical studies. But as it was, what he had to say reached a wider, more articulate public. Since it conflicted with the mores of the times just as the Darwinian theory of evolution in an earlier day offended theological dogma, the response was immediate and strong. He was criticized and reviled in the press by professors of medicine, clergymen, essayists, and editors. Overnight he achieved the unenviable reputation of a "moral nihilist" and came to be regarded as the leader of a small,

---

[2] This degree, the *philosophiae licentiatus,* is perhaps peculiar to Swedish institutions of higher learning. It represents work in advance of the American M.A. It involves comprehensive oral and written examinations, comparable to the qualifying examinations most American Ph.D. candidates must pass before their candidacy for this degree is accepted and before they begin research on their dissertations. Usually *fil. lic.* examinees present an outline of their prospective dissertations for evaluation when they undergo these examinations. Later, when they have completed their proposed research, they undergo an official "disputation," i.e., a defense of their thesis before an examining committee of professors, to obtain the *fil. doctor.* (Ph.D.) degree.

suspect intellectual sect known as neo-Malthusians. In addition Uppsala University Academic Consistory felt constrained to take disciplinary action against him. After hearing his own statements, the consistory decided to proceed no further and concluded its action with a mild censure.

Wicksell defended himself ably and with courage in articles and tracts, all of which added further to his notoriety. However, in this process he felt the need to make a more methodical study of population questions. He felt goaded by his critics' assertion that he, a mathematician and natural scientist, had very unwisely taken a stand on economic problems without having sufficient insight into them. For competent advice in these matters he turned to David Davidson, then a *docent* (assistant professor) in economics and fiscal law at the University of Uppsala. Davidson launched Wicksell on his career in the social sciences by lending him a personal copy of Malthus's *Principle of Population*. From this as a starting point, the study of classical political economy in its entirety was but a short step for Wicksell. This he pursued in conjunction with mathematics until he went abroad to study economics in 1885.

Wicksell's intellectual antecedents go back to the classical economists, particularly to the writings of Malthus, J. S. Mill, and Ricardo, which he studied intensively during his first stay abroad. However, he also derived much stimulation from the writings of some distinguished contemporaries, notably from Jevons, Menger, L. Walras, and Böhm-Bawerk. At any rate his scientific work is more closely related to the doctrines of the foregoing than it is to those—now mostly forgotten—professors whose lectures and seminars he once mentioned as having attended while abroad; namely, Leroy-Beaulieu and Desmoulins in Paris, Knapp and Brentano in Strasbourg, Wagner in Berlin, and Menger and Singer in Vienna.

Wicksell's most productive period as an economic theoretician began upon his return to Sweden in 1890 and lasted approximately to the eve of World War I, at which time his major works had already been written. However, the first decade of this period, while very productive, was also a very troublesome one for him and his young family, especially from a financial point of view. It must be remembered that from 1890 to 1899 when he received his first small academic appointment, he had no regular academic position. During this time he was obliged to pursue further studies and research in order to qualify for the professorship he eventually obtained in 1901. He was also without any grants, except in 1896 when he received a modest sum from a government fund to begin his monetary studies in Berlin.

Although it is true that he received additional funds from the Lorén Foundation, these were given to him for the purpose of financing the publication of his scientific works.

To maintain his family he corresponded on social questions with a number of Swedish, Norwegian, and Finnish newspapers. He journeyed on extensive lecture tours, lecturing for a fee on various social reform topics to public audiences associated with the labor, socialist, and temperance movements in Sweden. He also published some popular tracts through the liberal-minded student association, Verdandi, at the University of Uppsala. These publications probably yielded him a small, irregular income. When the opportunity arose he accepted occasional high-school teaching and private tutorial assignments. Yet, despite these efforts, he did not earn enough for his family's needs and found it necessary increasingly to go into debt with his elder sisters.

Wicksell's first scientific work, a long article, "Kapitalzins und Arbeitslohn," was published in *Conrads Jahrbücher* in 1892. This was soon followed by his first major treatise, *Über Wert, Kapital und Rente,* a gem of economic analysis on the basis of the marginal utility and the general marginal productivity theories, a work later reprinted by the London School of Economics and Political Science, 1933, and translated by S. Frowein as *Value, Capital and Rent* (London, 1954). Although this work became a basis for the increasing international recognition he achieved, it was received with indifference at the time of its publication both in Germany and in Sweden. One reason for this was that German economists, under the dominance of the historical school, objected to the elegant mathematical formulation he had given to its main arguments. Wicksell tried to have the work accepted as a doctoral thesis at the University of Uppsala, but this was refused.

Wicksell then turned his attention to public finance, and in May, 1895, he obtained a *fil. lic.* degree in political economy and public finance. Soon thereafter he obtained his doctorate, also in 1895, on a much shorter work he had written, *Zur Lehre von der Steuerincidenz.* This work was incorporated as the first chapter of his second major work, *Finanztheoretische Untersuchungen* (1896). In this book Wicksell tried, *inter alia,* to solve an old problem of public finance by means of a novel approach; namely, to establish the criteria for justice or equity in taxation. His chapters dealing with this topic have been translated by J. M. Buchanan as "A New Principle of Just Taxation," in R. A. Musgrave and A. T. Peacock, *Classics in the Theory of Public Finance,* Macmillan, London, 1958, pp. 72-118.

About this time Wicksell applied for a *docentur* (assistant professorship) in economics to the philosophy faculty at the University of Uppsala where he hoped for an appointment without the necessary legal degree. Under special dispensation this might have been granted. But this faculty took the view that (1) the subject belonged to the faculty of law, (2) Wicksell lacked the training in humanities required by the faculty of philosophy, and (3) his activity on behalf of neo-Malthusianism and other social reforms indicated that he was more of a propagandist than a promising and sound pedagogue. The merits of his scientific achievements apparently were not even reviewed. He then turned to the faculty of law but was told that his lack of a legal degree disqualified him for a post requiring that he teach fiscal law first of all and economics only as a secondary or optional subject.

Consequently all avenues to an academic position were closed to him unless he studied for a degree in fiscal law. Upon his return from monetary research in Berlin in 1896, he enrolled for courses at the University of Uppsala leading to the required degree, *utr. jur. kand.* (LL.B., with specialization in fiscal law). At a considerable sacrifice both financially and in terms of energy he obtained this degree in 1899 in less than the normal time. Only then was he appointed a *docent* at Uppsala.

In the meantime, 1898, he had also found the energy to complete his epoch-making third treatise, *Geldzins und Güterpreise,* translated in 1934 as *Interest and Prices.* This book propounded his famous theory, revised on important points in his later monetary writings, that monetary equilibrium, or the height of the general level of prices, is essentially "labile." The price level is likely to move in a cumulative fashion from its initial position, i.e., to glide into an inflationary rise or deflationary decline, according to whether the "natural" rate of interest rises above or falls below the bank-controlled market rate of interest.

Later Phases of Wicksell's Career

Wicksell served only one year as a *docent* at Uppsala University, for by 1900 an additional position in fiscal law and economics was opened at Lund University, and he agreed to fill this post on an "acting" basis for the time being. When a board was appointed to fill the post permanently by competitive examination, Wicksell filed his application.

The roles played by Wicksell and his competitor, G. Cassel, as well as by the examining board and by the high officers of Lund University in the matter of this appointment—effected in Wicksell's favor at associate professor's rank in 1901—make a very interesting and dramatic story.[3] Suffice it to say here that the examining board was divided. One of its three members, his colleague David Davidson from Uppsala, preferred Wicksell because of his scientific merits, which were clearly superior to Cassel's. Another member was, to say the least, lukewarm toward Wicksell but neither could he approve Cassel, who lacked the required law degree. The third member was clearly in Cassel's favor because Cassel was fifteen years younger than Wicksell, because he was more "practical" in his outlook, and because, unlike Wicksell, he had not acquired a nationwide reputation as a radical and an avid fighter for social reform.

Rumors of the dissenting views of the members of the board came to the notice of the faculty, among whom the conservative members opposed and the liberal-minded favored Wicksell's appointment. From the faculty these rumors spread to the students and the public. All of a sudden, the question of this appointment became an issue of academic freedom, with a victory for Wicksell being regarded as a victory for freedom. At this point Cassel withdrew his application saying in the public press that in these circumstances the appointment was not likely to be decided strictly on scientific merits as distinct from the alleged social outlook of the two applicants.

Wicksell had kept unusually quiet in these proceedings. However, in such a simple matter as signing his application, which was to be forwarded to the King, he took a stand that might have cost him his career. Custom dictated that it should be signed "your humble servant." Wicksell, for many years an advocate of a republican form of government, as opposed to a monarchical form, could not abide this. After much worry and soul-searching, he signed simply "respectfully." [4] This was noted by higher university authority which raised the question whether his application, so signed, had the appropriate legal form to make it possible to forward it. Yet they eventually forwarded it.

The board, now left with only one applicant, recommended Wicksell chiefly on the basis that he had a degree in fiscal law besides his doctorate in economics. In 1904 when the senior professor of economics and fiscal law at Lund (the "lukewarm" member of the examining board) retired, Wicksell was elevated to the full professorship by vote of the faculty. He served in this capacity until 1916 when, at the mandatory retirement age of sixty-five, he became an emeritus.

---

[3] This story has been recounted in a superb manner in Gårdlund, *op. cit.*, chap. vii; and Wicksell, *op. cit.*, pp. 20-24.

[4] Wicksell, *op. cit.*, p. 21.

Wicksell's years at Lund were very productive despite the heavy teaching burden he had to assume. In 1901 the first volume of his *Lectures on Political Economy* was published. This work represents an expansion and reformulation, with considerable modifications in capital theory, of what he had presented in *Value, Capital and Rent* in 1893. In 1906 the second volume of *Lectures on Political Economy* —*On Money* came out. It exhibits an advance and a further development of the simpler monetary analysis he had presented in *Interest and Prices* in 1898. Both volumes have gone through a succession of editions in Sweden and have been translated into German, 1913-1922, English, 1934-1935, Spanish, 1947, and Italian, 1950.

Wicksell also contributed a steady stream of several significant articles every year to Sweden's leading economic journal, *Ekonomisk Tidskrift,* from its founding in 1899 in Uppsala by his colleague, David Davidson. In addition he wrote a number of articles and reviews for foreign journals in Austria and Germany.

This scientific activity is remarkable in the light of the teaching burden he had to carry. He worked alone without any assistant or *docent* until 1909 when such a position was created and F. H. Brock accepted it. Most of his teaching was devoted to fiscal law, a subject which was not congenial to him and in which he never achieved eminence, as he did in economics. Yet the courses he offered in economics were many, demanding, and nonetheless well attended. However, his students were mostly undergraduates specializing in law. In fact, during his teaching career Wicksell only had an opportunity to train a mere handful of graduates for advanced work in economics. This occurred after 1909 when one of his followers and admirers, the late Professor Emil Sommarin, obtained a new chair in economics at Lund opened under the auspices of the philosophy (not the law) faculty, and attracted capable students to Wicksell's courses. It is clear that Wicksell's energies were not used to best advantage by his university, a matter of loss to an earlier generation of Swedish economists.

Soon after his retirement Wicksell moved from Lund to a small suburb of Stockholm, a city he loved apparently with as much ardor as Frenchmen feel for Paris. There, with the aid of a fund collected in his honor from friends and admirers, he built a small villa for his wife and himself. It was there that he was to spend the last and most peaceful decade of his life.

After his retirement he remained intellectually very active, as well as energetic in his endeavors to influence Swedish economic policies during and after World War I. His influence on measures that were adopted during the period 1916-1926 was hardly ever direct or decisive.

Yet it was discernible. His role was mostly that of a gadfly; if it had not been for him and some like-minded colleagues, worse counsels might well have prevailed.

Post-Academic Activity—World War I and After

On reaching retirement Wicksell did not give up his scholarly habits in order to enter directly into the political debates of the times. He remained a man of science, content to stay out of politics in the hope of being able to influence behavior in that theater by presenting the public with his printed or spoken appeal to facts and to reason. He continued to write a large number of articles, mostly on monetary problems, as well as several reports for various parliamentary commissions of inquiry on which he served.

He also took a lively interest in the activities of the Swedish Economic Association, of which he had been a member ever since the 1890's. Here he found an appreciative following, especially among the younger economists who looked upon him as an inspiring and genial teacher, for he always took a very active part in the many meetings and discussions he attended.

Now that sufficient time had passed and the general level of understanding of social questions had been raised in the interim, several of the ideas Wicksell had espoused in the 1880's and 1890's, and for whose advocacy he was then regarded as a radical or a visionary, had become quite widely accepted. In these circumstances and in the cosmopolitan environment of Stockholm, he became increasingly regarded as the Dean of Swedish economics. When he expressed himself, as he did on a surprisingly wide variety of issues, his remarks were more and more accepted as representing the thinking not only of a respected individual, but of a significant element of the economic profession in Sweden.

This investiture of his congenial personality with public significance was probably indispensable for such influence as he wielded over Swedish economic policy. At least it guaranteed that his advice would receive notice in proper quarters. His criticisms or recommendations could not safely be ignored even if most of them, as concrete proposals for action, were rejected. Political power was in the hands of persons who did not share, or did not properly understand, most of his views. It is also true that several of his suggestions were mainly intended to force a reëvaluation of existing policy or of policy measures about to be adopted rather than to propose alternative measures. Yet on more than one occasion he argued eloquently for measures of his own devising which might have been applied with beneficial effects.

In retrospect it is regrettable that these were also for the most part rejected. Had they been acted upon with sufficient determination, they would have helped considerably in reducing the Swedish inflation of 1915-1920 to much smaller proportions.

Both during and after World War I, Wicksell insisted that the proper goal for Swedish monetary policy should be a gradual restoration of the 1914 level of prices by application of deflationary credit and fiscal techniques. The more Swedish prices rose from this level with the passage of time (to levels almost four times as high during the autumn of 1920), the more impractical and unattainable did this aim seem to his colleagues, not to mention the public generally. To this objection he answered: Let the restoration occur gradually over a number of years. To facilitate this process he thought that a "Restitution Commission" should be set up to review past transactions in long-term contracts and to arrange for compensation for creditors from the real gains their debtors had made by being able to pay off contracts in money of substantially depreciated value in the course of the inflation years.

Wicksell never worked out this proposal in detail. What he had in mind was that society must not sanction and perpetuate the arbitrary redistribution of wealth in favor of debtors that a protracted inflation brings about. He was particularly concerned that small creditors, who generally fare worse than big ones in such circumstances, should be given compensation or restitution for the losses they had suffered. His meaning is perhaps best made clear by quoting from a reply he wrote to those of his colleagues who considered his demand for return to the 1914 level of prices as impractical.

In 1914, i.e., at the beginning of the war, mortgages on fixed property in Sweden amounted to about 4,590,000,000 crowns. . . . Now is it 'practical' to deprive the owners of these claims of half their wealth (which in most cases was acquired with *at least* as much propriety as was the real estate of the debtors), by keeping the value of money at half its pre-war level, so that, without the slightest justification, property-owners might be made a present, calculated at the old values, of 2,250,000,000 crowns? To me it seems a dreadful injustice, which can never be practical.[5]

At this juncture we cannot stop to consider the merits and difficulties of this policy aim. Most of his colleagues regarded it, properly, as a visionary aim, although they acknowledged that it was motivated by the loftiest considerations for social justice. Yet this aim provides a background against which his more practical policy planks can best

---

[5] *Ibid.*, p. 30.

be understood as techniques for arresting inflation if restitution of a prewar price level proved impossible of accomplishment.

Wicksell's anti-inflation program consisted of nine proposals, which he did not present all together but intermittently during the period 1915-1925. When placed in juxtaposition, these proposals add up to a well-integrated inflation control program which was far in advance of the times. In combination they remind one of the more comprehensive economic control programs that were developed in the course of World War II.

First he argued for retention of the free-exchange standard which was introduced at the outbreak of the war when Sweden, along with most other European countries, abandoned the gold standard. To block the inflation which was traceable to a persistent gold inflow to Sweden from neighboring countries in payment for an alarmingly increasing Swedish export surplus, he urged vigorous application of the so-called "gold exclusion" policy, of which he, along with Davidson and to a lesser extent Cassel, was the chief architect.[6]

Secondly, to alleviate war-born shortages of foods and industrial raw materials in Sweden, and to make the Swedish price level practically independent of external price levels, he advocated imposition of a series of export duties. Proceeds were to be used to subsidize procurement by a government purchasing commission of essential foods and raw materials in foreign markets. These commodities were then to be sold in the domestic market under applicable provisions for consumer rationing and materials allocations at prices reflecting import costs minus tax subsidies from the export duties.

In the third place he contended for restriction of credit for plant expansion in the country's overextended export industries. This, he thought, could best be achieved by rationing bank and other credit by a control commission. The latter should see to it that credit for fixed capital investment would only be extended for essential uses in building up and strengthening Sweden's domestic-market industries.

Fourthly, all during the war, he urged that the Riksbank (Sweden's central bank) should raise its discount rates much higher than it did and that it should engage in heavy open-market selling operations until the rise in domestic prices subsided. To reinforce this last step, he pleaded for a change in existing bank legislation to permit the

---

[6] The "gold exclusion policy" involved explicit permission for the Riksbank (the Central Bank of Sweden) to stop buying and selling gold in unlimited quantities at the fixed prewar mint price in order instead to buy and sell gold at the then lower market prices and in quantities limited by its own requirements or discretion. This policy also included, at least implicitly, power on the part of the Riksbank to restrict and ultimately to prohibit importation of gold altogether.

Riksbank to pay interest, at rates of its own choosing, on demand deposits left with it by other banks and by government agencies. This, in turn, would force private banks to follow suit and raise interest rates, particularly on time deposits, which would tend to stimulate private saving and to reduce private spending for consumption purposes.

As a fifth plank he urged the government to refrain from monetizing the increasing public debt through borrowing directly from the Riksbank, and to borrow instead, first as much as possible from the nonbank public, and secondly from private banks. His seventh, eighth, and ninth measures involved the following: (*a*) Tightening of consumer rationing and materials allocations, and extending these regulations to all essential commodities in short supply; (*b*) letting the government use its powers of investigation in order to locate, and its powers of eminent domain to purchase and bring to market at fair values, private hoards of essential commodities in short supply, which were being held for speculative gains; and (*c*) strengthening the wartime excess-profits tax, and retaining it in peacetime on a stand-by basis, for use during speculative booms.

Very little of the foregoing program was adopted, and that little was not executed with much vigor or persistency. The gold exclusion policy became fairly effective during the last year of the war. Half-hearted attempts were made at credit rationing. Consumer rationing and materials allocations were applied selectively over too narrow a field of commodities and services to achieve the intended aim of arresting the upward price spiral.

Yet this failure to adopt Wicksell's policies does not measure his influence and that of some of his colleagues. That influence cannot be fully accounted for. It is undoubtedly true that his suggestions and criticisms stimulated thought and attracted wide attention. By doing so they forced opponents of his measures to defend their positions before the bar of an alerted public opinion. This may have prevented adoption of less rational policies, considered at the time, which promised extraordinary short-term gains to the country's major export industries in particular.

As the wartime and postarmistice inflation eventually gave way, during the winter of 1920 and the year 1921, to drastic deflation—reducing Swedish wholesale prices from an index value of 363 in October, 1920, to an average of 162 in 1922, 157 in 1923—Wicksell apparently relented in his demand that the 1914 price level be restored to a wholesale price index of 100.

The large-scale unemployment and mass bankruptcies that accompanied the deflation convinced him that the cost of inviting further deflation in order to regain the 1914 level of prices was out of all proportion to the gain that might result from such a course of action. This would most directly benefit the few individuals who were still living on fixed incomes established in prewar days and persons who had managed to realize their inflation gains before the deflation gathered momentum. It would not help those who had been forced to dispose of capital assets for depreciated money in order to maintain themselves during the preceding years of rising costs of living. And wageworkers in particular could hardly be expected to be enthusiastic about additional deflation, which would only lengthen and intensify unemployment in their ranks.

On these grounds Wicksell gradually changed his aim from one of prewar price restoration to one of postwar price stabilization at whatever level of prices promised to be tenable after some inevitable economic adjustments had run their course.

If 1921 and 1922 had been ordinary depression years not afflicted by certain economic maladjustments which were the direct heritage of the war, Wicksell might have been anxious to apply an antideflation policy he had advocated in 1907, long before the war, as a means of mitigating unemployment and financial distress in times of poor trade. The essence of this policy was to give industry sufficient inducement to maintain a moderately high as distinct from a low level of employment by producing durable and storable commodities to stock in depressed times. These could be disposed of later at a price advantage in the recovery period. But this required that industry be given ample credit facilities at low or negligible interest rates. In view of the risks involved in this proposal—namely, that the collateral of commodity inventories might have to be held for considerable periods, after which it might not be salable at prices sufficient to repay the loans—the banks by themselves would not have been able (because of solvency considerations) to finance such a production scheme adequately. Therefore, the banks would have to be assisted in this task by the government, which would have to underwrite or assume the ultimate risk of losses that might arise on such production loans.

But 1921 and 1922 were not "ordinary" or "usual" peace years, and the unemployment that arose was dealt with by somewhat extraordinary means, chiefly by the provision of national government credit on easy terms for provincial and local governments to set a series of public works programs in action. By 1923 deflation had spent its force and recovery was under way in conditions of remarkably stable prices. This in turn led to an increasing demand by financiers and others, including many of Sweden's economists, that the country give up its inconvertible paper standard and return to the allegedly safe and sound prewar gold standard.

Here Wicksell at first took sharp issue with the majority, including most of his colleagues. Ever since he had written *Interest and Prices* in 1898, he had advocated an international free-exchange standard. This system was to function under organizational and operational safeguards comparable to those which we find in the present International Monetary Fund. These were intended to guarantee substantial stability of foreign exchange rates and provide at the same time orderly procedures for adjustment of such rates by majority-approved measures of devaluation and the like, when persistent balance-of-payments disequilibria developed in particular countries. To his mind an international free-exchange standard was far superior to the automatic gold standard in being more amenable to rational monetary management. Under the conditions he laid down, the free-exchange standard would also provide approximately the same stability of exchange rates that was the glory of the gold standard.

For a decade most of the world had been on national inconvertible paper standards without the benefit of international monetary organization and orderly, rational monetary management procedures. The exigencies of war finance had brought most national paper currencies into bad repute. Considerable inflation had affected all of them. In several countries this process got entirely out of hand, as in Germany and some other central- and east-European countries. But by 1923-24, the inflation and its aftermath of deflationary adjustment had lost most of their force. The time seemed ripe and the general nature of economic conditions seemed propitious for attempting monetary reorganization on a stable basis. Then why, asked Wicksell, revert to the gold standard with its several fundamental flaws when a superior system was attainable by a properly managed international free-exchange standard?

It was his hope that such a standard would be adopted, or at least that an approach to it would be made, in the course of the postwar international monetary conferences in Brussels in 1920 and in Genoa in 1922. This hope was doomed to disappointment. The only resolution for the world's monetary problems brought forth by these conferences was gold-exchange standards for the smaller and financially weak nations tied to the gold standards of the major nations.

It was probably this disappointment that induced Wicksell, in April, 1924, to give his blessing, reluctantly, and with many reservations, to Sweden's return to the prewar gold standard as promising greater monetary stability than had been experienced under the ineptly managed inconvertible paper standard. He found some comfort in the thought that the gold standard adopted by parliament in 1924 was *not exactly like* that which had been in use until 1914. The new standard provided more scope for monetary management than the old. In particular, the new standard contained a provision which extended power to the Riksbank to restrict and, if need be, prohibit importation of gold, so that inflation from a persistent gold inflow might be averted.

The foregoing sketch of Wicksell's impact on Swedish economic policy, carried out by conservative cabinets and equally conservative parliamentary majorities of the time, reveals the main features of his position. Wicksell waged his fight for an economic policy mainly through his contributions to the major organs of the Stockholm daily press as well as to Sweden's economic journals. Through these media he reached a wider audience than had been possible for him in his past teaching and in his participation on government commissions of inquiry.

After the resumption of the gold standard in 1924, Sweden's monetary problem receded into the background for the time being. This afforded Wicksell a respite. During 1925 he still published some important articles on monetary questions, but actually he was preoccupied with revising the monetary analysis he had published in the second volume of his *Lectures*. In chapter xi, it will be shown what progress he made on this task. He did not live long enough to complete this work. In the spring of 1926 he was severely chilled at a public function. The result was a virulent lung inflammation. He died in a matter of days, on May 3, 1926. His wife survived him until 1928, and his one remaining son, Sven Dag, who left no heirs, until 1939.

CHAPTER II

Synopsis of Wicksell's Contributions to Economics

Before entering on the extended treatment that follows, a synopsis of Wicksell's contributions to economics will be useful as a focus for the separate discussions of various aspects of his work to which subsequent chapters are devoted. Moreover, a summary of his work is in order because his contributions, major and minor, are numerous and range over almost the entire field of economics.

To be meaningful such a synopsis must be set forth against a background which reveals the state of economic theory as Wicksell found it and reacted to it. It must also show the most immediate consequences of his labors in terms of their impact on contemporary economic thought. This calls first for a brief review of the main lines of doctrinal development that occurred between 1848 and 1890,[1] which link classical economics with the "marginalist" or neoclassical schools.

When Wicksell began his studies, about 1885, marginal utility and marginal productivity analyses had attained status as "the new economics" for the leading economists of that day. Yet, at that time these theories were neither fully developed nor coördinated one with another, as they were to become during the 1890's. Wicksell played a significant role in this development. Perhaps it was precisely because of the tentative and sketchy form in which he left several of his investigations that Wicksell succeeded in stimulating so many able

---

[1] These dates are selected for convenience, 1848 denoting the culmination of the classical school with the publication of J. S. Mill's *Principles of Political Economy*, and 1890, when the first edition of Marshall's *Principles of Economics* appeared, marking the beginning of an era which was to last into the 1930's, during which the "neoclassical" school exercised a dominant influence over economic thought.

16

economists of the succeeding generation, not only in Sweden but else-where, to efforts which resulted in substantial theoretical progress. In that sense contemporary economics owes him a large debt, which is difficult to specify and which transcends what one finds in his own writings.

The State of Economic Theory about 1890

At the time Wicksell began his creative work, the field of economic theory, apart from the new, ascendent marginal utility school, was divided between several opposing camps. The classical tradition, epitomized by J. S. Mill's *Principles of Political Economy* (1848), still dominated the thinking in England and the United States. It was characterized by a cost theory of value and a residual theory of distribution. According to the latter, labor received its subsistence or conventional standard of living from the wages fund. Landowners received the proceeds of a natural monopoly, the ownership of supramarginal land, a share determined by prices or by the level of demand. Finally, capitalist-entrepreneurs received the remainder of the product (or its equivalent in value terms) as a residual. This residual, however, could not in the long run fall below a certain positive minimum equal to the supply price of abstinence or saving, plus wages for the labor of management, plus, where applicable, a risk return.

In France, the classical heritage had become somewhat modified, many would say vulgarized. This was partly the consequence of Bastiat's "harmony" interpretation of the classical cost doctrine, which he extended to land rent as representing the "cost" of ancestral labors of appropriation and of clearing for cultivation. In part it was also due to a strong emphasis, by those following the tradition of J. B. Say, on usefulness or use value as the basis of value theory in contrast to labor cost.

In Germany and central Europe generally, except for Vienna, academic economics was dominated by the German historical school. Its orientation was primarily empirical and antitheoretical. In the same area, however, nonacademic economics was increasingly coming under the sway of Marx and the "scientific socialist" interpretation centered on an exploitation theory of distribution derived from the classical labor theory of value.

It was against this mixed background that the new "subjective value" or "marginalist" schools had been making headway, especially in Lausanne, Vienna, northern Italy, and England. Their development was foreshadowed in the works of Cournot, von Thünen, Gossen, Mangoldt, August Walras, Longfield, Jenkin, and Dupuit, which were received intermittently over some decades, approximately between 1825 and 1865. These forebears had laid the groundwork for a subjective interpretation of value, and for a theory of functional distribution imputing distributive shares according to the marginal productivity of coöperating factors. But their works did not attract much attention and discussion upon publication, with the result that they soon fell into oblivion, only to be rediscovered more than a generation later, in the 1880's and 1890's, by the chief proponents of the marginalist doctrines.

As is well known, it was to the independent efforts of Carl Menger (*Grundsätze der Volkswirtschaftslehre*, 1871), W. S. Jevons (*Theory of Political Economy*, 1871), and Léon Walras (*Élements d'économie politique*, 1874), that the marginal utility doctrine owed its rise. Especially in the hands of Walras this doctrine was developed into an explicit general equilibrium analysis of prices, production, and allocation of resources. For its time, this new orientation represented a revolutionary development in the realm of economic speculation.

This new movement in economics was soon strengthened by gaining additional and prominent adherents, such as Marshall, who adopted its approach in his *Economics of Industry* (1879), and Edgeworth, who embodied its spirit in his highly speculative *Mathematical Psychics* (1881). In 1886 the marginal utility analysis received further elaboration in Böhm-Bawerk's long essay, "Grundzüge der Theorie des wirtschaftlichen Güterwertes." Three years later this doctrine became equipped with an explicit but defective theory of imputation in Wieser's *Der Natürliche Wert*. Shortly after that Böhm-Bawerk published his *magnum opus, The Positive Theory of Capital* (1889), which attempted to explain the phenomenon of interest on subjective grounds as well as to relate the latter to real capital viewed as the time dimension of production. This work also attempted a substantial reconstruction of the theory of production. Finally, in 1890 Marshall published his *Principles of Economics* which, except for its rejection of Austrian capital theory, represented an incomplete synthesis and a substantial elaboration of the new doctrines. This work came to dominate academic instruction in economics both in England and the United States for at least a generation afterward.

By this time the theoretical edifice of the marginalists seemed to be fairly complete. But it lacked the symmetry that coördination of effort among its several architects might have given it. Moreover, the latter were now beginning to fall out with one another. The reasons were several. Menger, Wieser, and Böhm-Bawerk were each working in separate specialties, apparently unable to arrive at a synthesis of their theories. Menger specialized in marginal utility theory and in a running battle over methodology with the German historical school, particularly with Schmoller. Wieser published little of substance after *Der Natürliche Wert,* which was noted mainly for its inconclusive attempt at imputation of distributive shares along marginal productivity lines. It was decades later that he wrote his speculative *Theorie der gesellschaftlichen Wirtschaft* (1913), in which he paid scant attention to problems of "pure theory" and concentrated instead on attempts at divining the trend of social and economic development. Because of divergencies between his own and Böhm-Bawerk's views on capital, the works of the latter could hardly pretend to be a synthesis of Austrian doctrines. Böhm-Bawerk, finally, did not go far beyond what he had achieved in *The Positive Theory of Capital* except for lengthy polemics with the Marxists on one hand, and with the productivity theorists of interest on the other.

Marshall and Edgeworth in England, while accepting the marginal utility theory of value, insisted on another determinant as well, real cost. Moreover, they were unable to accept Böhm-Bawerk's theory of a determinate time structure of production as well as his abstruse analysis of the technical superiority of present over future goods. Marshall had set out on a career of economic analysis in which his *Principles of Economics* remained the first installment for more than thirty years. Edgeworth, on the other hand, was more fragmentary and selective in his expression than Marshall. Consequently, there was little or no reason to hope for an integration of the new thought from the British economists.

The Lausanne school, centering around Léon Walras and his followers, Pareto and Barone, seemed more likely to perform the synthesis. Theirs was the general equilibrium approach and the mathematical-functional analysis of multiple and mutual causation or interrelations. But they, in turn, were estranged by certain aspects of Austrian theory, especially by Böhm-Bawerk's treatment of production and capital.

To Wicksell, in 1892 and 1893, the time must have seemed ripe for an attempt to consolidate the gains made by the foremost representatives of the new doctrines into a coördinated system, and it was to this task he devoted his efforts in *Über Wert, Kapital und Rente* as well as later in his *Lectures-I.*

In the less systematized branches of economics—monetary theory, business cycles, and public finance—the situation about 1890 can briefly be characterized as follows: The crude or "simple" quantity theory was the dominant monetary doctrine, although it was adhered to with increasing dissatisfaction and misgivings, because of its failure to account in any adequate manner for variations in the circuit velocity of money and its impact on society. Moreover, an inordinate amount of intellectual energy that might have found better use was devoted to polemics concerning monetary standards, currency, and banking reform.

Business cycle theories consisted mainly of monetary and credit explanations of crises, and of occasional echoes of the underconsumption thesis. The turn of the century had yet to arrive before this complex phenomenon was to be investigated systematically on hypotheses attributing it mainly to variations in investment in durable real capital and to other nonmonetary causes. As it happened, Wicksell was one of the pioneers in this effort.

With certain notable exceptions—A. Wagner in Germany and Mazzola, Pantaleoni, and others in Italy—public finance remained a rather neglected field. Its theoretical content, as distinct from its more ample descriptive and prescriptive content (the "canons" of taxation), was centered around a theory of tax incidence which had received very little development since the time of J. S. Mill. The essence of that theory was that taxes, regardless of type or whom they were levied on, had their ultimate incidence on "the economic surplus." For it was held that real wages tended toward a subsistence level equilibrium, below which they could not be driven in the long run, for instance, by excise duties on consumption goods. Analogous minima applied to the incomes of entrepreneurs and capitalists. If taxes temporarily reduced the returns of workers, capitalists, or entrepreneurs below these minima, the result would be an appropriate, often painful and difficult, reduction of the supply of the productive factor in question, which, in due time, would restore its return to its equilibrium or "natural" level.

In brief terms, the foregoing summary describes the intellectual environment in the general field of economics to which Wicksell reacted when he began his studies in the 1880's.

Wicksell's Contributions to Economic Science

As a creative theoretician Wicksell enriched the economics of his generation in the several ways outlined below.

CONTRIBUTIONS TO ECONOMIC THEORY—STATIC ANALYSIS

The marginal productivity theory of distribution. Wicksell was one of the founders of the marginal productivity theory of (functional) distribution of incomes to owners of factors of production. Chronologically he was the first writer to prove, in *Über Wert, Kapital und Rente* (1893), that distribution becomes entirely determinate when the product is fully distributed or exhausted by imputation of distributive shares to coöperating factors according to their respective marginal productivity. Nevertheless, he was satisfied to let the credit for this discovery go to Wicksteed who, independently, proved the same theorem by means of a more complete demonstration one year later in his work *Coördination of the Laws of Distribution* (1894).

The theory of price in imperfect competition. Wicksell's work in this field contributed in several ways to the development of the contemporary theory of imperfect competition.

1. Wicksell followed the footsteps of Cournot whose analyses of monopoly and duopoly he adopted. By linking the latter with the analysis of isolated exchange, he succeeded in laying the basis for the theory of bilateral monopoly, for he demonstrated that under certain assumptions both prices and quantities of goods exchanged in isolated barter become determinate.

2. His analysis of market imperfections in retailing came remarkably close to some of the characteristic findings of the modern theory of monopolistic competition without the benefit of some of the conceptual tools developed after his time and apparently indispensable for further progress in this realm. Thus he was able to account for the tendency toward overcrowding in the retail field because it invited entry of too many firms of less than optimum scale. He also noted the existence of differentiated markups, of product differentiation, and a tendency for consumer demand to be less than perfectly elastic for retail services, because consumers develop a form of attachment for the services of particular retailers.

3. He emphasized that in the most significant markets of the real world "free" or perfect competition was absent and, instead, monopoly tendencies were in the ascendency for technological and other reasons. In this manner he contributed to that change in emphasis which has occurred in price theory since his time; namely, a change from treating "free competition" as if it were the prevailing market form to treating imperfect competition as a family of related and widely prevailing market forms.

4. He provided theoretical sanction for authoritarian intervention in the pricing process. He demonstrated that even if perfect competition might possibly be made to rule on all markets, the resulting production-consumption equilibrium would not be one, contrary to what some distinguished contemporary theorists held, in which economic welfare would be maximized, as long as the prevailing distribution of wealth remained essentially unchanged. In such circumstances, as he pointed out, a set of uniform prices imposed by authority that favored recipients of low incomes as compared with those of high incomes, would result in an increase of total utility in contrast to what would be experienced under competitively established prices.

5. The foregoing led him to conclude that all monopolies and all industries tending strongly toward formation of joint monopolies or "showing unmistakable signs toward formation of cartels and trusts," as he put it, were ripe for being taken over by local or national governments to be operated as

public enterprises. And it was precisely for public enterprises that he formulated the ingenious principle that they should be managed in their production policy according to the marginal cost-pricing rule. In other words, they should produce and sell the output for which marginal costs equal the prices paid by the public, regardless of whether all of their production costs would be met in such conditions or whether some of the latter would have to be met by subsidies from general tax revenues.

The theory of capital and interest. Wicksell's most important contribution to static economic theory was his revision and reconstruction of Böhm-Bawerk's capital theory. He reformulated the latter lucidly on the postulate of a stationary state and then proceeded to generalize it by: (1) including land within its scope; (2) introducing into its treatment the assumption of variable production coefficients or factor proportions; and (3) by extending the analysis of capital beyond the confines of a hypothetical one-commodity economy into a multiple-commodity general equilibrium treatment.

As a result Böhm-Bawerk's cumbersome trinitarian ("three grounds") explanation of interest was transformed into an explicit theory of interest as the marginal productivity of waiting, coördinate with the marginal productivity theories of wages and rent. In this connection he also arrived at the conclusion that saving is likely to prove interest-inelastic.

However, his chief innovation in capital theory was his elaboration of a new, consistent concept of capital structure, which amounted to a method for quantifying real capital both: (4) as a determinate time structure of production capable of variation in several dimensions, "width" and "height"; and (5) as a quantification in value terms, a conception he referred to as "the stratification of capital through time."

The value of Wicksell's formulation was that it made the impact of capital accumulation on the national dividend and on the relations between distributive shares more accessible to theoretical analysis than they were in earlier versions of "Austrian" capital theory and in "non-Austrian" conceptions of real capital as an aggregate of producers' goods.

CONTRIBUTIONS TO ECONOMIC THEORY—DYNAMIC ANALYSIS

Distributive shares and the national dividend in conditions of capital accumulation and technological change. Wicksell was the first among modern theorists to subject the question of relative and absolute distributive shares to rigorous analysis. His treatment, which was stimulated by Ricardo's famous chapter, "On Machinery," assumed a perfectly competitive society with a constant labor force and quantity of natural resources. His demonstrations showed the impact on the national dividend and on distributive shares of:

1. Net investment without technological change. This increases the national dividend and eventually reduces the relative share of capitalists as production becomes capital-intensive.

2. Technological change without net capital formation. This always increases the national dividend as long as competition remains strong and it

generally increases the relative share of one of the productive factors more than that of the rest, depending on whether the innovation increases the productivity of capital, or land, or labor more than that of the other two factors.

3. Technological change and net capital formation. These two forces increase the national dividend and *may* bring about large-scale displacement of labor by real capital with a concomitant reduction of labor's relative share, *if* the innovation is very laborsaving and thus renders fixed capital and equipment more profitable—in absolute terms—than before.

Wicksell's work in this area clearly anticipated by almost three decades several of the conclusions of J. R. Hicks in his *Theory of Wages* (1932).

The Wicksell effect. In his work on distributive shares, Wicksell stressed a force which is a partial offset to the decline of interest that is bound to occur if net accumulation is continuous and other factors are constant in quantity. This phenomenon had also engaged the attention of the classical economists, notably J. S. Mill, in their speculations concerning the tendency toward a zero rate of interest and, presumably, a stationary economy. This was the observation that a certain portion of net real saving is absorbed in rising real wages and rent during an interval of capital formation. This appeared to be a strong guarantee against a zero rate of interest, for partial wage-absorption of savings could be counted on to prevent creation of the extraordinarily large quantity of real capital that would be required to drive its marginal productivity toward zero. Wicksell was also preoccupied with this same phenomenon in several demonstrations. For this reason partial wage-absorption of savings is here labeled the "Wicksell effect."

In working on this problem he was able to prove that this effect is a phenomenon uniquely associated with changes in the factor real capital. He also showed that the marginal productivity principle has full application to real capital only at the microeconomic level, where the private marginal productivity of capital equals the rate of interest. But at the macroeconomic level a discrepancy arises between the social marginal productivity rate of real capital and the rate of interest, with the latter remaining somewhat higher than the former.

Wicksell's labors in this area were effective in the sense that his demonstrations were a first attempt, which stimulated others to more successful efforts, to study the dynamic process of capital formation in detail. The Wicksell effect pointed essentially to the existence of a series of problems connected with adjustments between the capital structure and (1) changes in the distribution of income; (2) changes in the magnitude and composition of total output (relatively more or less capital goods or consumption goods when total output varies); and (3) changes in the income dispositions of individuals (relatively more or less saving versus consumption expenditures when total income varies).

The foregoing, more or less simultaneous, complex adjustments are called forth by variations in the capital structure itself. These are adjustments which apparently are required to maintain equilibrium or to prevent the "vertical maladjustment" that von Hayek stresses. As such the Wicksell effect at the real level is a force opposed to that of "forced saving" at the monetary level of analysis of cumulative processes or price level movements. If Wicksell had juxtaposed these two forces on a common plane of discourse, it is conceivable that he may have arrived at a capital-structure-maladjustment thesis of the business cycle similar to von Hayek's. For von Hayek's "vertical maladjustment" or, in the later versions of his thesis, his "Ricardo effect," represents the swamping of the Wicksell effect that necessarily occurs by the increasing momentum of "forced saving" in an upward price spiral.

However, as is shown later in this chapter, Wicksell apparently would not have subscribed to the "capital shortage" or "vertical maladjustment" theories of the business cycle that his researches on the problem of capital formation seem to have stimulated in the minds of some of his followers, such as G. Åkerman and F. von Hayek.

Monetary theory. Wicksell's greatest contribution to dynamic economic analysis was undoubtedly made in the field of monetary theory. Here he became the originator of the modern aggregate demand-supply or savings-investment approach to monetary phenomena, an approach from which the contemporary income-employment analysis was developed about a decade after his death.

How great his originality was in this field can best be seen if it is borne in mind that monetary theory in the 1890's, when he began his investigations, had not advanced appreciably beyond the pattern set by Ricardo in the *High Price of Bullion* (1811) and in his *Proposals for an Economical and Secure Currency* (1816). The simple quantity theory dominated monetary discussions. Its leading exponents were mostly concerned with questions of currency reform, the object of which was to obviate price fluctuations by controlling the quantity of money.

Wicksell drew his inspiration largely from the bullionist-antibullionist polemics of the early nineteenth century and from Tooke's forceful criticisms of the quantity theory around the middle of that century. Wicksell succeeded in transcending the classical preoccupation with currency and the mechanism of payments and he relegated variations in the quantity of money to a secondary place. He approached the same problem that traditional quantity theorists had dealt with—namely, what determines the value of money and how its value may be stabilized—from the novel standpoint of how cash balances and their rate of turnover (chiefly their income velocity) are affected by changes in aggregate demand. He developed an explanation which enabled him to relate changes in the value of money or in the general price level as responses to (or as dependent variables of) autonomous, not necessarily coördinated forces. These acted (1) on aggregate individual income dispositions (consumption expenditure versus saving), and (2) on entrepreneurial production decisions—and investment decisions—relating to how much to invest in production of output, and to what proportion of the output shall be in the form of consumption goods or "present goods," and in the form of capital goods or "future goods."

Since entrepreneurial decisions are guided by profit expectations, which are expressed in Wicksell's "real rate of interest" (an analogue of the contemporary concept of marginal efficiency of capital), while individual income dispositions are affected by the "agio of present over future goods and services," or by the "money rate of interest," he centered his explanation of price level fluctuations on the behavior of these two rates. His cumulative price fluctuations are, however, necessarily attended by corresponding changes in the level and distribution of money income and in the magnitude and composition of current output. Unless one assumes perfect foresight and complete absence of economic frictions, changes in the level and distribution of income are necessarily accompanied by changes in the level of employment and in its distribution as between employment in the production of capital goods and of consumption goods. Consequently the level and distribution of both income and employment respond to changes in the relation of investment to saving, and Wicksell regarded investment as a magnitude which would readily increase or decrease in response to changes in the real rate of interest.

(3) Hence, as early as 1898 in *Interest and Prices,* Wicksell anticipated much of the analysis found in Keynes's *Treatise on Money* (1930).

(4) If we consider some modifications he introduced into his monetary analysis during the last years of his life, it can be said that his revised doctrine anticipated the type of analysis that was developed by D. H. Robertson in *Banking Policy and the Price Level* (1926).

(5) Probably more important than the foregoing is the fact that the framework for monetary analysis which he left behind was found to be sufficiently broad and flexible to serve as the basis for the work of the "Stockholm School" of contemporary employment-income and price-structure analysis.

Business cycle theory. Wicksell ranks as one of the first theorists to develop a coherent real-investment explanation of the trade cycle. Yet it must be admitted that, contrary to what was the case with most of his contemporaries who wrote in this field, he did not devote himself to an extended, systematic investigation of business cycles, but dealt instead with this problem in concise theoretical analyses.

1. He distinguished carefully between the trade cycle and monetary crises. Crises, which generally accompany and complicate industrial fluctuations, he considered to be the primary consequences of inept monetary management of elastic credit systems under criteria—often misleading—provided by the traditional gold standard for the guidance of central bank monetary management.

2. On the other hand he viewed the trade cycle as the sequence of responses economic systems (subject to endogenous growth factors coördinated with one another in a precarious internal balance) make to the irregular impacts they receive from time to time from exogenous forces acting upon them, chiefly from technological change. As he put it, "the principal and

sufficient cause of cyclical fluctuations should . . . be sought in the fact that in its very nature technical or commercial advance cannot maintain the same even progress as does . . . the increase of needs . . . owing to the organic phenomenon of increase of population, but it is sometimes precipitate, sometimes delayed." (*Lectures-II*, p. 211.)

3. As he saw it, technological change and commercial advance raise the real rate of interest or the expected yield on newly created real capital and consequently determine the demand for investment. The prosperity phase of the cycle is characterized by savings being increasingly invested in fixed capital (by "the conversion on a large scale of liquid into fixed capital," *Lectures-II*, p. 209), and by the investment demand for the latter exceeding the supply of savings.

The upper turning point is reached when production becomes saturated with real capital at a given stage of technology. The downturn is often preceded by a crisis, which is due to the sudden cessation of the rise in commodity prices that occurs when investment demand begins to decline. It is characteristic of the downturn that savings, which are reduced in volume but nevertheless do not cease in this period, are almost entirely invested in an increasing accumulation of inventories or in "mobile real capital." Inventory accumulations, in turn, supply the basis for the subsequent recovery, the impulse for which is provided by new innovations and by commercial advance. These inventories make it possible to increase consumption when employment revives and also to provide the initial raw materials for expanding investment in fixed capital, which ushers in prosperity.

Wicksell's theory of business cycles had much in common with that of Arthur Spiethoff and to a certain extent, because of its emphasis on technological innovations, with that of Schumpeter. However, Wicksell's writings in this field, dating from 1890 onwards, antedated theirs by many years.

Public finance and theory of social economy. Wicksell's work on taxation records a certain advance of the theory of shifting and incidence of taxes over the development it had received by the classicists and by Cournot. It has already been related how, while working on these problems, he originated the marginal cost-pricing principle as the best criterion of production policy (the one that would result in the greatest contribution to the general welfare) for public enterprises.

Perhaps equally original, although less influential than the foregoing, was his attempt to elaborate a theory of equitable or just taxation by extending the marginal utility analysis to the problems of budgets and revenue acts. The basic principle for which he found surprisingly wide application in this field was the benefit principle of taxation. In his hands the latter could be extended also to include taxes levied according to ability to pay as representing effective techniques for raising revenues in a democratic society, provided these forms of taxation were supported by more than a bare majority of the citizens.

His "theory of social economy" was never formalized or completed. As applied both by him and by most of his contemporaries, this theory or concept was practically synonymous with what we nowadays refer to as a "theory of economic progress." However, his writings reveal that his own outlook on the conditions necessary for economic progress would have had the following character:

1. On grounds of maximizing the output of goods and services with given economic resources he urged considerable extension of socialized production in areas where private enterprise develops unmistakable monopoly tendencies.

2. In addition he would have placed heavy reliance on expansion of government welfare and developmental services, particularly in the field of education, in order to amplify and equalize economic opportunities for youth regardless of its income status in the community. These services were chiefly to be supported by the progressive types of taxation he advocated. He also thought a democratic society would voluntarily give overwhelming support to progressive tax legislation for the foregoing commendable expenditure objects.

3. In looking ahead toward a future, more rational, economic development of society, Wicksell visualized that the great majority of productive activities in an effectively organized "social economy" would be carried on under the auspices of highly competitive private enterprise, because nothing would be gained, and possibly much might be lost, by socializing production in areas where private enterprise remains "freely competitive." But this private production would be supplemented by many types of government services, especially in matters relating to the improvement and conservation of the human as well as the material resources of the economy. However, like J. S. Mill, he also held that the distribution of income and wealth in such a society would largely be a matter of "social institution."

He visualized that a relatively egalitarian distribution of income would be achieved by applying the fiscal powers of taxation and subsidization to mitigate the results of primary income distribution according to marginal productivity of economic resources. In his opinion, however, one of the prime prerequisites for the attainment of a social economy of this "mixed" (quasi-socialized, quasi-liberal) type was the prior achievement of an optimal relation between population and economic resources.

The foregoing reveals how substantial and varied were Wicksell's contributions to economic theory. By contrast, Wicksell expressed himself only in a fragmentary fashion on questions of method and scope in economics. However, what he had to say in this area is of sufficient interest to merit treatment in the following section.

Wicksell's Views on "Method and Scope" in Economics

In contradistinction to some of his distinguished contemporaries, notably Menger, Wicksell apparently did not consider the problem of methodology in economics to be very vital, at least not until the science had received further development. This is the reason he never attempted to deal with this problem systematically, and, except for his inaugural lecture upon his promotion to full professorship at Lund University, in September, 1904, devoted to "Aims and Methods in Economics," [2] he was content to comment on it only in passing in a few of his writings. In the following a few of his most characteristic remarks concerning the scope, method, and aims of economics have been gathered and juxtaposed.

His definition of economics "as a practical science" was in keeping with his reform-oriented approach to his subject:

. . . the definition of political economy as a practical science is the theory of the manner of satisfying human needs which gives the greatest possible satisfaction to society as a whole, having regard to future generations as well as the present. . . . As soon as we begin seriously to regard *economic phenomena as a whole* and to seek for the conditions of the welfare of the whole, consideration for the interest of the proletariat must emerge; and from thence to the proclamation of equal rights for all is only a short step. . . . *The very concept of political economy, therefore,* or the existence of a science with such a name, *implies, strictly speaking, a thoroughly revolutionary programme.*[3]

Despite this challenging definition most of his writings in economics are formal, highly abstract, theoretical treatises and essays which do not seem to be directly related to "the thoroughly revolutionary programme" his definition points to.

In this lecture he expressed the view that economics, relatively the most mature of the social sciences, could at best be compared with physics as of the early eighteenth century. It could offer but few laws or theorems likely to command universal assent together with a considerable variety of controversies concerning even a large number of its fundamental concepts. This notwithstanding, he averred:

. . . I would be surprised if the bitterly waged battles concerning method in science would not ultimately prove that all science, all human knowledge, is in substance obtained by the same method. To call one science empirical, another exact, another speculative or abstract is not warranted. All real science is empiric insofar as its point of departure as well as its goal must be reality, experience, and exact is every method which leads to the goal. . . . If the goal can be gained by direct observation, all the better, but generally our inquiries go beyond our resources of direct observation,

² His lecture, "Mål och medel i nationalekonomien" (Aims and Methods in Economics), was published in *Ekonomisk Tidskrift*, 6 (1904), 457-474.
³ K. Wicksell, *Lectures on Political Economy*, vol. I, pp. 3-4; italics supplied. Hereafter cited in text and footnotes as Wicksell, *Lectures-I*.

and at this point an element, necessary in almost all sciences, begins to take over, speculation, abstraction, hypothesis. . . .[4]

Once, as I hope and believe, we come to recognize that our goal on earth is to spread the greatest possible happiness to all, regardless of class, race, sex, language, or religion, then one will make the pleasant discovery that *the economic side of this problem has already in essence found its solution . . . and that the science of political economy* despite all, even in its present retarded position, the consequences of unfortunate circumstances, *possesses resources and means to make the average material conditions for human happiness greatly superior to the present ones.*[5]

But it was precisely because of the underdeveloped and controversial nature of economics that he found it necessary to seek a solid theoretical foundation for economic policy:

It will *not do* to treat questions relating to economic policy, to trade and industry . . . as if they were metaphysical speculations in which each person can adopt the point of view which appeals most to his temperament— and still more frequently to his private interests. We are here concerned with substantial quantities, measurable magnitudes. . . . To obtain an explanation of their relations which would be convincing to every thinking and unprejudiced person cannot be said to be outside the scope of economic inquiry but must, on the contrary, be its ultimate goal.[6]

It was for these reasons he adopted an approach explicitly patterned after the manner of Walras's *Élements,* a formal approach of successive analytical approximation to reality, enriched with mathematical demonstration of all major conclusions wherever feasible. For this approach he rightly claimed the following advantage: "by adopting it, it becomes easier to escape the criticism so often and with so much justice advanced against the older economists, that the range of validity of their conclusions was not always clearly established." [7]

He then set himself a working plan based on a tripartite division of the subject matter, the first part to be theoretical, the second, applied (on the basis of existing institutional conditions), and the third to be concerned with "social economics" or economic policy. It was in this third part that the application of theory and practical precept— the aim being the maximization of social welfare—under assumptions involving radical change or reform of existing institutions, was to be investigated.

---

[4] Wicksell, "Mål och medel i nationalekonomien" (Aims and Methods in Economics), *Ekonomisk Tidskrift,* 6 (1904), 464-465.

[5] *Ibid.,* p. 474. Italics supplied.

[6] Wicksell, *Lectures-I,* p. xxvii.

[7] *Ibid.,* p. 9.

This working plan, as in the case of Marshall, proved too vast to be executed during Wicksell's lifetime, partly because of the high standards of performance he set for himself. In fact, it was clear to him many years before his death, that he would not be able to finish either the second or the third part, as a statement in the first edition of *Lectures-I* in 1901 indicates.[8]

This meant that his energies would largely be devoted to completing the theoretical part of his work plan. In reference to the latter, he stated clearly the method he preferred to use: "The theoretical part was to issue in a 'statement of economic laws of the connection between economic phenomena, in which, in order to discover or demonstrate these laws, we must necessarily proceed from certain simplifying assumptions.'" [9]

As to his assumptions, abstractions, and method of successive approximation in general, he laid down the following conditions: ". . . the assumptions (must be) founded on reality, i.e., contain at least some elements of reality . . . for otherwise all reasoning about them would be sterile. . . . Further, the conditions from which we abstract must be relatively unessential, at least as regards the question under consideration." [10]

As one reads his works one finds that he was not always able to satisfy these criteria. But, at any rate, he scrupulously observed the fundamental rule of scientific etiquette: he was at all times careful to make explicit the nature of his abstractions and the number and character of his assumptions. To this should be added that his disinclination to construct suitable hypothetical models, and his terseness, were occasionally a hindrance to what he was endeavoring to communicate.

One may question the validity of his rationalist method in view of his aim, the maximization of social welfare. It is altogether probable that the question of social progress cannot be satisfactorily answered exclusively in terms of a rationalistic approach. It is quite possible he may have made more headway on that problem had he been less averse to empirical investigations and historical studies.

His possibly excessive reliance on aprioristic methods must then be understood as a reaction both to the antitheoretical nature of German historicism, and to the methods of dialectical materialism employed by socialist theoreticians. The first appeared to him as excessively empirical and largely sterile. The second impressed him as

---

[8] *Ibid.*, pp. 7-8.
[9] *Ibid.*, p. 9.
[10] *Ibid.*, p. 9.

doctrinaire in application and as arbitrary and unreliable for purposes of scientific prediction; within its own premises, it lacked a reliable method of deciding how many and what elements of the social scene to include in its analysis. Furthermore, it did not offer a recognizable method for weighting or assigning causative significance to the several variables in a problem subjected to the dialectical analysis.

Finally, as will be made clear, despite his preference for aprioristic reasoning, such explicit treatment as he gave to several questions of social reform and of the broader theme of social progress, did in fact not proceed without the benefit of empiric observation and considerable reflection on the past course of social history with an eye to estimating its most probable future trend and configuration. However, these issues or problems could not, in the nature of the case, be permitted to intrude themselves, except incidentally, in his formal work on economics.

CHAPTER III

Theory of Value

The Marginal Utility Explanation of Value

Wicksell's treatment of marginal utility theory per se was a work of interpretation and critical appraisal. While he adopted this principle as the best explanation of value extant, he viewed it as an incomplete value theory which needed further development. Thus he was at pains to point out that, even as an explanation of market values or of relative prices, marginal utility theory was subject to significant limitations. These had to do with the nature and interrelationships of commodities on the one hand and with the relations between commodity value-magnitudes and the size of consumer budgets on the other hand.

At the same time in another sphere, that of public finance, Wicksell accorded marginal utility theory much wider scope than did most of his contemporaries. As will be shown more clearly later, Wicksell approached public finance almost entirely from the perspective of the "interest" or "benefit" principle. In substance this principle amounts to a consistent application of marginal utility estimations to taxes or revenue measures as well as to public budgets or expenditure objects. Yet, as he emphasized, marginal utility calculations are most meaningful when they are carried on in real terms. They become meaningful also in terms of relative prices, but only on the assumption that money has, or is so managed as to have, constant value. However, except in the very short run, this is not likely to be the case in the world in which we live. To the contrary, economic experience has thus far occurred in an environment characterized by monies of fluctuating rather than constant values.

Thus in his monetary analysis Wicksell was concerned to show how marginal utility calculations are perniciously affected by fluctuations in the value of money. As he viewed them, these fluctuations were chiefly the consequences of the pursuit of irrational types of central bank policies. Misguided monetary policies yield market or bank rates of interest which deviate from the real rate of interest, i.e., from the actual rate of preference of present over future goods or utilities. Guided by the bank rate of interest, individuals, as income recipients in deciding on how to allocate their incomes between saving and consumption spending, are likely to misjudge the actual rate of preference of present over future goods. Simultaneously another set of individuals, entrepreneurs, are apt to misread the level and the most probable trend of the real rate of marginal value productivity (or of marginal efficiency) of capital by using the prevailing bank rate of interest as a bench mark. This is bound to affect or distort their investment and output decisions, and to make the latter progressively less compatible or less consistent with the income-allocation decisions of the great body of consumers. At the same time central banks, because they are financial institutions rather than utility-maximizing individuals, cannot be guided directly by the marginal utility calculus in deciding on the scope and contents of credit policy. Moreover, as properly functioning, responsible central banks, they *ought not* to make these decisions primarily on the basis of how their profit positions would be affected. Without the benefit of utility-and/or profit-maximizing criteria for determining monetary policy, central banks are in fact left without direct and clear-cut criteria for their policy decisions. Instead they are forced to resort to trial-and-error methods of applying their policies and to indirect, often indistinct, and after-the-fact indications concerning the correctness and efficacy of policies recently adopted as imperfect guides to current policy decisions, which are to remain in effect over some period in the future.

The Nature of Equilibrium Market Prices

In the first approximation, the task of value theory is to explain market prices, and only at a later stage in the analysis—by bringing observations obtainable from production theory into focus—to account for how market prices tend to be transformed into long-run equilibrium values. This was and remains the characteristic approach in the theory of price formation.

The study of equilibrium market prices proceeds traditionally on several simplifying assumptions and conditions. Observations are generally limited to a particular consumption period for a closed economy in which all persons possess an initial quantity of goods and services, which remain fixed in quantity during the period in question (because supply variation from the sphere of production is eliminated by abstraction). Moreover, while tastes and wants vary as between persons, for each particular individual they are assumed to be predetermined and to remain unchanged during the period. The fixed quantity of goods and services implies that total real income in this economy is constant. So are individual real incomes except for such subjective modification as the latter may undergo as a result of exchange.

In these circumstances the only problem that arises is for each person to maximize his satisfaction by trading less preferred units from among his fixed resources for resources offered by others for which he has greater preference. This trading process is greatly facilitated if some one commodity serves as *numéraire* or as a standard of value in terms of which the exchange ratios of all other commodities can be expressed as prices.

If there are many individuals in the economy, and if resources are so distributed that the quantities owned by the wealthiest person are of a second order of magnitude, or are infinitesimal, in relation to the total quantity traded in the market by all other individuals, then exchange takes place under conditions of "free" or pure competition. As a result of the trading that occurs a set of equilibrium market prices emerges. In the early phase of trading prices may vary considerably, but eventually they tend to become stable and uniform for each commodity on the market, at a level, the equilibrium level of price, at which supply equals demand for each commodity. Furthermore, if the price of any commodity deviates temporarily from its equilibrium level, it is soon driven back to that level by an appropriate variation in its supply in the same direction and variation of its demand in the inverse direction to the price deviation.

In this familiar abstract situation, what determines and explains the various market equilibrium prices? Wicksell's answer was also, with certain reservations, a familiar one; namely, that these prices are determined by the tendency of each individual to maximize his total utility by trading until, for each commodity remaining in his possession, its marginal utility to him is proportional and equal to its price. Like many of his contemporaries, Wicksell was fond of expressing this conclusion mathematically. To that end he construed the individual's total utility as a function of all the commodities on the market and of their terms of exchange or prices in *numéraire*. Maximization of this utility function was then expressed as occurring when the partial derivatives of the function with respect to each commodity are proportional to the commodity's exchange value.[1]

There would seem to be little room for doubt about the validity of the marginal utility doctrine as applied to most market situations if it is granted that the maximization postulate is the ruling motive and stimulus underlying the observed propensity to "truck and barter," and if it is further granted that those who participate in this process possess, on the average, the requisite degree of rationality and persistence to conduct their trading in the manner outlined above. Yet, as Wicksell stressed, even here on its "home grounds," this theory is subject to several important qualifications. These center around (a) the nature of interrelations between commodity demands and supplies, (b) the technical character—size and indivisibility—of many commodities in relation to individual demand functions, (c) the impossibility for individuals to measure relative marginal and total utility in any other than an ordinal sense, and (d) the less than freely or purely competitive market situations in which a significant and increasing proportion of total exchanges or trade takes place.

Similar qualifications on marginal utility theory were also noted and emphasized in the writings of several of Wicksell's contemporaries, notably in the works of Marshall, Edgeworth, Pareto, and Wicksteed.

Interrelations of Demand and of Supply of Commodities

Marginal utility theory is most easily illustrated and applied to commodities that are "independent" from the standpoint of demand or supply. These are commodities which are not subject to a high degree of joint (complementary) or of competitive (substitutive) demand or supply. In all other cases buyer decisions with respect to any particular commodity are affected by the prices of its close substitutes or complements, as the case may be. In addition, sellers' supply (and production) decisions proceed on the basis of comparisons of composite marginal value products with joint marginal costs of production for joint products.[2] In cases of strong complementarity it is clear that the marginal utility calculus cannot meaningfully be applied to one or another of the complements taken by themselves. In such cases it is often advisable to expand the definition of "commodity" and then proceed to apply the calculus to the group as such rather than to its individual components.

Wicksell's work on joint demand and joint supply was not very

---

[1] Wicksell, *Lectures-I*, pp. 46-49, 65-67, 78-81.
[2] *Ibid.*, pp. 84-85.

systematic. A primary reason for this was that he did not possess the convenient concept of cross-elasticity of demand and supply by which to make more precise the meaning of "commodities independent of each other as regards consumption." [3] As a result his treatment is somewhat inconclusive. One gathers that marginal utility evaluations can be directly applied to commodities "independent" of each other, but not if they are too independent, for: "Where, on the other hand, two commodities cannot replace each other in consumption, but either wholly or in part satisfy different needs, it becomes a question whether their relative utilities can be measured by or compared by any common standard." [4]

By "independent" he evidently meant commodities that are not close substitutes or complements. But his most interesting comments, which qualify the utility calculus by pointing to the possibility of unstable price equilibria, refer to commodities which are "to a greater or less extent capable of acting as substitutes." [5] It was with reference to these that he brought out very clearly the possibiliy of a perverse response of supply (or demand) to a change in price of a particular commodity. At the same time, despite his familiarity with Pareto's stress on complementarity in *Manuel d'économie politique,* Wicksell neglected its analysis while concentrating on that of substitutes.

His discussion of joint demand and supply was more complete than Marshall's treatment. To some extent it anticipated the later Hicks-Allen analysis of substitution and complementarity in demand and supply of goods, and the analytical separation of income and substitution effects of changes in relative prices.[6] In this respect Wicksell stood at the threshold of the contemporary perspective which conceives of demand and supply relations as variable over a considerable range. At one extreme this range is limited by perfect substitutability and at the other by perfect complementarity. Within this range there may arise stable as well as unstable market price equilibria even under the purest of competition, depending on the relative position and slope or elasticity of the demand and supply functions.

Technical Character of Commodities—Size and Indivisibility

Marginal utility theory assumes that individual demand functions for particular commodities are continuously and incrementally variable. This implies that the supply variations by means of which marginal

---

[3] *Ibid.,* p. 57.
[4] *Ibid.,* p. 17.
[5] *Ibid.,* pp. 56 ff., 60-63; Wicksell, *Value, Capital and Rent,* pp. 86 ff.
[6] Cf. J. R. Hicks, *Value and Capital* (1939), pp. 31, 32, 36.

utilities of commodities are compared must be of a second order of magnitude relative to the budget of the individual consumer or household. This condition holds approximately for a host of consumption goods, but not for the majority of those which are included in the category of durable consumers' goods. The indivisibility of the latter rests more on technical than on economic grounds. Whatever its cause, it tends to make individual marginal utility evaluations with respect to houses, automobiles, and the like, exceedingly crude.

Wicksell recognized three types of discontinuity and indivisibility which affect the analysis of demand: (1) when prices are so high that some consumers are forced out of the market and some sellers are completely sold out; (2) when prices are so low that sellers withhold supplies on the basis of reservation demand; and (3) when commodities represent large and indivisible units even after allowances are made for quality differences between such units. In reference to the first two types he said: "In such circumstances . . . marginal utility *has ceased* to regulate the quantities of goods demanded and supplied by such persons." [7]

But if marginal utility has ceased regulating supply and demand in such cases, he failed to state what does regulate them. As to the third variety of discontinuity, he held: "Determination of market price in the ordinary sense is impossible and business is reduced to more or less isolated exchange . . . in which price . . . is indeterminate." [8]

This was undoubtedly an overhasty resolution of the problem of indivisible goods. It is doubtful whether one can say, for instance, that the automobile market proceeds on the basis of isolated exchange. Yet from a consumer standpoint it is obvious that the purchase of a car represents a relatively large outlay for an indivisible commodity as compared with the purchase of a pound of coffee.

Measurability of Utility

Whether and to what extent utility is measurable is a curious problem in economics. Leading theorists of the last two generations have been careful to point out that interpersonal utility comparisons were out of the question. They have also stressed that even at the subjective level, it is impossible for an individual to measure utility, whether total, average, or marginal, in the manner he can measure length and weight. Nevertheless, much of their treatment of utility

---

[7] Wicksell, *Lectures-I*, p. 69; italics supplied. As for quality differences between large, indivisible commodities, he insisted these facilitated the application of marginal utility calculus to such goods; see his article, "Verteidigung der Grenznutzenlehre," *Zeitschrift für die gesammten Staatswissenschaften*, 56 (1900), 584.

[8] Wicksell, *Lectures-I*, p. 71,

and demand proceeded on reasoning or illustrations which implied that utility is measurable in the cardinal sense. This is certainly the impression created by illustrations of individual demand functions by histograms or by smoothed curves. The same holds for numerous mathematical interpretations of individual demand for particular commodities as first partial differentials of multidimensional total utility functions, and for the conclusion that prices tend to proportionality with the marginal utility assessments for various commodities by buyers on the margin of indifference in the market.

Wicksell was no exception to this rule. He agreed that interpersonal utility comparisons cannot be made. He insisted that it is only different degrees of utility to the same person that are compared, and that in these comparisons it is not the maximum, nor the average, but the least important use values or utilities of goods that are compared. He averred further that some crude sort of interpersonal utility comparison might be possible if property and incomes were distributed in more egalitarian fashion.[9]

He was also aware of the indifference ratio or marginal rate of substitution technique of analysis in this field, but he made no use of it. This technique was foreshadowed in some of Cournot's diagrams. It was subsequently developed by Edgeworth, then adopted and used extensively by Pareto, only to fall into disuse until it was revived, years later, by A. Bowley in his *Mathematical Groundwork of Economics* (1924). But even in Bowley's work its application as a solution of the measurability problem was not in evidence. Its implications for such a solution had to await the work of J. R. Hicks and R. G. D. Allen in the early 1930's. They worked out the contemporary, explicitly relativistic theory of consumers' choice, and then discovered that as early as 1915 Eugen Slutsky had arrived at a similar theory in a long-neglected article written for *Giornale degli Economisti*.[10]

Imperfections of the Market

MONOPOLY, DUOPOLY, AND MONOPOLISTIC COMPETITION

The conclusion that equilibrium prices will be proportionate to the force of individual marginal utility estimates of commodities in the market assumes that the market is perfectly competitive. At the very least, it is implied that no buyer or group of buyers exercise monopsony power over sellers who may, without disturbing the buyer-calculus, be either competitive or monopolistic. It is only in a purely competi-

[9] *Ibid.*, pp. 30, 33; Wicksell, *Value, Capital, and Rent*, pp. 49 ff.
[10] Cf. Hicks, *op. cit.*, p. 19, n. 1.

tive market that sellers and buyers both take the temporarily ruling market prices as data and adjust their individual demands and supplies accordingly. But when sellers or buyers, singly or in combination, become aware that they can influence prices by curtailing or expanding their demand or supply as the case may be, then the resulting equilibrium prices will no longer be proportional to the marginal utility assessment of commodities. Even to attempt to express to what prices will be proportional in such cases in the older terminology becomes quite cumbersome as compared with the great convenience afforded for such expressions by the current concepts of marginal revenue and marginal cost, which were introduced by R. F. Kahn and P. Sraffa in the closing years of the 1920's.

Perhaps this was the reason writers of the last generation left an impression that price determination under imperfect competition was in some fundamental sense different under free competition. The lack of a suitable set of concepts for dealing with these problems, even if some of the later concepts were implicit in their mathematical discussions of monopoly pricing, may have been the primary reason why their observations were in the main confined to conditions of pure competition. This also explains why their insights into the nature of imperfect markets, though often penetrating, lacked precision and definiteness.

Wicksell contributed to bridging the apparent dichotomy between freely competitive and monopoly price determination by bringing into the body of his discussion a fairly complete treatment of Cournot's problems of monopoly, duopoly, and polyopoly. He also stressed the pervasive nature of imperfect markets and he made a definite advance in this field by clearly showing the connection between the theory of isolated exchange and the phenomenon of bilateral monopoly.

He considered market imperfection to be the greatest stumbling block for marginal utility theory: "But the most important objection [to marginal utility theory of value] . . . is no doubt the fact that our assumption of *free competition* is and can only be *imperfectly realized.*" [11]

Along with Marshall and others of his period, Wicksell emphasized that free competition endures only in fields where economies of scale are insignificant, or where the production function is homogeneous and linear. His standard examples of free competition were wholesale trade and agriculture. Everywhere else he recognized the presence of market imperfections in varying degree.

His treatment of monopoly in *Lectures-I* offered very little out of

---

[11] Wicksell, *Lectures-I*, p. 71.

the usual. His observations were restricted to a monopoly operating under constant cost. On the other hand, he developed the implications of monopoly in the field of taxation at length in *Finanztheoretische Untersuchungen,* a matter which we shall reserve for discussion later on. In general one may say that Wicksell's treatment of monopoly, duopoly, and the transition to polyopoly by entry of new firms amounted essentially to a restatement of the position Cournot had taken on these topics and to a defense of Cournot's point of view against some objections brought forth by Edgeworth and Barone.

In his discussion of multimonopoly, Wicksell stressed the likelihood of the several monopolists combining, and he concluded, somewhat hastily, that the combined sellers would behave like a single joint monopoly. As later analysis indicates, this need by no means be the case. Many forms of combination are possible, from complete mergers to loose cartel arrangements, including also such forms as producer and consumer coöperatives. It is clear that the production and pricing policies of these dissimilar types of organizations are not likely to follow the same pattern, and do not consistently resemble those of pure monopoly.

Wicksell also recognized that there exists a variety of mixed and weaker types of monopolies which are related to and yet are distinct from the foregoing "strong" or "pure" cases of market imperfection. He referred to the latter as imperfect or partial monopolies. Today we would classify most of these in the category of monopolistic competition, a market structure he considered to be particularly prevalent in the retail field. His observations of this phenomenon amounted to a contribution which, at least at the verbal level, anticipated several of the characteristic conclusions on the monopolistic competition analysis of the early 1930's.

In the retail field Wicksell found market imperfection to rest on three grounds: joint costs, location advantages, and consumer ignorance. Retail store managements perform essentially retail merchandising services for their customers. So far as any particular lot of merchandise among the various lots that are handled in such stores is concerned, these services are a joint product occasioned as much by the presence of other merchandise as by the particular lot in question. From the store management's point of view the performance of retail merchandising services involves outlays or costs. These become overhead expenses which cannot rationally, but only arbitrarily, be charged to the various lots of merchandise, perhaps in relation to the relative values of particular lots or in relation to their rate of turnover or sale, or some combination of these elements.

Secondly, each retail store has a location advantage in its immediate neighborhood. This is largely what accounts for overcrowding in the retail field. The relative ease of entry of new, small firms (small capital requirements) and the prospect that propinquity alone will attract customers from already established firms, constitute strong inducements for new retail establishments to spring up. The result is likely to be that at any given time and place there will be too many overly small retail firms for the good of consumers and store owners alike. The effect of this condition is a combination of retail prices higher than a more rational allocation of resources to this type of marketing service would have called for, and a higher incidence of business failures than would be likely in the absence of crowding.[12]

Thirdly, consumer ignorance and inertia preclude any effective "shopping" on their part, which might result in more uniform retail markups and prices. In addition there is a service aspect to differentiated retail markups. Staple articles, equally familiar to most consumers, sell at low and relatively uniform markup. Complex and unusual goods, the quality of which can in most instances not be fully known to the consumer, move at substantially higher markups. One important reason for this is that in such cases the retailer gives the consumer the benefits of his personal services as an expert buyer.

It is strange that Wicksell did not enter into a discussion of consumer coöperatives. He only mentioned in passing that they may have a constructive role to play in correcting some of the wastes of imperfect competition.

The correct remedy [for too many retailers and excessively high retail prices] unless one of the competitors such as a great store manages to overshadow all the others, is clearly the *formation of some form of organization among the buyers*. But so long as such an association does not exist—and between persons in different positions in life and without more intimate bonds, it is extremely difficult to establish—the anomaly must remain that competition may sometimes raise prices instead of always lowering them as one would expect.[13]

The foregoing was one of the few, brief comments he had to make concerning consumer coöperatives. Yet during his lifetime, consumer coöperatives grew from very modest beginnings in Sweden to dominate a significant portion of the country's retail and wholesale trade. Because of his reformist tendencies and also because the behavior of such organizations, when strong, differs from that of ordinary profit-

---

[12] *Ibid.*, pp. 86-88.
[13] *Ibid.*, p. 88. Italics supplied.

motivated industrial and trade organizations, and thus must have posed a theoretical challenge, one would expect Wicksell to have given the coöperative movement more attention than he did.

The writer made an inquiry about this in private correspondence with the late Professor Sommarin, who explained the reasons for Wicksell's apparent indifference to the coöperative movement. At the turn of the century when that movement was introduced in Sweden, it was heralded by its enthusiasts as a social panacea. This only served to arouse Wicksell's skepticism. During the early years of its development there were numerous business failures among local coöperative stores. These were due to a combination of untoward circumstances. Many of the failures were the consequences of incompetent and sometimes venal management. Other failures were due to an attempt to satisfy rash demands for concrete benefits (patronage dividends) which were pressed by customer-members whose hopes had been unduly aroused by propagandists for the coöperative movement. Because of this unconvincing performance Wicksell apparently lost interest in the coöperatives and discounted them heavily as a meliorative force of any significance.

ISOLATED EXCHANGE AND BILATERAL MONOPOLY

Perhaps the most interesting work Wicksell did in the field of value theory was on the problems of isolated exchange and bilateral monopoly. As to the former, he was preceded by Edgeworth, who dealt with isolated exchange both in his *Mathematical Psychics* (1881, pp. 29 ff.) and in an article he wrote on the same topic for *Giornale degli Economisti* (February, 1891). Wicksell's earliest treatment appeared in *Über Wert, Kapital und Rente* or *Value, Capital and Rent* (1893), pp. 61 ff.

Marshall adopted Edgeworth's analysis and summarized it in Note XII of the Mathematical Appendix in the third (1895) and later editions of his *Principles of Economics*.

Wicksell returned to this problem again in *Lectures-I* (1901 and later editions), pp. 49-52, where he restated the conclusions he had reached in his earlier treatment in nonmathematical form.

However, the problem of isolated exchange and the related one of bilateral monopoly received very little additional attention after the 1890's until A. Bowley revived interest in both in his *Mathematical Groundwork of Economics* (1924). Wicksell's contribution to the theory of bilateral monopoly was received in the form of a review he wrote of Bowley's work for *Ekonomisk Tidskrift* (1925). This lengthy review attracted the attention of Schumpeter and others and at their urging it was subsequently translated into German and published in *Archiv für Sozialwissenschaft* (1927).

Since 1927 the bilateral monopoly problem has received increasing attention because of its importance in contemporary institutional circumstances. For instance, many contracts signed between labor unions and large employers in the process of collective bargaining partake of the nature of bilateral monopoly negotiations. The limits within which such bargains are likely to be effected have recently been the object of penetrating analysis by Professor Fellner in an article on "Wages and Prices under Bilateral Monopoly," *Quarterly Journal of Economics* (August, 1947) and also in his comprehensive treatise, *Competition Among the Few* (1949).

1. *Isolated exchange.* Edgeworth's treatment had succeeded in narrowing the alleged complete indeterminacy of value in isolated barter to more manageable proportions. Since no individual voluntarily trades at a loss, exchange value must be determined within a bargaining range, lying within the limits of the no-gain, no-loss exchange ratios for both traders. Within this range, however, there are other exchange ratios possible at which each is trading at some gain to himself. The locus of those bargains, within the no-gain exchange ratio limits, from which it is impossible to deviate to the advantage of one party without hurting the other party defines the "contract curve." Quantities of respective commodities traded, and hence their exchange ratios, were considered to be indeterminate over the range of the "contract curve." Edgeworth thought it conceivable, though unlikely and purely coincidental, that barter might take place at an exchange ratio of equal gain to each trader, that ratio being on the curve. He thought it more likely that one party would gain relatively more than the other at barter, depending on the relative bargaining skill or strength of the two parties.

By a slightly different approach Wicksell also found that the equal gain ratio for each of the traders would be located on the contract curve. But this ratio would only be realizable by coincidence. On the other hand he found that a maximum joint gain ratio for both traders would not be located on the contract curve and would be likely to be outside the bargaining limits, at which one or the other trader exchanges at no gain. Thus he concluded that: "price determination in isolated exchange is an indeterminate problem, i.e., cannot be solved solely on the assumption that both parties desire the greatest possible profit." [14]

---

[14] Wicksell, *Value, Capital and Rent*, pp. 61-62; see also A. Bowley, *Mathematical Groundwork of Economics* (Oxford, 1924), pp. 62 ff.

It was almost thirty years later before he reverted to this topic in the far more significant guise of an analysis of the determination of price and output under conditions of bilateral monopoly.

2. *Bilateral monopoly.* Wicksell's work on bilateral monopoly was confined to a remarkable review article of Bowley's *Mathematical Groundwork of Economics* (1924), written for *Ekonomisk Tidskrift* in 1925, under the title "Mathematisk Nationalekonomi" (Mathematical Economics). In this article Wicksell managed to (*a*) discourse on the value of mathematical method for theoretical work in economics, (*b*) restate and defend Cournot's analysis of imperfect competition against his posthumous critics, Bertrand and Edgeworth, (*c*) chide Bowley for having uncritically adopted some of Edgeworth's conclusions vis-à-vis Cournot, (*d*) discuss and criticize Pigou's tax-and-subsidy scheme for industries of increasing and of decreasing returns, (*e*) criticize Bowley's treatment of bilateral monopoly and make a contribution of his own to its analysis, (*f*) comment favorably on the distinction between "inferior" goods and their price and output behavior as compared with that of ordinary goods, and (*g*) appraise favorably the prospects of the indifference-concept as a device of analysis in the field of value theory. Only Wicksell's work under item (*e*) will be discussed here. The other aspects will be disregarded.

Although isolated exchange and bilateral monopoly have some features in common, their differences are perhaps more important. In contrast with isolated barter, where each party has an initially fixed supply of some commodity, bilateral monopoly involves production. Consequently, the analysis of the latter is not limited to considerations of market price alone. It involves at least a short-run determination (*a*) of commodity prices, (*b*) factor prices, (*c*) of output of product, and (*d*) of factor quantity used or of employment. In addition, bilateral monopoly exists in an economic environment which is generally characterized by other market structures involving a greater degree of competition. Thus bilateral monopoly cannot in the long run offer terms to either party which are inferior to those available in surrounding, more competitive, markets by more than the cost of movement into or access to such markets. There is no similar "lower limit" externally imposed, as it were, under isolated barter.

Moreover, bilateral monopoly involves an extra degree of freedom compared with isolated exchange among consumer-traders because buyer-monopsonists are generally not purely competitive sellers of their own products. To that extent they have relief from or room for adjustment to possible harsh terms imposed by factor-monopolists. For, within limits of elasticity of product demand, factor-buyer-monopsonists operating in imperfect product sales markets can alter their end-product prices by varying the volume of their output. No similar adjustment or "shifting" is possible in isolated barter. As contrasted with the latter, it would only be under exceptional circumstances that monopsonists involved in bilateral monopoly relations with factor-monopolists might be forced to "trade at no gain."

Finally, contemporary analysis of bilateral monopoly proceeds on the basis of a set of cost and revenue concepts which were not made explicit and did not become widely accepted in economics until the early 1930's with the development of the theory of monopolistic competition. The character of the conceptual apparatus requisite for these purposes has been stated clearly and concisely in Professor Fellner's article "Wages and Prices under Bilateral Monopoly." [15]

Bowley's treatment of bilateral monopoly in 1924, and Wicksell's response to it the year following were both less complete and less explicit than are most contemporary treatments. In part, this was due to the simplifying assumptions on which their analysis proceeded. But most of it was probably due to the fact that the analogues of marginal-cost, marginal-value-product, marginal-to-marginal-cost, and marginal-to-marginal-value-product concepts, which are essential to the contemporary discussion, were left on an implicit basis in Bowley's and Wicksell's application of the differential calculus to aggregate value product and aggregate cost functions in their treatment of the bilateral monopoly problem.

The situation to which they addressed themselves did not differ as greatly from that of isolated barter as do modern labor-management relations between organized employers and organized labor engaged in collective bargaining. For present purposes trader A at isolated barter is simply replaced by a manufacturer who is a monopsonist with reference to the market in which he procures his factors of production. Trader B was also replaced by a factor-monopolist, in this case one particular laborer, a skilled artisan. To add a touch of realism to his discussion, Wicksell in his review mentioned that he remembered reading of a case in the works of Babbage where a doll manufacturer succeeded after extensive search in finding an Italian artisan noted for his skill in painting remarkably lifelike dolls' eyes. Since this artisan was the only man in the city of London in possession of this rare skill, he was, indeed, a factor-monopolist. Thus the problem was one of finding how the monopsonist would determine his output and selling

[15] W. Fellner, "Wages and Prices under Bilateral Monopoly," *Quarterly Journal of Economics*, LXI (August, 1947), especially pp. 505-508; for a more extended treatment, cf W. Fellner *Competition Among the Few* (1949), chaps. ix and x.

price and the factor-monopolist his price or wage and his labor supply offer.

Bowley's analysis was of the following type. The manufacturer-monopsonist, knowing the demand function for his end-product as well as its production function, decides to offer a wage rate, π_1, a piece rate, for the quantity of labor he needs to produce output X_1'. This X_1' quantity of output is the output which the manufacturer calculates as most likely to enable him to maximize his profit. The wage rate he offers is determined by the magnitude of his marginal value product function for the labor quantity requisite for production of X_1' output.

But when the monopsonist offers wage rate π_1, the factor-monopolist independently decides to supply a quantity of labor X_1''. This quantity is likely to be different from X_1', which the manufacturer hoped to obtain. The factor-monopolist's supply offer of X_1'' is determined so as to maximize his income in the sense that $\pi_1 X_1''$, his income, becomes a magnitude which, relative to the disutility associated with delivering the X_1'' labor quantity, makes the difference between income received and disutility incurred a maximum.

Since X_1'' need not be, or is not likely to be, equal to X_1', Bowley concluded that: "There may be a value for which $X_1' = X_1''$, but without collusion it will not be obtained." [16] In other words, in bilateral monopoly, employment, factor prices, output, and end-product prices are all indeterminate unless both parties collude. Wicksell's objection to this was: "If the manufacturer can set the wage rate, then, contrary to the assumption, the worker has no longer a monopoly. . . . That wageworkers will only work so and so much for a certain wage offer constitutes no monopoly on their part. One must rather assume that the workers themselves determine their wage, and, if so, they have a primary, a real monopoly." [17]

Then Wicksell proceeded to an analysis of what amounts to a case of noncollusive bilateral monopoly under factor-monopoly domination. This, he thought, embodied the essence of noncollusive bilateral monopoly, rather than a particular and not unimportant variety of the more fully developed theory of bilateral monopoly.

Now, if the worker-monopolist can decide his own piece rate of wages according to income-maximizing criteria, then all that remains for the manufacturer-monopsonist (*sans* effective monopsony power in this situation) to do is to decide his rate of output and his product-

---

[16] A. Bowley, *Mathematical Groundwork for Economics*, p. 62.

[17] Wicksell, "Matematisk Nationalekonomi" (Mathematical Economics), *Ekonomisk Tidskrift*, 27 (1925), 122.

price according to profit-maximizing criteria on the basis of his taking the piece rate of wages as a datum. Since it is a piece-rate wage that is under consideration, the production function becomes so simple that it may be ignored in this problem. It is assumed that the manufacturer and the worker both know the rate of output per unit of time that the worker is willing and able to produce at various possible piece rates.

If the wage rate (the determination of which is considered later) is taken as a datum, then the output quantity, x, and the price, p, at which the manufacturer maximizes his profit depend on the demand function for his product. Output x would reach its maximum magnitude if he offered his output free, i.e., when p is zero. On the other hand, if he prices his output high enough, no output at all will be sold, or x will then be zero. The units in which both price and output are measured span these limits in order to make the analysis general. Thus $x = 1.00$ only when $p = 0.00$, and $p = 1.00$ only when $x = 0.00$. The actual x and p to be determined will lie between these limits and will be expressed as fractions of their respective maximum (unitary) amounts. In consequence, a very general demand function was used, namely: $x = 1 - p$. The situation in question is illustrated in figure 1.

Given the wage-rate, π, the manufacturer's profit, y, is determined by: $y = (p - \pi) \cdot (1 - p)$, i.e., by the difference between his aggregate value product and his aggregate cost. Since π is a datum or a constant, if we differentiate this expression with respect to p and then equate the differential to zero, we obtain the solution for p and x which will make the manufacturer's profit a maximum: $dy/dp = 0.00 = (1 - 2p + \pi)$, hence $p = (1 + \pi)/2$, and $x = (1 - \pi)/2$.

The situation now depends on the worker's determination of his piece-wage-rate. For this purpose it is assumed that the worker knows the manufacturer's marginal value product function, i.e., his labor demand. The worker's income, which is to be maximized per unit of time, depends on his output or productivity times the piece rate of wages, per unit of time, and may be written: $w = \pi(1 - \pi/2)$, or $2w = \pi - \pi^2$. If one ignores multiplication by the constant 2, and if one differentiates this expression with respect to w and equates the differential to zero, one obtains the piece rate which maximizes the worker's income. This rate is expressed in the same units as p; namely, $dw/d\pi = 0.0 = 1 - 2\pi$, or $\pi = 1/2$, and with this the problem is solved. For when $\pi = 1/2$, $p = 3/4$, and $x = 1/4$. As a result, the manufacturer's maximized profit is $y = 1/16$; the worker's maximized income, here the lion's share of the total value product, is $w = 1/8$, and the

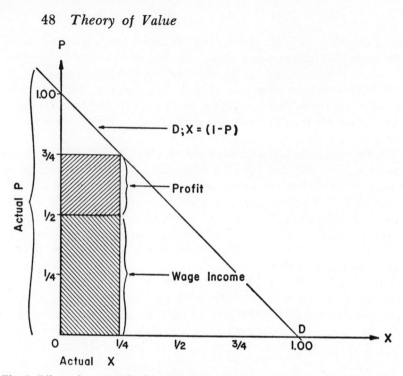

Fig. 1. Bilateral monopoly determination of output, wages, and profits under factor-monopoly domination.

aggregate value product is $y + w = 3/16$. Thus Wicksell found that price and output of end product, and price and input (i.e., employment or quantity of services supplied) of factors of production, are entirely determinate in noncollusive bilateral monopoly as long as the factor-monopolist is the dominant party.

Having demonstrated this, he then turned to the opposite case of monopsonist domination. As Bowley and others have pointed out subsequently, this case is symmetrical with its opposite number and is equally determinate. But for some reason Wicksell failed to reach this solution and concluded that product and factor prices and outputs in noncollusive bilateral monopoly dominated by the monopsonist would not be determinate except by a stratagem:

The employer, on the other hand, cannot take the initiative by setting a certain selling price and output quantity, for in that case it is to the worker's advantage to demand the highest possible wage which the employer can be induced to pay. It may be possible for the employer to depress the worker's wage rate by use of a stratagem, namely if, apparently contrary to his interest, for every concrete wage level he sets a selling price (according to the usual maximization rule) *as if* the wage rate had been higher, e.g., twice as high as the wage actually paid.[18]

This fell short of the recognition that the dominant monopsonist in such a situation determines the factor quantity he will use for which his marginal value product function equals (or intersects with) the function which represents the marginal-to-marginal cost of labor to him. The latter is a variable that bears the same relation to the monopsonist's marginal cost function x (which expresses the supply function of labor) as his marginal cost function bears to his average cost function.

At any rate, on the stratagem-assumption Wicksell was able to show —although his demonstration was defective—that the roles of the employer and the worker would be reversed. If the employer sets his price *as if* the wage rate were twice as high as actually is the case, then, as the foregoing calculations indicate, $p = 1/2 + \pi$; the worker's income $w = \pi(1/2 - \pi)$, and this income is maximized when $\pi = 1/4$. The selling price of the output, p, would be the same as before, namely $p = 3/4$, and the quantity of output would also be the same, namely $x = 1/4$. But the monopsonist's profit would now be greater, $y = 1/8$, while the worker's income would be smaller, $w = 1/16$, and the aggregate value product would remain the same, namely, $y + w = 3/16$.

But Wicksell rejected this tentative demonstration as illegitimate under the rationality postulate which underlay all of his analysis, and which would have precluded the worker from acting on the manufacturer's stratagem. Thus he concluded: "One can consequently say that in this case it is the worker who attains a real maximum and the employer a relative maximum. The great importance of the problem is easily recognized if we replace one worker with a strong union with tens of thousands of members and one employer by a syndicate of employers within a certain branch of production." [19]

This was a premature conclusion. It implied that the motivation and maximization problem would be as simple for a strong union and a well-united group of employers as for a single worker and his employer. This was an oversimplification. Collective bargaining, apparently, involves a composite of several maximization problems at the same time. The complex relations between multiple ends and means or strategies of collective bargaining have not yet been unraveled to the point where we are in possession of a theory or an explanation of the proportions in which the several ends are likely to be attained in given circumstances.

---

[18] *Ibid.*, pp. 122-123.
[19] *Ibid.*, p. 124.

Secondly, his conclusion implied that bargaining strength is not likely to be as great on the side of organized employers as on the side of organized workers or other firmly united suppliers of factors of production. Certain observations he had made earlier in *Value, Capital and Rent* concerning the possibility of a combination or joint monopoly of capitalists depressing the wage rates of freely competitive labor may have made him prone to infer that the relative strength of the factor-monopolist in a bilateral monopoly situation is always greater than that of the monopsonist producer of end products.

But it is also likely that his reasoning was influenced by the circumstance that employers have on the whole used different and less dramatic methods to exert their monopsony power than have been applied by workers to exert their monopoly power. Lockouts are far rarer than strikes, and they are probably also less effective. Furthermore, a lockout represents a deliberate assumption of a risk by employers which, in the case of a strike, is forced upon them. Both result in a production stoppage which, particularly if it is protracted, involves great risks for employers who sell in monopolistic markets. During the stoppage their "administered" price structures, market quotas, and the like may crumble or change independently of the outcome of the dispute. On the other hand, factor-monopolists who operate in bilateral monopoly markets have, in the absence of collusive agreements, hardly any other effective method for pressing their requirements than that of withdrawing temporarily the supply of the factor in question in full and then restoring it when a settlement has been reached, on the basis of an all-or-none offer to monopsonist-buyers. This does not mean that bargaining strength and ability to maximize is necessarily unequal between the contending parties but rather that their methods for using them are apt to be different.

It was Bowley who, shortly after Wicksell's article had been translated, posthumously, into German, carried on to the next advance in the study of bilateral monopoly. He accepted Wicksell's solution for the case of factor-monopolist dominance and then demonstrated an equally determinate solution for monopsonist dominance. Further, he showed that there was a determinate solution for end-product price and output and for factor quantity or employment, but not for the wage or factor price, if both parties collude for the maximization of joint gains from the outset. This leaves the division of joint gains between them to be settled with the settlement of the wage or factor price on the basis of relative bargaining strength.[20]

---

[20] Cf. A. Bowley, "Note on Bilateral Monopoly," *Economic Journal*, XXXVIII (1928), 651 ff.

The wage rate would be indeterminate, depending on relative strength, over a range limited at its lower end by the factor-monopolist's average cost, and at its upper end by the monopsonist's average value product for the factor quantity requisite for producing the output that maximizes joint gains. Within this range, Bowley pointed to the existence of an "ideal" if improbable solution. This would be a wage rate determined by the equality or intersection of the factor-monopolist's marginal cost function with the monopsonist's marginal value product function. At that factor price the relative share of joint gains for each party would be justified on purely economic grounds, i.e., in abstraction from considerations of relative bargaining strength.

Professor Fellner has pointed out that this "ideal" wage rate may conceivably be established without collusion. But any other rate than the ideal one for the uniquely determined joint-profit-maximizing-factor-quantity would require an all-or-none clause to make it stable. The reason is that at a wage lower than the "ideal" one, the factor-monopolist would offer a smaller supply than the maximum-joint-profit-supply of the factor, unless he were prevented from doing so by an all-or-none agreement. At the same time the monopsonist would be inclined to demand a larger factor quantity than the joint-profit-supply. Finally, Professor Fellner's analysis establishes the unexpected conclusion that the joint-profit-maximizing output of collusive bilateral monopoly "is the 'competitive output' in the sense that the bilateral monopoly relationship *per se* does not distort the competitive pattern of allocation, provided it does not change the production functions." [21]

This completes our discussion of Wicksell's contributions to what J. S. Mill might have called "some peculiar cases of value." In view of the likelihood of unstable market equilibria even under free competition for goods with close substitutes or complements, and in view of the even greater perplexities of value and output under "imperfect competition" of various types, it was to be expected that a man of Wicksell's candor and reformist tendencies would take a strong position against those who insisted on reading into a system of free competition the achievement of maximum social welfare.

Free Competition and Maximization of Social Welfare

Wicksell dealt repeatedly with the question of whether total utility or welfare is maximized under free competition. He mentioned this problem briefly in *Value, Capital and Rent* (pp. 75 ff.); he devoted an entire section to it in *Lectures-I* (pp. 72-83); and he wrote extensive

---

[21] W. Fellner, *Quarterly Journal of Economics,* LXI (August, 1947), 507.

comments on it in three separate reviews of Pareto's works (*Cours d'économie politique,* tome I and tome II, and *Manuel d'économie politique*) which he published in *Zeitschrift für Volkswirtschaft, Sozialpolitik und Verwaltung.*

He traced the doctrine that welfare tends to be maximized in a regime of free competition to the Physiocrats and the Manchester School. While the majority of marginal utility theorists objected on various grounds to this view or dissociated themselves from it, there were two notable exceptions, L. Walras and V. Pareto, who upheld it. It was Walras who made an emphatic claim for it in Lesson 10 of his *Elements of Pure Economics* (p. 143); namely, that all participants in exchange in a freely competitive market obtain the greatest possible satisfaction of their needs if they deal with each other at uniform prices, or as he put it: "The exchange of two commodities for each other in a perfectly competitive market is an operation by which all holders of either one, or of both, of the two commodities can obtain the greatest possible satisfaction of their wants consistent with the condition that the two commodities are bought and sold at one and the same rate of exchange throughout the market."

Pareto made substantially the same claim in more technical language in his *Manuel,*[22] and it was particularly to Pareto that Wicksell's criticism was addressed. Wicksell's attack proceeded by pointing out that in order to compare utilities of various persons we must have some means of measuring them. To that end we may in the first place abstract from individual differences in tastes and assume that all have the same capacity for enjoying the good things of life. But even on this assumption we would not be entitled to infer that their marginal utilities with respect to various commodities will be the same unless, as an approximation, we also assume away differences in wealth. If all were equally well-to-do, then with approximately equal wants and capacities for enjoyment, they might all at the same time be able to maximize their satisfaction under free competition, or free competition would then tend to bring about the maximization of welfare.[23]

But it was obvious to Wicksell that in questions of this type it was illegitimate—an unwarranted use of abstraction—to disregard differences in wealth. In the absence of economic equality, the most that could be said for free competition is that individuals maximize their satisfaction relative to market prices by exchanging until they reach relative satiety *at those prices.* But this is no proof that under a dif-

---

[22] V. Pareto, *Manuel d'économie politique* (Paris, 1909), pp. 354 ff., Appendice, pp. 617-631.
[23] Wicksell, *Lectures-I,* pp. 77, 80-81.

ferent, an authoritarian or decreed system of uniform prices, it might not be possible, even probable, that individuals will in the aggregate attain a greater measure of welfare. In fact, mathematical analysis of the conditions of free exchange leads to the inference that "in normal cases there can always be found a system of uniform prices at which exchange will produce a larger sum of utility than at competitive prices." [24]

In his review of Pareto's *Cours* (1897) Wicksell reinforced this conclusion by visualizing a situation where pure competition is universal and remains such except for labor which organizes. But aggregate income in this society remains constant both as and after the workers organize. Labor, being the vast majority of the population and having a smaller per capita income than capitalists and landowners, succeeds in raising the wage level 10 per cent at the expense of the other classes. In this situation Wicksell concluded that

. . . there is at least a *strong presumption* that total utility for *all classes* or all of society has increased over what it was in universal free competition, since the 10 percent income increment for labor constitutes a greater marginal utility gain than the marginal utility loss of 10 percent of the incomes of capitalists and landowners. . . . [Whether labor's gain] is greater than the loss sustained by other classes . . . we cannot measure and cannot say with certainty—but its probability is enhanced by the virtual certainty that in the reverse case total utility would be less, the gain by capitalists and landowners (a relatively wealthy minority) being smaller than labor's loss.[25]

He further said: "Broadly speaking there is a contradiction in denying this possibility (of combination on the part of one group or class increasing the total utility for all classes) whilst on the other hand admitting that a changed distribution of property might be to the advantage of the most numerous class in society." [26]

This is, of course, an argument that modern welfare economics regards as insoluble for lack of adequate measurement criteria, but nonetheless it is one it supports on the basis of the same presumptive evidence Wicksell cited.

However, it was from the standpoint of production rather than that of value and distribution under existing property relations that Wicksell considered free competition to yield optimal results in the sense that it would tend to maximize the social product in a closed economy.

[24] *Ibid.*, p. 80. See also Wicksell, "Verteidigung der Grenznutzenlehre," *Zeitschrift für die gesammten Staatswissenschaften*, 56 (1900), 587.
[25] Wicksell, "Vilfredo Pareto, 'Manuel d'économie politique,' " Tome II, a review, *Zeitschrift für Volkswirtschaft, Sozialpolitik und Verwaltung*, VI (1897), 162.
[26] Wicksell, *Lectures-I*, p. 77.

. . . in matters of production pure and simple—i.e., when we abstract both from the distribution and the pricing commodities, as if the prices within the economy in question were determined on the international market— the present mode of production, which is in substance based on free competition and which is for the most part guided by considerations of private gain, does bring about, at least in theory, the maximum amount of production and of value, just as much as one might expect from rationally guided production in some imaginary collectivistic society.[27]

Yet, even in this respect maximization of social product under free competition was subject to qualifications. In an open economy it may be frustrated by migration both of labor and of capital. Hence this theorem applied only to a closed, or to the world, economy as a whole. Only in such conditions would the circumstance that private gain often tends to diminish rather than to increase gross product be neutralized:

The transition to productive enterprises with reduced gross output would *never occur on a general scale in a closed* economy but only partially, here and there. For the services of labor and capital which would be released by this tendency would find employment in the remaining [old] enterprises, and would develop the latter to a greater intensity. In due course a new equilibrium would emerge, actually at a *higher*, not a lower [total] gross output.[28]

But even in a closed economy, maximization of social product under free competition was subject to a serious qualification. Freely competitive production will not bring about this result in cases where production occurs under increasing returns. In such circumstances attainment of optimum output requires intervention into free competition by subsidy or otherwise so as to motivate firms to expand until they are producing at least cost. Since the resulting industrial expansion may give rise to monopolies, industries or enterprises subject to increasing returns may be particularly suited for socialization, or at any rate for operation under comprehensive public regulation.[29]

This, then, was a broad premise for intervention by public authority both in the production and distribution of the social product in

---

[27] Wicksell, "Vilfredo Pareto, 'Manuel d'économie politique,'" Tome II, a review, *Zeitschrift für Volkswirtschaft, Sozialpolitik und Verwaltung*, XXII (1913), 142.

[28] Cf. Wicksell, "V. Pareto, 'Manuel d'économie politique,'" p. 161; *Finanztheoretische Untersuchungen* (Jena, 1896), pp. 125-138; *Lectures-I*, pp. 129, 131, 133; and Marshall, *Principles of Economics* (1890), Book V, chaps. xii and xiii, which Wicksell referred to in this matter.

[29] Wicksell, "V. Pareto, 'Cours d'économie politique,'" *Zeitschrift für Volkswirtschaft, Sozialpolitik und Verwaltung*, VI (1897), 161; *Finanztheoretische Untersuchungen*, pp. 125-38; and Marshall, *op. cit.*, chaps. xii and xiii, which he cites in this matter.

the interest of the community as a whole. To Wicksell there was nothing sacrosanct about the results of free competition. But as to ameliorative intervention he urged caution and circumspection, as well as application of democratic procedure, in order to make reasonably sure the cure would not be worse than the disease.

. . . an encroachment on free competition, if it is to [increase satisfaction or welfare] must be effected in *the right direction*. Unrestricted liberty is infinitely to be preferred to a misguided system of restriction and compulsion. Insofar as the government of a country is based on democratic principles, there is a certain, though not always reliable, guarantee that such measures will be introduced only when they are to the advantage of the vast majority; whereas when commercial and industrial policy are in the hands of a privileged minority, there is a strong presumption to the contrary.[30]

There are strong resemblances between Wicksell's position on the maximization of social welfare with those of Marshall and Pigou. Yet there are differences as well. One of these concerns his implicit rejection of the doctrines associated with the concept of consumers' surplus. The references he made to Marshall in his writings show that he was familiar both with the concept and the welfare speculations to which it led. But whatever his reaction to it may have been, he refrained from written comment on it, except for a page in his review of Bowley's *Mathematical Groundwork of Economics*. There he addressed himself more specifically to the early Pigovian position on the "marginal supply curve." In that connection, Pigou has given rise to a doctrine that a subsidy and tax scheme might be used to advantage to transfer more resources into industries subject to increasing returns at the expense of those subject to diminishing returns. The result would be an augmentation of the national dividend.

Wicksell admitted that the Pigovian subsidy and tax scheme may readily increase the national dividend in an open economy where the rents earned in industries of diminishing return accrue to absentee owners living in other countries. But, he averred, if the economy is a closed one, then there is no guarantee that the real gain obtained from subsidizing industries of increasing return may not be fully offset, and perhaps more than offset, by loss in output of industries of diminishing return.[31]

Wicksell's comments were too brief to reveal his position. Perhaps there are ways of preventing a net loss in real product or in total utility under the scheme, if other and possibly greater difficulties did

[30] Wicksell, *Lectures-I*, pp. 81-82.
[31] Wicksell, "Matematisk nationalekonomi" (Mathematical Economics), *Ekonomisk Tidskrift*, 27 (1925), 112-113.

not stand in the way. Relative gain or loss could presumably be measured by some index reflecting a consumer consensus concerning the increased magnitude and changed composition of the national dividend. It is less certain that taxes and demand would obligingly adjust to the changed composition of the national product in an appropriate manner. The scheme, if taken seriously, as it was not, might have brought about·rationing of some commodities while others would be relatively abundant or in surplus. It is conceivable that under this arrangement average consumers might find themselves obliged to forego butter and to keep their electrical household appliances and lights in operation 24 hours a day in order to maximize their positions.

By contrast, Wicksell's preference for socializing monopolistic industries and firms, i.e., those most likely to be subject to increasing returns, ·seemed more likely to make a substantial contribution to the general welfare with a minimum of inconvenience for the vast majority of all concerned.

CHAPTER IV

The Marginal Productivity
Theory: A First Approximation

Method and Assumptions

Wicksell approached the synthesis of his system, "the interdependence of production and exchange," by the method of successive approximation, proceeding after the manner of Walras through the
following stages of analysis: (1) production without capital in a one-
commodity stationary society; (2) production with a given quantity
of capital in the same society; (3) one-commodity production in a
society dynamic by reason of capital accumulation; (4) production as
in the former case with the added influence of technological change;
and (5) production of two, and later of more than two, commodities
in a stationary society with a determinate capital structure.

In elaborating these analyses, he made use of several limiting assumptions. The ones most frequently encountered in his writings
will be listed, although, as will be obvious, all of them were not
intended to apply to one and the same but to different situations.
Apart from the convenience for reference that such a list affords, it
brings out more clearly than anything else how restricted his framework of analysis was. This makes it all the more remarkable that,
despite this framework, he was able to make considerable contributions to certain dynamic problems. His most frequently used assumptions were the following:

(*a*) The total quantity of each of the three factors—labor, land,
and capital—is given in a closed economy, and factor units within the
same factor category are of uniform quality and are perfect substitutes
one with another.[1]

---

[1] Wicksell, *Lectures-I*, pp. 104-105.

(*b*) Factor proportions are freely variable, and an increase in any one factor in a combination, the others remaining constant, is subject to diminishing returns.[2]

(*c*) Production functions are simple and similar for all producers; they are generally assumed to be homogeneous and linear, but not always.[3]

(*d*) There is complete elasticity of factor supply to every producer or firm, a condition which is also expressed by the assumption that factor owners have no reservation prices concerning factor service. In Wicksell's words: "The utility of the various factors of production, after a certain amount has been set aside for the owner's direct consumption becomes so insignificant . . . that it need not be taken into account in comparison with the indirect utility derived from their productive employment." [4]

(*e*) Prices of commodities to be produced are given.[5]

(*f*) Free competition prevails universally, except where some other type of market condition is explicitly postulated.[6]

(*g*) In *Lectures-I* for as long as the discussion relates to "production without capital," a one-year uniform production period is assumed. During this period workers and others maintain themselves from independent means in order to receive their appropriate undiscounted marginal product shares of output at the end of this period. Production without capital is also said to mean that such simple capital goods as may be indispensable for any type of production, crude hand tools and implements, do exist but they are free goods. Both of these features are dispensed with when the role of capital in production is discussed. Then the period or time dimension of production also becomes variable and is among the unknowns to be determined. Furthermore, wages and rents are then considered to be advanced to the owners of labor and land services, and the capitalists receive as their product share, interest, or the discounts on the previously undiscounted product shares of labor and land. Wages, rent, and interest are all expressed in real terms, except in certain phases of the monetary analysis.[7]

(*h*) Except where otherwise noted, stationary conditions, which are taken as given initially but may be disrupted while some change is

---

[2] *Ibid.*, pp. 99, 113-115.
[3] *Ibid.*, pp. 116, 125.
[4] *Ibid.*, p. 103.
[5] *Ibid.*, p. 104.
[6] *Ibid.*, p. 112.
[7] *Ibid.*, pp. 108-110.

taking place, are restored with the establishment of new equilibrium relations.[8]

(*i*) Most of the analysis of capital is presented in terms of simple interest because the investment period or time structure of production is generally said to be short. However, when longer periods and more complex production structures are under discussion, it is understood that instantaneously compounded interest must replace simple interest, and the mathematical expressions which accompany the exposition are, accordingly, to be modified to logarithmic form.[9]

The foregoing apparatus was, of course, best fitted for economic reasoning at the level of comparative statics. In fact, most of Wicksell's work did not transcend this level of analysis except in two fields, those of capital and monetary theory.

Supply of Factors of Production and Laws of Return

The problems connected with the supply, or more particularly with changes in the conditions of supply, of productive agents were for the most part excluded from view in Wicksell's treatment because of his use of assumption (*a*); namely, that the total quantity of these agents was given. To the extent that variations in factor supplies were admitted into his analysis, they were introduced as variables in a general equilibrium situation. In such a position, although there can be no doubt that factor supply conditions play an important role, this role is no longer clearly discernible or easy to isolate in the interrelatedness of numerous variables.

In his dynamic analysis, the only factor supply problem he treated at length was that of capital. With respect to the latter he succeeded in developing a theory of the consequences of capital accumulation which was far in advance of those espoused by the most outstanding among his contemporaries. As to land, there was no particular problem since its supply was regarded as fixed by nature.

The supply of labor, outside his general equilibrium analyses, received only indirect attention in his studies of population. In *Läran om befolkningen, dess sammansättning och förändringar* (*The Theory of Population, Its Composition and Mode of Change,* Stockholm, 1910), a tract which embodies his mature thought on this subject, he developed a concept of a population of optimum size. He discussed the conditions under which such a population size may be attained, and,

---

[8] *Ibid.,* p. 152.

[9] *Ibid.,* pp. 156, 162, 178 ff., 205, 274 ff.; Wicksell, *Value, Capital and Rent* (London, 1954), pp. 121 ff., 123, 137 ff., 143-144.

once attained, how it might be maintained at that size relative to the economy's resource development. Implicitly, an optimum population involves a corresponding (though smaller) labor force. Since he assumed that owners of factors of production have no (or, if any, very low) reservation prices to limit the supply of factor services to production, this entire labor force is, presumably, supplied to the market under a regime of free competition. To be sure, he did not deny the existence of "non-competing groups" within the aggregate supply of labor. Nor was he unaware of the existence of leisure as an alternative to work, and of how this is likely to result in backward sloping supply curves of labor at wage rates in excess of certain critical levels. He was also aware that the efficiency or productivity of labor rises and falls, within wide limits, with the wages received.[10] But all these influences were "provisionally" assumed away by his treating the total quantity of labor as given and by his considering all units of labor to be homogeneous and perfect substitutes for one another.

Perhaps there was a certain candor about his habitual reference to men and acres of uniform quality and given quantity. Apparently he did not consider economic theory in his time to be sufficiently developed to deal fruitfully with the complications that arise from changes in the conditions of factor supply, except with respect to the factor real capital. We may admit that this was an inadequate way of meeting this problem, but, when all is said and done, very little more than this was achieved by his celebrated contemporaries, Marshall and others, despite their long discourses on labor and land, wages and rent.

Wicksell made the transition from factor supplies to the theory of production as such in a few strokes of the pen. If a country with fixed factor quantities is a small, closed economy "in which everything was produced and exchanged with the outside world on common account," at prices given by the world market, then its production problem simplifies to a technical one of maximizing its output. If the international market is purely competitive, this comes to the same as maximizing the exchange value of its output. In that case "the distribution of its output or its equivalent obtained by exchange would be an independent question and would be regulated by other than purely economic considerations." [11]

This was Wicksell's view of how production would be managed in a world of rationally directed small collectivist (not necessarily socialist) economies. But if there is free competition and private

---

[10] Wicksell, *Lectures-I*, pp. 104-105.
[11] *Ibid.*, p. 105.

enterprise, then, *ceteris paribus*, it becomes "everybody's business to produce, not as much as possible, but as *cheaply* as possible, i.e., in such a way as to maximize his net profit. This again depends on his costs of production . . . on the share of the product demanded by the factors of production. It is therefore bound up with the problem of distribution." [12]

In this manner the door was opened for the marginal productivity theory of distribution. But consideration of the latter presupposes knowledge of the relation of enterprise outputs to inputs of factor units, i.e., a knowledge of the so-called laws of return.

Actually, Wicksell's treatment of these "laws" was unsystematic and inconclusive. It was more or less incidental to his preoccupation with marginal productivity theory. In a section in *Lectures-I* (pp. 108-33) mainly devoted to clarifying the concept "marginal productivity" and to demonstrating the product exhaustion theorem under conditions of "production without capital," he *uses*, but does not explain, diminishing returns to any factor in a combination when it alone is increased. He also uses the assumption of a linear and homogeneous production function. In his exposition he comments on confusions which have arisen between profitability and returns. These affect the discussion of diminishing returns, and he asserts that the law of diminishing returns is difficult to verify experimentally. With reference to Marshall's emphasis on increasing returns, he concludes these can only represent short-run phenomena in production which will inevitably, in the long run, be overwhelmed by the tendency to decreasing returns (cf. p. 111). He discusses returns to scale very briefly, chiefly to demonstrate that distribution according to marginal productivity becomes impossible or results in overdistribution in such cases. In the opposite case, decreasing returns to scale, distribution according to marginal productivity results in underdistribution and induces fragmentation of enterprises. Hence he concludes that constant returns to scale, or the existence of optimal or least-cost production conditions for some attainable level of output, are required for distribution according to factor marginal productivity to be determinate or to exhaust the product without any residual.

It is surprising that with his awareness of the relation between increasing returns to scale and imperfect competition, his critical attitude toward Marshall's "law of increasing returns" and toward Pigou's related subsidy and tax scheme, he did not work out a brief, systematic treatment on a topic so central to his theory of production.

One reason which may have contributed to this omission on his

[12] *Ibid.*, pp. 105-106.

part was that he operated with an emasculated concept of the competitive firm. His firm—except when he was discussing monopolistic competition, taxation of monopolies, and so forth—was conceived as a most simple, atomistic production unit. It was a firm in which, alternately, laborers, landowners, capitalists, or "a fourth party" were considered capable of acting in the role of the entrepreneur. For "firms" of that simple type, the Marshallian categories of prime and supplementary costs, of internal and external economies, economies external to the firm but internal to the industry, and the like could only have slight meaning. Consequently, he did not deal with these matters to any appreciable extent. For the freely or purely competitive case, his analysis was practically limited to the statement quoted above; namely, that in competition it is everybody's business not to produce as much as possible, but as cheaply as possible.

Far more successful and interesting was his treatment of marginal productivity theory. His contributions in that connection should, however, be approached from the standpoint of his exposition in *Value, Capital and Rent,* rather than from the more compressed version he gave it in *Lectures-I.*

The General Marginal Productivity Theory and the Product Exhaustion Theorem

The development of a determinate imputation theory by the mid-1890's may, to present-day economists, seem more like a pleasing curiosity than the achievement it must have represented at that time.

That Wicksell played a significant role in the development of imputation theory has long been recognized, as J. R. Hicks, among others, has pointed out.[13] The extent of his contribution compared with that of others to this doctrine has been more fully stated by G. J. Stigler whose discussion probably represents the best contemporary treatment of this subject.[14] A backward glance at some representative varieties of distribution theories which preceded the one developed in the 1890's on the basis of marginal productivity will help to place Wicksell's labor in an appropriate historical context.

IMPUTATION THEORY PRIOR TO 1890'S AND UP TO 1900

Classical distribution theory solved the problem of imputation of product shares to participating factors of production by means of one determinate and two residual shares. Real wages were determined by the cost of labor's subsistence, rent—a differential residual—by

---

[13] J. R. Hicks, *Theory of Wages* (London, 1932), Appendix, pp. 234-239.
[14] G. J. Stigler, *Production and Distribution Theories* (New York, 1941), chap. xii.

the difference in fertility (and/or service-producing aspects) of intensively cultivated or used land and marginal land, and profits by the problematic remainder of total product, after subtracting the former two shares. To followers of this tradition, who dominated the scene when subjective value theories began gaining ground in the 1870's, the new tendencies in economic analysis must have appeared as a futile preoccupation with the minutiae of supply and demand.

Even Walras's demonstration of static general equilibrium in *Élements d'économie politique pure* (1874) apparently had no substantial immediate impact on distribution theory. However, it did contain a determinate, nonresidual solution of the distribution problem for the economy as a whole. For if products were priced according to the force of marginal utility evaluations, if competition unfailingly reduced prices to the level of production costs, and if these costs were incurred in relation to the output contribution of agents of production, then the distribution problem had found its solution. In such conditions the total product of the economy had become "exhausted" or fully distributed as shares to participating factors of production. Moreover, these factor-shares were in this situation determined not arbitrarily, nor as remainders or residuals after the shares of certain factors had been determined on a derived demand basis, but all the factor shares were determined simultaneously on a derived demand basis.

But even if this solution was determinate, it left much to be desired since it failed to explain how changes in the relative size of factor shares are determined. It was of little value to know that distribution is determinate in stationary general equilibrium for those who were concerned with the relations of factor-shares in the nonstationary economic conditions of the real world.

F. von Wieser, in *Der Natürliche Wert* (1888), attempted, unsuccessfully as it turned out, to solve this problem. To that end he availed himself of a derived demand explanation of factor prices, an alternative cost doctrine, and a set of simultaneous equations which purported to state the "productive contribution" of the several factors, not their marginal, but their total, productive contribution. Concerning this, Wicksell, a few years later, made the following appropriate comment:

Wieser suggests that in order to find out the share of the total profit or, as he expresses it, "the productive contribution" of the different productive factors, one should place side by side a sufficient number of different but actually occurring combinations of the same productive elements, so as to be able to estimate according to the principle of simultaneous equations the proportion of each element which is everywhere equal, from the known value of the total sum. For instance, "to reduce the entire number of expressions which offer themselves to the shortest possible form," one would obtain, for three means of production x, y and z, the following equations:

$$x + y = 100$$

$$2x + 3z = 290$$

$$4y + 5z = 590$$

where $x = 40$, $y = 60$ and $z = 70$."

Now it is clear that, proceeding in this way, however great the number of equations may be, we shall learn nothing more than we knew already, namely that when competition is free the remuneration for, or the share in the proceeds of, one and the same "means of production" must be approximately the same in all transactions. The above equations tell us this and nothing more, as can easily be seen. If, therefore, Wieser meant by his expression "productive contribution" (*produktiver Beitrag*) merely the remuneration actually obtained from the different factors of production— the reward for common labor, the rent for land of equal quality, the average capital interest, and so on—then he has stated a true, but self-evident rule. If he meant something else, then his "solution" must *a priori* be declared false.[15]

The problem had to be recast. It should be possible to go from Walras's solution for general equilibrium in the economy as a whole to one for the firm or the industry. Böhm-Bawerk made some attempts in that direction, as recorded in "Exkurs VII" in the later editions of *Positive Theorie des Kapitales*. Proceeding from perfect factor complementarity to partial factor substitutability—the substitute elements being subject to opportunity costs to the firm because of their value in alternative employments—he succeeded in finding certain ranges or limits within which imputation could be carried out. No replaceable factor element would receive less than its opportunity cost in alternate employments, nor more than the total product minus the sum of opportunity costs of other replaceable elements in the combination. But its specific share would be determined by its particular degree of irreplaceability or complementarity within the combination. His solution was indeed difficult to "add up," for the sum of the

---

[15] Wicksell, *Value, Capital and Rent*, Preface, p. 24. In one of his major articles written some years later, "Zur Verteidigung der Grenznutzenlehre," *Zeitschrift für die gesammten Staatswissenschaften*, 56 (1900), 591, Wicksell very candidly pointed out what was amiss with Wieser's attempt at imputation. He found that Wieser had assumed the technical coefficients of production to be variable and to be among the unknowns of the problem to be determined in the earlier part of his textual discussion. But later when Wieser set up his simultaneous equations, he assumed, rather inconsistently, that these coefficients were predetermined or were among the known rather than among the unknown factors of the problem.

specific shares of the various factors, calculated on the foregoing basis, may readily be either greater or smaller than the total product and would only be equal to it by coincidence.

Since then it has been pointed out repeatedly—for instance in *Lectures-I*, p. 133—that the early attempts at imputation by the subjective value theorists foundered, except in general equilibrium, because they assumed perfect factor complementarity or fixed production coefficients also at the microeconomic level of analysis of the firm. They further endeavored to ascertain the factor's total contribution to output directly rather than indirectly via its rate of marginal productivity. Therefore, when Wicksell in 1893 in *Value, Capital and Rent* elaborated a marginal productivity analysis of wages, rent, and interest on the assumption of variable factor proportions and diminishing returns to each factor when it alone is increased in a combination containing other agents, the solution of the imputation problem crept into his treatment almost without his being aware of it, or at least without his giving great emphasis to it. He closed the preface of that work with the following concise statement of its solution:

> In order to discover this [namely, how and why the participation of different elements of production receives precisely such and such a reward], *we must, instead of looking at the quantities* [of factors of production] in question themselves, *consider rather their changes* (as, by the way, Wieser himself points out later, but with little consistency); that is to say, *we must approach the subject from the standpoint of the differential calculus.*
>
> This means that if we conceive the total proceeds of production as a real (stable) function of the participating factors of production (which must be regarded as approximately true) then obviously thrift requires that each factor shall be employed in such quantities that the falling out of a small portion of this quantity would diminish the result of the production by an amount equal to the share in the proceeds which belongs to this quantity. That is to say, *so long as this condition is not fulfilled, it will always be more remunerative for the entrepreneur* of the business, whoever he may be, *to employ either more or less of the elements of production in question.*
>
> *Mathematically expressed,* this means that *the share in the proceeds of the different factors of production must be proportional to the partial derivative of the above-mentioned function in respect of the factor in question as variable;* and *in this simple formula lies indeed the true solution of the problem,* provided that at the same time the special position of capital as an element in production is sufficiently considered.[16]

It was not until several years later, 1900 and 1902, when he was prompted to write in defense of Wicksteed's demonstration of the

---

[16] Wicksell, *Value, Capital and Rent,* p. 25. Italics supplied.

product exhaustion theorem of 1894 against criticisms by Walras and Barone, and then in recognition of Barone's more general solution of 1896 (see below, p. 74) that Wicksell became fully aware that he had already developed a solution to this problem very similar to Wicksteed's, however a year earlier than the latter, in 1893.

Perhaps this entire matter would have receded into oblivion if it had not been for a controversy that ensued concerning both the priority of discovery and validity of this theorem. The roles of Edgeworth, Marshall, Barone, Pareto, Walras, and Wicksteed in that polemic are entertainingly presented by Stigler. Aside from some private correspondence with Walras about this, Wicksell was not a direct participant in this controversy, for the articles he wrote about it were in Swedish and presumably did not come to the attention of the world at large.

However, this polemic scored a victory for the marginalist theories over the older tradition, for it forced upon the attention of others that the distribution problem had found a consistent and elegant determination, albeit on assumptions which would rarely be realized in the world in which we live.

WICKSELL'S DEMONSTRATION OF THE MARGINAL
PRODUCTIVITY THEORY OF DISTRIBUTION

Wicksell's best work on this subject is found in *Value, Capital and Rent* (pp. 146-153). There his immediate problem was one of presenting a synthesis of the Böhm-Bawerkian capital theory with the marginal productivity theories of wages, rent, and interest. In accord with his capital concept of that time, he regarded capital as a quantity of means of subsistence to be advanced for a return of real interest by entrepreneur-capitalists as real wages and rent to laborers and landowners during the requisite production period. With a certain quantity of labor and land given, and all of capital invested in advances, capital could conveniently be expressed as a function of time, namely of the length of the production period during which it suffices to sustain laborers and landowners. The product for any particular firm and the output of the economy as a whole (by summation of the products for all the firms), could be expressed as a function of a combination of three variables: time; quantity of labor services; and quantity of land services. The marginal productivity of these three factor services, capital (or time), labor, and land, could then be directly expressed as the partial derivatives of the production function with respect to each of these factors treated as continuously changing variables.

Within this analytic framework, he assumed the existence of an economy with the following given resources: the total quantity of labor (or number of laborers) was represented by the quantity A, the total units of land by another quantity B, and K as the total quantity of real capital. These resources were subject to private ownership, and their owners enjoyed full freedom of contract with respect to them. Concerning this society he asked, according to what principles will production be carried on, and what will be the relation between wages, rent, and interest? If capitalists are entrepreneurs, in a regime of free competition (which is assumed throughout) they will try to maximize the interest return, z, on their capital. This is done by their advancing the latter as real wages and rents to laborers and landowners for a production period of optimum length, t, expressed in years. What it will be depends on the annual real wage per laborer, w,[17] on the annual rent per unit of land, r, as well as on the quantities of labor and land hired, and on their productivity. All factor payments are made either in units of product or in their equivalents in *numéraire*.

At this stage, the production function was expressed as $p = f(t,h)$, where p was the annual product per laborer, and h, one of the unknowns to be determined, was the optimum size land unit per laborer. The product per laborer, p, was in turn directly related to the average length of the production period, t; the average investment period was $t/2$ because production was thought of as continuous. Each new input unit of capital (i.e., unit of advanced means of subsistence) remains invested for the production period, t, while at the same time units invested earlier become disinvested by wear and tear as output of product begins arriving. Thus at any given time, the period during which all capital inputs in use (those added to production earlier as well as those added most recently) are invested, and for which, on the average, any given input unit is invested, is $t/2$.

The product per worker per production period (as distinct from p, the annual product per worker) was denoted by s, a magnitude which was not used much in the subsequent treatment. The relation of s to p was $s/t = p$. On the basis of these relations, Wicksell set up as his first expression an equation for the product per laborer per production period, as follows:

---

[17] Following a precedent set by Stigler, the letter w is used here to denote wages rather than the letter l (an abbreviation for the German "Lohn," the noun for wage) which Wicksell used. This is the only change made in his notation, chiefly for ease of recognition. But this change should be borne in mind when passages in his works are cited where his l's are used.

(1) $$s = [t(w + hr) (1 + zt/2)].$$

This states the value of the product in terms of annual real wages and rent per laborer and land unit, times the real interest accrued on wage- and rent-advances of subsistence during the average investment period, times the production period. If we divide both sides of this equation by t, we get a second expression, the equation for the annual product per laborer:

(2) $$p = (w + hr) (1 + zt/2).$$

This is one of the fundamental relations which, together with its derivatives, dominates the greater part of Wicksell's demonstration.

If laborers are entrepreneurs, then the laborer is the fixed factor, and the size of the land unit, h, as well as the length of the production period, t, is variable. At the level of his purely competitive firm, each laborer-entrepreneur must take z, the rate of interest or discount, and r, the annual rent per land unit, as constants given by the market. His problem then is to find the values or magnitudes of h and of t which will make w, his annual real wage, a maximum. By differentiating (2) partially with respect to t and h, while treating w as a constant, two relations are obtained:

(3) $$\partial p/\partial t = (w + hr) z/2 \text{ and}$$

(4) $$\partial p/\partial h = r(1 + zt/2).$$

Here (3) indicates that under maximizing behavior, the production period is extended by labor-entrepreneurs until its marginal product, $\partial p/\partial t$, equals the real interest that must be paid for the requisite subsistence advances for real wages and rent. And (4) shows that each entrepreneur will incrementally increase the land unit used per laborer until its marginal product, $\partial p/\partial h$, equals the requisite annual rent increment times interest thereon.

But if (2) is restated, by multiplying out its right member, as

(2.1) $$p = w + hr + wzt/2 + hrzt/2$$

and if (3) is similarly restated as

(3.1) $$\partial p/\partial t = wz/2 + hrz/2$$

then it becomes clear that the last two terms in (2.1) are equal to $t(\partial p/\partial t)$. Using this equality together with the root for r in (4); namely, $r = (\partial p/\partial h) (1 + zt/2)^{-1}$, for substitution in (2.1) yields us the following equation:

(2.2) $$p = w + h(\partial p/\partial h) (1 + zt/2)^{-1} + t\partial p/\partial t.$$

This last expression shows that land, h, receives its discounted marginal product, capital (expressed here by transformation as a function of time) its marginal product as real interest on advances of subsistence as real wages and rent, and that labor, the fixed factor, receives its wage-share, w, of the product, p, as a residual.

Now in order to let the argument proceed from the level of the individual firm to that of the economy as a whole, it must be recognized that w and r will no longer be given at the macroeconomic level of analysis, but instead they will be variables which reach a determinate magnitude through the action of the freely competitive market only when the following relations hold:

$$(5) \qquad K = (t/2) A(w + hr),$$

the aggregate capital equation, which states that the quantity of real capital (subsistence means) available, K, must just suffice for wage and rent advances to all available labor and land for a one-year investment period at the rates of w and r which are determined when this equality holds, and

$$(6) \qquad h = B/A,$$

the land-labor equation, which states that the entire area of economically usable land, B, must be made available to all the A laborers in the optimal ratio of h land units per laborer. This solves the problem, for now five independent equations determine simultaneously the five unknowns, w, r, t, z, and h.

At the next stage of the analysis, the production period and labor were made the variable factors and land the fixed one. But now a variable number, n, laborers are engaged on large tracts of land. The former land unit per laborer, h, now becomes a fraction, $h = 1/n$, and the annual product per laborer, p, must be restated as the output, q, per large land tract plus its manpower complement. This requires that the production function be changed from $p = f(t,h)$ to $q = nf(t,h)$, and consequently $q = np$. This also requires restatement of equation (2) and its derivatives in terms of q. Since $p = q/n$, its differential (or the marginal product of the land-unit-per-laborer) is

$$(7) \qquad \frac{dp}{dh} = \frac{d\left(\dfrac{q}{n}\right)}{d\left(\dfrac{1}{n}\right)} = q - n\frac{dq}{dn},$$

which states that the marginal product of a large tract of land equals the total product of such a tract worked by n laborers minus labor's distributive share, and hence the marginal product of land is equal to rent of land as a residual.

At this point in his exposition in *Value, Capital and Rent* (pp. 149 ff.), Wicksell broke the sequence of his main argument to turn his attention to the rent doctrine of Ricardo and von Thünen. To that end he changed one of the previous conditions. He let the production period become constant and the real interest rate equal to zero. On that basis equation (2) reduces to $p = w + hr$, and since $p = q/n$, when this expression is multiplied by n it becomes:

$$(8) \qquad\qquad q = nw + r.$$

This states that the product of the large tract equals the real wages and rent expended on its production. By substituting for r the right member of (7) (where r is an implicit residual), in (8), and simplifying, one obtains

$$(9) \qquad\qquad dq/dn = w.$$

This shows that the optimum allocation of labor to each large tract of land occurs when such a number of men are employed on it that the marginal product of each laborer in the group employed on each large tract of land equals his real annual wage. In this manner, between equations (7), (8), and (9), Wicksell showed the classical rent doctrine to be a special case of the general marginal productivity theory.

Having gone this far, Wicksell did not resume his main argument but turned instead to a critique of Walras and to a demonstration of general equilibrium relations in which Böhm-Bawerkian conceptions of capital were included as a major ingredient. But in a long footnote in *Value, Capital and Rent* (p. 152), he left some expressions to indicate how his earlier discussion might be carried out. Stigler's comment on this seems justified: "Wicksell's mode of presentation in *Über Wert, Kapital und Rente* (Value, Capital and Rent) unfortunately obscures the fact that he is presenting the first complete mathematical formulation of the marginal productivity theory of distribution." [18]

However, Stigler was sufficiently interested in Wicksell's presentation to proceed from that footnote and make explicit by means of some transformations the elegant proof of the product-exhaustion theorem which Wicksell left on an implicit basis. We shall make use of some of Stigler's formulations in the following.

Using (4) in the form of (4.1) $r = (\partial p/\partial h)(1 + zt/2)^{-1}$; modifying

---

[18] Stigler, *op. cit.*, p. 293.

(9) to allow for the fact that the production period again is a variable, so that (9) receives a discount term and is written in the form of (9.1) as $w = (\partial q/\partial n) (1 + zt/2)^{-1}$, and finally substituting these values of r and of w in 2.1), we obtain

(10) $$p = (\partial q/\partial n) (1 + zt/2)^{-1} + h(\partial p/\partial h) (1 + zt/2)^{-1} \\ + wzt/2 + hrzt/2.$$

Equation (10), however, is only another expression of the original (2) in terms of discounted marginal product shares. But this expression must now be restated in terms of one and the same product unit, q, so as to eliminate the difficulty that arises from the first term of its right member being expressed in units of q whereas the remainder are in units of p. To that end (10) is multiplied by n, and an equivalent in units of q must be found for the factor $h(\partial p/\partial h)$ in the second term of the right member of (10). This is done by differentiating the product equation, $q = np$, partially with respect to h, so as to obtain $\partial p/\partial h = n(\partial p/\partial h)$. When (10) is multiplied by n, its second term at right becomes $nh(\partial p/\partial h) (1 + zt/2)^{-1}$. But this term may now be rewritten as $h(\partial q/\partial h) (1 + zt/2)^{-1}$, for since $n(\partial p/\partial h) = \partial q/\partial h$, then $nh(\partial p/\partial h) = h(\partial q/\partial h)$. Now (10) can be restated as (10.1) in which the last term $hrzt/2$ is simplified to $rzt/2$ because multiplication by n cancels out h in that term inasmuch as $h = 1/n$:

(10.1) $$np = q = n(\partial q/\partial n) (1 + zt/2)^{-1} + h(\partial q/\partial h) (1 + zt/2)^{-1} \\ + nwzt/2 + rzt/2.$$

Now, however, if (8) is rewritten to allow for t and z being variables, then it takes the form of

(8.1) $$q = (nw + r) (1 + zt/2).$$

By differentiating this equation partially with respect to t, we obtain an equivalent of (3) in terms of q, which we designate as (3.2) $\partial q/\partial t = (nw + r) (z/2)$, and which may also, for convenience, be written as (3.2) $\partial q/\partial t = nwz/2 + rz/2$. By means of this last expression, the last two terms at right in (10.1) can be gathered into one and stated as the share of capital in the form of $t(\partial q/\partial t)$, for just as earlier, between (2.1) and (3.1) $wzt/2 + hrzt/2 = t(\partial p/\partial t)$, so here, for the same reason, between (2.1) and (3.2) $nwzt/2 + rzt/2 = t(\partial q/\partial t)$. Thus (11) is obtained.

(11) $$q = n(\partial q/\partial n) (1 + zt/2)^{-1} + h(\partial q/\partial h) (1 + zt/2)^{-1} + t(\partial q/\partial t).$$

This expression clearly demonstrates the product exhaustion theorem when factors are remunerated according to their marginal productivity. The only remaining relation to be accounted for is that the marginal productivity share of capital, $t(\partial q/\partial t)$, must be equal to the discount applied to the otherwise undiscounted shares of labor and land, as shown in

$$(12) \qquad n(\partial q/\partial n)\,(zt/2) + h(\partial q/\partial h)\,(zt/2) = t(\partial q/\partial t)$$

which expresses this condition, namely that the sum of the undiscounted marginal productivity shares of labor and land when multiplied by the discount factor, $zt/2$, should equal the marginal productivity share of capital.

Stigler stated this condition but did not proceed to test it. This can be done as follows. From the development of (10), (10.1), (8.1) and (11), it is clear that nw and r have been transformed in (11) to $nw = n(\partial q/\partial n)\,(1 + zt/2)^{-1}$ and $r = h(\partial q/\partial h)\,(1 + zt/2)^{-1}$. Each of these may also be written in the following form: $nw + nwzt/2 = n(\partial q/\partial n)$ and $r + rzt/2 = h(\partial q/\partial h)$. The respective left members of these two equations may now be used for substitution at left in (12). Further, it is clear that as between (10.1) and (3.1), $t(\partial q/\partial t) = nwzt/2 + rzt/2$, the right terms of which may now be used at right in (12).

Thus in order for the condition expressed in (12) to hold, the following should be an equality:

$$(12.1) \quad (nw + nwzt/2)\,(zt/2) + (r + rzt/2)\,(zt/2) = (nwzt/2) + (rzt/2).$$

This is actually the case, subject to one qualification, namely, that the equation is only approximately satisfied since Wicksell calculated in simple interest, whereas, as he recognized (*Value, Capital and Rent,* p. 143, note) instantaneously compounded interest should be used. But the error involved in using simple interest is, however, small. If $n = 100$ laborers, if annual rent per large tract of land, $r = \$1,000.00$; if the production period is $t = 1$ year, and the interest rate, $z = 0.05$ or 5 per cent, then the left member of (12.1) comes to \$2,588.75, whereas the right member comes to \$2,525.00. For the short production period used here, the error is negligible. It amounts to 2.6 per cent of the value of the true aggregate share of capital, or, alternately, since capital advanced for the investment period, $t/2$, is \$50,000, the share of capital as a discount on the shares of labor and land at left equals 5.13 per cent on the principal sum invested, whereas its marginal productivity rate at right is exactly 5.00 per cent on the same sum.

This concludes our account of Wicksell's demonstration of the product exhaustion theorem. We must now turn to such use as he made of it and to the social significance he ascribed to it.

THE SIGNIFICANCE OF THE PRODUCT EXHAUSTION THEOREM
IN WICKSELL'S WORK

In his own later works—some articles cited below and through three editions of *Lectures-I*—Wicksell did not elaborate and complete his own original demonstration of the product exhaustion theorem as set forth in *Value, Capital and Rent,* but used instead the substance of the demonstrations given it by Wicksteed and Barone in 1894 and 1896 respectively.

Wicksteed based his analysis on a homogeneous and linear production function. For this he was criticized by Edgeworth, Pareto, Walras, and Barone,[19] because of the unrealistic character of the production function on which his demonstration depended. They denied that factors of production have the requisite degree of divisibility and can be reproportioned at will to permit the product to increase in proportion to the increase in all factors.

Wicksell took occasion to explain Wicksteed's demonstration to his Swedish audience in a long article.[20] In defense of marginal productivity theory in general, and particularly as an answer concerning indivisibilities, he held that the necessary degree of divisibility to ascertain and measure marginal products arises at the margin of production. Specifically, in defense of Wicksteed and contra Walras, he stated:

Walras claims he has developed the marginal productivity theory in a more generalized fashion, and holds that as long as there is competition entrepreneurial profit tends to zero. In that he is clearly wrong. In addition to competition, production must be independent of scale, or total product a homogeneous and linear function of factor inputs. If not, even with free competition and economies of scale, profit in large enterprises will not tend to zero, for either the small firm then runs at a loss or the large one at a net gain. Must we assume constant productivity for the proof? I think not. If we assume diminishing returns to all the factors, linearity is still preserved; so is homogeneity, since all factors simultaneously and equally suffer decrease of productivity with additional inputs.[21]

With the publication of the third edition of Walras's *Éléments* Barone's work on the theorem of 1896 came to his attention. Barone's proof was more general than Wicksteed's since it assumed no particu-

[19] *Ibid.,* pp. 341-344, 356-373 *passim.*

[20] Wicksell, "Om gränsproduktiviteten såsom grundval för den nationalekonomiska fördelningen" (Concerning Marginal Productivity as the Basis for Economic Distribution), *Ekonomisk Tidskrift,* 2 (1900), 305-337.

[21] *Ibid.,* p. 308.

lar property of the production function other than that it must have a maximum or that the related cost function must have a minimum attainable by variation in scale and in factor proportions.

In a second article,[22] Wicksell admitted that he had failed earlier to notice that Barone's minimum cost condition was not the same as Wicksteed's production function, although, he added, at the point of minimum cost, firms operate at constant returns and will continue to do so provided competition is maintained. Then he added some reflections on the tenuous relation between competition and increasing returns to scale. Finally, in the second and subsequent editions of *Lectures-I,* he adopted Barone's condition and stated the theorem on an "either-or" basis, either Wicksteed's function or Barone's optimum production condition.[23] This was as far as Wicksell progressed with this problem.

In substance, the product exhaustion theorem requires only that the production function have an attainable maximum, rather than that it must be homogeneous and of the first degree. Whether its maximum shall be achieved depends on (*a*) the existence of some indivisible factor of production in each firm, for instance, the entrepreneur, and (*b*) on the relation of the size of the market to that of the firm. What is required in that respect is that the market must be large enough for the firm to exhaust its "economies of scale" while it still behaves competitively. To the extent that these conditions are fulfilled, distribution, in the absence of artificial restraints on competition, will be according to marginal productivity, and the sum of the distributive shares will "exhaust" the product. Thus this theorem has validity in a limited sphere and is not entirely an academic museum piece as some observers have been inclined to claim.

As one views Wicksell's work as a whole one surmises—though it is difficult to substantiate this—that the product exhaustion theorem was in part at least a blueprint for his vision of "economic" as distinct from "social" distribution in the more rational mixed economy of the future. There are a number of indications to this effect. In view of his awareness of the connection between increasing returns and imperfect competition, it is clear he did not think the theorem had much immediate application in contemporary society. Yet his interest in it was not entirely theoretical. The pointed distinctions he drew in the introduction to *Lectures-I* between economic and social distribution is evidence to the contrary. In this he followed directly in the tradition of

---

[22] Wicksell, "Till fördelningsproblemet" (Concerning the Problem of Distribution), *Ekonomisk Tidskrift,* 4 (1902), 424-433.
[23] Wicksell, *Lectures-I,* p. 126.

J. S. Mill. He was also close to the classical writers in another respect, namely, in the double meaning in which he used "stationary conditions."

Static assumptions served him very well as devices of analysis, but he used them also as a speculative forecast on the trend of history. For instance, he stressed repeatedly that the inventions of the nineteenth century represent a unique epoch in history, not likely to be repeated or exceeded in terms of productivity by future inventions. To this must be added his emphasis on the neo-Malthusian aim of a stationary population, and his conviction that natural resources, fixed in quantity, had for the greater part already been brought under intensive exploitation. All in all, this indicates that he thought stationary conditions less remote than we, living in the dawn of the atomic age, have reason to believe.

Assume for a moment, with him, that the world economy would approach stationary conditions in the next century. If so, its imperative economic problem would be one of approximating more closely than now the maximization of output relative to consumers' wants. Today's condonable wastes may become misdemeanors under the laws of a future generation. Among the worst of these wastes are those associated with the increasing scope and significance of private monopoly and imperfect competition. Wicksell had no doubt that a more enlightened generation would place monopolies under public operation and would proceed to counteract the wastes of imperfect competition by appropriate public regulation. But whether under public operation or regulation, how should these enterprises and market structures be administered? In his view, the marginal productivity theory had a rational answer to this problem, one which cannot be ignored with impunity. And what about nonmonopolistic, competitive enterprise? Since these already maximize production consistent with freedom of consumer choice, he saw no reason for interfering with their behavior, and none for incorporating them into the public economy. He thought nothing would be gained and possibly a good deal might be lost by so doing. But, for a society in which (1) monopolies had become public enterprises operated on a marginal-cost-pricing basis, (2) state regulation as to price and output policies had been imposed on firms operating under looser forms of imperfect competition, and (3) all remaining production (possibly the bulk of it) is in the hands of freely competitive private enterprise, the product exhaustion theorem would evidently not be simply an aid to analysis; it would become an approximation to the actualities of this society's production arrangements.

Was this utopian? Probably so, since most long-run speculations seem to acquire more or less of that attribute. But was it more so than some recent prescriptions by Oskar Lange, A. P. Lerner, *et al.* concerning economic relations and rational economic conduct in a socialist or "welfare state" society?

However, if there seemed to be a strong possibility that the future society would realize the design of "economic distribution" in its production arrangements, this did not at all mean that actual distribution in that society would parallel its economic distribution.

To what extent and for what fundamental reasons social distribution would have to intervene and modify the consequences of distribution according to marginal productivity of factors, was an inquiry to which Wicksell devoted much of his energy and ingenuity with interesting results. Some of these are discussed in chapter vi and in those parts of chapter xii which deal with his theory of economic progress. However, since economic progress depends to a considerable extent on an adequate rate of capital formation, we must first turn to his theory of capital and interest for his views on one of the major premises for economic growth.

CHAPTER V

Theory of Capital and Interest

Wicksell's work in capital theory was focused on the process of capital formation, on its consequences for the relations between distributive shares, and on its implications for economic stability. One might say that his aim was to advance insights into this problem-nexus which might afford man a measure of control over society's real capital comparable to that which pursuit of natural science has yielded him over the forces of nature.

Studies of capital theory frequently present considerable difficulties of exposition and demonstration. This is particularly true of analyses which terminate in more or less elaborate attempts to conceive of society's real capital as a multidimensional capital structure. In equilibrium all dimensions of such structures become determinate. But it is otherwise when they are subject to dynamic change (expansion and development) between successive equilibria separated from one another by intervals sufficiently long to allow the forces set in motion by that change to spend their energy and to modify their dimensions in predictable ways. Attempts to deal with these matters systematically often give rise to long treatises, difficult to follow, as witness two of Wicksell's followers in this line of inquiry, G. Åkerman in *Realkapital and Kapitalzins* (1923-24), vols. 1 and 2, and F. von Hayek in *The Pure Theory of Capital* (1941).

By comparison, Wicksell's own treatment of this subject (particularly in *Lectures-I*, pp. 147-166, 202-206) seems incomplete as does also a more recent discussion of it by Lindahl (*Studies in the Theory of Money and Capital*, 1939, pp. 296-309). Here I must follow a com-

promise course. First, I trace the evolution of Wicksell's conceptions
of capital before he arrived at his structural view of capital. Then I
shall endeavor to explain his capital structure and its characteristic
mode of behavior more completely than he did. Finally I shall show
the most direct links between his treatment and those of Akerman and
von Hayek, however without following their example of discussing
alternate patterns of capital structure development at length.

Evolution of Wicksell's Concept of Capital

Wicksell devoted a section of *Value, Capital and Rent* (pp. 97-106) to
a discussion of Böhm-Bawerk's definitions of capital and to his attempt
to quantify capital in terms of the production period in Books I and
II of his celebrated *Positive Theory of Capital*. He praised Böhm-
Bawerk for limiting the category of real capital to material goods, and
he agreed that all claims and titles to capital goods, all personal abilities and land, should be excluded from this classification. But he took
Böhm-Bawerk to task for his distinction between "social capital"
(means of production or producers' goods, excluding labor subsistence)
and "private capital" (all means of acquisition excluding land, including producers' goods, durable consumers' goods, means of subsistence
for advance of real wages and rent to laborers and landowners, and
metallic money). Wicksell found this distinction to be untenable and
questioned why rented houses, lending libraries, and the like should
not be counted among social capital simply because they have the form
of consumption goods. They contribute to the production of services
just as much as raw materials included in "social capital" contribute
to the output of consumption goods. Then he concluded that "social
capital simply consists of the sum of private capitals," [1] and proceeded
to set up definitions of his own.

He adopted Böhm-Bawerk's perspective as the basis for his definitions, namely the view that the time-consuming, capital-using process
of production represents the functional and essential aspect of the
phenomenon of real capital. Consequently definitions of capital must
be so drawn as to afford insights into this function. The criterion he
applied in segregating capital from noncapital was in substance that
only objects or goods which are modifiable by the round-about processes of production belong to the category of capital. These are goods
which yield a finite series of services which can be extracted from them
over a variable time interval, a shorter or longer period. It was for
this reason, primarily, that labor or personal abilities and land had to
be excluded from capital. Labor can only yield its services in an un-

---

[1] Wicksell, *Value, Capital and Rent* (London, 1954), p. 104.

changeable *day-to-day* sequence over a finite period of years, and the same applies to land with the additional qualification that it yields an infinite rather than a finite series of services. Furthermore, neither the services of labor nor those of land can be stored *as such;* they can only be stored indirectly in the form of real capital. On this basis he set up two definitions: (*a*) Capital in the inclusive or broad sense—all produced goods that yield interest and/or quasi-rents; (*b*) capital in the narrow sense—nondurable, rapidly worn out or used up (*verbrauchbaren oder schnell abgenutzten*) producers' goods and inventories of consumers' goods, as long as the latter are *not* in the hands of consumers.[2] The distinction between capital in the "broad" and in the "narrow" sense, admittedly never easy to maintain, was drawn on the basis of durability. All durable goods (not in the hands of consumers) which were excluded from capital in the "narrow" sense (because of their *long* durability) and which were not counted among "land" proper, were referred to as "rent-goods" (*Rentengüter*).[3]

Thus in the 1890's Wicksell's category of "capital" consisted of "rent-goods" plus "capital in the narrow sense." The distinguishing features and reasons for separately classifying the former were:

1. Very durable goods are quite like land because they yield almost infinite series of services over a time interval which cannot easily be modified.

2. In stationary conditions, no rent-goods are produced, but those extant will be perpetually maintained.

3. Once in existence rent-goods earn quasi-rents, their yield, which is *not* determined directly by the interest rate, and which is independent alike of their original and of their reproduction cost.[4]

There remained the problem of providing a place for metallic money. It was listed in both categories. For society as a whole it is a rent-good, its yield in service to the community being far in excess of the interest paid on money loans. For the individual it is a capital good in the "narrow" sense of the term.

However, some years later (1901 and subsequently), this double classification of capital was blotted out in *Lectures-I.*

. . . the term (capital) . . . includes all auxiliaries to production with the exception of natural forces in their original form and direct human labor . . . it includes the houses and buildings in which work is carried on . . . the implements, tools, and machinery with which it is conducted . . . livestock . . . raw materials which are worked up, and finally—not the least

---

[2] *Ibid.,* p. 105.
[3] Wicksell, *Value, Capital and Rent,* p. 105.
[4] *Ibid.,* pp. 105-106; *Interest and Prices,* p. 126.

important category—the provisions and other commodities which must be saved up or otherwise held ready if labor is to be supported during the period while work is in progress.[5]

This more comprehensive definition conforms better with the usage we are accustomed to, and, as he put it, thus defined, capital may be viewed either from a "cross-section perspective" as an aggregate of producers' goods, or from a "lengthwise section" perspective as a continuous flow or maturation of saved-up labor and land into finished consumption goods.[6]

For himself, he elaborated his capital theory almost entirely from the longitudinal perspective, and from that angle of approach real capital was analytically conceived of as "saved-up labor and saved-up land in combination." [7]

It must be admitted that his definition was unnecessarily restrictive in excluding from capital all durable consumers' goods (in the hands of consumers) and consequently from saving and investment all expenditures made on such goods. Moreover, while he finally included very durable producers' goods, formerly called "rent-goods," in his definition of capital, it must also be admitted that in that category they led an uneasy existence as it were. True to his earlier standpoint, his entire analysis of capital structure, and all of his illustrations and examples of the behavior of real capital, were stated in terms of real capital of relatively short durability or short maturation terms of one, two, and three years.

As will be shown later, in viewing real capital as "saved-up labor and saved-up land in combination," Wicksell and others working in the "Austrian" tradition, by no means intended to deny that current production of capital goods requires and receives, besides the services of the "original factors" (direct or "uninvested" labor and land services), also services of preëxisting capital goods. From a "cross-section" view of production, preëxisting capital goods are legitimately viewed as another factor of production, coördinate with labor and land. But from a "lengthwise section" view, these goods also must be regarded as consisting of labor and land services "saved up" from earlier periods. Yet, the conception that "a capital instrument as a whole can be regarded as a *bundle* of such investments (of 'saved-up' labor and land services)

---

[5] Wicksell, *Lectures-I*, pp. 144-145.

[6] Wicksell, *Interest and Prices*, pp. 125-126; concerning some interesting comparisons between the lengthwise and the cross-section perspectives of real capital and the associated explanation of interest, see also his comments on Léon Walras's interest theory in the article "Professor Cassel's System of Economics" in Appendix I, *Lectures-I*, pp. 226-227; 236-237.

[7] Wicksell, *Lectures-I*, p. 151.

successively 'maturing' over the different periods of its lifetime," [8] does not require that we should be able, even approximately, to express society's real capital as a certain quantity of such "saved-up" services. This conception was entirely an analytic device. It was used chiefly to stress two fundamental ideas; namely, that maintenance of an existing quantity of real capital requires replacement-investment, or requires some draft on or diversion from the total quantity of labor and land services which otherwise would be available in their entirety for producing consumption goods. Secondly, net capital formation (over and above mere capital maintenance) requires a greater diversion of resource services from consumer goods production.

Given that these diversions of resource services are necessary to maintain and to create capital, then the value, and in a certain sense also the time dimension, of the real capital maintained and/or created by these means can be expressed by the quantities of resource services invested in production of capital. The value of this capital then equals the quantities of those resource services, times their prices, times the compound rate of interest applicable over the period they must remain invested before the corresponding capital goods render or "mature out" a corresponding quantity (and value) of capital goods services in production.

Since real capital is required to sustain several production stages, one can express the quantity of real capital in society (which for the moment is assumed to be stationary, and operating at full resource utilization, with perfect competition on all markets) by the length of the average production period its capital quantity sustains. In substance this was the quantification of real capital in a time sense which Böhm-Bawerk attempted when he defined his period of production as follows:

According to what has been said, the production period of a consumption good is, strictly speaking, to be reckoned from the moment in which the first hand was laid to the making of its first intermediate product right down to the completion of the good itself. In our times when unassisted production has almost disappeared, and one generation builds on the intermediate products laid down by earlier generations, the production period of almost any consumption good could, in any strict calculation, trace its beginning back to early centuries. [9]

---

[8] E. Lindahl, *Studies in the Theory of Money and Capital* (New York, 1939), p. 298. Lindahl's discussion of alternate ways of dealing with durable capital (pp. 296-309) is referred to as a more complete treatment of this topic.

[9] E. von Böhm-Bawerk, *The Positive Theory of Capital*, W. A. Smart's translation (New York, 1891), p. 88.

Although Wicksell at first accepted this quantification of capital apparently he was not very happy with it. Nor was it long before he formally rejected the production period (1895) and substituted for it a derived measure of capital; namely, the weighted average investment period, or investment period for short. The latter was defined as the time interval between the input of a unit of real capital by purchase or payment of wages to labor (and rent to landowners) for the quantities of labor and land services used in producing this unit of real capital, and the replacement of this unit by the sale of finished consumption goods. Since several successive investments of labor- and land-services may readily have to be made over a succession of periods before the capital goods, or the requisite intermediary products, are ready to yield services in the production of consumption goods, each of these investments had to be weighted by the rate of interest applied to the time interval or number of periods it had to be invested, before it is released by the sale of finished consumption goods to the production of which it has contributed.[10]

This investment period was also related in a definite manner to the production period (defined for capital in the "narrow" sense only); namely, if production and investment are continuous and if the same number of workers and acres of land are engaged throughout this period, then the investment period is exactly equal to one-half the length of the average production period.

In what sense was the investment period an improvement over its progenitor? It implied that its virtue consisted in the closer quantitative relation that obtains between the investment period and the accumulation or decumulation of capital (in the "narrow" sense). Under continuous replacement and production, on the average, only half the real capital in existence during any production period is invested during that time interval. It cannot be denied that the investment period correlated more closely with the quantity of capital invested, and that the lengthening of this period reflected more directly changes in the rate of real saving or capital formation, than did the average production period. Yet the vagueness of this entire construction remained in compounded form, a vague time expression for an ambiguously defined category of capital goods. But it is to Wicksell's credit that he never tried to conceal the shortcomings of this conception; in fact, he emphasized them, as the following statement indicates:

It should perhaps be pointed out here that the assumption that the average period of investment is independent of the interest rate, *only applies*

---

[10] Wicksell, *Finanztheoretische Untersuchungen,* pp. 29 ff.

strictly speaking where several different capital investments relate to one and the same future act of consumption. In the opposite case, where one or more factors of production are invested in a single capital good, it may easily be seen that the average period of investment will be dependent on the rate of interest . . . waiting is not a simple quantity, but is . . . a complex; "average waiting" as a rule exists only as a mathematical concept without direct physical or psychic significance. But it should nevertheless be retained as a concise general principle reflecting the essence of productive capital.[11]

Wicksell used the average investment period for a number of years mainly to state the relation between the current output of means of subsistence and the corresponding, vaguely defined, quantity of capital. Thus if K is the quantity of capital in the "narrow" sense, and t the average investment period expressed in years, then K/t represents

. . . the amount of capital that becomes free in the course of a year, the amount, that is to say, of finished products which are available each year to pay for the services of labor and land (or other rent-earning goods) and it constitutes the *annual* wages and rent fund. K itself, the value of the whole of 'circulating' capital, can be regarded as the *aggregate* wages and rent fund, although it is not all free and liquid at any one moment, but becomes so only over a period of time. . . .[12]

If either Böhm-Bawerk's quantification of real capital as the average production period or Wicksell's quantification of real capital in the "narrow" sense as the average investment period were to show clearly the relationship between the interest rate and the quantity of capital as reflected in a lengthening or shortening of these periods, other factors constant, it would be desirable to obtain empirical measurements, or estimates, of the length of these periods in given economic conditions. However, Wicksell admitted that such measurements were impossible. "We are merely concerned with obtaining a *sufficiently clear perspective of the general direction in which economic forces operate, and we are not attempting any quantitative estimates. . . .* We are supposing . . . that once capital has been invested it becomes free only when the finished consumption goods find their way into actual consumption." [13]

Instead of the average investment period he developed a clearer time quantification of capital, his capital structure conception, which represents the final development of his perspective on capital. It is true that he never referred to this conception, as we do, as a "capital struc-

[11] Wicksell, *Lectures-I*, p. 184.
[12] Wicksell, *Interest and Prices*, p. 130.
[13] *Ibid.*, p. 128; italics supplied. Cf. also *Lectures-I*, pp. 166-183.

ture." Instead he characterized it in words of closely related meaning as "the stratification of capital through time" (*Lectures-I,* p. 151) and as "the technical dimensions and composition of capital" (*Lectures-I,* p. 202). The emphasis of this concept is on the future rather than on the past. The "stratification" amounts to a statement of the reproduction cost of existing real capital. It avoids most of the difficulties experienced with the attempts to express capital quantitatively by means of the investment period and production period. But, like the former, it cannot be measured empirically. Because Wicksell's contributions to capital theory are associated with his development of this conception, it calls for systematic treatment here.

Wicksell's Structural Concept of Capital and the Rate of Interest—Static Analysis

In order to get a clear view of Wicksell's structural concept of capital and of his interpretation of interest as the marginal productivity of waiting, it is best to go back to simple hypothetical cases. To that end we compare the conditions of a society producing initially without real capital with the conditions that emerge as this society begins to create capital. We shall imagine that this society is a closed economy of simple enterprises of optimum size, operating under perfect competition.

At the outset all its productive resources consist of a certain quantity of labor, designated as A, and of land, B. These resources are used entirely for producing consumption goods or "subsistence," here designated as C. At real wage rates of w and rent rates of r per unit of labor and land service rendered (determined by the marginal productivity of labor and land respectively) the economy's total output, C, has a value of $C = Aw + Br$. In this society the production period is one year long, as in many types of agriculture, and owners of the factors of production are paid their respective shares of subsistence at the end of each period. Between periods they live on the subsistence they received as annual real wages and/or rent at the end of the previous period. They also maximize the utility of this real income by exchanging varieties of subsistence among each other on the basis of marginal utility evaluations. The resource pattern of this society is shown in figure 2. Initially, as determined by prevailing wage and rent rates, resources of the quantity and value shown were entirely devoted to production of C.

Stationary conditions prevail all along until they are temporarily disrupted during one or more production periods in which this society undertakes net capital formation. But once a postulated amount of

Aw uninvested services of labor   +   Br uninvested services of land

Fig. 2. Resources of society before formation of capital.

capital has been created and a corresponding capital structure has been developed, the community returns to stationary conditions by ceasing further net formation of capital and by maintaining the capital created by replacement investment.

Now, in year I, some factor owners decide to produce simple capital goods of one year's durability or maturation period. They do this because they are convinced these goods will yield a net marginal product by which they wish to increase their real incomes.

Since the economy has only $(A + B)$ resources, one-year capital goods can only be produced if the factor owners in question practice abstinence. If they are laborers, they can do this by working less than an entire man-year in subsistence production, and by using the time thus set free for producing these capital goods. Of course, to the extent that they do this, they must reduce their customary consumption of subsistence. If they are landowners, they can practice abstinence by devoting less than the full land acreage available to them to subsistence production, in order to make some acre-years of land services available for capital goods production. Since production of capital goods requires inputs of both labor and land services we must assume that those among abstinence-practicing factor owners who have only labor services available exchange man-hours of labor services for acre-hours with other factor owners who only have land services available.

To create one-year capital goods requires that a portion, perhaps 10 per cent, of the total $(A + B)$ resources be withdrawn from production of C to be invested ("saved up") in production of capital goods of one year's maturity term. As a result perhaps output of subsistence declines to $0.9C$ in year I.

Let the resource services invested in one-year capital goods be designated as $A_{0,1}$ labor services and $B_{0,1}$ land services, and the resulting capital goods as $(A_1 w + B_1 r)$. Let the marginal productivity of invested resource services be greater than those of coöperating uninvested ones so that society's output with capital goods rises in the ratio $1.05/1.00$ as compared with what it was before. The cost of the invested resources then is $(A_{0,1} w + B_{0,1} r)$, and their value when ready for use in production in year II, in which they "mature out" their services, is greater than this cost by reason of their relatively greater marginal produc-

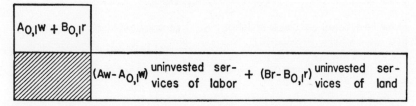

Fig. 3. Uninvested resources and resources set aside for investment in a one-year capital structure.

tivity. The society's resource pattern can now be depicted as in figure 3.

At the end of year I a quantity and value of $(A_1w + B_1r)$ services of one-year capital goods are available to coöperate with the remaining uninvested labor and land services, $(Aw - A_{0,1}w + Br - B_{0,1}r)$, in producing consumption goods. The marginal productivity of the $(A_1w + B_1r)$ services of capital goods is somewhat greater, for opportunity cost reasons, than that of a corresponding quantity of uninvested labor and land services. If the use of these capital goods raises output in the ratio $1.05/1.00$ as compared with what it was prior to creation of real capital, then their net marginal productivity is $(1.05/1.00 - 1.00)$ or 0.5 in units of output (C) or 5 per cent, and this determines the interest rate z, which must be paid to induce factor owners to "save up" some of the A and B resources for capital investment. Thus the marginal productivity of the $(A_1w + B_1r)$ capital goods is greater than that of a corresponding quantity of uninvested land and labor by $z(A_{0,1}w + B_{0,1}r)$.

With the given distribution between invested and uninvested resources, this higher real income level can be maintained indefinitely without further net abstinence by annual reinvestment of $(A_{0,1}w + B_{0,1}r)$ labor and land services to replace wear and tear on the existing quantity of one-year capital goods (fig. 4).

However, if in year II or later some factor owners, while maintain-

$A_{0,1}w + B_{0,1}r$	
$A_1w + B_1r$	$(Aw - A_{0,1}w) + (Br - B_{0,1}r)$ uninvested services of labor and land

Fig. 4. Uninvested resources and maturing services of a one-year capital structure.

ing the one-year capital goods, decide to create capital goods of two years' maturation term, then they would have to practice net abstinence anew for a succession of two years. This abstinence may not be as great as that associated with the creation of one-year capital because as long as the latter is maintained it produces a net addition to the output of subsistence which would not otherwise have been available. In any event, to create capital of two years' maturation term means that some factor owners must in a given year practice net abstinence, i.e., they must set aside some quantity of labor and land services previously uninvested, say $(A_{0,2}w + B_{0,2}r)$, to be invested in two-year capital. The next year they must again be prepared to invest an equal quantity of resource services, while that which was invested the year before has now aged one year and may be designated as $(A_{1,2}w + B_{1,2}r)$. As a result, at the end of the second or beginning of the third year, a new quantity and value of $(A_2w + B_2r)$ services of two-year capital goods are available to "mature out" in production in coöperation with the services of preëxisting one-year capital goods, and with the remaining (and reduced) uninvested services of labor and land. When the one-plus-two-year capital structure of this society is completed, its net real income will be greater than before. This greater income can be enjoyed in perpetuity without further net abstinence if the requisite quantities and values of $(A_{0,1}w + B_{0,1}r)$ and $(A_{0,2}w + B_{0,2}r)$ of labor and land services are invested each year in replacement of both types of real capital. The distribution of productive resources for a society with a two- and one-year capital structure may be depicted as in figure 5.

Obviously, these diagrams will increase in height and in width by additional steps as capital goods of longer maturation terms than two years are introduced into the "structure," while at the same time the

$A_{0,2}w + B_{0,2}r$		
$A_{1,2}w + B_{1,2}r$	$A_{0,1}w + B_{0,1}r$	
$A_2w + B_2r$	$A_1w + B_1r$	$Aw - (A_{0,1}w + A_{0,2}w) + Br - (B_{0,1}r + B_{0,2}r)$ uninvested services of land and labor

Fig. 5. Uninvested resources and maturing services of a one- and two-year capital structure.

proportion of uninvested to invested quantities of labor and land services will decline.

In these and later "capital structure" diagrams, invested quantities of resource services are given double subscripts, such as $(A_{0,1}w + B_{0,1}r)$, $(A_{1,2}w + B_{1,2}r)$, $(A_{2,3}w + B_{2,3}r)$, etc. The first subscript indicates in what year the corresponding quantity of resource services was invested, and the second the maturation term, in years, of the capital goods in which it was invested. Thus $(A_{0,1}w + B_{0,1}r)$ means that a certain quantity of both labor and land services, for which real wages and rents of w and r rates respectively are paid, has just been invested or transferred over from the category of uninvested labor and land services into capital goods of one year's maturation term. Similarly, $(A_{2,3}w + B_{2,3}r)$ indicates that a certain quantity of labor and land services was invested two years ago in capital goods of three years' maturation term.

The services that the corresponding capital goods render or "mature out" in production, per annual production period, are indicated by single subscripts, which show the maturation term of these capital goods. Thus $(A_4w + B_4r)$ shows that the structure contains a group of capital goods of four years' maturation term, and that these goods render one year's service during the production period. The value of these services will necessarily be greater than the value of services of uninvested labor and land and/or of labor and land just invested, i.e., with zero accrued investment time, as will be shown presently.

The quantity and value of uninvested labor and land services, sometimes referred to as services of "the original factors of production" or as services of "current" labor and land, are indicated without subscripts as $(Aw + Br)$. In an economy with a growing capital structure and a fixed supply of "original factors," the services of the latter are a declining proportion of total coöperating productive resources, shown as

$$Aw - (A_{0,1}w + A_{0,2}w + \ldots + A_{0,n}w) + Br - (B_{0,1}r + B_{0,2}r \ldots + B_{0,n}r)$$

All groups of *capital goods*, regardless of maturity term, *always render in current production the "mature" services of their "oldest" invested or saved-up labor and land element*. Take a group of capital goods of four years' maturation term as an example. Production of gasoline may be a possible case in point. This requires exploration and geological surveys to locate oil fields, which we may consider as taking place in year I. In year II test drilling occurs and engineering and construction work takes place to set up the first few wells. In year III more wells are constructed and perhaps also pipelines to transport the crude petroleum to centrally located refining facilities. In year IV, to process the new petroleum adequately, additional refining capacity has to be developed. Finally, in year V, an additional output of gasoline and other finished petroleum products, the "mature" fruits of these investment activities, becomes available.

If we assume, as Wicksell often did, perfect foresight on the part of investors, we might for simplicity consider that the requisite total investment was parceled out over the four-year period in equal annual amounts; namely, in amounts of $(A_{0,4}w + B_{0,4}r)$ of previously uninvested labor and land services. On the assumption of perpetual maintenance, the relations between these parcels of investment in the capital goods of four years' maturation term may, for any current annual production period, be illustrated as follows:

$A_{0,4}w + B_{0,4}r$ equals a value and quantity of services of current labor and land being invested during the current period as replacement in due course (i.e. four years hence), for the "oldest saved-up labor and land services," the $(A_4w + B_4r)$ services of these capital goods, which are received or "mature out" in current production.

$A_{1,4}w + B_{1,4}r$ equals $(A_{0,4}w + B_{0,4}r)(1 + z)$ services of labor and land which were "current" a year ago when they were invested, and on which, in consequence, a year's interest has accrued.

$A_{2,4}w + B_{2,4}r$ equals $(A_{0,4}w + B_{0,4}r)(1 + z)^2$ services of labor and land which were "current" two years ago when they were invested, and on which two years interest has accrued.

By parity of reasoning, it is clear that $(A_{3,4}w + B_{3,4}r) = (A_{0,4}w + B_{0,4}r)(1 + z)^3$ and that $(A_4w + B_4r)$, the extant four-year capital goods, equal $(A_{0,4}w + B_{0,4}r)(1 + z)^4$.

It is because capital goods of long maturation terms yield up the services of their "oldest" (hence most valuable) quantities of invested resource services in current production that, *in equilibrium, the marginal productivity of services of capital goods of long maturation terms must stand in a compound rate relationship to the marginal productivity of services of capital goods of short maturation term.* (Cf. *Lectures-I, p.* 160.)

If the use of one-year capital goods together with services of uninvested labor and land raises the level of output in the ratio of 1.05/1.00 as compared with what this level was when no capital goods were in use, then the net marginal product of one-year capital goods is 0.05 or 5 per cent of output. As long as this yield on one-year goods continues, foresighted capitalists will not invest in two-year capital goods unless they realize a yield of 0.1025 per annum, which equals $(1.05^2 - 1)$. If their net yield is less than this, it would be to the capitalists' advantage to invest the same amount and value of resources in additional one-year goods. Because of this rule, and on the assumptions that (1) interest is determined by the net marginal productivity of capital goods of shortest maturation term (here one year), (2) interest is compounded annually, and (3) the rate of interest, z, remains constant during the years implied in the maturation terms, we can now express the value of services rendered by four-year capital goods in the following equivalent ways:

$$(A_4w + B_4r) = (A_{0,4}w + B_{0,4}r)(1 + z)^4, \text{ or}$$
$$= (A_{1,4}w + B_{1,4}r)(1 + z)^3, \text{ since}$$
$$(A_{1,4}w + B_{1,4}r) = (A_{0,4}w + B_{0,4}r)(1 + z), \text{ or}$$
$$= (A_{2,4}w + B_{2,4}r)(1 + z)^2, \text{ since}$$
$$(A_{2,4}w + B_{2,4}r) = (A_{1,4}w + B_{1,4}r)(1 + z), \text{ or}$$
$$= (A_{3,4}w + B_{3,4}r)(1 + z), \text{ since}$$
$$(A_{3,4}w + B_{3,4}r) = (A_{2,4}w + B_{2,4}r)(1 + z).$$

If $z = 0.05$, the values of services of 4-, 3-, 2-, and 1-year capital goods can clearly be expressed in terms of their required annual replacement investments as follows:

$$(A_4w + B_4r) = (A_{0,4}w + B_{0,4}r)(1 + z)^4 = 1.215506 (A_{0,4}w + B_{0,4}r)$$
$$(A_3w + B_3r) = (A_{0,3}w + B_{0,3}r)(1 + z)^3 = 1.157625 (A_{0,3}w + B_{0,3}r)$$
$$(A_2w + B_2r) = (A_{0,2}w + B_{0,2}r)(1 + z)^2 = 1.102500 (A_{0,2}w + B_{0,2}r)$$
$$(A_1w + B_1r) = (A_{0,1}w + B_{0,1}r)(1 + z) = 1.050000 (A_{0,1}w + B_{0,1}r).$$

Now we shall make a *special assumption*, which simplifies the following discussion. We assume that annual replacements for the various groups of capital goods are all equal, or in other words that

$$(A_{0,1}w + B_{0,1}r) = (A_{0,2}w + B_{0,2}r) = (A_{0,3}w + B_{0,3}r) = (A_{0,4}w + B_{0,4}r).$$

On this basis it is possible to express the value of current capital goods services as well as the value of the capital structure itself (as of the beginning of any current production year) in terms of the relatively simple annual replacement investment $(A_{0,1}w + B_{0,1}r)$, for its capital goods of one year's maturation term.

The gross value or gross marginal product of the services of the one- to four-year capital goods above equals their sum at right, namely $4.525631(A_{0,1}w + B_{0,1}r)$. To obtain the net value or net marginal product of these services, we deduct the required annual replacement investments, namely $4(A_{0,1}w + B_{0,1}r)$ and obtain $0.525631(A_{0,1}w + B_{0,1}r)$. With capital goods of one-, two-, three-, and four-year maturation terms plus $[Aw - 4A_{0,1}w + Br - 4B_{0,1}r]$ services of current or uninvested labor and land, the community's capital structure can be shown as the sum of quantities of resource services invested for various terms, which lie above the double-ruled abscissa in the accompanying diagram. Its productive resources engaged in current production, namely its services of capital goods of varying maturation terms and its uninvested services of labor and land can be shown as rectangles lying below the abscissa (fig. 6).

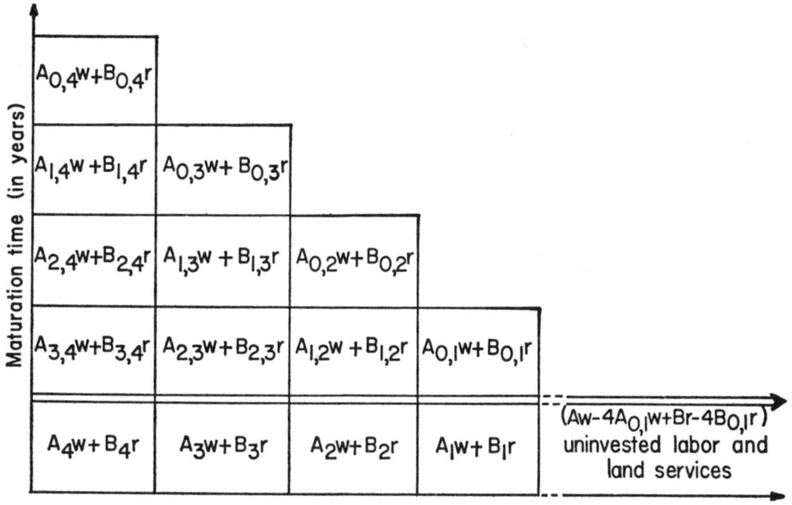

Fig. 6. A four-, three-, two-, and one-year capital structure and uninvested resources.

In figure 6 the uninvested services of labor and land, a finite quantity, are not shown in full so that the proportion between these and invested quantities of resource services cannot be read directly from the illustration. Hence the break in the base axis prior to the statement of the uninvested services. The arrows on both the double-ruled abscissa and on the time axis indicate the possibility of expanding the capital structure by introducing capital goods of greater than four years' maturation term and thus pushing the rectangular representations of groups of capital goods of four and less than four years' maturation term further to the right along the abscissa.

The present value (at the beginning of any production period) of the capital structure shown above, a value we designate as K, is evidently the sum of the values of the various quantities of resource services invested for various numbers of years and shown above the abscissa. By using the equivalents in replacement investment terms of these values and by using the special assumption stated above, we can now state these values as follows:

The present value of quantities of resource services invested in four-year capital goods is:

$$(A_{3,4}w + B_{3,4}r) + (A_{2,4}w + B_{2,4}r) + (A_{1,4}w + B_{1,4}r) + (A_{0,4}w + B_{0,4}r) =$$

$$(A_{0,4}w + B_{0,4}r) [1 + 1(1 + z) + 1(1 + z)^2 + 1(1 + z)^3] =$$

$$4.310125(A_{0,1}w - B_{0,1}r).$$

Similarly, the present value of quantities of resource services invested, respectively in three-year, two-year, and one-year capital goods are:

$$(A_{2,3}w + B_{2,3}r) + (A_{1,3}w + B_{1,3}r) + (A_{0,3}w + B_{0,3}r) =$$

$$(A_{0,3}w + B_{0,3}r) [1 + 1(1 + z) + 1(1 + z)^2] = 3.15250(A_{0,1}w + B_{0,1}r),$$

and

$$(A_{1,2}w + B_{1,2}r) + (A_{0,2}w + B_{0,2}r) =$$

$$(A_{0,2}w + B_{0,2}r) [1 + 1(1 + z)] = 2.0500(A_{0,1}w + B_{0,1}r), \text{ and}$$

$$(A_{0,1}w + B_{0,1}r) (1) = 1.000(A_{0,1}w + B_{0,1}r).$$

By adding together the values of resource services invested in these four groups of capital goods, we obtain the present value of the capital structure as

$$K = 10.412625(A_{0,1}w + B_{0,1}r).$$

We have previously seen that the net marginal product of the services rendered in current production by the various groups of capital goods was $0.525631(A_{0,1}w + B_{0,1}r)$. If we divide this quantity by K, we obtain z, the rate of interest, namely, $0.525631(A_{0,1}w + B_{0,1}r)/10.412625(A_{0,1}w + B_{0,1}r) = 0.05 = z$. Hence the net marginal product per production period of the capital goods in the structure equals interest at rate z per cent on the value K of services of resources invested in the structure. Thus the interest income of the community, a net addition to the income it enjoyed before capital goods were in use, is Kz. The community's total real income, measured in subsistence, is now $C + 0.525631(A_{0,1}w + B_{0,1}r) = Aw + Br + Kz$ respectively of real wages, rent and interest, whereas before capital formation began, this income was substantially smaller; namely, $C = Aw + Br$ real wages and rent.

In this connection, it may be instructive to see how a given capital structure can also be expressed in an investment-time sense by means of the weighted average investment period Wicksell employed in his earlier work. In the "structure" we have shown above, the unweighted average investment period for the four groups of capital goods is clearly $(4 + 3 + 2 + 1)/4 = 2.5$ years of investment of the equivalent of $4(A_{0,1}w + B_{0,1}r)$ services of resources which might otherwise be uninvested. A more accurate expression of this time quantity is obtained by using the weighted average investment period, in which the interest-accruals on resource services invested for terms of one or more years serve as weights. On that basis, using the values shown above, the weighted average investment period of our structure comes to $(4.31 + 3.15 + 2.05 + 1.00)/4 = 2.625$ years of investment of the equivalent of $4(A_{0,1}w + B_{0,1}r)$ resource services.

Perhaps a word should be added on the determination of the rate of interest as the net marginal (value) productivity rate of real capital. In the model we have used, we have shown that the investment demand for real savings, a demand based on the anticipated (here by assumption, the foreknown) marginal value productivity of capital goods, was exerted by the very factor owners who supplied the real savings or practiced abstinence. To them alone belong the corresponding capital goods and the net returns the latter bring in. However, even if we had used a different model, one in which there exists a consumption demand (based on time preferences) for real savings in addition to an investment demand, the result would have been similar. Consumption loans could then be treated as a subtrahend from total real savings, so that the supply of savings for investment in capital goods is stated net of the demand for consumption loans. The level of the rate of interest would still be determined by the net marginal (and value) productivity of capital goods because in equilibrium, entrepreneurs equipped with perfect foresight would not offer more than that rate as a supply price for real saving. Because of competition among entrepreneurs and because of opportunity costs applicable to the use of savings in alternate investment opportunities, savers, who would also be aware of these facts, would not have to accept less than the net marginal (value) product of invested savings as a rate of interest. And consumers, if they are to obtain loans at all, would have to meet the opportunity costs established by alternative uses for savings, and particularly as established in the market for investment in capital goods.

However, in our illustrations above, we have let real wages and rents respectively remain at their initial rates of w and r despite the fact that the total quantity of uninvested resource services has in the meantime declined by the equivalent of $4(A_{0,1}w + B_{0,1}r)$. This is an unrealistic assumption we have made use of in order to keep the description of Wicksell's capital structure on static premises within reasonable bounds of space. To the contrary, Wicksell was keenly aware that capital goods, like other factors, are subject to diminishing returns, and that if they alone increase, other factors constant, the marginal productivity of these other factors would increase in proportion to its decline on real capital. It was precisely at this point of his analysis that he made a notable discovery. He found that as the marginal productivity of real capital declines in societies where this factor increases faster than other factors do, *forces are set in motion which make investment in capital goods of progressively longer maturation terms more profitable than in goods of short maturation term.*

To get a closer look at the implications of this insight, we need to study the capital structure in process of development or on dynamic premises.

The Behavior of Wicksell's Capital Structure—Dynamic Analysis

As noted earlier, Wicksell spoke of real capital as having both "technical dimensions" and "composition." Before we enter on the discussion of its "dimensions," it will be best to dispose of its "composition."

The "composition" of real capital refers to the proportion in which saved-up labor and saved-up land enter into its make-up. This proportion varies directly with changes in the relative levels of the rates of real wages and rent, but in equilibrium it is always determinate when those rates are given. It is then determined by adding to the saved-up labor component until the net marginal value product of labor-capital equals that of saved-up land. In the discussion which follows we shall assume that real wages and rent are equally affected by such changes in the "dimensions" of the capital structure as we wish to demonstrate and that therefore the "composition" of real capital remains optimally adjusted throughout.

Now Wicksell spoke of his structure or "stratification of capital through time" as possessing "width" and "height," or a vertical and a horizontal dimension, and as being capable of change (mostly expansion) in both of these dimensions. "Width" referred to the proportion of total original factor services, $(A + B)$, that must be invested annually in replacement of the structure's groups of capital goods of various maturation terms. In figure 6, "width" is equal to the ratio of

$(4A_{0,1}w + 4B_{0,1}r)/(Aw - 4A_{0,1}w + Br - 4B_{0,1}r)$. In the more general case where a capital structure may have capital goods of 1 to N years maturation terms, and where the annual replacement investments needed to maintain the various groups of capital goods are not assumed to be equal, this ratio would be $(A_{0,1}w + B_{0,1}r + A_{0,2}w + B_{0,2}r + \ldots + A_{0,N}w + B_{0,N}r)/[Aw - (A_{0,1}w + A_{0,2}w + \ldots + A_{0,N}w) + Br - (B_{0,1}r + B_{0,2}r + \ldots B_{0,N}r)]$.

The "height" or vertical dimension of a capital structure is more difficult to express. "Height" refers to the length of the maturation terms of the various groups of capital goods. If goods of different maturation terms are arrayed, as in figure 6, in descending order of length of terms from highest to lowest, the result will be triangle-like capital structure diagrams as shown in figure 7.

Here we have graduated the time axis in logarithmic unit distances as more appropriate than an arithmetic scale for representing the quantities and values of resources invested in long-maturation as compared with short-maturation capital goods which stand in a com-

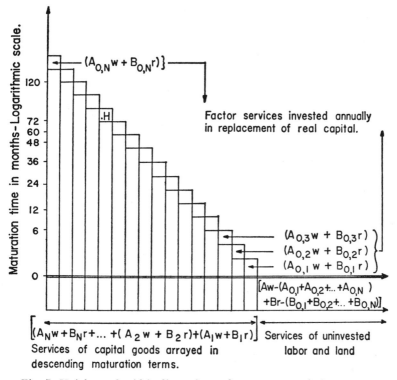

Fig. 7. Height and width dimensions of an *n*-year capital structure.

pound rate relationship to one another. The "height" of the structure above is best represented as the center of gravity, point *H*, of the triangle-like area enclosed between the double-ruled abscissa, the step-like maturation hypotenuse, and the maturation-time axis. Point *H* equals approximately 72 months on the time scale.

If we knew the maturation terms of all groups of capital goods in the structure and also the number of goods in each group as well as the net marginal productivity of capital or the interest rate, we could compute the weighted average investment period for this structure. Such a computation should give us a value equal to that of point *H*, about 72 months. Hence the center of gravity of capital structure triangles and the weighted average investment period of these structures are the same.

If we regard the maturation terms of capital goods as continuously variable, from a few days to many years, and if we state the time axis in arithmetic units, we obtain a capital structure diagram in which the former step-like maturation hypotenuse is replaced by a smooth curve of constant slope (fig. 8). The slope of this curve reflects the compound rate of growth of the marginal productivity of capital goods of long- as compared with those of short-maturation terms.

Again, the "height" of this structure is shown as the center of gravity,

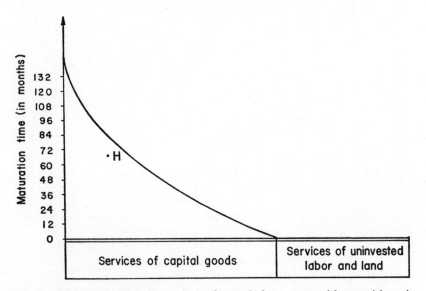

Fig. 8. Height and width dimensions of a capital structure with an arithmetic time scale.

point *H*, of the area enclosed between the curvilinear maturation hypotenuse, the double-ruled abscissa, and the time axis.

Now, concerning structures of this type, "expansion in width" in its pure sense meant a proportionate increase in all preëxisting groups of capital goods of different maturation terms. Such expansion could be shown by broadening the capital goods "bars" in figure 7. Hence "widening" would not change the slope of the maturation hypotenuse (as measured from the point where the lower end of the hypotenuse touches the abscissa). It would merely shift the latter to the right. As a result the area enclosed in the triangle-like figure would increase, and the amount of uninvested resource services available would decrease. The rectangle below the double-ruled abscissa beginning at the lower end of the hypotenuse, which represents the quantity of uninvested factor services, would decrease in length, by as much as the base of the triangle is broadened by "widening."

But it is also clear that "expansion in width" would not change the level of the center of gravity, *H*, of the expanded capital structure. In our diagrams, point *H* would simply move laterally to the right as the structure is widened.

"Expansion in height," however, means raising the center of gravity of the capital structure. In its *pure form,* growth in the vertical dimension means raising point *H only vertically* by increasing the proportion of capital goods of long terms at the expense of those of short-maturation terms within the structure. This is done by under-maintaining, over some periods, some of the short-term goods, which are thus allowed to decline in quantity, and by shifting the labor and land services which used to be invested in annual replacement of these goods to create additional capital goods of long maturation terms. However, if this is carried out on a large scale and over a long succession of production periods, it could result in such growth in the height of the structure and shrinkage in its base that its center of gravity is not only shifted up vertically but also to the left laterally, closer to the time axis.

Once the desired degree of height expansion has been accomplished, the completed shift of investment from goods of short to longer terms will have steepened the slope of the maturation hypotenuse and will have released to join the supply of uninvested factor services some quantities of labor and land services previously invested as annual replacement for the larger number of short-term goods then in existence. The reason for this is, of course, that the annual replacement requirement per unit of resource services invested is smaller on capital

goods of long term than it is if the same quantity of resource services
is invested in capital goods of short term.

Figure 9 shows how pure height expansion is achieved by a shift
of invested resource services from capital goods of short- to long-
maturation terms. Hypotenuse I-I shows the nature of the capital
structure prior to height expansion. Hypotenuse II-II shows the structure after the investment shift. The center of gravity has moved
upwards from approximately point H_1 to H_2 as a result of this action.

Wicksell's analysis was centered on the "pure" cases of height ex-

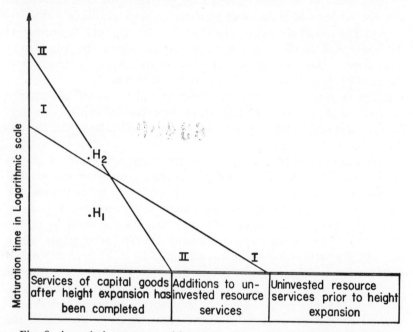

Fig. 9. A capital structure with an expansion in its height dimension.

pansion, like the one just illustrated, to the neglect of a "mixed" case
which should be considered in passing. If a community maintains all
its existing capital goods and then decides to expand its structure by
net investment only in capital goods of longer maturation terms than
that of the group among preëxisting goods with the longest term,
the result will be an expansion both in the width and height dimensions, as shown in figure 10.

The original maturation hypotenuse, I-I, has shifted to the right
and become longer in hypotenuse II-II. But the latter consists of two
segments, a lower and longer one which has the same slope as I-I,

and an upper segment of steeper slope than I-I. As a result of this change, the center of gravity is shifted both upward and to the right, from point H_1 to H_2 approximately, and the supply of uninvested factor services is reduced somewhat compared with what it was prior to this "mixed" expansion of the structure.

The reason, apparently, that Wicksell did not consider this case is that he thought of capital structure expansion as following a relatively

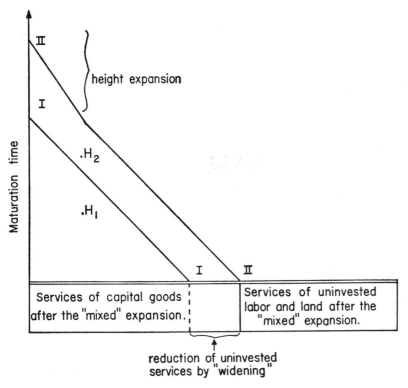

Fig. 10. A capital structure subject to expansion in both its height and width dimensions.

fixed pattern or sequence which would make mixed expansion rather unlikely. He considered it typical for capital structures first to be expanded by "widening." But with other factors constant, widening alone of the capital structure must before long reduce the marginal productivity of real capital and hence the rate of interest. This re-duction occurs first and to the greatest extent on capital goods of short-maturation terms because they are ordinarily present in any given structure in larger numbers than goods of long-maturation term. Proportionate expansion of all capital groups, consequently, expands short-term goods quantitatively more than the rest, and hence reduces their marginal productivity more than for the rest. This *disrupts* the compound rate relations between marginal productivity of capital goods of short and of long term which prevailed until equilibrium was disturbed by net capital formation to expand the structure.

Since the marginal productivity of long-term goods has fallen less than that of short-term ones, the former now represent superior investment opportunities. It is this which eventually stimulates the shift of investment from goods of short to those of long-maturation terms and brings on the "pure" type of height expansion of the structure. Thus height expansion occurs with a time lag behind widening. Moreover, it occurs as a result both of the decline in interest that has taken place and as a result of the yield discrepancies which have developed between capital goods of long and of short term, both of which phenomena were caused by the previous "widening."

But height expansion, which releases into the uninvested category some resource services formerly used in replacing short-term goods, counteracts the decline in interest rate and rise in real wages and rent which occurred during widening. However, vertical expansion, *by itself,* was not considered powerful enough to restore the interest rate, wages and rent, to their preëxpansion levels. This, which had important implications for the theory of distribution, may possibly be made clearer by the following example.

A community has a total quantity of 150 units of $(A + B)$ man-years of labor services and acre-years of land services available per annum for production. Over a period of years, this community has provided itself with a structure of three-, two-, and one-year capital goods, consisting of 10 units of three-year goods, 30 units of two-year goods, and 60 of one-year goods. These capital goods now supply an equivalent number of years of capital goods services per annum; namely, $10(A_3w + B_3r) + 30(A_2w + B_2r) + 60(A_1w + B_1r)$ years of capital goods services per annum. The net marginal productivity of one-year goods is 0.05, that of goods of two-year maturation term is 0.1025, and of three-year term, 0.157625, all in proper compound rate relationship to one another, and the interest rate is, therefore, 5 per cent. To maintain this capital structure requires replacement investment annually of

$$10(A_{0,3}w + B_{0,3}r) + 30(A_{0,2}w + B_{0,2}r) + 60(A_{0,1}w + B_{0,1}r)$$

quantities and values of factor services, leaving $(150 - 100)(A + B) =$

$50(A + B)$ man-and-acre years per annum as uninvested resource services.

This community decides, after some time, to *expand its capital structure, at first in* the *width* dimension, and only *later in height.* We shall ignore how many production periods are involved in accomplishing the desired amount of "widening," and what happens to the relative levels of interest, wages, and rent during this transition period. But we assume that the community has carried out a 10 per cent widening of its initial capital structure.

This means that once this is accomplished there are 66 units of one-year, 33 of two-year, and 11 of three-year capital goods, all of which mature out capital goods services in current production. To maintain this widened structure now requires investment annually of $110(A + B)$ man-and-acre years of original factor services, leaving only $40(A + B)$ man-and-acre years per annum as uninvested resource services.

The rates of wages and rent are, of course, determined by the marginal productivity of uninvested land and labor. All land and labor units are homogeneous and interchangeable, hence the wage and rent rates are everywhere the same, regardless of whether a particular quantity of labor or land is engaged directly in producing finished consumption goods or in producing annual replacements for the various capital groups in the structure.

Now, it is precisely in the finishing of consumption goods that the supply of uninvested resource services has decreased due to widening. Hence the marginal productivity of uninvested services in that branch of production must have increased, while that of coöperating capital goods, which have increased in quantity, must have decreased. With marginal productivity of uninvested labor and land and hence with wage and rent rates having increased in consumption goods production, this means that wage and rent rates have increased likewise in production of capital goods replacements, and the interest rate has fallen, because perfect competition prevails.

But while the marginal productivity of capital goods as a whole has fallen, it has not fallen uniformly. It has fallen most on one-year goods, which increased most in the process of widening. Let us say that their net marginal productivity has declined from 0.05 to 0.04, and that the net marginal productivities of two- and three-year goods have declined *relatively less but by the same absolute amount,* from 0.1025 to 0.0925 for two-year goods and from 0.157625 to 0.147625 for three-year goods.

The going rate of interest, determined by the net marginal (value) productivity of capital goods, is tending toward the net productivity of one-year goods, i.e., toward 4 per cent. If we discount the net marginal productivities or yield rates of two- and three-year goods by this interest rate, we óbtain their capitalized values. Accordingly, that of two-year capital is 2.256, as compared with 2.05, which it was in the equilibrium that prevailed prior to structure expansion. That of three-year capital is 3.6906 now as compared with 3.1525 previously. But that of one-year capital remains 1.000 now as before because its net yield has fallen from 0.05 to 0.04. Thus capital goods of three- and of two-year maturation terms now commend themselves as superior investment opportunities to capitalists. As a result, some capitalists begin to shift investments out of one-year and into three- and two-year capital goods, and it is thus that "height expansion" begins.

In the aggregate, owners of 12 units of one-year capital goods decide to shift their investments in these goods over a period of years into three-year capital. This requires some abstinence on their part. For the investments they are shifting did, after all, bring a 4 per cent net return, whereas the goods they are shifting them into will not be completed and begin bringing the anticipated higher return until four years hence. However, the investment shift is accomplished in the following stages.

In Year I, some capitalists decide not to replace three units of one-year capital so as to shift the corresponding replacement investment of $3(A_{0,1}w + B_{0,1}r)$ into $3(A_{0,3}w + B_{0,3}r)$ thus laying the basis for creating 3 additional units of three-year capital goods. At the end of this year the structure consists of 11 three-year, 33 two-year, and 63 one-year goods, plus the uncompleted investment in new three-year goods. This structure can be maintained by replacement investment of the equivalent of $107(A + B)$ man-and-acre years of services per annum, rather than 110. Thus the incomplete investment-shift has already released $3(A + B)$ man-and-acre years of services to be added to the preëxisting $40(A + B)$ such units of uninvested resource services.

In Year II, capitalists decide not to replace an additional 3 units of one-year capital, so as to shift a new quantity of $3(A_{0,1}w + B_{0,1}r)$ into $3(A_{0,3}w + B_{0,3}r)$ and so as to permit what was shifted into three-year goods the year before to become $3(A_{1,3}w + B_{1,3}r)$. Now the structure has 11 three-year, 33 two-year, and 60 one-year goods, plus investments two-thirds completed in new three-year goods. This structure can be maintained by annual replacement investment of $104(A + B)$ man-and-acre years of services. This releases three more such units of services to the uninvested category, which now is $46(A + B)$ man-and-acre years of services per annum.

In Year III, 3 more units of one-year capital are not replaced, to permit the corresponding resources to become $3(A_{0,3}w + B_{0,3}r)$, and to permit similar quantities of resource services invested in three-year goods respectively two years ago and one year ago to become $3(A_{2,3}w + B_{2,3}r)$ and $3(A_{1,3}w + B_{1,3}r)$. Now the structure can be maintained by annual replacement investment of $101(A + B)$ man-and-acre years of services per annum, increasing the uninvested quantity of such services to $49(A + B)$ per annum.

During Year IV, an additional 3 units of one-year capital are not replaced, in order to use the corresponding resource services as replacement-investment for the 3 new three-year capital goods which are now adding their $3(A_3w + B_3r)$ capital goods services in current production. But the transfer of these last 3 units of one-year capital investments has not been a *net* transfer, like the former transfers were, for in their place now stand 3 new three-year capital goods performing more valuable services in production. Also this last transfer involved no net abstinence, for the new three-year goods have a gross marginal productivity of 3(1.147625) as compared with the gross productivity of the last three one-year goods transferred, namely 3(1.0400), so they more than pay their way. The structure now contains 14 three-year, 33 two-year, and 54 one-year capital goods, and as such it can be maintained in perpetuity by annual replacement investment of $101(A + B)$ man-and-acre years of services, leaving $49(A + B)$ man-and-acre years of services per annum in the uninvested category for direct production of consumption goods. At this point we assume no further adjustments are made in the structure and the economy returns to stationary equilibrium.

Now it is clear that whatever levels wages and rents had reached during "widening," when only $40(A + B)$ man-and-acre years of services per year remained uninvested, can no longer be maintained. They must be reduced at the same time as the rate of interest now must rise above the 4 per cent level to which it had fallen prior to height expansion.

Ultimately, when full equilibrium has been restored, which may involve further small investment shifts between the various capital goods groups, the correct compound rate relations between the marginal productivities of the capital groups will have been restored. These adjustments will have raised the marginal productivity of one-year goods above 4 per cent, perhaps to 4.75 per cent and reduced that of three-year goods below 14.76 per cent, until all differences in yield per time interval of investment are eliminated. In the end the interest rate will be higher than 4 per cent but lower than the original 5 per cent. Wages and rent will be slightly higher than before expansion began, and the structure will have expanded both in width and height but in greater proportion in the latter dimension.

Perhaps enough has .been said to demonstrate the behavior traits of Wicksell's capital structure. However, the foregoing, or something very much like it, is what he had in mind in discussing it in *Lectures-I* (pp. 158-163), although there he expressed himself in too crabbed a manner to make himself as clear as would have seemed desirable in view of the importance this conception had in his economic thought.

However, since Wicksell elaborated this structural conception of capital within the "Austrian" orientation in capital theory, in a measure it shared the fate of the entire genus of "Austrian" capital concepts; namely, it became an object of protracted, and sometimes heated, theoretical controversy.

Wicksell and the Controversy in Capital Theory

The controversy concerning the theory of interest and capital, 1933-1938, between F. H. Knight, F. A. von Hayek, F. Machlup, N. Kaldor, *et al.*, has reopened some questions which were also debated vigorously at the turn of the century between Böhm-Bawerk, J. B. Clark, F. von Wieser, I. Fisher, and J. Schumpeter, to mention only the leading participants. There were others who joined in this polemic only infrequently and incidentally, among them Wicksell, Léon Walras, and Marshall. Wicksell's stand was relatively neutral. He was far from uncritical of Böhm-Bawerk's analysis and, as time went on, he withdrew most of the objections he at one time raised against Walras's capital theory, which he then treated as the prototype of the "non-Austrian" approach in this field.

WICKSELL ON WALRAS'S CAPITAL THEORY
AND WICKSELL'S THEORY OF INTEREST RATES

Wicksell's views on Walras's capital theory are of importance because they bring out his theory of the short-term rate of interest, as distinct from that of the long-term rate determined by the behavior of his capital structure.

Wicksell's evaluation of Walras's analysis of capital and interest was initially stated in his first major article in economics.[14] What he said there was repeated in substance in the closing pages of *Value,*

---

[14] "Kapitalzins und Arbeitslohn," *Jahrbücher für Nationalökonomie und Statistik,* 59 (1892), 852-874.

Capital and Rent (pp. 167-8), later in *Lectures-I* (pp. 185 ff.), and finally in a review he wrote of Pareto's *Manuel d'économie politique* in 1914.[15] His recantation vis-à-vis Walras is found in his essay "Professor Cassel's System of Economics," first published in *Economisk Tidskrift* in 1919, which has been translated and appended to *Lectures-I* (see pp. 236-237 and 226-227 in that order).

He interpreted Walras's analysis of the theory of production as an expansion on his theory of exchange (with commodity supplies given). From this perspective, production is viewed as a set of exchanges, mediated by derived demand for agents of production, which arises between owners of factors of production and owners (presumably the entrepreneurs) of the commodities resulting from production. Thus owners of labor-, land-, and capital-goods-services offer these to entrepreneurs in exchange for portions of the resulting output. With perfect competition on all markets factor owners are presumably rewarded in products according to the marginal productivity of the services they supply.

But Walras himself held that this sort of exchange fails to determine the level of rate of interest unless the economy be progressive rather than stationary.[16] He inclined to the view that a stationary economy has no market in which the values of its capital goods are determined, for there is no net saving and no net production of capital goods. Hence the equations of exchange in such an economy supply no data on, nor do they determine, the values of its capital goods. In a progressive economy, however, new capital goods are made. These supply services or have yields as well as current production costs. Entrepreneurs will demand capital goods up to the point where their yields equal the supply price of saving. Their yield discounted by the supply price of saving determines their value. Under perfect competition that value must equal their current production cost. With the rate of interest and value of new capital goods thus determined, the value of preëxisting capital goods of similar types is also determined, namely by discounting their yield rates by the supply price of saving.

But, said Wicksell, it is clearly wrong to imply that there is no market for capital goods in a stationary economy. Such an economy has to produce enough new capital goods to replace the ones which wear out in production. Hence interest must emerge because capital

---

[15] Wicksell, "Vilfredo Pareto 'Manuel d'économie politique,'" *Zeitschrift für Volkswirtschaft*, XXI-XXII (1914), 132-151.

[16] See a passage to this effect in L. Walras, *Abrégé des élements d'économie politique pure* (Gaston Leduc edition; Paris, 1938), pp. 226-227.

goods have a net marginal productivity. As for Walras's dynamically based interest theory, he considered it not to be materially different from a theory of rent, chiefly because it ignored the time function of real capital in production. This, he went on to say, in turn is due to Walras's antiquated conception of real capital.

Walras considered only durable producers' goods to be real capital and excluded from this concept all the things Wicksell referred to as "circulating capital"; namely, raw materials, goods in process, and, most important of all, means of subsistence not in the hands of consumers. As for the durable goods in Walras's formulation of the problem, Wicksell conceded that the equations of exchange would determine the level of their rents or quasi-rents. But they would not determine their values, which depend on their current reproduction costs. These costs, however, stand in no determinate relation to their rents or their original costs. He also found that Walras's view that owners of factors of production are paid from the proceeds of completed production implies that factor owners maintain themselves while production is in process. In this, he said, Walras is clearly wrong; e.g., carpenters and others cannot wait for their wages until the houses they work on are finished and sold. Labor in particular must be paid its real wages out of products (subsistence means) made during earlier production periods. By excluding these products from his concept of capital Walras is forced to ignore the time service capital supplies to production. It is the quantity of available subsistence means which, more than anything else, determines the time that can be taken in production.

For many years this was the substance of his evaluation of Walras's capital theory and of the closely related one of Pareto's. It is not known when Wicksell came to the conclusion that: (1) within his own framework of analysis Walras had been wrong about requiring a progressive economy for the determination of interest; (2) Walras's method led to a perfectly satisfactory determination of the short-term interest rate, and must be considered as an alternate explanation, which both completes and is completed by analysis such as Böhm-Bawerk's or his own. In the article referred to he went on to say:

We can *either* adopt Walras's method of taking a cross section through social production at a moment of time, and thus consider only the coöperating factors existing at the moment. In that case, no doubt, the demand for finished products constitutes an indirect demand for raw materials and the factors of production by means of which the finished products are produced. At the same time there is a demand for new capital goods, and their present yield is the basis for their estimated future yield. *We can thus gain a clear insight into the mechanism by which the loan interest is determined at each moment of time.*[17]

Alternatively, we can take a longitudinal section through social production and refer everything back to the "original factors" in conjunction with "waiting" or time. If so, the indirect demand for productive factors from the consumers' side "becomes a mere metaphor," and we can "resolve everything into production directed toward the future." The fact that such a longitudinal section extends indefinitely in time in both directions, future and past, is of no practical importance, since its major portion lies between finite limits. Then he went on to say:

For him (Walras) the capital *goods* themselves are factors of production, just as much as labor and the forces of nature, and the rate of interest . . . is considered as the ratio between the expected yield of capital goods now being made (= the price for their services as factors of production minus the necessary amortization costs) and their own costs according to present prices. . . . Savers and entrepreneurs strive to maximize this ratio, and equilibrium is reached when it is the same for all alike. In this way Walras constructs an extraordinarily coherent and rigorous system. . . .[18]

Then he made the following statement concerning the relation between the anticipated interest rate and the level of the loan rate of interest which is of importance for his monetary theory, while, at the same time, he withdrew an earlier objection to Walras's analysis:

Clearly, *Walras's method does not yield the actual rate of interest which the future reveals, but the anticipated interest rate on which the level of the loan rate is directly dependent at any moment of time.* At this point I must withdraw an objection which I previously made against Walras—i.e., that his theory of interest necessarily presupposes a progressive type of society. Walras indeed said so himself, but the truth of the matter is that *it is just as applicable to the stationary state, and in fact gains thereby in rigour. The underlying assumption is that the factors of production will have the same relative values or prices in the future as they have at the present moment. Actually, this is true for the stationary state but it does not hold for the progressive economy. . . .*[19]

In the light of what has been said earlier, this passage fits into Wicksell's theory of interest about as follows. In equilibrium, short- and long-term interest rates, calculated in real terms or in *numéraire*, are equal and their level is determined by the marginal (value) pro-

---

[17] "Professor Cassel's System of Economics," *Lectures-I*, Appendix 1, pp. 236-237; italics in last sentence supplied.

[18] *Ibid.*, p. 226. Italics in the original.

[19] *Ibid.*, p. 227.

ductivity of real capital. In this connection it .makes no particular difference whether we regard society's real capital as an aggregate of producers' goods or as a capital structure of "saved-up labor and land in combination." In either case, it is the same quantity of real capital we are talking about.

However, during a dynamic process or movement between equilibria, the short-term rate may diverge from the long-term one (both still calculated in real terms), although it gravitates toward the level of the latter. Other things equal, the behavior of the short rate then depends most immediately on changes in the quantity and marginal productivity of capital goods of short-maturation terms, while the level of the long rate is determined by the slower moving changes which are occurring in the various dimensions of society's real capital viewed as a capital structure.

But the many varieties of interest rates we observe in the money markets of the world in which we live are calculated in money terms. After making allowances for risk premia and for imperfections in the money markets themselves, which affect the levels of these differentiated rates, we can distill the corresponding "pure" interest rates.

The trend-level of the latter is generally referred to as "the" rate of interest, here as "the loan rate of interest." The loan rate can diverge from the corresponding interest rate calculated in real terms because of changes which are occurring in the value of money. But the loan rate "is directly dependent at any moment of time" on, or gravitates toward, "the anticipated interest rate" on capital goods calculated in real terms, or on the anticipated "real" rate of interest.

Incidentally, as von Hayek seems to have been the first to notice,[20] the first sentence in the passage above contains the germ of the distinction between *ex post* and *ex ante* determinants of savings, investment, income, and interest, made famous by Myrdal. But now we must consider certain general "non-Austrian" objections to capital theories of Wicksell's type.

WICKSELL AND THE OPPOSITION TO THE "AUSTRIAN" SCHOOL

"Non-Austrian" theories of capital and interest include all those in which the time aspect of real capital is not emphasized and is not treated as one of the fundamental determinants of investment or the demand for capital. This, of course, includes Marxist as well as non-Marxist doctrines which are more or less opposed to the "Austrian" time approach.

In their attention to the "theorem of the declining rate of profit"

---

[20] F. A. von Hayek, *The Pure Theory of Capital* (London, 1941), p. 44, n.

and its connection with "the changing organic composition of capital," Marx and his followers have arrived at insights into the process of capital formation and its implications for economic stability which have features in common with those developed by "Austrians" in their analyses of the behavior of capital structures, and those developed later also by "non-Austrians" in their attention to the relations between "widening" and "deepening" of capital. This notwithstanding we shall bypass Marxist capital theory because it is based on an unscientific postulate, an exploitation theory of distribution.

Among "non-Marxist-non-Austrian" capital theories we shall only discuss those of some American writers, mainly J. B. Clark and F. H. Knight, who engaged Böhm-Bawerk and his followers, von Hayek in particular, in protracted controversy. Although J. B. Clark wrote at the turn of the century and F. H. Knight elaborated similar arguments a generation later, it will be convenient to ignore minor differences in their position, and to paraphrase the latter as the Clark-Knight thesis as follows:

1. Capital is a permanent fund of wealth embodied in perishable capital goods. A production period may be attached to the use of capital goods, but it is irrelevant for the problem of interest, since there is no discernible relation between such a period and the level of interest.

2. Production or investment periods, hence also capital structure concepts, of Austrian theory have neither beginning nor end and involve indefinite regression of time into the past or progression into the future.

3. Capital goods coöperate with labor and land in the production of new capital goods regardless of whether the latter are intended as replacements or as net accretions to the preëxisting stock of such goods. Hence any period concept relating to capital goods and the associated distinction of land and labor as "original factors" is untenable.

4. Capital in the sense of a permanently maintained fund synchronizes consumption and production. There is, therefore, no "waiting" involved. It is real abstinence, rather, that is necessary for net additions to be made to the permanent fund. It is impossible for society to disinvest its permanent capital fund, whereas the individual can disinvest, however, only if some other individual is willing to invest.[21]

The Clark-Knight analysis results in a theory of interest closely

---

[21] J. B. Clark, *Distribution of Wealth* (New York, 1899), chaps. ix, x, xviii, xix, and xx. Cf. also the following two of Knight's several articles on this subject: "Prof. Hayek and the Theory of Investment," *Economic Journal*, XIV (1935), 77 ff.; "On the Theory of Capital—Reply to Mr. Kaldor," *Econometrica*, VI (1938), 82 ff.

related to that of Walras, as described in Wicksell's words above. Capital, which in their definition includes all forms of wealth or sources of income except human abilities, is conceived as a permanent fund or value. This fund is "permanent" only in a stationary society, but the same can be said for the value of a Wicksellian capital structure in such a society. This "fund" represents the capitalization of the future yield of these sources of income discounted by their net marginal (value) productivity rate, which is established at the margin where alternatives of consumption versus investment of real income are compared. This fund is considered to be "permanent" also in another sense; namely, that for purposes of comparison of alternative investment opportunities, the rational investor converts the expected net yields of various income sources into "perpetuities," in order to decide which affords the best investment opportunity on the basis of the resulting value calculation relative to cost.[22] Consequently, the rational investor always provides for the permanent maintenance of his real capital or income sources both in a physical and in a value sense in a static society. If and when he decides to disinvest he expects to hand his real capital on intact to his buyer, another investor. Society cannot rationally and does not voluntarily decide to disinvest or reduce this permanent fund of value, for to do so would be to diminish welfare, particularly in the future.

That the "fund" may not be permanent in dynamic conditions is granted, but this really has no bearing upon idealized and rational investor behavior. To be sure, in dynamic conditions the fund can increase or decrease, and its value may change independently of changes in the physical quantity of real capital. But these things are due to matters over which rational investors have no control, such as uncertainty, risk, variation in the value of money, destruction of capital in warfare, by natural disaster, and the like.

The advantage of this conception of capital is its simplicity. It can be applied to the firm as well as to the economy as a whole, and it results in a concept which is more readily quantifiable in value terms empirically than the "Austrian" capital structures.

The Clark-Knight objections to Austrian "production periods," "investment periods," to "real capital = saved-up labor and land in combination," and their insistence that capital goods production always involves the coöperation of existing capital goods along with the

---

[22] Cf. F. H. Knight, "The Quantity of Capital and the Interest Rate," *Journal of Political Economy* (August, 1936), 444-465; and his article "Capital and Interest" reprinted in W. Fellner and B. F. Haley, eds., *Readings in the Theory of Income Distribution* (Philadelphia, 1946), p. 396 *et passim.*

services of labor and land, no longer represent any real issues in this controversy, as von Hayek has pointed out.[23] These "Austrian" conceptions were devices of analysis not intended to be applied in empiric research.

The capital structure figures we have used above can readily be adapted to the coöperation of existing capital goods in production of new ones without changing the end results. As Lindahl, among others, has shown, all this requires is additional terms for the coöperating capital goods in the structure figures and in the equations describing the value relations of the services these goods render to their own capitalized values or maturation terms.[24]

Another contradiction between these two capital perspectives which is probably more apparent than real relates to the Clark-Knight emphasis on the well-nigh automatic maintenance of real capital, for "society does not disinvest," etc., as opposed to the "Austrian" emphasis on the nonautomaticity of this maintenance. It requires diversion of productive resources from production of consumption goods to produce the annual replacement requirements of real capital, and even greater diversion to make net additions to real capital. Moreover, "Austrian" writers point to instances where existing capital is undermaintained. This occurs not only in such obvious cases as war and its immediate aftermath, but also in peacetime years of rapid investment expansion in certain branches of production at the expense of the maintenance requirements for other branches, and at times when overexpanded industries are shrunk back to more proper size by undermaintenance and the like. What really is at issue here is how much uncertainty and imperfection of foresight one should admit in dynamic conditions. If uncertainty is slight and foresight very great, the foregoing "malinvestments" as "Austrians" might call them would not occur, and society's capital would not only be maintained, whether "automatically" or not, but would also increase by a positive rate of net investment.

A related point made by Clark, and the only one of Clark's many points Wicksell answered, but without mentioning its author by name, was the claim that capital synchronizes production and hence there is no "waiting" involved in its replacement or creation. To this Wicksell replied:

---

[23] F. A. von Hayek, "The Mythology of Capital," *Quarterly Journal of Economics* (February, 1936), reprinted in *Readings in the Theory of Income Distribution.* See especially pp. 356, 361, 362, 374, 382.

[24] E. Lindahl, *Studies in the Theory of Money and Capital* (New York, 1939), pp. 301-309.

That wages (real wages) are paid in products more or less *simultaneously produced* signifies nothing from an economic point of view. The present laborer has, as a rule, nothing to do with the manufacturing of these products; they are the final result of a series of processes whose various phases of labor have, as a rule, been paid for. The fruits of these productive processes belong . . . to the capitalist entrepreneur and may be employed as he chooses, either for *new production*—in which case he maintains, or even increases, his capital—or for *his own consumption*.[25]

In this connection it will be convenient to consider together two other objections Wicksell answered, those by Lexis and by Brisman. Lexis contended that longer production processes are not more productive than short ones, and that economic history is largely a record of the progress of labor-saving techniques which shorten the process of production. Brisman held that the "Austrian" interpretation of investment as "the wise selection of roundabout methods" is either a tautology or else an instance of circular reasoning. He concluded this can only mean the selection of profitable processes, and, in turn, a process is "wisely selected" only if it is at the same time profitable.[26]

Wicksell's answers were brief. Labor-saving techniques no doubt shorten the production time per task in any particular firm or on any particular process. However, looking at the economy as a whole, introduction of labor-saving methods have as a rule meant subdivision of former single processes into a greater number of production stages. This has expanded the time dimension of production as a whole, with an attendant increase in output, as experience shows. Moreover, at any given time there are longer processes available which could be but are not adopted because at the given configuration of interest, wage, and rent rates, these would not yield a sufficient surplus of product to be profitable.

As for investment viewed as the wise selection of production processes, this is an interpretation of the end result of entrepreneurial investment behavior. In order to minimize costs and maximize profits,

---

[25] Wicksell, *Lectures-I*, p. 190.

[26] Cf. W. Lexis, "Über Wert, Kapital und Rente," Rezension, *Schmollers Jahrbuch*, XIX (1895), 332 ff.; S. Brisman, "Kapitalet och kapitalräntan" (Capital and Interest), *Ekonomisk Tidskrift*, 14 (1912), 89-121; "Professor Wicksells framställning av kapitalet och kapitalräntan" (Professor Wicksell's Treatment of Capital and Interest), *Ekonomisk Tidskrift*, 14 (1912), 157-170; "Ännu några ord om kapitalet och kapitalräntan" (Once More Concerning Capital and Interest), *Ekonomisk Tidskrift*, 14 (1912), 399-416. Wicksell's replies are found in *Finanztheoretische Untersuchungen*, pp. 32 ff., addressed to Lexis; and in "Kapital und kein Ende" (Capital—Ad Nauseam), *Ekonomisk Tidskrift*, 14 (1912), 309-322, to Brisman. Most of his reply to Lexis was repeated by Böhm-Bawerk in "Einige strittige Fragen der Kapitalstheorie," *Kleinere Abhändlungen* (Vienna, 1922), pp. 123 ff., and in *Positive Theorie des Kapitales* (4th ed., Jena, 1921), vol. II, "Exkurse" I-IV, inclusive.

entrepreneurs endeavor to select and combine the factors of production in optimal proportions. This involves a selection of the production process most appropriate for the purpose at hand. To deny the existence of this tendency is to deny the profit motive as an active force in a private enterprise economy.

The foregoing issues between the Clark-Knight and "Austrian" capital doctrines involve, as we have seen, either relatively small points, or else are resolvable in terms of how strictly one construes "stationariness" and how much uncertainty and imperfection of foresight one is prepared to admit in dynamic conditions.

Was there, then, no real or irreducible issue between these two schools? We believe there was; namely, the "Austrian" affirmation, and the Clark-Knight denial of a direct or discernible relationship between the time dimension of real capital as a determinant of investment, or the demand for capital, and via the latter, a relationship between this time dimension and the rate of interest. We also believe that "Austrian" theory has come off with the victory in this polemic, and has gained adherents outside its own camp. Our reasons for these contentions are the following:

1. The "Austrian" time perspective on production explains an important circumstance, which is not necessarily denied in other quarters but is rarely emphasized there. That is that current consumption, which sustains current production of near-future consumption goods, plus production of capital-replacement and net-investment goods, proceeds largely (consumption of services being the major exception) on the basis of output produced in the recent past. The quantity of past consumption output available, then, places a strong limit on how far and in what directions the economy can in any short space of time further extend its production of output for the future. This is not as readily perceived from the Walrasian or the Clark-Knight orientations in capital theory.

2. Böhm-Bawerk and his followers, Wicksell, Åkerman, and von Hayek with their "structural" analyses of real capital, have succeeded in pointing out that society's real capital is permeated with complementarity. Production or capital structures consist of many parts interrelated with one another in complex ways or in several "dimensions." These structures are capable of harmonious change, only if the change occurs slowly and in ways which do not introduce increasing imbalances between the component parts. Most of the time, they grow via the process of net investment. But the rate of net investment is capable of rapid change, independently of the structure's requirements, as income recipients change their allocation of income between

consumption spending and saving. This often produces deep-seated maladjustments, to which is traceable much of the uncertainty and lack of foresight which would prevent Clark-Knight's rational investors from maintaining capital as a permanent fund of value.

These relations are mostly lost sight of when real capital is regarded simply as an aggregate of producers' goods.

3. Wicksell's discovery that as capital formation proceeds, other factors constant, investment in capital goods of long-maturation terms becomes relatively more profitable than in goods of short term, and that therefore investment will progressively be shifted to goods of long term, with the result that wages and rents rise and interest declines less than they would otherwise do, constitutes an important hypothesis. It is this hypothesis, which Lindahl characterized as Wicksell's most important contribution to capital theory,[27] that makes it possible to establish a direct link between the time dimension of real capital and demand for investable funds, hence, also a direct link with the rate of interest. If this hypothesis is true, and it seems to have gained adherents very widely, then the Clark-Knight denial of this link cannot be other than false.

Now, it is true, this same insight has been adopted from Wicksell or from one of his followers by writers who generally do not use the "Austrian" approach or terminology in their capital theories. Examples are N. Kaldor, K. Boulding, and despite his protestations to the contrary, J. R. Hicks.[28]

Precisely what occurs and why in the process of capital formation remains an unresolved problem on which Wicksell, apart from the foregoing hypothesis, had many observations to make. We turn to some of these now, those which record his reaction to Böhm-Bawerk's

---

[27] Cf. Lindahl, *Studies in the Theory of Money and Capital*, p. 310 n.

[28] N. Kaldor, "Annual Survey of Economic Theory; The Recent Controversy on the Theory of Capital," *Econometrica*, 5:3 (October, 1937), see especially pp. 221 ff.; K. E. Boulding, "Time and Investment," *Economica* (May, 1936), pp. 196 ff., also his *Reconstruction of Economics* (New York, 1950), pp. 193 ff.; and J. R. Hicks, *Value and Capital* (New York, 1939), pp. 216 ff. While Hicks has much to say in criticism of "Austrian" capital theory in this work, and while he launches his own investigations into this subject from an entirely different point of departure, he comes to the conclusion, nonetheless, that a decline in the rate of interest (usually the consequence of more rapid growth of capital than of other factors) "tilts," as he puts it, "the production plan" in favor of outputs remote in time and against current and near-future outputs. Moreover if the interest-rate reduction is great enough not only will production plans be revised in favor of later outputs, but the quantity of current inputs and of near-future inputs may also be reduced. Couched in entirely different terminology, we believe this observation comes very close to Wicksell's, that a decline of the rate of interest favors investment in capital of long rather than short maturation and induces a shift among preëxisting investments from capital of short to long maturation.

explanation of the "agio," and his speculations on the relations between interest and capital accumulation in the very long or in the "secular" run.

The Rate of Interest and Accumulation

In the previous discussion we have assumed a given rate of real saving. As a consequence it is chiefly the demand side of the explanation of the interest rate which has received attention. At the turn of the century the fashion was to say that the demand explanation accounted for the "existence" as distinct from "the level of the rate" of interest. Once the demand for capital had been accounted for and could be considered as given, "the level of the interest rate" was viewed as determined by the supply of saving.

The rate of interest becomes a variable only in dynamic conditions. But, apart from this, the interest rate represents a separate problem from that of real capital since an interest rate can exist even in an economy which has no capital in the sense of a productive agent. This was usually expressed by saying that interest was not coextensive with capital.[29] This had already been pointed out in Böhm-Bawerk's discussion of "Darlehnzins" (interest on consumption loans), but the credit for having made it explicit and very clear rests with I. Fisher in his work *The Rate of Interest* (1906).

Böhm-Bawerk attempted to account for both the existence and the level of the rate of interest, or the "agio," by his famous "three grounds." These were (1) underprovision of present want and increasing estimation of future provision, (2) subjective underestimation of the future, and (3) technical superiority of present goods. The first accounted for the demand for consumption loans by those whose present wants were undersupplied. This demand acted as a subtrahend from the total net saving which would otherwise be supplied to production. The second ground explained the necessity of offering a reward for saving and the reason why the supply of saving would be scarce. A premium must be given in terms of future commodities or money of similar kind but in greater quantity than the present goods individuals are induced to give up or lend, both because many persons view the future as better provided for than the present, and because the future is uncertain for all. The first and second grounds acted cumulatively with reference to each other. Because of the first ground, the agio is higher than it would be otherwise. Were it not for consumer loans, the entire supply of saving would be available for productive investment at a lower rate of interest.

---

[29] Cf. Wicksell, *Lectures-I*, p. 169.

The third ground explained both entrepreneurial demand for saving and why, in view of the fact that large savers are generally not persons who undervalue the future, their savings are not obtainable at a lower agio. The technical superiority of present goods consists in their ability to sustain the use of more productive roundabout processes. By reason of competition, entrepreneurs are willing to offer an agio for such goods according to the incremental productivity of the capitalistic processes they make possible. Because of the possibility of employing present goods in a similar manner themselves, wealthy lenders would, as a matter of opportunity cost, not have to accept a return on their saving less than this market agio.

In *Value, Capital and Rent* (pp. 106-15), Wicksell rejected the first ground, accepted the second, and also the third which, however, he construed as a productivity explanation of interest not very different from that of von Thünen. In *Lectures-I* (p. 207) he rejected both the first ground and a particular emphasis Böhm-Bawerk had placed on the third ground. He retained the second provisionally while stating that economics is much in need of a rational theory of saving. His objections centered around the following points.

Attempts to explain a value difference between present and future goods of the same quantity and quality as due to a difference in their marginal utilities suffer from two deficiencies. Both the supply and the period of consumption of future goods are indeterminate. Marginal utility calculations presume a definite consumption period.[30]

The first ground—differences in provision of means of satisfaction at different times—is inconclusive. The young may have reasons to expect greater provision in the future; the old may have opposite expectations. Whether the agio on consumption loans would be positive or not depends on which set of expectations outweighs the other.

The third ground—technical superiority of present goods—leads to the inference that production periods would be lengthened indefinitely. This is not the case, for although longer processes are as a rule more productive, they are not adopted unless they are also more profitable. Whether they are or not depends on the relation of wage and rent rates to the rate of interest, and on the latter relative to the extraproductivity of the longer processes in question. Wicksell pointed out "Böhm-Bawerk's real error—his cardinal error, as Bortkiewicz calls it—is that at this point in his exposition he seeks to solve the problem of the *existence* of interest—as distinct from its actual rate—without referring to the market for capital and labor." [31]

---

[30] *Ibid.*, p. 169.
[31] *Ibid.*, p. 171.

Wicksell considered the second ground—subjective undervaluation of the future—to be universally valid. But he did not think that it was a sufficient reason for a positive rate of interest, nor a guarantee that the supply of real saving would be interest-elastic. A high interest rate increases the yield on present saving, but it also increases the saver's future income. This reduces the marginal utility of this income to him, hence a drop in the interest rate may not reduce the supply of saving. He conceded that the motives for saving are complex and not well known. Yet he emphasized, contra Cassel who feared that saving would be brought to a stop as the interest rate declines while this rate is still positive, that "progressive accumulation of capital must be regarded as economical so long as *any rate of interest, however low,* exists." [32]

This argues that a close-to-zero rate of interest is never likely to occur, not only not in the existing society, but even in one where we abstract from technological change and from all noneconomic forces which might tend to increase the demand for capital or tend to decrease its supply, and where we assume savings to be interest-inelastic. However, Wicksell never committed himself on the degree of this inelasticity. Apparently what he had in mind is that there is some sort of geometric or logarithmic relation between the amount of real capital required to reduce the level of interest and changes in this level. In other words, if a quantity x of additional real capital is required to reduce the interest rate from 6 to 5 per cent, it might well require a quantity x^2 to reduce it further from 5 to 4 per cent, and so on. Hence the quantity required to reduce it in some future generation to 1 per cent, for instance, would be so enormously large as to be unlikely to occur.

Yet, he felt that, in view of the great formation of capital which had occurred throughout the nineteenth century (a rate of capital accumulation greater by far than the rather rapid rate of population increase which was also experienced in that century), it was surprising, not that interest rates had declined at the end of the century to about half the level they had held at its beginning, but that they had not declined even further.

By way of explanation of this circumstance, he adduced the following reasons: (1) society is not stationary but subject to rapid technological change; (2) the rate of population growth is still positive even if it is declining, and (3) the actions of government frequently result in capital consumption and outright capital destruction, as in times of war. In this connection he pointed to a difference between "capi-

---

[32] *Ibid.*, p. 209, cf. also p. 241,

talist" and "collectivist" societies which also helps to explain why the interest rate had not declined further in the former. He felt that the capital-consumptive activities of governments were at least in part motivated by the class interest of capitalists: ". . . it cannot be denied that capitalists as a class will gladly welcome all measures destructive of capital such as armaments and war—for which they will largely be compensated by the state's contractual obligations, and which will help to raise the rate of interest. This constitutes a not inconsiderable political danger, as Adolph Wagner pointed out." [33]

By contrast with this state of affairs he had the following view of the future of the rate of interest in a "collectivist state":

The collectivist state will be quite unaffected by a lowering of the rate of interest as such, since all sources of income would be more or less common to the whole community, and, in such a case, the other sources would necessarily increase in a more than corresponding degree.[34]

. . . a collectivist society would afford a much better guarantee for the rapid accumulation of capital than does the existing individualistic society. The capital saved by united efforts would equally benefit all individuals and the whole of society in the future; and the failure of some enterprises would be of little importance, if those which succeeded yielded a correspondingly greater return. Though this is opposed by current opinion, it is precisely in a collectivist society that we should expect a progressive accumulation of capital until production was fully supplied with new capital and the national dividend reached its technical maximum—assuming that interest in the well-being of future generations was not less than in existing society.[35]

The foregoing long-run speculations postulated the continuance of a highly competitive private enterprise economy. Except for occasional and brief crises, which, he thought, derive in the main from the aberrations of traditional monetary policy and are remediable by introducing more rational policies, in his study of capital Wicksell almost always assumed this economy would operate at the level of full employment. Moreover, his analysis was almost always carried on in real terms. Perhaps this was the primary reason he had so much difficulty, except in his monetary theory, when he attempted to reason about saving and the process of capital formation in conditions of less than full employment, as the following indicates:

Real, productive saving . . . always assumes the form of real capital. In the normal course of business this process is clearly visible. . . . At the close of a boom, paper credit often seems to make up, in part (though actually

[33] *Ibid.*, p. 212.
[34] *Ibid.*, pp. 212-213.
[35] *Ibid.*, pp. 211-212.

it does not), for the shortage of real capital—and *still more in a period of depression when investment in fixed capital hardly pays, but savings continue,* though perhaps at a slower pace. *The process of capital accumulation is here not a little enigmatic. It must continue in some real form, since there is no other; but in what?* [36]

At this juncture, it would no doubt have been helpful to him if he had become acquainted with N. Johannsen's doctrine of "impair saving" as expressed in some works this very original thinker published in 1903 and 1908,[37] but, apparently he never came across them.

Wicksell's difficulty, one which was shared by most of his contemporaries at this level of analysis, was that he operated with a "real" concept of saving, i.e., "real saving." Obviously, whatever form "real saving" takes, it is always invested in something. This accounts for the tendency in Wicksell's time to treat "real saving" as synonymous with capital formation. There is nothing wrong with this procedure per se, for instance, if one is only concerned with the consequences of changes in the total quantity of real capital. But in dynamic problems concerned with the form of "real saving" at the height of a boom or during a recession-depression sequence, this concept is treacherous. It shields entirely from view that the resulting capital accumulation may not be of the intended or desired variety. Some of it may take the form of "unintended lacking," to use one of D. H. Robertson's felicitous terms.

Nevertheless, Wicksell made some valuable contributions to the analysis of the process of capital formation in dynamic conditions, his real-savings concept notwithstanding, as will be shown in the next chapter.

---

[36] *Ibid.*, p. 217. Italics supplied.

[37] N. Johannsen, *Der Kreislauf des Geldes* (Berlin, 1903), and *A Neglected Point in Connection with Crises* (New York, 1908).

CHAPTER VI

The Wicksell Effect and the Theory of Capital Formation

Background and Nature of the Wicksell Effect

At the secular level of analysis a problem emerged which was of deep concern to most of the classical writers. This was the question of the ultimate fate of the rate of profit or interest on capital. If capital keeps increasing faster than the population, this rate will necessarily decline, and if it ultimately reaches zero, this would probably usher in the stationary state. However, in the very process of capital formation, they pointed to the existence of tendencies which would be a strong guarantee against a zero rate of interest.

Capital is created by the investment of real savings, i.e., subsistence means, which purchase the services of land and labor, which, in turn, produce the capital goods in question. Creation of real capital, particularly of the more durable types such as canals, railroads, factories, and the like, is a time-consuming process. At full employment, with given rates of real wages and rent, net creation of capital can occur only if the rate of real savings exceeds the rate at which the labor force increases, the quantity of land or natural resources being given. In these conditions net capital formation necessarily requires that some labor and land services, until then engaged in production of consumption goods, must be transferred from these industries into the ones producing capital goods. Thus competition for additional labor and land between individual capitalists intent on producing more capital goods and others intent on producing consumption goods as before, forces them to bid up the rates of wages and rent. This rise in wages and rent *absorbs* a corresponding amount of the real savings intended for transformation into real capital. The result is that a smaller quantity of real capital is created than was intended and would have been created if wages and rents had remained constant.

It was indeed conceivable that this "partial wage absorption of real saving" might occur on such a scale, while the interest rate is still *positive*, as to reduce effective net capital formation to a rate corresponding to the subsistence requirements imposed by the rate of growth of the labor force. If that happened, there would be no reason to assume that this rate of interest, presumably reduced to a much lower level than was common in the nineteenth century, would decline further below this "equilibrium level" toward zero. This, in substance, was J. S. Mill's position on this problem;[1] his formulation stimulated Wicksell to make further inquiries.

In fact, Wicksell was so much preoccupied with this problem, which we refer to as the "Wicksell effect," that over the years, 1892-1923, he gave it four different demonstrations,[2] chiefly mathematical, supplemented by a few enigmatic interpretive comments.

Clearly, the Wicksell effect occurs only under dynamic conditions. Once creation of capital begins and sets in motion the forces whereby real wages and rents rise, it is no longer certain whether the assumption of perfect foresight, usually made in stationary conditions, has been retained or dropped. If it is retained, we have to imagine that individual capitalists foresee the results of their aggregate action and the amount of "wage absorption of savings" which this brings about. This, however, is a strange assumption to entertain about individuals with reference to the results of their aggregate action in a dynamic process. If this assumption is dropped, on the other hand, then we must operate on the basis of imperfect foresight. We must then take into account that the realized creation of capital will be smaller than the intended one, because capitalists did not clearly foresee how much wage absorption of their savings would occur.

Imperfect foresight introduces considerations of uncertainty and risk, and the likelihood of capital gains for some and losses for others.

---

[1] Cf. J. S. Mill, *Principles of Political Economy* (Ashley ed.; New York, 1920), Book 1, chap. 5, no. 3, pp. 67-68; no. 9, pp. 79-90; Book 4, chap. 3, no. 2, pp. 713-714.

[2] Wicksell's demonstrations of "wage absorption of real saving" and the resulting discrepancy between the private and social marginal productivity of real capital occur first in his article, "Kapitalzins und Arbeitslohn," *Jahrbücher für National-ökonomie und Statistik*, 59 (1892), 857-858; then in *Value, Capital and Rent* (1893), translated (London, 1954), pp. 137-39; *Lectures-I* (1901), translated (London, 1938), pp. 177-180; and finally in his article "Real Capital and Interest," first published in *Ekonomisk Tidskrift* (1923), now translated as Appendix 2 of *Lectures-I*, see particularly pp. 269 ff. and pp. 291 ff.

Perhaps these influences will have a greater effect on their subsequent investment behavior than the "wage absorption of savings" they experience. In other words, on this point the problem needed more clarification than Wicksell gave it. However, in what follows, we shall assume, as seems to have been his practice, that although entrepreneurs may not fully foresee the amount of wage absorption of savings which occurs in a period of net capital formation, they are nonetheless able to "adjust" to this force without losses.

We may visualize this as follows. As more and more capital is created, other factors constant, the marginal productivity of real capital declines. In order to avoid losses, entrepreneurs, as borrowers of real savings, must be permitted to renegotiate their contracts as to the rate of interest to be paid to capitalist-savers at the *end* of the period in question in terms of the then prevailing (lower) net marginal (value) productivity of real capital. If not, they would have losses on the basis of having borrowed real savings at the higher interest rate in effect at the beginning of the period when there was less capital in existence.

However, as long as the net marginal (value) productivity of real capital remains positive (as we assume throughout) although it decreases, the earnings-rate of capitalists' real savings also remains positive (though it will be smaller than the rate of net marginal productivity or the interest-yield on real capital). Hence capitalists have no losses, in fact the contrary. Their absolute income increases, although at a diminishing rate, while their relative share of total income probably declines. At the same time both the absolute and relative income shares of labor and land increase. With this as background, we now proceed to Wicksell's demonstration and discussion of this phenomenon.

Demonstration and Implications of the Wicksell Effect

In his second demonstration of "wage absorption of savings," in *Value, Capital and Rent* (pp. 137-142), which we use here because it is the clearest of the several treatments he gave to this topic, Wicksell proceeded on the following assumptions. A society which is initially stationary has a fixed quantity of man-years of labor services per annum available for production, A, and acre-years of land services, B. To simplify matters he treated land as a free good which would be combined in optimal quantities or units, h, per laborer per annum. Perfect competition rules throughout. The production function, similar for all firms, is homogeneous and of first degree, $p = f(t,h)$, assuring diminishing marginal returns to any factor that increases when other factors are constant. Since land is a free good, we need not take it into consideration, and consequently we obtain a series of equations similar to, but simpler than, the ones used in chapter iv.

The equation stating the output, p, per laborer per annum in real terms was: (1) $p = w + wzt/2$. Taking capitalists as entrepreneurs, we determine the output equilibrium for their firms (all of optimum size) by differentiating (1) with respect to t as if w were a constant, and setting this differential equal to zero. Differentiation yields us (1.1) $dp/dt = wz/2$. Substituting this value of $wz/2$ in (1) restates the latter as (1.2), $p = w + t(dp/dt)$, from which it is clear that (1.3) $w = p - t(dp/dt)$.

The aggregative or macroeconomic equation for real capital was (2) $K = (A/2)wt$. It summarizes the conditions for stationary equilibrium, namely:

1. That the average period of investment is determined by the condition that in equilibrium the annual wage per laborer times the number of laborers, Aw (which represents the demand for real saving or capital), fully uses up the quantity of real capital, K, as subsistence advances, and that

2. the equilibrium real wage, w, is determined by the marginal productivity of labor measured via equation (1.3), as a residual between the product per firm, p, and the capitalist's share thereof, $t(dp/dt)$. The latter is so determined relative to w as to

3. maximize the capitalist's competitive return, z, or the interest, on his fully invested capital.

Since perfect competition prevails, there will be no profit anywhere, and capitalists are assumed to live entirely on their interest incomes so that their consumption is not included in or does not trench on K.

Now capitalists supply net real saving by consuming less than their real-interest incomes, in order to increase these incomes in the future. Their real savings are invested as subsistence advances to capital goods producing laborers. Thus the community's real capital increases by dK or rises to $K + dK$. As a result the production period is lengthened by dt to $t + dt$, and real wages increase by dw. Moreover, the annual product per laborer in the various firms increases by dp. But since p is a function of t, the rate of increase in this product can also be expressed as $(dp/dt)dt$. With a total of A number of laborers and their free land units engaged in production, this means that the social product increases by $A(dp/dt)dt$.

To determine the effect of the increase in real capital, one must obtain dK as a total differential of (2) with respect to w and t, i.e., (2.1) $dK = A/2(wdt + tdw)$. Further one must obtain dw as a differential of (1.3) with respect to t, i.e., (1.4) $dw = - t(d^2p/dt^2)dt$.

Now, to apply the marginal productivity principle or "Thünen's law," as Wicksell used to refer to it, in this situation, the increase in the social product, i.e., the social marginal product of real capital, $A(dp/dt)dt$, must be divided by the increase in real capital, dK. Simplifying by canceling terms and by substituting the equivalent of dw from (1.4), one obtains the following alternate expressions of equation (3):

$$(3) \qquad \frac{A\frac{dp}{dt}dt}{dK} = \frac{2\frac{dp}{dt}dt}{wdt + tdw} = \frac{2\frac{dp}{dt}dt}{wdt - t^2\frac{d^2p}{dt^2}dt} = \frac{2\frac{dp}{dt}}{w - t^2\frac{d^2p}{dt^2}}.$$

Because of diminishing returns, d^2p/dt^2 is always negative by its very nature. Hence, $-t^2(d^2p/dt^2)$ in the denominator of the last expression is algebraically a positive quantity added to its other term, w.

On the other hand, the interest rate, obtained by solving (1) for z, is (1.5) $z = 2(p - w)/wt$. Using the equivalent of w in (1.3) in this equation for z and simplifying, one finds that the rate of interest can also be stated as

$$(1.6) \qquad\qquad z = \frac{2\frac{dp}{dt}}{w}.$$

Consequently,

$$\frac{2\frac{dp}{dt}}{w - t^2\frac{d^2p}{dt^2}},$$

the social marginal productivity rate of real capital, is always smaller than

$$\frac{2\frac{dp}{dt}}{w},$$

the interest rate, when capital varies in quantity, other factors constant.

This is connected with the fact that this increase in the national capital is *accompanied by an increase in wages which partially swallows it up*, with the result that the lengthening of production actually achieved always falls short of the lengthening of production possible when the rate of wages remains unchanged.[3]

Thünen's doctrine of the determination of the rate of interest by the yield

---

[3] Wicksell, *Value, Capital and Rent*, p. 137. Italics supplied.

of the last portion of capital applied, gives, when taken with reference to the whole capital of the community (reckoned in money or consumption goods) *too low a value.*[4]

Looking back at the second expression in (3); namely,

$$\frac{2\frac{dp}{dt}dt}{wdt + tdw},$$

it is easy to see why this discrepancy must arise. When the quantity of capital is constant, tdw in the denominator equals zero, and the remainder of the expression equals the interest rate. But when capital increases by net real saving, wdt shows the amount of extra advances of real wages that is required for extending the production period by dt. Thus tdw shows the net absorption of real saving per production period, which occurs because the marginal productivity of labor rises relative to that of capital. If the quantity of capital were to decrease by net real dissaving, the same discrepancy would arise, i.e., the social marginal productivity rate of capital will still be less than the interest rate. The reason for this is that in such circumstances dt is negative and wdt measures the amount of capital consumption by a reduction in the wages-fund which occurs consequent upon a reduction of the production period by dt. But tdw will then also be negative and measure the decline in real wages that corresponds to the decline in the marginal value productivity of a constant quantity of labor when capital diminishes in quantity.

The social marginal productivity rate of a varying quantity of real capital must, consequently, always be smaller than the interest rate, because the social marginal product of capital, $2(dp/dt)dt$, inevitably involves a division by $(wdt + tdw)$ to be stated *as a rate*. The rate of interest, on the other hand, is simply the ratio between the social marginal product of capital and the social marginal product of labor (expressed as the competitive rate of real wages),

$$\frac{2\frac{dp}{dt}dt}{wdt} = z.$$

It is the real wage times the production period which represents the medium of investment, or the principal, of capital here. And it is with reference to the latter that the yield or marginal value productivity of capital is expressed as a ratio, i.e., expressed as a rate of interest.

Thus, to what extent "absorption" will occur either of net real sav-

---

[4] Wicksell, *Lectures-I*, p. 177.

ing into greater real wages, or of labor power, as measured by declining real wages into increasing interest incomes, depends on whether real capital is increasing or decreasing, and on the relative magnitudes of *tdw* as compared with *wdt*.

This, then, was the nature of the Wicksell effect. Its author did not apply it in reverse to consider the possibilities of absorption of labor power in declining real wages and increasing interest incomes if the quantity of labor increases while that of real capital remains constant. Wicksell used this proof only for two purposes, (1) to clear up a point of controversy in the doctrine of interest between Böhm-Bawerk and von Thünen, and (2) to stake a claim to the effect that the "absorption" and "rate discrepancy" are phenomena *uniquely* associated with quantitative variation in the factor real capital, and they do not arise when other factors vary, capital being constant.

Wicksell's Application of the Demonstrated Effect

The first point was concerned with Böhm-Bawerk's critique of productivity theories of interest. As is well known, Böhm-Bawerk held that these theories failed to explain why capital or waiting has a *net value* productivity as contrasted with merely a net physical productivity. It was up to productivity theorists, he felt, to explain why competition does not eliminate interest, despite the net physical productivity of capital, by reducing equilibrium prices to the point where the use of capital returns only its replacement value but nothing beyond that by way of a net value or interest income.[5]

Wicksell's comments were a countercriticism to which, incidentally, Böhm-Bawerk made no satisfactory reply. If we assume a stationary state, said Wicksell, then the issue disappears because the marginal-physical and marginal-value productivity of capital are alike. However, in dynamic conditions, both Böhm-Bawerk and productivity theorists like von Thünen are partly right and partly wrong, depending on how, or at what level, the marginal product of capital is measured. If the supply function of real capital is given in terms of a schedule of net real saving, then the marginal productivity of capital measured in *numéraire* at the level of the firm, determines the rate of interest by means of determining the firm's demand for real capital. If we add these demands for all firms in the economy, we obtain the aggregate demand for capital. On this basis one can hold that the rate of interest is determined by the marginal productivity of capital. If that is what

---

[5] Wicksell, *Interest and Prices* (1898), translated (London, 1936), pp. 161 ff. and E. von Böhm-Bawerk, *Positive Theorie des Kapitales* (4th ed.; Vienna, 1920), vol. 1, pp. 116, 283, 457.

von Thünen and Böhm-Bawerk had in mind, then they are both right and may be considered as saying the same thing. But if they meant that this is also applicable at the macroeconomic level of analysis, i.e., if they meant that the social marginal productivity rate of the community's real capital as a whole (viewed as a quantity of net real saving) determines the rate of interest, then they are both wrong, for, as Wicksell's demonstrations showed, the social marginal productivity rate of real capital is always less than the rate of interest.[6]

It was his second point—that the Wicksell effect is uniquely associated with quantitative variation in capital and is absent when other factors vary, capital constant—which, because it sounded so paradoxical, stimulated further discussion and induced others to inspect this peculiar relationship more closely. Wicksell supported this contention by a vague line of augmentation rather than by "rigorous" proof:

. . . the analogy between interest . . . and wages and rent . . . is incomplete. With labor and land . . . the law of marginal productivity applies . . . both to the economy as a whole and to every private undertaking. . . . But this theory applies to capital as usually conceived, only when we look at it from the point of view of the private entrepreneur, to whom wages and rent are data determined by the market. If we consider an increase in the total capital of society, then it is by no means true that the consequent increase in the social product would regulate the rate of interest.[7]
. . . The explanation of this curious divergence [between the interest rate and the social marginal productivity rate of real capital, always lower than the former] is quite simple. Whereas labor and land are measured each in terms of its own *technical* unit [e.g., working days or months, acre per annum] capital, on the other hand . . . is reckoned . . . as a sum of *exchange value*— . . . . In other words, each particular capital good is measured by a unit extraneous to itself. . . . If capital also were to be measured in technical units, the defect would be remedied and the correspondence [between the social and private marginal productivity of each of the three factors] would be complete. But in that case, productive capital would have to be distributed into as many categories as there are kinds of tools, machinery, and materials, etc., and a unified treatment of the role of capital in production would be impossible.[8]

This explanation left much to be desired. So far as the partial absorption of net real saving into rising real wages and rents is concerned, it does not matter whether the productivity of capital goods is measured in horsepower—or other modes of expressing energy—per

---

[6] Cf. Wicksell, *Value, Capital and Rent,* pp. 111-113, 136-138; *Lectures-I,* pp. 147, 167, 177, 180, 269-270, 291-292.

[7] Wicksell, *Lectures-I,* p. 148.

[8] *Ibid.,* p. 149.

unit-period of service, or in money terms, any more than it matters to the wages of carpenters, whether their physical productivity is measured in man-hours of work or in square feet of construction. Physical or technical productivity is not per se an economic phenomenon, whereas wage absorption of real saving is. Moreover, whether or not "absorption" would occur, depends on market conditions, rather than on energy calculations as such.

As for the unique relation between the Wicksell effect and variation in real capital, a general argument would have to adduce reasons why a similar effect does not arise when labor or land vary, real capital being constant. One general ground for this is that the services of labor and land cannot be stored directly *as such*. They can only be stored in the form of real capital.

However, in competitive conditions, today's labor must offer itself today, and each day, on the labor market at the price which reflects its marginal value productivity. If the community's stock of accumulated subsistence remains of a given size while the quantity of labor increases, then real wages will fall in proportion to the decline in labor's marginal value productivity, while the interest rate and the distributive share of capital increase. There has been no "absorption" of net real saving because no such saving has been undertaken. Neither has there been any "absorption" of labor-power or of real wages into capital-income in the sense that the social marginal productivity rate of labor is less than the now lower real wage rate. The two are equal, and each factor receives its changed marginal value productivity rate of remuneration.

The reason for this, is, of course, that today's labor becomes fully effective, without leakage or loss, in creating product. When it is paid according to its marginal value productivity, there is no "extra" or "unpaid" labor performed whereby its social marginal product may be divided to yield a social value productivity rate which is less than the wage rate. The same holds for land.

But this is not true of net real saving in the form of an increasing accumulation of subsistence goods, not only because such goods are more or less storable, but also because both their production and consumption take time. If the real wage level rises during these periods, it is clear that some additional quantity of subsistence goods is absorbed in extra labor consumption. When net real dissaving and disinvestment occurs, it is likewise clear that the social marginal productivity rate of real saving (now changing negatively) will be less than the rising interest rate because of another kind of "absorption." Now it is labor power or its equivalent in real wages, that is partly being absorbed by (*a*) the decline in the national dividend caused by disinvestment, and (*b*) the larger relative share of the latter which accrues to capitalists as increasing interest income when the quantity of capital decreases, other factors constant.

To demonstrate that social marginal productivity of capital is less than the interest rate, where labor increases and capital is constant, while at the same time the social and private marginal productivity of labor, at the end of the period, are equal, would have required modification of the simple production function Wicksell used. This function would have had to be changed so as to show, in particular, at what rate marginal productivity of labor changes negatively as it increases, capital constant. This requires greater clarification of the problem than Wicksell gave it. While it would not be difficult to develop a suitable model for this case, we shall use his own model, which suffices for demonstrating that the absorption phenomenon is uniquely associated with variation in real capital.

Referring to equation (1.2) $p = w + t(dp/dt)$, and assuming that the production period, t, is two years, we may postulate that the marginal product per annum per laborer, was initially $0.9p$, and that of waiting or real capital $0.1p$. Since labor is paid its marginal value productivity, here equal its marginal physical product since value is expressed in *numéraire*, then the annual real wage per laborer must be $w = 0.9p$. However, in view of equations (1) and (2), the interest rate must be

$$z = \frac{2(p - w)}{wt} = \frac{t\frac{dp}{dt}}{K} = \frac{2(0.1p)}{2(0.9p)} = 0.1111$$

or 11.11 per cent.

Now we assume that labor increases by some increment, dA, for example by 3 per cent of the initial quantity available, A, and because of this its marginal productivity declines by 1 per cent. At the same time the marginal productivity of capital rises by the decline in labor's marginal productivity multiplied by the change in the production period (a small decrease), which results from the increase in the quantity of labor. We assume wage and interest rates adjust, as they should under perfect competition, immediately to changes in the productivity of capital and labor. Using subscripts of zero ($_0$), to indicate initial conditions, and subscripts of unity ($_1$), for conditions which result from the increase in labor, initially we have then:

$$p_0 = w_0 + t(dp/dt) = 0.9p_0 + 0.1p_0.$$

The initial labor quantity, A_0, increases by $dA = 0.03A_0$ to $A_1 = 1.03A_0$. The initial production period was $t_0 = 2.00$ years, but due to the increase in labor (with K a constant, so that $K = A_0 w_0 t_0/2 = A_0 \cdot 0.9 p_0 \cdot 2/2 = 0.9 A_0 p_0$), it now changes to $t_1 = t_0[A_0/(A_0 + dA)] = 0.971 t_0 = 1.942$ years. The marginal productivity of labor now becomes: $0.9 p_0 \cdot 0.99 = 0.891 p_0 = w_1$. The marginal productivity of capital is a residual between the annual product per laborer in the firm and labor's share thereof, i.e., $t_0(dp/dt) = (p_0 - w_0)$, and now the latter changes to $t_1(dp/dt_1)$, a residual between the initial product per laborer in the firm and the new reduced real wage or product share of labor, adjusted for the attendant reduction in the production period. Thus $t_1(dp/dt_1) = (p_0 - w_0) \cdot [t_0/(A_0 + dA)] = 0.109 p_0 \cdot 0.971 = 0.1058 p_0$. The new level of the firm's annual product per laborer, p_1, must equal the sum of the new levels of marginal product of labor and capital respectively:

$$p_1 = 0.891 p_0 + 0.1058 p_0 = 0.9968 p_0$$
$$= w_1 + t_1(dp/dt_1).$$

Hence, p_1 is smaller than p_0, which is proper since we are dealing not with the total output per firm (which has risen due to the use of more labor in the firm) but with the annual product *per laborer per firm*.

Now the social product of the extra labor is

$$A_1 p_1 - A_0 p_0 = (A_0 + dA)p_1 - A_0 p_0 = 1.03 A_0 \cdot 0.9968 p_0 - 1.00 A_0 p_0$$
$$= 0.0267 A_0 p_0.$$

This social marginal product of labor, when divided by the increase in labor should, if "Thünen's law" is to be applicable, equal the new real wage rate, w_1, which it does: $0.0267 A_0 p_0/0.03 A_0 = 0.890 p_0$, which $= w_1$ as shown above, except for a discrepancy of $0.001 p_0$ due to rounding of decimals.

This, or any similar model, demonstrates the full applicability of "Thünen's law" both at the microeconomic and macroeconomic level of analysis to other factors than capital, in a frictionless, perfectly competitive society. It follows from the relations stated above that at the new level of social product, $A_1 p_1 = 1.0267 A_0 p_0$, the national dividend has risen 2.67 per cent above its former level. The interest rate, z, is now 12.11 per cent as compared with 11.11 per cent before. The absolute product share of labor is $A_1 w_1 = 0.9177 A_0 p_0$, which represents an increase of 1.9 per cent above its former level of $0.9 A_0 p_0$. The absolute share of capital is $K z_1 = 0.1090 A_0 p_0$, an increase of 9.0 per cent over its former level of $0.10 A_0 p_0$. Further, the new level of social product, when recomputed in terms of p_1, shows that the relative share of labor is $A_1 w_1 = 0.8939 A_1 p_1$ compared with its initial relative share of $0.90 A_0 p_0$, a decrease of 69/100 of 1 per cent. The relative share of capital is $Kz_1 = 0.1061A_1p_1$ compared with its former share, $0.10A_0p_0$, registering a gain of 6.1 per cent, all in accord with what one would expect under the assumed conditions.

Moreover, despite the "absorption" phenomena observable in the Wicksell effect, there is no "exploitation" involved. Whether net real saving or dissaving occurs, other factors constant, or whether the quantity of labor (and land) increases or decreases, real capital constant, the wage rate and interest rate *at the end of the interval* are exactly equal to the marginal value productivity, at its changed level, of each factor respectively.

There remain, however, some technical issues raised by the Wicksell effect which should be disposed of before we proceed to the role it played in the investment theories of Wicksell and of some of his followers.

Technical Issues Raised by the Wicksell Effect

ÅKERMAN AND THE PROBLEM OF MEASURING REAL CAPITAL

In *Realkapital und Kapitalzins*,[9] G. Åkerman endeavored to redeem "Thünen's law" to full applicability to capital, saying that the Wicksell effect was largely the consequence of improper formulation of the problem by its author. He held it is not legitimate to apply the marginal productivity principle by dividing the social marginal product of real capital by the corresponding amount of net real saving. Instead it should be divided by the amount of concrete capital that has been created during the period.[10]

Åkerman's point is unassailable insofar as the new level of the interest rate can be no greater in the long run than the marginal value productivity of the new "concrete" capital created by investment of net real saving. Neither had Wicksell denied this; to the contrary he stressed it. The objection did not meet, far less resolve, his problem, which was one of explaining the consequences of real capital accumulation for the national dividend and its distribution. That the actual capital created would not, except in very unusual circumstances, be equal to the quantity of saving involved, was obvious. But what was not obvious, as Wicksell pointed out in reply, was how one should infer and express quantitatively the "concrete" capital resulting from investment directly from the net real saving: "The author now says that von Thünen's thesis may hold even for social capital if only we

---

[9] G. Åkerman, *Realkapital und Kapitalzins* (Stockholm, 1923), vol. 1, pp. 151-153.
[10] *Ibid.*, p. 152.

take into account the increase in 'concrete' capital, i.e., the amount of labor recently invested to the value of the previous increase in capital. This should probably prove to be correct, if only we could always, so to speak, catch hold of this concrete capital." [11]

Again, this brings out the obstacles to clear thinking that inhere in real level analyses of saving and investment. At that level there is no choice but to treat the quantity of net real saving as the approximate equivalent of the increment in real capital, dK.

F. A. VON HAYEK'S NONABSORPTION CASE

F. A. von Hayek[12] has brought forth a criticism of the Wicksell effect, more serious than Åkerman's, because it is intended to show that partial wage absorption of real saving is *not a necessary* consequence of the variation in the quantity of real saving, other factors constant. His example for an otherwise stationary society in full equilibrium at full employment is that some individuals indulge in a single, unforeseen act of net real saving. For a time they lay by a store of consumption goods by consuming less than their real income. Then they direct some of their laborers to work on making intermediate products, rather than finished ones. During this period, they pay these laborers the same real wages as before by investing their hoards of consumption goods. In the end, net investment has occurred without any "absorption" of net real saving. Corresponding to the latter there is now an increment in capital goods produced at no increase in real wages. Neither has there been any hitch in the flow of consumption goods and consumption expenditures, for the capitalists who hoarded subsistence goods, kept buying them currently at the same rate as before. But they did not consume these goods themselves; instead they practiced real private abstinence. No doubt a reduction occurred in the current output of finished goods, while some workers produced capital goods. But that reduction was offset by an equal flow of dishoarded subsistence goods from the capitalists. *Ergo,* net real saving can occur, and so can net formation of real capital, *without* any absorption of the saving in rising real wages.

The legitimacy of this case must be admitted. The essence of the matter is that it is a *planned act of net saving and net investment* deliberately timed and arranged so as not to interfere with the net flow of consumption goods output and consumption expenditure. The same persons who do the saving also do the investing, short-circuiting the usual exchange process in the labor market whereby the savings are

[11] Wicksell, *Lectures-I*, p. 268.
[12] F. A. von Hayek, *The Pure Theory of Capital* (London, 1941), pp. 273 ff.

transformed into real capital. The investment process is initiated and completed by simple acts of managerial direction to certain workers within the savers' own enterprises.

Such planning of investment by the same party which causes the net real saving to occur should be possible, perhaps even on a large scale, in a socialist state. The state as primary, possibly sole, investor-saver, can presumably induce some of its servants to practice real abstinence and take the place of the capitalists in von Hayek's illustration, while at the same time the planning board arranges for direct investment of these savings. The real wages of those who are not induced or commanded to practice abstinence need obviously not increase in such circumstances. Consequently, the entire quantity of net real saving may be made effective without "wage absorption" in a corresponding quantity of Åkermannian concrete capital. But in private enterprise economies, where those who do the saving are generally not the same persons who do the investing, the likelihood of such an undisturbed transition into a period of net capital formation is very small, and the probability of Wicksell's absorption effects is correspondingly great.

But now we must turn to the role this "effect" and other elements of Wicksell's observations on capital formation came to play in business cycle theory.

Wicksell's Structural Theory of Capital Formation and His Approach to the Problem of Business Cycles

It is true that Wicksell did not elaborate a comprehensive theory of capital formation nor of business cycles. What he did along these lines was rather to work up analyses of several phases of the complex problem of capital formation, among which the Wicksell effect was one, and also to develop a fruitful perspective on business cycles. He never succeeded in coördinating these several elements with one another. That was largely left to his followers. Since the "elements" of a theory of investment he left us cut across the entire corpus of his work in economics, it may be useful to list them here in the order in which he might have related them to one another.

These "elements" are the following: (1) his capital structure conception capable of determinate modes of change in at least two dimensions, width and height; (2) his analysis of the effect of accumulation of real capital (*in abstraction from the process* by which it occurs) on the national dividend and distributive shares; (3) his four demonstrations of the Wicksell effect, which represent the first attempts to deal with the process of capital formation at the real level of analysis; (4) his dynamic monetary theory with (*a*) its emphasis on cumulative processes or price level movements, (b) its stress on the boom phenomenon of "forced saving," (c) its acute explanation of crises; and (5) his articles on the trade cycle. The latter clearly suggested, first, that the business cycle is very largely a phenomenon of real investment connected with the development of capital structures. Secondly, his statements conveyed the idea that this development is not uniform but is disturbed in compound fashion by changes in "real factors," such as technological progress, population growth, etc., which are unpredictable both as to timing and incidence. Furthermore, his treatment suggested that these disturbances generated by actions of and reactions between "real factors" are in turn amplified or accentuated by the influence of "monetary factors." In the remainder of this chapter, we shall deal mainly with certain relations between items (2), (3), and (4, b), in this list.

The foregoing indicates that it was implicit in his position that the trade cycle reflects some breakdown or maladjustment in the development of capital structures. On his general methodological grounds, this implied that proper understanding of such maladjustments required first a theory to explain under what conditions the structure development would, on a priori grounds, be harmonious or tranquil. Once such a theory is at hand it would serve as a suitable framework for studying, especially empirically, particular causes and types of maladjustment.

He developed a perspective on the process of capital formation which can most clearly be described by a metaphor. We can liken this process to a tube with an intake end which is somewhat larger than its outflow end. The latter is connected at the base with one of the walls of a tanklike structure, the capital structure, made of flexible materials so as to be capable of both simultaneous and separate expansion in all of its dimensions. The intake end of the tube is loosely connected with a cistern containing the community's real savings. The level of real savings in this cistern can vary upwards or downwards, and the rate of investment of the savings varies according to whether the intake or suction end of the tube is partially or fully immersed in the cistern's fluid of savings. Let us also imagine that the intake end of the tube, besides being initially larger than the outflow end, can be stretched to any desirable extent so as to make it possible to pump real savings out of the cistern at any desirable rate. Furthermore, we may assume that the tube itself is also elastic so that it can expand or contract and that its outflow end, though always smaller than the inflow one, can also expand and contract, and so can the aperture which connects it with the capital structure, so as to accommodate various rates of inflow.

If the intake end is only partly immersed in the cistern, then there will be an even smooth flow of real saving through the tube. This creates an equivalent amount of real capital at the outflow end; namely, capital goods destined to maintain the dimensions of the capital structure as replacement investments for the services the goods in that structure mature out into current production.

If the intake end is immersed further, perhaps fully, in the cistern then the rate of intake of real saving exceeds the replacement requirements of the structure. This greater inflow of real savings is subject to "wage absorption" or to the Wicksell effect while going through the tube, but emerges as a quantity of "concrete" real capital at the outflow end, which though smaller than the intake of real savings, is still greater than the capital replacement requirements of the structure, i.e., net capital has been formed. But once the net capital goods arrive, they begin to expand the dimensions of the structure in various ways, and thus affect both the size of the national dividend and the relative sizes of the shares of real wages, rent, and interest in which it is distributed.

Wicksell thought that what goes on both inside the tube and inside the structure when net capital formation occurs was of first importance. He thought that fruitful hypotheses concerning these matters could be generated by repeated observations of what is or what might be taking place at each end of the tube. His own work exhibited at least one connection between phenomena observable at both of its "ends." It pointed, namely, to a mutual set of relations between (1) the Wicksell effect when the rate of net saving is taken as given; (2) net formation of real capital, when the rate of accumulation of this real capital is taken as given; and (3) the rate of interest.

As we have seen, sustained net formation of real capital expands the capital structure both in width and height, but not uniformly. As the growth of real capital, other factors constant, reduces the rate of interest, this induces expansion preponderantly in the "height" dimension. Now then, the lower the interest rate we start from, the greater will be the future structure expansion in the vertical dimension and the less will be the subsequent decline of the interest rate.

On the other hand, the Wicksell effect shows that the greater the rate of net real savings, other factors constant, the more will this saving be absorbed in rising wages and rents, and the smaller will be the effective capital formation, and, a fortiori, the smaller the decline it causes in the marginal productivity of capital. This decline will be all the less if the nonabsorbed real saving is chiefly invested in the height dimension of the structure. Thus wage absorption of real saving and height expansion of capital structures are forces which reinforce each other in retarding the decline of the interest rate. This poses a paradoxical problem of the following type.

With a given rate of net real saving, height expansion prevents a wage and rent rise which would have occurred with width expansion alone. Yet, the wage and rent rise which was thus obviated implies also that further height expansion will not be undertaken until wages and rents do in fact rise further. Bearing in mind that technological change, which profoundly affects these relationships was excluded by assumption at this stage of his analysis, the question arises: Is it possible that the two influences may at some point neutralize each other and bring about the peculiar result of a constant rate of interest, despite a stationary technology and labor force, *in conjunction with continuous accumulation* of real capital?

But this is only one of a host of questions which arise concerning the relations between the "cistern," the "tube," and the "structure." To Wicksell's imaginative mind other questions of the following nature (to which, incidentally, he gave no answers) are likely to have arisen:

1. What conditions determine the proportion in which a given rate of net real saving will be absorbed and will become effective real capital?

2. Within what ranges of decline in interest and rise in wage and rent rates lie the optima that determine the proportions in which nonabsorbed net real saving will be invested, on the one hand in the height, and on the other in the width dimensions of the capital structure?

3. With an initial structure given, how much, or what rate, of net accumulation of real capital for a given period with attendant expansion in structure dimensions is required to (*a*) raise the national dividend by some given amount or rate, and (*b*) change the distribution of the rising dividend into relative shares of determinately varying size?

4. What conditions determine the rate of net saving that may be expected to occur when the national dividend is rising at a certain rate and its distribution is changing in a determinate manner due to structure expansion of changing proportions in several dimensions?

5. What further conditions as to net real saving in (4) are required to equate (*a*) the nonabsorbed portion of the rate of net real saving

with (*b*) the rate of real capital accumulation necessary to sustain the capital structure expansion that is requisite for (*c*) attaining the postulated rise in social product corresponding to the rise in national dividend in (3), and (*d*) to give the increasing social product the composition of output that (*e*) corresponds to the variation in consumption expenditure and saving which occurs when the national dividend is rising and its distribution is changing in a determinate manner due to structure expansion?

It is evident that Wicksell's problem even in its simplified form was complicated enough to defy exact and systematic treatment without introducing into it other types of simultaneous dynamic change such as would be due to variations in technology, growth of the labor force, changes in tastes, etc.

Åkerman's and von Hayek's Development of Wicksell's Capital Structure Analysis

Even in its first approximation Wicksell's problem of the theory of investment was fated to increase in difficulty. In 1923, his former student, G. Åkerman, in *Realkapital und Kapitalzins,* showed that the capital structure has multiple dimensions and degrees of freedom of structural variation. Among these dimensions are the durability (as distinguished from the maturation-term) and the automatism (i.e., the labor-saving quality) of capital goods of which the capital structure is made up. Åkerman pointed out that "durable" and/or "automatic" capital goods represent a particular organization of the homogeneous investment units or inputs of "saved labor and land services" with which Wicksell worked. By using more or less of such inputs at the time of construction, one can make capital goods more or less durable and/or automatic. Rational investment action demands that they be made as durable and/or automatic as is "worthwhile" at the time of construction. With given interest, wage, and rent rates, and a given production function showing the relation between inputs used in construction and the resulting increase in durability or automatism of capital goods, the optimum durability or automatism of these goods is determined by: using inputs up to the point where the marginal value product (properly discounted for the maturation term involved) of the service the good will render during its last unit period of service, equals the corresponding marginal investment cost, i.e., the price of extra input units needed for the purpose.

Optimum durability and automatism, like the maturation periods of Wicksell's conception of real capital as "variable capital," vary inversely with the rate of interest and directly with the rates of wages and rent.

Further work along these lines in the 1920's and later by F. A. von Hayek has added an indefinite number of "dimensions" to the Wicksellian capital structure by elaboration of the related concept of the "structure of production." Its possibilities of variation are expressed as follows: "The datum called the supply of capital can thus be adequately described only in terms of the totality of all alternative income streams between which the existence of a certain stock of non-permanent resources [Hayek's synonym for real capital], together with the expected flow of input, enables us to choose." [13]

Von Hayek's conception represents the logical completion of the Wicksell-Åkerman structures. While it was inspired and developed on the basis of Böhm-Bawerk's descriptions of "roundabout" methods of capitalistic production, it is also evident that it draws on and incorporates the more stylized Wicksell-Åkerman conceptions. Von Hayek's "structure of production" is an advance over the capital structure concepts of his predecessors. It is more realistic than theirs in the sense that its many dimensions stamp as futile any attempt to follow its internal changes in detail. Moreover, it relates structure changes more explicitly to changes in consumer income dispositions.

Von Hayek's production structure depicts real capital as organized in a number of production stages so proportioned to one another as to yield a certain flow and composition of output by employing input units of labor and land. As long as the flow and composition of output matches the rate and expenditure pattern of income by income recipients, all is well. But if the output and expenditure streams fail to match, a maladjustment develops within the structure. The adjustments which are then called for take time to execute and cannot keep pace with the relatively rapid changes which are likely to take place in the expenditure stream. Further, complementarity dominates the relations of the parts to the whole of the structure, so that needed adjustments have wide ramifications. Most adjustments to fit the output to the expenditure stream require net investment (or disinvestment). This tends to raise (or lower) the consumption expenditures of the recipients of factor payments in advance of a similar rise (or fall) in the flow of consumption goods. The excess profits (or losses) which then accrue on consumption goods induce a shift of labor and land inputs, or of so-called "permanent resources," from the higher to the lower stages of production (or the reverse). This makes it unlikely that the revision of the production structure will be completed which might,

[13] *Ibid.,* p. 147.

at a later time, have yielded the requisite flow and composition of output. Moreover, even in the absence of monetary complications, but far more so in their presence, there seems to be something inevitable about this, a perverse tendency to dislocation or disequilibrium:

> All that is required for our theory to apply [i.e., for maladjustments to develop within the production structure], is that when incomes are increased by investment, the share of additional income spent on consumption goods during any period of time should be larger than the proportion in which the new investment adds to output of consumption goods during the same period of time. And there is, of course, no reason to expect that more than a fraction of the new income, and certainly not as much as has been newly invested, will be saved, because this would mean that practically all the income earned from the new investment would have to be saved.[14]

Thus one arrives, at the end of the journey, as it were, at von Hayek's well-known capital shortage thesis of the business cycle. An analogous, although less-developed thesis was propounded by G. Åkerman in Volume II of his *Realkapital und Kapitalzins* (1924).

On the basis of what has been said above, it seems likely that Wicksell might have arrived at a capital shortage thesis of his own, for his analyses of the process of capital formation pointed in that direction. But, if so, there would have been one major difference between his and von Hayek's diagnosis as to monetary conditions. In that field Wicksell stood for price stabilization.

This, of course, makes a considerable difference in how Wicksell and von Hayek would have wanted to deal with a depression. Economists who insist on price stabilization do not have to seek the cure for depressions in rapid downward flexibility of wage rates, as do those who favor the neutral money policy.

However, there were other differences between their analyses than those concerned with norms of monetary policy. One of these, of particular interest here, has to do with the relations between two opposed phenomena in their doctrine, namely the Wicksell effect on the one hand, and "forced saving" on the other.

The "Wicksell Effect" versus "Forced Saving" or versus von Hayek's "Ricardo Effect"

"Forced saving" is a short-run, monetary phenomenon usually characteristic of the boom phase of the trade cycle. It is imposed on all persons in varying degree whose money incomes fail to keep pace with the rise in the price level during an inflationary price spiral. The

---

[14] *Ibid.*, p. 394.

Wicksell effect, on the other hand, is a less dramatic force acting more or less imperceptibly at the real level of analysis, with effects that are likely to be discernible only in the long or medium run. On a priori grounds it is clear that these two tendencies are oppositely related to one another. But, more than that, one can observe the interaction between them in a number of theoretical treatments or "models" of hypothetical business cycle sequences, particularly sequences of the "self-generative" type.[15] Illustrations of their interaction can be obtained by imposing the Wicksellian categories and terminology on descriptions of the sequence which connects the "full recovery" (i.e., full employment) phase of the trade cycle with its "upper turning point" or the end of its boom phase.

Let us assume an economy with stationary technology and labor force, in which net capital consumption occurs, with the consequence that there is some "absorption" of labor power or its equivalent in real wages, into increasing interest incomes of owners of real capital. For short, let us call this a case of "interest absorption of real wages." The "forced savings" sequence also involves an absorption of real wages. But the essential difference between "forced saving" and "interest absorption of real wages" is that in the "forced savings" case, the absorption of real wages occurs *despite* the net real saving or capital formation that goes on simultaneously. This seems to contradict the Wicksell effect, for other things equal, as long as there is some net real saving, there will be some wage absorption of the latter since the labor force is constant and its marginal productivity rises relative to that of real capital. But the contradiction is only apparent.

The essence of the Wicksell effect is that it postulates harmonious adjustment of the composition of the net national product and of the structure of production (or the structure of capital) to the rising real wages implied in the partial absorption of net real saving.

The forced savings sequence, on the other hand, implies a disturbance of the output and income expenditure equilibrium by net credit creation. Credit expansion makes the commodity composition of the national dividend diverge from the income disposition of income recipients as between consumption spending and savings in such a manner that the capital structure expands more, by net investment, than it would have done on the basis of "voluntary" savings alone. The "real" investment which corresponds to the extra expansion of the

[15] See particularly F. A. von Hayek, *Prices and Production* (London, 1934), chap. 4; his *Profits, Interest, and Investment* (London, 1939), chaps. 1 and 7; R. F. Harrod, *The Trade Cycle* (London, 1936), chaps. 2 and 3; and J. R. Hicks, *A Contribution to the Theory of the Trade Cycle* (London, 1950), chaps. 7, 9 and 12.

structure is obtained by a reduction in the output of "wage goods" relative to the rise in money wages.

At this point we have to anticipate some of the discussion of chapters x and xi in order to indicate the sequence or process that develops within the simple economy we have assumed. We impose a "pure credit" system on the economy, which means that all payments are effected by transfers of bank credit, and that the banks are capable, without any restraint, to maintain a given loan rate of interest by extending as much credit as the community may come to demand at the given loan rate. For our purposes, however, under the pure credit system, calculations or comparisons must now be made in two standards, in money terms and in real terms, perhaps suitably expressed in Keynesian "wage units." The "pure credit" banks have from habit or instinct adopted either the "neutral" money policy von Hayek insists on, or its equivalent in Wicksellian terms, i.e., they charge a loan rate of interest at which *ex ante* savings and investment are equal.

Full employment equilibrium prevails and wage absorption of net real savings occurs. Evidence of this may be seen in the fact that labor's relative share and real wages rise in relation to the rising national dividend. Net real saving may equal 10 per cent of the national dividend measured in wage units. If wage absorption amounts to 20 per cent of the net real saving, the resulting net real investment comes to 8 per cent of the national dividend measured in wage units. The marginal productivity of the resulting real capital formation must be sufficiently high, in wage unit terms (i.e., as the analogue of Wicksell's "natural" rate of interest), so that when it is expressed in money terms, it equals the loan rate of interest at which entrepreneurs borrowed the net money savings which corresponded to the net real savings. Other things equal, this means that the "natural rate" of interest must be higher in wage unit terms than the loan rate when the latter is expressed in similar terms. This is as it should be, or as is required by Wicksell's demonstrations concerning relations between the rate of interest, here equal to the "natural rate," and the social marginal productivity rate of capital, here equal to the "loan rate," both in wage unit terms. We may say then, that the loan rate in money terms, which maintains this monetary equilibrium, and thus is the "normal" loan rate, expresses the social marginal productivity rate of the net money savings.

Forced saving may now come about in this situation in the same manner it does in Wicksell's discussion of cumulative processes (see *Lectures-II*, pp. 192-93); namely, by a rise in the "natural rate," which is not accompanied by a similar rise in the loan rate. Technological improvements may occur, and if so the marginal efficiency of capital or the "natural rate" of interest rises, although we may assume that the banks continue maintaining the same loan rate of interest as before. Consequently net investment demand increases while, for the time being, "voluntary" savings remain at the old rate and volume. The extra investment demand is financed by net credit creation by the banks. Entrepreneurs pay over the extra funds as money wage increases in order to attract a larger number of workers into production of capital goods.

Wage absorption of net real saving need not, therefore, cease. To the contrary, it increases by the entrepreneurs' actions, at least at first. Investment is now provided for by a mixture of "voluntary" savings and net additional credit. To the extent that wage absorption rises, to that extent are labor money incomes increased while the concurrent output of wage goods remains constant at first. But eventually the output of wage goods decreases as more workers are transferred from the "lower" to the "higher" stages of production. If prices of wage goods had been constant at rising money wages, they will now begin rising. With each income-expenditure round prices of wage goods will rise in cumulative fashion as long as the banks continue to provide a perfectly elastic supply of credit at the preëxisting loan rate.

It may take a few "rounds" of this sequence before the decline in real wages begins to overtake the "wage absorption of real saving," but it is inevitable that this occurs sooner or later. At the end of the boom von Hayek's "vertical maladjustment" is close at hand for either one of two reasons:

1. The cumulative rise in consumption goods prices and the accompanying rise in windfall profits for their producers overtakes the price rise that has occurred on capital goods. The "lower production stages" are thus put in a position to outbid the "higher stages" for workers. The result is that planned extensions of the "higher stages" of the structure of production cannot be completed.

2. At declining real wages, labor has progressively become a favored substitute for increasingly dear real capital, and the boom collapses because of a decline in investment demand. It requires at least an investment demand as great as earlier, and more likely an investment demand which keeps on increasing, to keep the boom going.

This last possibility, which represents an alternative version of von Hayek's monetary overinvestment and capital shortage thesis, has been labeled the "Ricardo" effect by its author. Thus, by relating the Wicksell effect to the forced saving which is implicit in Wicksell's own discussions of upward cumulative processes or price level movements, one arrives, by easy stages, at von Hayek's "Ricardo" effect.

In view of the insights that were made available by the concern of Wicksell and his followers about the process of capital formation, it may be appropriate to close this chapter with some reflections on the reasons for the eclipse of capital structure analyses and capital shortage theses of the trade cycle.

Eclipse of Capital Structure Analysis and Capital Shortage Hypotheses of Business Cycles

For their time, approximately 1920-1935, analyses of the Wicksell-Åkerman-von Hayek type represented outstanding achievements both in capital and business cycle theory. Since then, and particularly with the arrival of the so-called "Keynesian revolution," very little more is heard of capital structure analyses on the one hand and capital shortage explanations of the upper turning point of business cycles on the other.

Instead of concerning themselves with the nature and requirements of elaborately conceived capital structures, contemporary capital theorists stress the brevity of the investor's horizon, limited as it is by uncertainty and shifting anticipations. Consequently major emphasis is placed on short-run analyses. As for real capital, it is usually treated as intermediate products possessing a certain productivity and competing on equal terms with other types of input at the margin of substitution. By and large, the interest rate has been demoted from its earlier role of determining the proportion of current resources which are to be used for production of "future goods" as compared with production of "present goods." Instead, this rate now has a less impressive and mixed status. It is widely regarded both as an opportunity rate or reward for giving up liquidity, and also as a time discount factor which bears a certain relation to the long-term marginal productivity rate of capital in a "free" market.

The decline that the capital shortage thesis has suffered is even more definitive. In many quarters, it has been replaced by a diametrically opposed theory, an underconsumption or shortage-of-investment-opportunity thesis, depending on which of its elements is to be stressed. In any case, the newer doctrine holds that whatever else may be the sources of our troubles, capital shortage is not one of them. This eclipse of capital shortage theses is apparently attributable to their failure to interpret the Great Depression in a sufficiently meaningful manner to suggest criteria for realizable economic policy. And this, in turn, seems to be due to causes chiefly of methodological origin.

The capital shortage thesis remained essentially of a long-run character. It became overrationalized on narrow premises. Questions concerning dynamic behavior of capital structure were asked from the standpoint of ascertaining what relations among its major variables must be fulfilled in order that growing structures could proceed majestically from one to another equilibrium through time. Solutions to these questions were sought on assumptions of atomistic competitive behavior, perfect foresight, perfect mobility, and absence of intervention and frictions obstructing the ends of maximizing behavior. The forces of dynamic change studied in this atmosphere were mainly those of capital accumulation and technological change. These were observed to generate patterns of short-period variations toward central and abiding relations.

When the problems of living society were to be diagnosed by contrasting its condition with that of the hypothetical society two things happened. Most of the contrasts were charged to the account of "frictions," and some of the behavior assumptions were carried forward. "Frictions" of two general types were noted: (1) those associated with alleged derelictions of monetary policy and intimately connected with these "the excesses of government finance"; and (2) those due to imperfect competition, especially rigidity resulting from the progress of trade unionism, and monopolistic pricing of commodities, often aided and abetted by legislative proscription on competitive behavior.

The transferred assumptions were those of atomistic behavior in areas not directly affected by "frictions," and investor behavior in general according to the pattern obtained under perfect foresight, qualified, however, by the influence of aberrant money policy on the prices supplied for the exercise of foresight.

The direct and implied suggestions for economic policy contained in the recent writings of F. A. von Hayek, L. von Mises, and W. Röpke are unrealistic. Essentially, they advocate the following: First, remove the defects of monetary policy by some specific reform such as adopting the "neutral money" method of management. Second, balance the government budget. Third, remove the market frictions or restore universal free competition. If these steps prove politically impossible, then, in view of the complexities and sensitivities of the production structure, do nothing and let nature take its course. The burden of these analyses is that the only way in which "boom and bust" sequences can be obviated and relative economic stability achieved, is by policies designed to prevent the development of the boom, which inevitably brings with it the complex structural maladjustment. This may be conceded, but only as a counsel of perfection.

If Wicksell had lived to see the Great Depression, he would almost certainly have deviated from the general position ascribed to the three well-known authorities above. First, he would have urged international price stabilization. But he would also have gone far beyond this to advocate various forms of intervention, for he had no optimistic convictions as to the restorability of free competition. In his own day he advocated a state-supported credit scheme to maintain employment in depressed times. This was to be done by inducing entrepreneurs to "produce to stock" aided by state-guaranteed credit, and spurred by the opportunity for making net gains in the ensuing recovery.

It stands to reason that in a purely competitive society, involuntary unemployment is not a problem except as a result of immobility of resources when the structure of production adjusts to a change in demand. It is further reasonable to assume that in such a society investment will be highly interest-elastic, and hoarding in excess of minimum transactions balances will not occur for lack of a proper or rational motive. But it does not follow that under conditions of imperfect foresight and great uncertainty, investment responds to the same extent to interest rate changes, and that hoarding would be irrational. Neither does it follow that certain modes of intervention, inadmissible under the assumptions of a fully "rational" society, must fail of accomplishing desired ends or must have uniformly baleful consequences in the less rational society in which we live.

It is at these points, under assumptions in several respects similar to those used in capital structure analysis, but with one important exception—admitting uncertainty and imperfect foresight into the analysis—that the Keynesian theory and its succession had something new to offer. Does this mean that capital structure theory was and is useless? Hardly. Even Keynesians use some of its results, as for instance, A. Hansen, when he discourses at the long-run level on the consequences of "deepening" and "widening" of capital.

This is precisely the point. In matters involving the long perspective, the so-called "new economics" (S. E. Harris' name for Keynesian analysis), has relatively little to offer that had not already come to attention in theories of capital structure. Granted that the problem of cyclical unemployment, which obviously is not independent of problems affecting the secular development of the community's productive resources, rightly takes priority over more latent questions, which become topical only in sustained periods of full employment. It is equally clear that steps taken to alleviate unemployment must have consequences for the secular development of resources. Hence there is a "structure problem" involved in all reëmployment programs. The problem then is not simply one of increasing the total investment demand on private and public account sufficiently to restore high-level employment, but there is also a problem or a series of such relating to the qualities or types of investments to be undertaken.

This is sometimes lost sight of; as, for instance, when it is claimed that a public works expenditure or a production subsidy of some large amount "costs society nothing" because the resources used were idle in the first place. This is true only in the obvious sense that their continued involuntary idleness constitutes a greater cost in foregone production than any incurred in their reëmployment. But it is not true in the sense that it is a matter of indifference whether the re-employment takes the form of leaf-raking or of constructing a hydro-electric power project.

In recognition of this it has become more and more customary to insist that once the necessity for countercyclical policy is well understood and accepted, its scope and contents must be decided according to some scale of "social priorities."

This raises a "structure problem" of the highest order. It is generally assumed that such priorities are to be decided by the democratically elected representatives of the people. This involves difficulties of choice among social objectives, as well as even greater difficulties of assigning some rank to the many possible objectives, and then deciding on the limits or relative size of projects falling in the various rank classes. There is, of course, no guarantee that a political assembly will arrive at a social priority scale and schedule that is (*a*) workable from the standpoint of harmony of ends, (*b*) internally consistent enough to make the achievement of harmonious ends probable, and (*c*) flexible enough to be adjustable without major breakdown to changes of foreseen type but imperfectly foreseen extent arising in its execution. But legislatures do, after all, struggle with problems of this type with varying degrees of success.

It is in this connection that a revitalized analysis, analogous to the capital structure studies in perspective and aim, but more realistic in assumptions and methods, may be of great service. Its difficulties will be both novel and great, for monetary returns and profit-maximizing behavior will often not be conclusive or admissible in many of its problems. But such cases are not unknown in contemporary theory. They have appeared and have received a fair share of attention in the literature on public finance.

CHAPTER VII

The Marginal Productivity Theory: A Second Approximation

One can clearly discern a thread of continuity between Wicksell's first and his later treatments of the distribution problem if his earlier analysis is considered as a study of distribution under conditions of capital expansion "in the horizontal dimension" only.[1] His later discussions develop this theme in a logical sequence of how the shares are affected solely by technological change, and finally by a combination of capital expansion "in the vertical dimension" and technological change. Accordingly, we have adopted this sequence as a mode of presentation here.

Effect on Distributive Shares of Net Accumulation of Capital "in the Horizontal Dimension"

It will save time to follow Wicksell's presentation of the shares problem in much the same form he gave it in *Value, Capital and Rent* (pp. 126-130, 138-140) because then we can use most of the equations of the previous chapter over again. The reason for this is that Wicksell developed his analysis of distributive shares on the same assumptions he used in dealing with the phenomenon of "wage absorption of net real saving."

In view of land being a free good, the production function, $p = f(t,h)$, actually simplifies to $p = f(t)$, and the net accumulation of real capital which occurs (*after* partial wage absorption of net real saving) was interpreted as resulting in a lengthening of the period of produc-

---

[1] Wicksell, *Value, Capital and Rent* (Jena, 1893), translated (London, 1954), pp. 126-130, 138-142; *Lectures-I*, pp. 133-144, 163-166.

tion. Consequently the marginal productivity of real capital, or of incremental lengthening of the production period, can be expressed as $dp/dt = f'(t)$, and the *rate of change* in the marginal productivity of real capital must then be $d^2p/dt^2 = f''(t)$. The simple production function used here is homogeneous and of first degree, and with the labor force constant, the marginal productivity of the increasing quantity of real capital is subject to diminishing returns or declines. Consequently, the rate of change in the marginal productivity of capital, d^2p/dt^2, is necessarily negative.

Now, whether labor's relative share; namely, the ratio of annual real wages per laborer per firm to the annual product per laborer per firm, (w/p), increases or decreases as the quantity of capital expands in width, depends on whether the derivative $d(w/p)dt$ varies positively or negatively. Likewise, whether the absolute share of capital, namely, the residual between the annual product and the annual real wage per laborer per firm, $(p - w)$, increases or decreases with continuous accumulation, depends on whether its time derivative, $d(p - w)dt$, is positive or negative.

As to the first, $d(w/p)dt = p(dw/dt) - w(dp/dt)$. By using the value of w in (1.3), namely, $w = p - t(dp/dt)$, and the value of dw/dt in (1.4); namely, $dw/dt = -t(d^2p/dt^2)$, for substitution in the right member of the foregoing differential equation, we obtain

$$(4) \qquad d(w/p)dt = -pt(d^2p/dt^2) + t(dp/dt)^2 - p(dp/dt).$$

Since d^2p/dt^2 is negative throughout, this makes the first term at right in (4) positive despite its negative sign. The second term is necessarily positive, while the third term, which represents the rate of change in capital's relative share, is necessarily negative as capital increases, the quantity of labor being constant.

Consequently, labor's relative share increases only if the first two positive terms at right in (4) exceed the third, negative one. Whether and when this will be the case cannot be said a priori. It depends on the production function, i.e., on how far production has been driven into the stage of diminishing returns as the quantity of real capital per laborer (and optimum land unit) per firm increases.

What matters here is the relative capital intensity of production and the downward or negative acceleration of the marginal productivity of capital, d^2p/dt^2. If production is only slightly capital-intensive, or, as it would have been expressed in 1893, if the production period is relatively short, then the utilization of capital cannot have proceeded very far into the stage of diminishing returns. The result is that as long as capital-intensity is slight, the relative share of capital increases with period extensions, while wages increase absolutely at the same time. The reason for this is that the intensive margin of utilization of labor is raised because the increase in capital leaves less labor per unit of capital to coöperate with the latter in production. This is also shown by the fact that the time derivative of wages, $dw/dt = -t(d^2p/dt^2)$, is positive.

But continuous net accumulation, with the labor force constant, will in due course make production capital-intensive. Then the relative share of labor begins to increase along with its absolute share. On the other hand, labor's absolute share will then increase more slowly than before because the marginal productivity of capital has declined to a smaller magnitude with the progressive rise in capital-intensity.

The circumstances controlling the rate of change in the absolute share of capital are: $d(p - w)dt = dp/dt - dw/dt$. Substituting at right in this expression the value of dw/dt in (1.4) and changing signs, as required, yields

$$(5) \qquad d(p - w) \, dt = dp/dt + t(d^2p/dt^2).$$

Here the first term at right is positive and the second, for familiar reasons, negative. The increase in capital's absolute share depends on whether the first term exceeds the second. Again, this cannot be decided a priori. The nature of the production function and the degree of capital intensity are the vital elements. As long as the latter is small, the absolute share of capital will increase. Then it is implicit, although Wicksell did not show it, that capital's relative share declines earlier than its absolute share with continuous accumulation. By (1.2), namely $p = w + t(dp/dt)$, the relative share of capital is $t(dp/dt)/p$, and this share must change as its differential with respect to time, i.e., as:

$$d \, \frac{t \, \dfrac{dp}{dt}}{p} \, dt = p \, \frac{dp}{dt} + pt \, \frac{d^2p}{dt^2} - t \left(\frac{dp}{dt} \right)^2.$$

Capital's relative share is at its maximum when this differential equals zero and may be written as:

$$p \, \frac{dp}{dt} = t \left(\frac{dp}{dt} \right)^2 - pt \, \frac{d^2p}{dt^2}.$$

Dividing both sides by p results in

$$\frac{dp}{dt} = \frac{t}{p} \left(\frac{dp}{dt} \right)^2 - t \, \frac{d^2p}{dt^2}.$$

On the other hand, the absolute share of capital is at its maximum when its differential assumes the form of $dp/dt = -t(d^2p/dt^2)$. It is evident that the diminishing coefficient dp/dt must have a greater value at the former than at the latter maximum, and that, therefore, the decline in capital's relative share sets in earlier than in its absolute share.

There is a sort of "distributive shares equilibrium" that arises when the production period is sufficiently extended to maximize capital's absolute share. This may be a point beyond which capitalists may no longer be induced to make more net saving available. This point coincides with a substantial gain in labor's share. But for labor itself, there is no maximum short of the product in its entirety, since here capital's share is determined as a residual. Was there any exception to this? Might not, for instance, labor's absolute share eventually also decline as capital accumulates?

Wicksell rightly maintained there is no exception; the national dividend and labor's absolute, later also its relative share, increase as long as there is free competition. However, he found that if either side combines, particularly if the capitalists combine to maximize the return to capital by increasing the length of the production period, they may succeed in depressing the wage of freely competitive labor substantially. But by then the character of the problem also changes.

As long as capitalists act in competition with one another, each takes the market rate of wages as a datum. Once they combine, the wage rate becomes an independent variable along with the production period. What the result would be was briefly sketched in *Value, Capital and Rent* (p. 129). Our earlier macroeconomic capital equation (2), namely, $K = (A/2)wt$, shows the relation between the wage rate and capital quantity more clearly if it is written in the form of (2a), $w = (2K/At)$. Solving (1), namely $p = w + (wtz/2)$, for z, we obtain $z = 2(p - w)/wt$ as the relation between interest, wages, and the productivity of period lengthening. If we substitute the value of w in (2a) into the right member of this last expression, and simplify, we obtain:

$$ z = \frac{2\left(p - \dfrac{2K}{At}\right)}{t\dfrac{2K}{At}} = \frac{A}{K}\left(p - \frac{2K}{At}\right) = p\frac{A}{K} - \frac{2}{t}. $$

This last expresses z as a function of two variables, of wages restated in terms of p, and of time, t, all other terms being constants. By partial differentiation with respect to p and t, we obtain: $\partial z/\partial p = A/K$ and $\partial z/\partial t = 2/t^2$, hence the total differential of z is: $dz = (A/K)dp + (2/t^2)dt$.

The problem for the capitalists was to maximize z in combination. This occurs when its differential equals zero. Hence, by the usual transposition: $Adp/Kdt = 2/t^2$. If this last is written in the form of $dp/dt = -2K/t^2A = -2K/At \cdot 1/t$, then we can substitute for $2K/At$ its equivalent in (2a), namely w, and thus obtain Wicksell's expression: $dp/dt = -w/t$.

Concerning this, Wicksell reasoned that since w and t must of necessity be positive, it is dp/dt that becomes negative. In other words, maximization of interest by combined capitalists can only be attained when lengthening of the production period results in negative returns, the social output being reduced far below that obtainable under a regime of competition. He conceded that such an interest-maximum was not practically attainable, but that as long as the capitalists combine, every possible period-lengthening will be advantageous to them, subject only to one limit. The latter takes the form of increasing expense for poor relief. When wages have been depressed below subsistence levels long enough, capitalists, in the interest of preserving an adequate labor force, have to make up the difference in poor relief.

One wonders which of the following statements of Adam Smith (perhaps both?) Wicksell may have had in mind:

Masters are always and everywhere in a sort of tacit, but constant and uniform combination, not to raise the wages of labor above their actual rate. To violate this combination is everywhere a most unpopular action. . . . Masters too sometimes enter into particular combinations to sink the wages of labor even below this rate. These are always conducted with the utmost secrecy, till the moment of execution, and when the workmen yield, as they sometimes do, without resistance, though severely felt by them, they are never heard of by other people.[2]

People of the same trade seldom meet together, even for merriment and diversion, but the conversation ends in a conspiracy against the public. . . .[3]

Rarely, if ever, have these observations of Smith's had the benefit of a better or more elegant demonstration.

This thought, that there are no assignable theoretical limits to how far a powerful factor monopoly, of whatever category, may press its advantage, recurs again and again in Wicksell's writings.[4] In chapter iii we have pointed out how this insight led him to certain premature conclusions concerning the nature of bilateral monopoly relations.

Yet to have distilled this demonstration as a contrast to the competitive case in an otherwise static framework of analysis is in itself some-

---

[2] Adam Smith, *The Wealth of Nations* (Cannan ed.; New York, 1937), pp. 66-67.
[3] *Ibid.*, p. 128.
[4] Cf. Wicksell, *Lectures-I*, pp. 141-143, 165, 267-268, 279.

thing of an achievement. Incidentally, it answers another part of the problem at issue; namely, whether the national dividend necessarily increases as accumulation proceeds. In his own words:

In any case it is to be noticed that production—so far as our assumptions hold—reaches its maximum, from a technical point of view, with universal competition. *Coöperation* [nowadays generally called "combination"] between workers to raise wages and between employers and landowners to lower wages—in the course of which some land must remain uncultivated— *would* both *lead to a diminution of product,* and only if coöperation results in social collectivism could the maximum product, physically and technically possible, again be reached.[5]

The practical inferences he drew from this part of his analysis of the relations between the shares may be seen from the following:

. . . we may proceed on the provisional conclusion that free competition is normally sufficient to ensure maximization of production. But this maximization may very well be associated with and even conditioned upon, a reduction in the distributive share of one of the factors. . . . This shows the serious error of those who see in free competition a sufficient means for maximum satisfaction of the needs or desires of all members of society.[6]

On the whole, it is a mistake to regard as obvious—as is so often done— that all healthy persons capable of work must be able to live by their labor *alone*. . . . On the contrary, it is quite conceivable that the total output of society may be large enough for all, but the *marginal* productivity of labor so small that labor has only a slight economic value. Even in a socialist state, under such conditions, the wages paid would only correspond to a part of necessary expenditure, whilst the rest would have to be found from the rent and interest of society.[7]

It was precisely this thought—that individuals in the mass should not be reduced to living from their labor *alone*—that dominated his reform program, particularly his fiscal reform program, as developed in *Finanztheoretische Untersuchungen,* as will be shown in chapter viii.

Effect of Technological Change on Distributive Shares

In proceeding to consider technological change and the complications it introduces in the relations between factor shares, Wicksell first oriented his discussion to a classical observation. This was Ricardo's dictum that adoption of labor-saving machinery will be to the ad-

---

[5] *Ibid.,* p. 142. Italics supplied.
[6] *Ibid.,* p. 141.
[7] *Ibid.,* p. 143.

vantage of employers even when its application results in a decrease of the national dividend, as long as the new technology increases their profits.[8]

Ignoring for the moment capital and its accumulation, Wicksell refuted this notion by means of a classic example. The factors are labor and land only. The innovation is some agricultural technique which makes pastoral agriculture more profitable in a region otherwise devoted to raising grain. Ordinarily this would cause heavy displacement of agricultural laborers, cottars, and yeomen. If Ricardo were right, the displacement would be permanent and would involve a lengthy and very difficult adjustment of numbers and appetites to reduced real product and real wages. Mill's dictum that a demand for commodities is not a demand for labor would never need a better illustration.

However, said Wicksell, if free competition prevails, although there will be a difficult short-run adjustment in store for labor, the gross real product will not decline, except partially and for brief periods while a varying number of entrepreneurs are rearranging their production. First of all, not everyone would adopt the new technique simultaneously. In the end, this means that all the farms will not be converted to sheep raising. The innovation, while displacing labor on the farms being converted, raises the productivity of sheep farming compared with what it was before. Thus, there will be more sheep in the national dividend. But under competition, the displaced laborers will also offer their services at lower wages to other producers, thus making grain farming more profitable than it was earlier. The result is that while the acreage devoted to grain farming is reduced, cultivation will be intensified on the better grades of grain farms. Thus, as the displaced laborers are absorbed at whatever wages in grain production, the output of grain also increases. *Ergo,* the national dividend has increased—there is both more mutton and more bread, perhaps with some wool to spare for export!

Thus, under competition, innovation does not reduce the national dividend, though it may be hard on labor and be an unmerited blessing for the landed gentry. However, this difficulty does not adhere to technology per se, but to the fact that new technology, while it raises average productivity, *does not necessarily raise the marginal productivity of all factors in equal proportion.* It may, as here, raise the productivity of land more than that of labor. What the consequences of this might be was indicated as follows:

---

[8] *Ibid.,* p. 135.

Nor is the result any different if we assume that wages are already at the subsistence level (and cannot according to this view, fall any lower). In reality, wages can not only be forced below it for a little, but can remain below it indefinitely if the laborers and their families make up the difference in poor relief, as happened in England. . . . If we assume . . . labor must . . . be somehow supported by the landowners, it would in fact be more advantageous for them to *reduce* wages to the point to which they would tend to fall as a result of free competition, and to add, by charity, enough to bring up these incomes to the necessary minimum; it would be better for them to do this than to insist that every laborer employed should earn a subsistence wage.[9]

. . . the evils here requiring a remedy relate exclusively to the problem of *social distribution of income* and *not* to that of the most economically advantageous method of production.[10]

In his subsequent discussion, the pathetic shadow of the eighteenth- and nineteenth-century British yeoman was consecrated to its sad past by the logic of probability: ". . . there is an overwhelming probability . . . that the great majority of inventions and technological improvements . . . may . . . tend to increase the marginal productivity of both labor and land together with their share in the product." [11]

Precisely how that probability was to be weighted and evaluated was a problem into which Wicksell did not enter.

Effect on Distributive Shares of Net Accumulation of Capital "in the Height Dimension" and of Technological Change

We have seen earlier how capital expansion "in height" counteracts and retards but does not stop or reverse the rise in wages and rent which continues until net investment stops. Now, however, if we introduce progressive or dynamic technological conditions in this setting, land and labor still constant, then the situation changes considerably. Wicksell described the possible consequences for distributive shares of technological change as follows:

But the position is different where, as may easily happen, *some technical invention renders long-term investment more profitable (absolutely) than previously.* The consequence must necessarily be—so long as no further capital is saved—a diminution in the 'horizontal dimension' and an increase in the 'vertical dimension', so that the quantity of capital used in the course of a year will be reduced; an increased quantity of current labor and land

---

[9] *Ibid.*, p. 141.

[10] *Ibid.*, pp. 141-142.

[11] *Ibid.*, p. 143.

will consequently become available for each year's direct production; and, although this need not necessarily cause their marginal productivity and share in the product to be reduced—since the total product has simultaneously been increased by the technical discovery—yet a reduction may clearly result. *The capitalist saver is thus, fundamentally, the friend of labor, though the technical inventor is not infrequently its enemy. . . . That the transformation of circulating into fixed capital, i.e., the change from short-term to long-term capital investments, may frequently injure labor is beyond doubt.*[12]

Thus technological change increases the national dividend under free competition because it increases the productivity of one or more, possibly of all, factors of production. This force was considered to be subject to an "overwhelming probability" of also increasing the marginal productivity of labor and land—though not necessarily in equal proportion. Yet, it was evidently subject to an even greater and more overwhelming probability of autonomously increasing, *absolutely*, the marginal productivity of capital, particularly capital of the long-vertical-dimensional type. Technological change is then capable of increasing the marginal productivity of this type of real capital, altogether apart from any decline in the rate of interest which may have been occurring due to continued accumulation of capital goods of short-maturation terms. Technological change may, consequently, not only retard the decline in the rate of interest which is to be expected when real capital increases, other factors constant, but it may indeed reverse this decline. At the same time wages and rents, because of the displacement of men and acres into "direct" production, may not only be prevented from rising, but may be forced to fall and to remain at a reduced level for some years while production is increasingly oriented to output of new, more durable types of fixed equipment. At full employment society's total resources are constant in the short run. Since they are at best capable of a slow rate of increase in the short run, this necessarily entails a simultaneous reduction in the output of wage goods.

The resemblance between this and J. R. Hicks' analysis of the same type of problem in his *Theory of Wages* is striking. Hicks admittedly drew on Wicksell's work,[13] but also made contributions of his own in relating the relative-share problem more directly to the theory of value by use of the concept of derived demand for factors, elasticity of derived demand, and elasticity of substitution between factors. Further, his discussion also brought the shares problem into

---

[12] *Ibid.*, p. 164.
[13] J. R. Hicks, *The Theory of Wages* (London, 1932), pp. 121 ff.

closer contact with monetary theory. It brought out the connection between real and money wages and the influence of money or credit in sustaining an abnormal rate of production of durable capital goods during the boom phase of the trade cycle.

Both of these features were lacking or were less in evidence in Wicksell's treatment. The demand problem was hidden from view by the assumption of given commodity prices. The monetary connection was excluded by calculating in terms of product or *numéraire*. That connection was, however, established in another context, in his monetary writings. But in the latter the relative-share problem no longer occupied the center of the stage.

Further, Hicks generated a very suggestive theory of inventions. In the first place there are inventions which are "neutral" or not stimulated by economic motivation. Such inventions may affect all shares equally. Secondly, there are inventions which are induced by the decline in the interest rate due to net accumulation, and by the search for labor- and cost-saving methods of production. These increase capital's relative share, however, generally without reducing but instead somewhat increasing labor's absolute share. Finally, there are inventions which are "very labor-saving" and which would have been profitable even without an antecedent decline in the interest rate, or without an antecedent change in "relative prices," as Hicks put it. It is inventions of the latter type that are likely to have the disastrous effects on labor which Wicksell spoke about. They would reduce not only labor's relative share but also its absolute share as well.

It may be debatable whether it is permissible to read "an induced invention that would have been profitable even in the absence of an antecedent change in relative prices" into Wicksell's "technical invention that renders long-term investment more profitable (absolutely) than previously," but the connection seems to be a very close one.

Yet one aspect of Wicksell's treatment of distributive shares invites criticism, his constant refuge in the assumption of free competition, especially in the last phase of his analysis.

Technological Change, Competition, and Obsolescence

The assumption of free competition may be tenable as long as the discussion concerns an economy in relatively quiet or stationary technological conditions and one where industrial enterprise is of small scale. But once we leave these conditions behind, the question of survival of competition in conditions of large-scale production and rapid technological change forces itself to attention.

It has been shown earlier that Wicksell, in his work on value theory and on the product exhaustion theorem, was well aware of the relationship between imperfect competition and large-scale enterprise. But in the present context, it seems even more necessary to reintroduce that relationship and to integrate the theory of markets or of market structure more directly with the relative share analysis. Wicksell failed to do this. If he had attempted such a treatment, it could hardly have failed to impress on him that temporary displacement of men and acres and consequent reduction in wages and rent are possibly not the most serious consequences of technological change. Equally serious, perhaps more so, are the tendencies toward monopolization and industrial concentration that follow in its wake.

These tendencies, in turn, bring forward forces, which if unchecked, threaten—in the interest of protecting existing investments against obsolescence—the very source of technological progress. They bring into view the possibility of contrived or enforced technological stagnation added to that of contrived scarcity, a very bleak prospect.

Also, one notes the absence in Wicksell's analysis of any treatment of the technological incidence on obsolescence and its effect on the risk element involved in capital formation.

CHAPTER VIII

Taxation and Public Finance

Wicksell's formal work in public finance was limited in scope, except for some popular pamphlets he wrote analyzing the Swedish revenue system in the 1890's and advocating a change to greater reliance on direct as compared with indirect taxes. He dealt only with problems of revenue or taxation, to the total neglect of the equally important problems of the uses to which revenues are put. By and large, he also ignored questions relating to the public debt, except for occasional comments which recorded his suspicion that capitalists as a class have a vested interest in expansion of public indebtedness for nonproductive purposes.

In the field of taxation he devoted himself to two types of problems. One was concerned with the theory of incidence and shifting of certain types of taxes. The other was a lofty speculation concerning the institutional premises necessary for devising revenue systems or for revising extant systems to effectuate "justice" in taxation to all groups of citizens.

Theory of Shifting and Incidence of Taxes

Judged by contemporary standards, Wicksell's work on tax incidence in *Finanztheoretische Untersuchungen* may seem both unspectacular and incomplete. But it should be borne in mind that his discussion, never revised, bears the date 1895. At that time even such concepts as elasticity of demand and supply were novelties which had not yet been applied in the analysis of taxes from the context in price theory in which they appeared in Marshall's *Principles of Economics* (1890). Studies of public revenues proceeded largely according to the pattern set by J. S. Mill in Book V of his *Principles of Political Economy*, which Wicksell selected as his starting point for introducing the marginal utility and marginal productivity calculus into public finance. In this field his first aim was to extend the analysis of exchange value and production he had performed for an economy assumed to consist entirely of freely competitive private enterprises in *Value, Capital and Rent*, to the governmental sector of such an economy.

Wicksell reacted critically to the survival of certain beliefs based on the classical doctrine of taxation, and attempted to refute or modify them. These held in substance that:

1. Taxes on monopoly products cannot be shifted because they fall on net monopoly profits.

2. Among the most vicious of indirect taxes are tariffs because they distort the allocation of resources, unless they are offset by similar levies on domestic production. Further, they are shifted to domestic consumers and to unprotected domestic producers at a negligible net gain to the treasury and with substantial gains only for the protected producers.

3. Taxes on wages whether direct or indirect, and excises on wage goods, are always shifted to employers, and ultimately employers shift them to the rent of land. The reason is that labor working at a subsistence real wage cannot absorb these taxes without diminution in numbers, which, if it occurs, forces employers eventually to bid wages up by the amount of tax. Although wage taxes thus appear to rest on employers, they are often able to shift them to landowners by reducing their demand for agricultural products. A corollary of this doctrine, which proved difficult to uproot in certain quarters, was that labor ought not to resist the imposition of excises on wage goods, because, in the long run, it was not the laborer but someone else who actually paid these taxes to the treasury.

In order to come to grips with these beliefs, Wicksell decided first to develop a more systematic approach to the theory of taxation than he found in the public finance literature of the 1880's and 1890's.

METHOD AND ORIENTATION FOR THEORETICAL
RESEARCH IN TAXATION

To Wicksell's mind, a matter of prime importance in studies of taxation, is to have a clear distinction between the meaning of "shifting" and of "incidence" of taxes. The "incidence" of certain taxes is often greater than the amount of such taxes which are "shifted." At best only 100 per cent of a commodity tax can be shifted by a price rise from the seller to the buyer. But the incidence of such a tax, whether it is fully or partly shifted, is generally greater than the tax itself, hence also greater than the revenue collected.

Let us assume that an ad valorem tax is fully shifted forward to consumers. As a result purchases of the commodity in question are reduced according to the elasticity of its demand. The incidence of this tax then consists of several elements, not all of which are capable of direct measurement. First, there is the tax on the reduced quantity purchased. This sum equals the revenue the tax yields to the treasury. Secondly, there is the loss of utility to consumers who formerly bought more of this commodity and must now find less preferred substitutes. This element of incidence is not directly expressible in quantitative terms. Thirdly, the sellers of the taxed commodity probably have a reduced rate of profit on the reduced sales volume. This is another loss imposed by the tax without a corresponding benefit to the treasury.

Consequently, one of the primary problems of taxation is to design levies with a minimum of incidence, i.e., with an incidence not in excess of the revenue raised. This is approximately the case only with direct net income taxes. But if their secondary effects are considered, it is not altogether certain this would be true even of them.

However, studies of tax incidence must proceed under certain rules of which the following seemed indispensable to him. They should proceed from the assumption (a) that a certain amount of revenue has to be raised. Then (b) how this revenue may be raised with a minimum of incidence and disturbance to economic relations should be investigated. This involves finding the direction and extent of probable tax shifting under different types of taxes. Then (c) the secondary effects of these taxes must be determined, for instance, to what extent they would induce substitution of untaxed or less taxed commodities and/or factor uses for the taxed ones. In the fourth place, (d) all questions concerning the use to which the revenue is to be put must be ruled out as irrelevant in questions of tax incidence. Finally, (e) he held that the incidence of a tax system as a whole cannot be ascertained in any absolute sense. It can only be determined in a relative sense to the extent that it is possible to classify revenue systems composed of several types of taxes according to their relative degree of regressiveness, progressiveness, and the like.

These suggestions as to method were probably all to the good, except for point (d) above. In studies of tax incidence it may be legitimate in the very first approximation to rule out all questions concerning the uses of the corresponding revenues. But this abstraction should not be maintained very long. For instance, it is decidedly relevant to the incidence of an excise tax on some commodity whether the revenue it yields is used for subsidizing production of the taxed commodity itself, or possibly for subsidizing the production of some of its close substitutes.

However, under the foregoing rules, Wicksell focused his studies in taxation on the following problems:

1. Taxation of monopolies.
2. Uniform taxation of production under free competition.
3. Nonuniform or differentiated-rate taxation of particular goods and services under free competition.
4. The alleged shiftability of taxes imposed on wages.

In this connection one circumstance deserves passing mention. Wicksell's work on the first of these problems, monopoly taxation, arrived at findings which are rather similar to those stated in Cournot's *Researches into the Mathematical Principles of the Theory of Wealth* (chap. vi, pp. 67-78, 1838). However, he developed his treatment independently of Cournot. As a statement in the preface of *Finanztheoretische Untersuchungen* informs us (p. vi), it was only later, after this treatise had gone to press, that he became aware of Cournot's work in Italian translation, the only version then in existence.

WICKSELL'S CONCLUSIONS ON INCIDENCE AND SHIFTING OF TAXES

As a rule Wicksell pursued his analysis of taxation under assumptions of a closed, stationary economy with free competition on all markets, with fixed production functions, and with all exchanges calculated in *numéraire* or in money of constant purchasing power. One obvious exception was the taxation of monopolies, in which the assumption of free competition had to be relaxed. His conclusions for the cases he studied were of the following tenor.

1. A tax—proportional, progressive, lump sum, or otherwise—on net monopoly profit, and by analogy, on net income in general even under free competition, is not shifted, and its incidence equals the revenue it yields. However, there are secondary effects of net profits and net income taxes. The net income which is reduced by the tax implies either decreased consumption demand, or diminished saving and/or diminished investment by persons subject to the tax. Consequently, the conclusion that such a tax cannot be shifted is subject to a qualification. It cannot be shifted if the aggregate demand for factors of production is not affected by the reduction of net disposable income.[1] This qualification was repeated in his discussion with G. Cassel concerning the "secondary" shiftability of taxes on net income.

---
[1] Wicksell, *Finanztheoretische Untersuchungen* (Jena, 1896), p. 35.

Cassel held that such taxes are shifted to rents in situations where workers and capitalists reduce their consumption of agricultural products as a result of the tax, and where, by assumption, agriculture does not have access to new markets, domestic or foreign, in which to dispose of its "surplus" products.[2]

2. A uniform tax per unit of output levied on all types of production under free competition acts at first as a tax on net real income. It reduces real wages, rent, and interest in about equal proportion. But the tax is partly compensated for by the subsequent expansion of output. The reason for this is that capitalists who at first maintain the same structure of capital now find it advantageous to increase this structure in the height dimension. As a result, real output increases and real wages, rent, and interest rise toward but do not quite achieve the levels they had prior to the production tax.

On this basis it seems that a uniform production tax is an effective way of making an otherwise stationary society progressive.[3] As Lindahl has pointed out, here Wicksell's argument was arbitrary and erroneous.[4] He fell into a trap of his own making by abandoning the stationary assumption with which he started, and by looking at the consequences of the tax solely from the point of view of private capitalists in terms of its analogy with a rise in real wages.

This confuses two things, a uniform decline in the productivity of all factors because of the tax, and the decline in the marginal productivity of capital, other factors constant, during a period of net capital formation. In an otherwise stationary society, there is no reason why capitalists should be motivated to net investment simply because all types of net disposable incomes have been reduced proportionally by a tax. As a result of the tax, the government has in effect acquired an equity in or has confiscated a part of their real capital equal to the discounted value of the proceeds of the production tax.

To be sure, they can make up for this loss by further net accumulation. But it does not follow from the imposition of the tax that they will do this. A similar option; namely, to increase the quantity and value of their real capital by net investment was also open to them in the initial stationary equilibrium, but was not acted on.

---

[2] Cf. G. Cassel, "Om skatteincidens" (Concerning Incidence of Taxation), *Ekonomisk Tidskrift*, 1 (1899), 316-328; Wicksell, "Om överflyttning av skatt" (On Shifting of Taxes), *ibid.*, pp. 211-232, and "Ytterligare om överflyttning av skatt" (More About Shifting of Taxes), *ibid.*, pp. 383-387.

[3] Wicksell, *Finanztheoretische Untersuchungen*, pp. 37 ff.

[4] E. Lindahl, *Die Gerechtigkeit der Besteuerung* (Lund, Sweden, 1919), pp. 175-178 and especially p. 177 n.

The division of the production tax between the three factors, as Wicksell pointed out, depends on the elasticity of substitution between them and on their relative elasticities of supply. The factor with the greatest supply elasticity should be able to shift some of its pro rata share of the levy onto the other two factors.

3. A fixed tax per unit of product, or an ad valorem tax of a fixed percentage of value of product, were both shown to be shiftable under monopoly conditions and to involve greater incidence than the revenue obtained, the more so for the fixed tax per unit than for the ad valorem tax.

4. Nonuniform taxes per unit of product (uniform for units of the same commodity, but of different rates for different commodities) were shown to be shiftable under free competition. Such taxes affect the output of particular commodities as well as the proportion in which factors of production are used. In part, such taxes are forwarded to consumers according to the inelasticity of demand for the good in question, in part they are carried backward to the factors of production according to the relative inelasticity of supply of the latter. After requisite substitution adjustments have been made, a new set of equilibrium relations arise. But how these differ from the ones in the initial situation with no differentiated commodity taxes is impossible to tell with sufficient precision to assess the incidence of a group of such taxes.

In this connection Wicksell found occasion to deal critically with the free-trade doctrine. In substance, he was satisfied with pointing out that the difference between tariffs and nonuniform domestic excise taxes is only a matter of degree. Both distort the pattern of resource use, and both have an incidence of unspecifiable extent and in excess of the revenue they bring. Yet advocates of free trade have not censured excises nearly so vehemently as tariffs. To prove his point, Wicksell showed that one of the elements of incidence of a tariff is to reduce prices of domestic products which no longer find as much of an export market as before. Then he reverted to the infant industry argument to show that there are circumstances under which a tariff regime may improve the resource utilization and raise the real national income of a virgin colony, whereas free trade in such conditions may merely benefit the landed interest. By these means he wanted to emphasize the relative truth of the free-trade doctrine against certain extravagant claims made for it by some of its adherents.[5]

5. His treatment of "a tax on wages" involved a concise review of the wages fund doctrine, and with it a refutation of the alleged shift-

---

[5] Wicksell, *op. cit.*, pp. 58 ff.

ability of the wages tax. Some of the best writing in *Finanztheoretische Untersuchungen* was directed against the sophistries involved in this doctrine. The tax was supposed to be shifted by diminution of the number of workers as wages net of the tax are depressed below subsistence levels. Concerning this, Wicksell asked, would not the same option—reduction in number of workers—be open to labor at the pretax equilibrium level of wages? If so, at wages in excess of subsistence, why should all of a wages tax be shiftable? As to J. S. Mill's query, whether it is better for workers to be taxed a shilling per week, the state using the revenue to hire labor on public works, or to be free of the tax and the state to discontinue the public works, Wicksell raised the counterquestions: Does the state hire workers for their own sake, or for the useful labor they perform? Assuming the tax of a shilling per man per week is spent on works projects, what compensation is this? Is not the working class out the extra work performed under such a regime at no gain to itself but rather to other classes?

He pointed out further, in questions of shifting of taxes, there is generally some possibility of escape from the tax by individuals unwilling to pay it. The nonsmoker pays no tobacco tax. But when it comes to a tax on wages, there is little possibility of escaping it for the great majority.[6]

The foregoing may suffice to reveal the character of Wicksell's theory of incidence of taxes. One service he performed was to hold up to the light the seamy side of indirect taxes. That, in turn, raised an even broader question: What, if any, are the standards or criteria of equity or justice in taxation? It was to this problem he addressed the second part of *Finanztheoretische Untersuchungen*.

Principles of Equity or Justice in Taxation

WICKSELL'S PROPOSED METHOD FOR ACHIEVING "EQUITY" IN TAXATION

Wicksell's attempt to ascertain the theoretical principles for a "just" system of taxation, or for an equitable distribution of the tax burden onto the citizens, was a contribution to marginal utility theory. It was an attempt to extend the scope of this theory over the entire field of public finance primarily by relying on the benefit principle of taxation. In order to understand what he was trying to do, it may be helpful to bear the following contrast in mind. He was *not* directly *concerned with the grand problem of equity in taxation under any and all conditions*. To deal with it, one must be able to set up uni-

---

[6] *Ibid.*, p. 75.

versally acceptable standards of equity not alone for taxation, but for other social relations as well, such as property ownership and distribution of wealth. The history of philosophy records many ingenious and valiant attempts to do this, none of which, however, have become universally accepted among those best qualified to judge, the philosophers themselves. Instead, he addressed himself to the narrower problem of what are the criteria of equity in taxation *in societies about which one can assume a nearly unanimous approval by their members of the existing distribution of income and wealth.*[7]

There are two reasons for this, one historical and the other analytic. Toward the close of the nineteenth century influential writers on public finance, such as J. S. Mill and Adolph Wagner, placed increasing emphasis on using the tax apparatus not only for raising revenue but also for broader aims of social reform, particularly for achieving a more egalitarian distribution of income. This was generally referred to as *"die sozialpolitische Gesichtspunkt der Besteuerung"* (the social policy orientation in taxation). Concerning this, Wicksell said in substance that if the taxing power is to be used to expedite income-equalizing reforms, by confiscation of certain types of wealth, by steeply progressive profits tax rates, by capital levies, and the like, then this shows clearly that the distribution of wealth is regarded as inequitable by those who wield political power. One cannot fruitfully consider the question of equity in taxation as long as property relations between groups of citizens are undergoing major changes. But when these changes have been carried out, the modified property and income relations must presumably rest on a pervasive social consensus. After that there should be no occasion to use the taxing power in a confiscatory manner against any groups of citizens.

But this condition that the distribution of wealth must be almost unanimously approved by the members of society carried with it, at least implicitly, another prerequisite; namely, that all members of society be effectively represented in parliaments, legislatures, and local government councils in which questions of revenues and public expenditures are decided. This was by no means the case in the 1890's. At that time the franchise in Sweden was denied not only to women but also to most urban workers, tenant farmers, agricultural laborers, and

---

[7] *Ibid.*, pp. 143-144. In a later work of his on taxation, Wicksell said emphatically: "I claim that the very concept of taxation *presupposes* that all incomes are equally justified." Wicksell, "Inkomstbegreppet i skattehänseende och därmed sammanhängande skattefrågor" (The Income Concept in Taxation and Tax Problems Connected with This Concept), *Betänkande om Inkomst- och Förmögenhetsskatt*, II (Report on Income and Property Taxes, II), *Statens Offentliga Utredningar* (Official Reports of the Swedish Government), 1923:70 (Stockholm, 1923), p. 65.

others who could not meet the relatively high property qualifications imposed on the franchise.

Wicksell advocated abolition of all property restrictions on the franchise and its extension to all members of society above a stipulated minimum age. But universal suffrage was in his opinion not enough to guarantee "effective" representation. The latter required an electoral system based on proportional representation rather than on simple majority representation for electoral districts with approximately equal voting populations. He thought proportional representation was ideally suited to effectuate his principle of voluntariness in taxation.[8]

Now, if all interest groups of citizens are adequately represented in the legislature, and if they or their representatives regard the existing distribution of income and wealth as satisfactory, i.e., if they are sufficiently satisfied with it *not* to endeavor to change it in important respects by use of fiscal powers, then the basis for devising an "equitable" system of taxation is at hand. But according to what criteria should such a system be designed?

The literature of public finance exhibits two apparently opposed principles for levying taxes on the citizens, namely the criterion of "relatively equal sacrifice," and the "benefit" criterion.[9] Since the "relative equality" of tax sacrifice, or the relative "ability to bear" taxes, cannot be measured exactly, it is best measured as between in-

---

[8] *Ibid.*, pp. 123-124; in addition, some of his other writings emphasize these points. Thus in his tract *Våra Skatter—Hvilka betala dem och hvilka borde betala?* (Our Taxes: Who Pays Them and Who Ought To?), written under the pseudonym of Sven Trygg (Stockholm, 1894), his last chapter advocates extension of suffrage to the workers in particular as a prerequisite for achieving a more equitable system of taxation in Sweden. In his pamphlet, *Den politiska rösträtten och skatterna* (The Political Franchise and Taxation) (Stockholm, 1898), he argued for universal suffrage and proportional representation, adding that proportional representation per se may not be of great consequence in general political questions, whereas it becomes a matter of considerable practical importance under his tax system which accords an effective veto right to parliamentary minorities.

[9] The names given to the two tax principles in the text are liberal and abbreviated translations of longer designations given them by Wicksell. Thus, what we call the "principle of relatively equal sacrifice," he called "das Prinzip der Gleichheit oder Verhältnismässigkeit der gebrachten Opfer," and, alternately, "Besteuerung nach der Leistungsfähigkeit" (taxation according to ability to perform or to pay). What we call the "benefit principle" he called "das Prinzip der Gleichheit oder Verhältnismässigkeit zwischen Leistung und Gegenleistung" (the principle of equality or proportionality between performance—i.e., tax payment—and counter-performance—i.e., value or benefit of government services), and alternately, "Besteuerung nach dem Interesse" (taxation according to "interest," meaning according to the person's or group's interest in the benefits conferred on him or it by services rendered by the government). Cf. *Finanztheoretische Untersuchungen*, p. 77.

dividual citizens by their incomes. Because personal incomes are subject to diminishing marginal utility as they increase in quantity, the "equal sacrifice" criterion is the principle which justifies progressive taxes on net incomes as the best available measure of "ability to pay" and hence of "relatively equal" sacrifice.

Wicksell had no quarrel with this and accepted the "ability to pay" principle as a perfectly *valid basis for distributing a given tax burden.* As we shall see, he gave ample scope to this principle in his system of "equitable taxation." But, pointing to the work of Sax and Mazzola, he decided to base his system on the "benefit" principle.

In this connection, however, Emil Sax as well as writers, mostly Italians, who have followed the path he opened up, placed a higher goal before themselves when they applied the idea of marginal utility and of value *not only to the distribution, but also to the determination of the concrete level of taxes.* By doing this they have indeed transformed, or wanted to transform, the entire problem of equitable taxation from an ethical into a purely scientific problem.[10]

The ability principle could not be applied directly to the determination of the total magnitude of public expenditures, nor to the proportions in which this total should be distributed over the many competing functions and services of the government. In the absence of clear criteria concerning this, there was the danger that the services of government, and with it public expenditures, would be expanded more and more without definable limit. If the corresponding increasing tax burden were strictly distributed according to "relative equality of sacrifice," in extreme cases this might result in complete equalization of incomes *after* taxes. This, in turn, might well have disastrous consequences for private initiative and economic incentives.

The benefit principle, on the other hand, can and should be applied to expenditures as well as to revenue measures. It is true that total benefits of government services cannot be measured by this principle any more than the total utility of any commodity. But to do so is neither necessary nor relevant. In questions of providing public services and arranging for their proper support, it is seldom necessary to decide whether an important group of services, such as defense or administration of justice, is to be continued or to be abolished totally. It is almost always a question of whether some should be expanded while others might be curtailed; and still further it is a question of whether taxes as a whole must be increased to accomplish this result,

---

[10] *Ibid.,* p. 86.

and if so, what taxes and by what increments. These problems are not essentially different from those faced by consumers in purchasing goods and services. Decisions of this type are properly subject to the marginal utility calculus.

However, the benefit principle does not imply that the tax levied on the citizen must be equal or proportionate to the benefits he receives from the services of the government. First of all, many of these services provide only general benefits which cannot be separated nor identified as being conferred on particular individuals. Police protection and public sanitation are good examples of this. But beyond this, all that is necessary to justify a proposed service and a corresponding public expenditure under the benefit principle is that the value of the additional service be considered at least equal to the tax required to support it. This very frequently means that some citizens receive more benefits from the service than others, even benefits greatly in excess of the tax they must contribute.

For instance, well-to-do families are taxed at progressive rates for the maintenance of "free" public schools. Since many of these families send their children to private schools, it is clear that they receive fewer benefits from the public-school system than do working-class families whose children probably would receive little or no schooling if it were not for the public system of education. To be sure, working-class families are also taxed for the support of public schools. But, they are taxed far less per family and less relative to their income than are wealthy families. Yet, on pure benefit principle grounds, one would expect the well-to-do, or their representatives in the legislature, to vote for school taxes, as long as they consider the benefits to themselves as individuals, or as a class, of a public system of education to be at least equal to the taxes which are imposed on them. Among these benefits are the security and comfort which comes from living in a community where public-school education is universal, where an informed public opinion scrutinizes and judges the actions of government as well as of individuals.

Now, it was Wicksell's idea that just as the distribution of wealth should rest on a nearly unanimous social consensus in rationally developed societies, so should questions of increases or decreases of taxes and of expenditures for government services in such societies also be decided, ideally on the basis of unanimous consent, and practically by "qualified majorities," i.e., on the basis of near-unanimity. He did not specify what he meant by "qualified majority." Essentially, he meant a vote by the elected representatives of the people substantially in excess of 51 per cent and as close as possible to 100 per cent. He spoke interchangeably of qualified majorities as two-thirds, three-quarters, and even 90 per cent of the representatives.[11]

This was the essence of his "principle of voluntariness and relative) unanimity in tax decisions";[12] namely, that decisions on public expenditures and on taxes should be made *simultaneously* in parliament.[13] Members of parliament should be guided in these decisions by considerations of marginal service benefit compared with the marginal tax or cost involved on proposed services, and these decisions should be subject to qualified majority approval. He recognized only three types of exceptions in which decisions were to be made by simple majorities, and *all other* expenditure and tax questions should be enacted by qualified majorities. The exceptions were concerned with (a) questions where only two mutually exclusive alternatives are open and a third one is not attainable or not possible, (b) matters of financing the government's "obligations," and (c) decisions on a classification in the initial budget proposal in which the various taxes and other sources of government revenues are provisionally "earmarked" or allocated as support for the several categories or groups of government services.[14]

Wicksell did not think these three types of simple majority decisions would occur very often, and in any case that they would arise only infrequently in questions concerning *taxation,* although this might not hold with respect to expenditures. The first exception would affect taxation only to the extent that the community holds certain types of income and forms of wealth to be unjust, and therefore properly subject to mildly or severely confiscatory forms of taxation. What he had in mind here was particularly taxes on inheritances, and on land value increments which are principally due to the growth of population and its concentration in cities. But even here he favored caution and averred that it would be far better for the community if decisions on

---

[11] *Ibid.,* p. 117.

[12] We have adopted this translation of Wicksell's phrase "Das Prinzip der (relativen) Einstimmigkeit und Freiwilligkeit der Steuerbewilligung" (*Finanztheoretische Untersuchungen,* p. 110 *passim*) from Duncan Black's recent article, "Wicksell's Principle in the Distribution of Taxation," in *Economic Essays in Commemoration of the Dundee School of Economics 1931-1955,* edited by J. K. Eastham (Dundee, Scotland, 1955), pp. 7-23, see particularly p. 10 and n. 4.

[13] *Finanztheoretische Untersuchungen,* pp. 115-116 and p. 156.

[14] Simple majority rule for decisions is prescribed in *Finanztheoretische Untersuchungen,* (1) when "one of two mutually exclusive alternatives must be chosen and a third is not attainable or possible," p. 111; (2) in the financing of "obligations" of the government, p. 118, particularly the payment of interest and amortization on the existing public debt, pp. 119-121; and (3) when the provisional allocation of government revenue sources to groups of government services and expenditure objects must be determined, p. 120.

these matters were taken by qualified majorities, provided the land-owners and prospective heirs to sizable fortunes directly affected would not be permitted to participate in the decision nor to block it.[15]

However, in questions of expenditures the first exception introduced an apparent contradiction in his system. Suppose a national health insurance bill is introduced and passed by a 60 per cent majority. In due course, this measure along with others comes before parliament's budget sessions with an estimate of its cost and some recommendation as to how it is to be financed. If the qualified majority required for its incorporation in the final appropriated budget is 90 per cent of the members, it is clear that the minority can block its passage at this stage by simply refusing to vote for any of several alternative tax or finance proposals made for the bill.

What saves his system from inconsistency is that in most such matters there is a third alternative, but this is not true for all expenditure-objects. In the present case, it is not a question of there being no health services available unless parliament enacts a health insurance act. The third alternative is that if no public health insurance is provided, the community may form voluntary associations to provide it, as compared with having to continue to rely only on private health services. And Wicksell would have added that if the proposed health insurance cannot obtain the qualified majority necessary to provide for its finance, then this is presumptive proof that this service does not belong among the objects of collective wants (properly to be served by government), but among the objects of private wants (properly to be served by private enterprise or by voluntary associations).

However, national defense is clearly an object of collective wants. Now if a bill proposing an expansion in defense activities receives a parliamentary majority smaller than the qualified majority and consequently is blocked by minority action when it comes to appropriating revenues for its support then there is no third alternative. Generally, it would be unrealistic to say that the desired defense expansion can be provided by private enterprise. Hence there are expenditure objects of collective wants which can be vetoed by recalcitrant parliamentary minorities. Wicksell was not unaware of this possibility,[16] but he developed his system on assumptions which would make it unlikely that minorities would exercise their veto power in an obstructionist manner.

The second exception to qualified majority decisions was the matter of "obligations of the government," particularly the contractual rate

---

[15] *Ibid.*, pp. 144-145.
[16] *Ibid.*, pp. 157-158.

of interest to be paid on its *existing* public debt, payment of pensions to retired civil servants, armed forces personnel, and the like. He held that the benefit-tax-cost calculus could not be applied here, because these were *fixed obligations,* and therefore decisions as to how these were to be financed should be made by simple majority vote. But decisions to *increase these obligations or to incur new ones,* for instance, by expanding the public debt for defense or public works purposes, were decidedly to be subject to qualified majority decisions. The reason was that capitalists as a class have a vested interest in expansion of the public debt, because the taxes they are apt to have to pay toward the interest payments on the debt are likely to be much smaller than the interest payments they receive from the treasury in their capacity of owners of government bonds.

Wicksell thought the types of "obligations" of government would be so few that they could readily be listed in the constitution. As for financing them, he thought that, first of all, revenues from government enterprises should be used for this purpose. To the extent that these might be insufficient, taxes based on the ability principle would have to be relied on. But the rates of these taxes must be varied in proportion to the greater-than-average benefits which certain groups of citizens or certain localities receive from the objects for which the obligations were incurred. Thus if the public debt was increased to build a bridge in a town, the taxpayers of that town, who receive the primary benefit from it, should contribute much more in income and property taxes than other taxpayers to paying interest and amortization on the corresponding debt. However, taxpayers generally would also be called on to contribute to its financing insofar as the benefits yielded are not entirely local in character.

The third exception, that the provisional allocation of taxes and other revenues to government services be decided by simple majorities, was necessary for the introduction of his principle of voluntariness of taxation into parliament. This provisional allocation would serve as an agenda for debates, compromises, and amendments on expenditure and tax items during parliament's budget sessions. The final, appropriated budget allocation of taxes and other revenues to expenditure objects was expected to be quite different from the provisional one. And this final budget was, of course, to be approved by a qualified majority.

Before we consider how he thought his "principle of voluntariness in taxation" would operate in a parliamentary setting, we must pause to inquire about the rationale on which his "equitable" system of taxation was based.

THE RATIONALE UNDERLYING WICKSELL'S TAX SYSTEM

It has been claimed, by Mr. Black for instance,[17] that Wicksell constructed his "voluntarist" tax system on the analogy of the market and as in line with the trend toward increasing liberty and democratic development in the political institutions of his day. In essence this position amounts to a claim that just as we voluntarily buy goods and services in the market, so should we arrange our system of taxation, by which we pay for government services, on a voluntary or consent basis insofar as that is possible. This claim cannot be denied nor ignored, for Wicksell did indeed express himself in this vein here and there in *Finanztheoretische Untersuchungen* in defense of his proposal.

Yet this explains only a small part of the nature of his system. We are inclined to believe that the major part of its rationale is accounted for by his reaction to changes which were enacted into Sweden's tax system prior to his writing *Finanztheoretische Untersuchungen,* and which, in large part, prompted him to undertake this volume. Secondly, he looked ahead to changes in the power relations between the working and the propertied classes, which were in their beginning stages in the 1890's. The tax system he devised was in no small measure addressed to a future period when these changes would have occurred.

In 1894 he wrote a tract, *Våra Skatter—Hvilka betala dem och hvilka borde betala?* (Our Taxes—Who Pays Them and Who Ought To?), in which he also propounded his proposal for an "equitable" system of taxation in an abbreviated form. However, the major part of that work was concerned with a survey of the nature of Sweden's revenue system. He found that about 90 per cent of total revenues were obtained from indirect taxes on commodities, mostly excise and tariff duties. These taxes were by no means limited to luxury goods, such as tobacco and alcoholic beverages. They extended to a wide variety of necessities such as sugar, meats, flour, etc. He also found that the proportion of revenues from indirect taxes to total revenues had increased. A landowner-dominated parliament had recently acted in its own class interest by abolishing some and by substantially reducing other taxes on rural and urban land and improvements. If the parliament had limited its action to this tax reduction alone, a budget deficit would have developed. To guard against that, it made up for its reduction in property taxes by raising the rates of several excises and tariffs, and by extending taxes of this type to certain commodities

---

[17] D. Black, "Wicksell's Principle in the Distribution of Taxation," in *Economic Essays in Commemoration of the Dundee School of Economics 1931-1955,* p. 10.

which had previously been free of tax. He concluded that the primary reason the landowner-interest had succeeded in perpetrating this injustice was that the working class was not represented in parliament.

However, he went on to say, the disfranchisement of the workers is unlikely to be permanent. Sooner or later they will acquire the right to vote, and since they outnumber other groups in society, their representatives will then outnumber those of other classes and come to dominate parliament. Unless a reform such as his proposed method for achieving equity in taxation is adopted as a preventive measure and written into the constitution, prior to the workers' accession to political dominance, they might, guided by the examples of those who preceded them in power, resort to extravagant expenditures for state services for which they pay almost no tax and impose taxes which will confiscate much of the wealth and will severely reduce the incomes of the propertied classes. Such measures are bound to result not only in the virtual cessation of further capital formation, but also in wanton destruction of existing capital on a large scale if property owners are forced to liquidate existing investments to meet greatly increased tax liabilities.

Capital destruction would amount to a catastrophe for a country such as Sweden, which was then suffering from chronic capital shortage, and was forced to borrow abroad to obtain the capital needed to build railroads, power projects, and to expand the country's forest products and engineering industries. It was *this* that he wanted to avoid with his proposal for an equitable system of taxation. His real concern was not to protect the middle and upper classes in their possession of property; it was rather to protect his country's slender capital resources from destruction. Moreover, he realized that changes in the distribution of income in favor of the working class were both inevitable and desirable. The thought in the back of his mind—made explicit in a tract he wrote a decade later, *Socialiststaten och nutidssamhället* (The Socialist State and Contemporary Society, Stockholm, 1905)—was that the workers have relatively little to gain from income redistribution per se, especially in the short run. On the other hand they have everything to gain from influences, such as technological change and growth of real capital, which increase productivity as a whole. Their strategy should consequently be one of making sure that they obtain an increasing share of the increasing social product that the future has in store. This, of course, is more directly a matter of wage bargaining than it is one of taxation. However, as a long-run policy a good deal can be accomplished by way of income redistribution by progressive inheritance taxes and by taxes on "unearned" land value increments.

Now, if labor's arrival to power is sudden, then some capital destruction probably cannot be avoided. Income and property relations between the working and other classes might be changed rapidly and drastically. But if, as he thought was more likely, the workers' rise to power would occur over a long period, as in one, two, or more decades, then changes in distribution of income and wealth between them and other classes, will for the most part have been completed during this interval. In that case society is likely to have adjusted to these changes without upheavals. The economy is also likely to have accommodated itself to them, not only without destruction of real capital but in a manner which provides for its continued and possibly increased growth.[18]

Once these changes have been completed and the leaders of the politically dominant workers recognize that nothing can be gained from further efforts at redistribution, i.e., that the then-existing income distribution is optimal or "equitable," then these same leaders may be persuaded to adopt and apply Wicksell's "principle of voluntariness and (relative) unanimity in tax decisions." If they do this, then the nature of parliamentary budget work also changes considerably. Taxes, traditionally viewed as evils to be avoided, are now seen in the light of a *quid pro quo* for government services of at least equal or greater value. This may indeed lead to an expansion of government services, which is often so bitterly opposed by groups who, under a system of simple majority decisions, cannot protect their legitimate interest and rights, but who would have that opportunity under his proposal.[19] The result may be that the government takes over all functions which it can perform better than private enterprise.

Since confiscatory use of the taxing power is no longer to be applied, there can be no serious objection to the requirement of qualified majority approval of tax and expenditure decisions. The veto power this gives to political minorities will be their primary means of protecting and promoting their legitimate interests. Why should minorities be protected by this special device? Since the income positions of the upper- and middle-class minorities have been modified to the point where no significant gain will accrue to the majority by disturbing them further, these minorities must have the means of maintaining their position and preserving their identity. Political minorities are indispensable in an economic sense, for most of the administrative,

---

[18] *Finanztheoretische Untersuchungen*, p. 122.
[19] *Ibid.*, p. 115 and Preface, p. vii.

entrepreneurial, and professional skills available to society are found among their members.[20]

Once his system was adopted, Wicksell assumed that no party in parliament would propose new government services or extensions of existing services *which would not appear to be useful and desirable* (apart from the tax costs involved) *to all other parties.* Proposals would, of course, not seem equally desirable to all parties, but the point is that no party would bring out measures which were offensive or hostile to other parties. It was by means of this assumption[21] he thought to obviate conflicts which might arise about some measures which were to be approved by simple majorities since it might be possible for a small minority to veto them in budget sessions. His reasoning on this point was as follows. If a proposed service seems desirable to all parties, then all that is required for its adoption is to decide how much of it is wanted and how it is to be financed. There are many ways of financing a proposed expenditure—by special taxes, by portions of general levies, by fees, by borrowing, and by combinations of these methods. It is expected that several methods of financing the proposed service will be considered in the budget session. Each participant must evaluate the benefit of the service to his constituents against the additional taxes they would have to pay for it under the various financing plans. He must vote for only those proposals for which the benefit seemed greater than or at least equal to the tax imposed.

Some finance plans will receive more votes than others, and many of the same persons who vetoed a proposal under one finance plan would be likely to vote for it on another which they consider more favorable to their constituents. Now, if in the opinion of all, the proposed service is desirable, if it is to be supported by taxes which no one regards as confiscatory, and if there are still enough representatives opposed to it to veto its passage because they feel its tax cost exceeds its benefits to their constituents, then, said Wicksell, the service is not unequivocally an object of collective wants. Then it had better be supplied by private enterprise or by voluntary associations. Consequently, objects of collective wants, which define the scope of government functions and services—except for those few functions which are exempt from qualified majority approval—are those, and those only, for which members of a thoroughly representative parliament will vote nonconfiscatory tax and other finance support on a nearly unanimous basis.

What has been said here about proposed new government services

---

[20] *Ibid.*, p. 159.
[21] *Ibid.*, p. 112-113.

or extension of existing ones, holds also for the replacement of one tax by another in the support of government services. It must be approved by a qualified majority.

But when it came to proposals for abolishing a government service and the corresponding taxes, Wicksell would, for the sake of simplicity, have let parliamentary minorities initiate these proposals and have them pass, unless a qualified majority overrode them.[22] Although this may be a very obvious corollary from the logic of qualified majorities, this gave much too much power to minorities and would in practice have given his system a tax-and-expenditure-reduction bias.

One may or may not be willing to grant the presuppositions on the basis of which Wicksell elaborated his system of "equitable" taxation. Nonetheless, it is clear that something like the perspective he and some of his followers, such as Lindahl,[23] employed in this field of study will eventually be necessary to reduce to order, rather than to leave to drift, the relations between the public (governmental) and the private enterprise sectors of the economy. Lines of demarcation, probably flexible ones, must eventually be established between activities which belong properly to "government" and those which properly belong to "business."

THE DECISION PROCEDURE IN WICKSELL'S SYSTEM OF TAXATION

Let us assume a society in which all interest groups are effectively represented and in which the distribution of income and wealth is approved by all groups. Labor is the dominant party and has agreed to try Wicksell's proposed system. In his own treatment Wicksell gave only the sketchiest indication of how he thought his proposal would operate in a parliamentary setting.[24] It is clear that he had not thought through this part of his problem and that he had no idea of the procedural difficulies it involved nor of the peculiar results it would lead to. Mr. Black is apparently the only scholar who has given this problem the benefit of careful analysis, and here we shall make use of several of his findings.[25]

The first difficulty that arises is that members of parliament must agree, by simple majority votes, on a preliminary allocation of the

---

[22] *Ibid.*, p. 120.

[23] E. Lindahl's book, *Die Gerechtigkeit der Besteuerung* (Lund, Sweden, 1919), carries forward Wicksell's treatment of this problem on a more realistic level of analysis.

[24] *Finanztheoretische Untersuchungen*, p. 117.

[25] D. Black, "Wicksell's Principle in the Distribution of Taxation," *Economic Essays in Commemoration of the Dundee School of Economics 1931-1955*, edited by J. K. Eastham (Dundee, Scotland, 1955), pp. 7-23.

government's various sources of revenue to its even more numerous services and expenditure objects. As Black points out,[26] if there were only twenty taxes, all of the same yield, and twenty different types of expenditures, each of the same amount, the number of possible combinations of expenditures and taxes would be 400. Clearly the number of different taxes and expenditures is much greater than twenty, and the problem is further compounded by the fact that the taxes do not have equal yields, and that several revenue sources in combination are used to finance many types of expenditures. It is doubtful that any contemporary legislature would be able to carry out this preliminary part of Wicksell's plan even with the aid of electric recording of votes and modern computing machines to list the very large number of expenditure-tax combinations to be voted on.

As Black puts it: "Wicksell's procedure would provide a position of stable equilibrium, but *only after a number of series of votes.*" [27]

Black shows clearly that Wicksell's qualified majority requirement introduces a very considerable restraint against increasing expenditures.

Let us adopt Mr. Black's method and imagine a parliament of only 100 members, and that the qualified majority required to pass tax-and-expenditure measures is 90 per cent of the members. Now we assume that the preference curves of the members of parliament have "single-peaked optima," and that we can array their expenditure-preference curves from lowest to highest. We also assume that each member places at least one motion in favor of that level of expenditure he thinks most desirable before parliament.

The enormous amount of parliamentary work this may involve becomes clear if we consider that parliament may then have before it 100 different motions on a proposed item. To determine conclusively which of the 100 motions will be adopted may involve 100 series of votes if members are free to reintroduce motions defeated in earlier votes. For 100 motions and an initial condition, the number of votes that may be required for determination of the issue is no less than 4,480 separate votes.

When parliament has 100 motions before it to change the initial expenditure a_0 by various amounts, a few members may have moved to decrease it, but others have moved to increase it by various amounts. But whether or not a_0 shall be increased at all depends on the relationship between the expenditure level corresponding to the optimum on the preference curve of the eleventh from the lowest among the 100

---

[26] *Ibid.*, p. 16.
[27] *Ibid.*, p. 14. Italics supplied.

arrayed preference curves and the expenditure magnitude a_0. If the expenditure level on the eleventh lowest preference curve is less than a_0, then a_0 will not be increased at all but will remain as it is, because then there will be no motion for increasing a_0 which will receive more than 89 votes, i.e., one less than the required qualified majority. If that expenditure level is greater than a_0 then a_0 will be increased, however, not to the level proposed by the majority, a_1, but to less by an amount found at the optimum on the eleventh lowest expenditure-preference curve.

Under a system of simple majority approval, the probability is that, in similar circumstances, the increase in a_0 would be determined by the expenditure level corresponding to the optimum on the forty-ninth lowest expenditure-preference curve. Black's conclusions concerning this seem entirely justified:

Here it is well to notice two distinct difficulties. . . . The first is that a position of stable equilibrium is only approached gradually. The result given by Wicksell's procedure at one vote must be expected to be upset when the matter is next discussed and a new set of votes taken. The next difficulty is inequity . . . in the general case [i.e., with simple majorities] there would be . . . a strong presumption in favor of a decision somewhere in the neighborhood of O_{50} [i.e., the fiftieth preference curve in the array]. *This would take into account the opinions held by all of the members. In contrast the final Wicksellian solution depends on the opinions of a handful of members who hold extreme views.* It protects a particular minority . . . who are least keen . . . to increase this item of expenditure and the associated taxes, but at the expense of the majority.[28]

On the other hand, if the valuations of members of parliament are complementary rather than independent, as was assumed above, then a further complication arises. Normally their valuations would be complementary, i.e., some members' willingness to approve of expenditures a, b, and c, and associated taxes, may very well be dependent on whether some other expenditures, e, f, and g are accepted. In such cases, Black concludes:

It can be shown that in these circumstances the expenditure chosen by Parliament in any particular line, and the corresponding tax, will *depend on the order in which the items of expenditure come before it for discussion;* and if a decision in regard to an item is made at one date and the matter is afterwards rediscussed, Parliament at this later date will in general alter its earlier decision, even though the members' preference functions remain unchanged.[29]

[28] *Ibid.*, p. 15. Italics supplied.
[29] *Ibid.*, p. 15. Italics supplied.

However, when it comes to curtailing a state service and reducing expenditures and corresponding taxes, Wicksell wanted to give the initiative to parliamentary minorities, who would automatically be successful, unless overridden by a qualified majority. In this matter Wicksell's meaning as to the procedure to be followed is ambiguous. As Black puts it:

Let us suppose, for instance, that the three motions a_1, a_2, and a_3 have been put forward, of which a_1 proposes a certain reduction, and a_2 a larger reduction, and a_3 a larger reduction still, in the height of a certain item of expenditure and in the associated tax. As against a_0 (the proposal that the existing state of affairs continue unchanged), a_1 say, gets a 100 percent majority, a_2 a 60 percent majority, and a_3 an 11 percent majority. It is not possible to tell from Wicksell's own words which of these three motions should be chosen. I think the simplest interpretation to give to his rule would be that *that motion is to be accepted which proposes the greatest reduction in expenditure*, provided it is able to get a minority of over 10 percent of the votes cast.[30]

What will happen depends again on how many motions are presented and on the expenditure levels corresponding to the optima of the members' preference functions arrayed from lowest to highest. Expenditure item a_0 will be reduced if its magnitude exceeds the expenditure level of the optimum of the eleventh lowest of the preference functions. Moreover, it will be reduced to the optimum of that function, for at any level higher than this motions for further reduction receive more than 10 per cent of the votes cast and cannot be overridden because opposing votes are short of the required qualified majority.

Even after giving Wicksell the benefit of the presuppositions on which he based his system, particularly the assumption that members of parliament will *not* propose expenditure and tax measures which are *hostile* or *offensive* to any political minority, Black's evaluation can hardly be gainsaid:

Inside Parliament Wicksell's principle, by requiring a high majority for an increase of expenditure and a very small minority for a reduction, would make increases in expenditure far more difficult and reductions far easier than with the normal requirement of a simple majority. The bias would be toward curtailment and reduction. . . . There is no doubt that the effect of his scheme would be severely restrictive of state expenditure. The principle would protect (certain) parliamentary minorities at the expense of the parliamentary majority.[31]

---

[30] *Ibid.*, pp. 16-17. Italics supplied.
[31] *Ibid.*, pp. 20-21.

However, in addition to this procedural proposal, Wicksell also elaborated a theory of how taxes of various types, i.e., based on different "principles," such as the confiscation, the benefit, and the ability-to-pay principles should be related to one another in an "equitable" system of public finance. This topic is the subject of the next section.

Wicksell's Theory of the Interrelationship between Taxes

A well-rounded theory of public finance, particularly one which stresses the need for simultaneous consideration of expenditures and taxes, should state the nature and justification for the various types of taxes to be used and the relations of these to one another. It should also explain the functions and expenditures the government is supposed to serve, and the relationship between the latter and the taxes. Wicksell never succeeded in writing such a theory.

After having stated his procedural plan for equitable taxation, he went on to comment on fees as a form of revenue, and on the principles according to which public enterprises should charge for their services. Then he briefly considered direct versus indirect taxes, as well as the problem of taxation versus an increase in the public debt. Finally he discussed taxes on inheritances and on unearned land value increments. His follower Lindahl elaborated these fragments into a comprehensive theory of taxation in *Die Gerechtigkeit der Besteuerung* (1919). Incidentally, this work received Wicksell's approbation since it was Lindahl's doctoral thesis and Wicksell was called in as one of his examiners. We shall follow Lindahl's procedure here and consider first taxes based on the confiscation principle, and then those based on the benefit and ability principles.

CONFISCATORY TAXES

Wicksell stressed the fact that there are certain types of private income and wealth in the existing economic order, which society regards as unjust and unjustifiable. Among these are inheritances of great estates, "unearned" increments in the value of land, gains accruing to big corporate enterprise from the possession of various degrees of monopoly power, speculative gains of certain types, and gains made by the debtor interest in the community at the expense of creditors and persons on relatively fixed-income status in the course of sustained periods of inflation. Since these aggravate the inequality in distribution of income and property and pose other serious problems as well, society has not only the right but also the duty to correct, so far as it can, their undesirable consequences. To that end society can and should confiscate them in part or whole, by certain types of taxes. In effect these are not "taxes" at all; rather they are the methods whereby society takes for the common good a portion of what has unjustly come into the possession of a few individuals.

Since these forms of wealth exist only in the form of capital or investments, the government's taking them, mostly in part, rarely *in toto,* posed a problem of possible capital destruction. If the proceeds of "confiscation-principle" taxes were used for the current outlays of government, a corresponding amount of social consumption of capital would occur. But if the yields of these taxes were invested in public enterprises of various type, then the total quantity of society's capital would not have suffered any reduction but only a change in form.

In his writings on public finance in the 1890's Wicksell took the position that proceeds of confiscation taxes, in addition to possible net revenues from government enterprises, should be used to pay interest and amortization in the public debt.[32] Later he changed his position and advocated that the yields of these taxes should be "funded" or invested by the state. The proceeds of the public investments which would be created in this manner should be used to provide a "social inheritance" or "dividend" for the citizens. It should be used primarily to provide full maintenance to impecunious youths with a proven capacity and an earnest desire for pursuing higher education, and for helping other young persons to set up homes or get a start in a business or trade.[33]

---

[32] *Finanztheoretische Untersuchungen,* p. 145.

[33] The "funding" of the yield of confiscation-taxes is stressed in Wicksell, "Inkomstbegreppet i skattehänseende och därmed sammanhängande skattefrågor" (The Concept of Income in Taxation and Tax Problems Connected with This Concept), *Betänkande om Inkomst och Förmögenhetsskatt* (Report on Taxation of Income and Property), II, *Särskilda Utredningar* (Special Reports), *Statens Offentliga Utredningar* (Official Reports of the Swedish Government), 1923:70, Finansdepartementet (The Department of Finance) (Stockholm, 1923), pp. 46, 57, 59. Hereafter cited as *Betänkande om Inkomst och Förmögenhetsskatt,* II (1923). The social dividend use of the investment yields of "funded" confiscation taxes was stressed in Wicksell's tract, *Socialiststaten och Nutidssamhället* (The Socialist State and Contemporary Society, Stockholm, 1905), pp. 21, 22, 29, 30, 32, 33, and 34. There he estimated that if the Swedish national income of that time were capitalized at 5 per cent, the national wealth of Sweden would amount to 9 billion crowns, and if this sum were divided by the 1.25 million couples of marriageable age, 25 years and over, it would amount to a sum of 7 to 8,000 crowns per couple as their per-family share of the national wealth. This sum, he averred, would be quite adequate for most of them to establish homes and/or to obtain vocational or professional training or go into small businesses of various sorts. The purchasing power of such a sum at that time probably exceeded but at any rate must have equaled the purchasing power of an equal amount of dollars now. Wicksell implied that thoroughgoing and steep taxation of inheritances would enable even a nonsocialist state to provide its marriageable couples in due course with a "social inheritance" approaching this amount, and he thought that, with

He thought that inheritance taxes should be made steeply progressive,[34] partly in order to complement other property taxes and thus
help make property taxes as a whole more progressive than they were.
He also felt that a reform of the right to bequeath wealth was needed.
Under the legislation of the times, 50 per cent of a wealthy man's
estate had to be willed or given to members of his immediate family;
only the remainder could be willed in other directions. This, said
Wicksell, is a severe restriction on "the right to give." He had in mind
that certain norms should be set up as to how much a wealthy person
should be able to leave to his widow and each of his children. This
should be sufficient only to support them in comfort and to provide
them with a reasonable start in life. He felt that it was a disservice
both to the individuals concerned and to society for wealthy men's
children to be "burdened" by large inheritances which "condemn them
to an aimless life of leisure." So, while he wanted to liberalize the
"right to give," he also wanted to restrict, by inheritance taxes, heirs'
"right to receive." [35]

What he seems to have had in mind with respect to large estates was
that the individual should be free to accumulate as large an estate as
he wishes. Under the kind of inheritance tax he advocated, the legator
would be aware that even though he bequeathed his entire fortune to
his widow and children, the state would step in and reduce the
amounts they would be permitted to receive to the norms mentioned
above. If the legator did not wish the difference between the value of
his estate and the amounts thereof which his heirs would be permitted
to receive to go to the state, he should be free to bequeath this portion
of it elsewhere, particularly to eleemosynary institutions, and notably
to institutions of learning. He feared that a steep inheritance tax
coupled with a narrowly circumscribed "right to bequeath" might
impair inducements to accumulation and savings, while such a tax
coupled with an expanded "right to give" would not be likely to have
this consequence.

The next form of wealth he thought properly to be subject to progressive taxation was "unearned" land value increments.[36] These are
a common phenomenon in growing urban communities as well as in
regions recently "opened up" to more intensive economic exploitation
as a result of expansion and improvements in networks of transporta-

---

appropriate policies to keep the increase of population within narrow bounds, a
socialist state would be able to achieve this more readily than one based on
private property and private enterprise.

[34] *Finanztheoretische Untersuchungen,* p. 150.

[35] *Ibid.,* pp. 146-148.

[36] *Ibid.,* p. 150.

tion and communication. Value gains that land has received up to the present should not be disturbed, but, from the time of enactment of this type of tax, all future "unearned" value increments should be taxed on a regular schedule, and not only at times of sale. However, care must be taken not to tax value increments due to or "earned" by the owners' effort.

In other words, if a given piece of land registers a substantial value gain between two successive assessments, and its owner can point to outlays he has made for improving this land, then the unearned-value-increments-tax should be applied in such a manner that the owner is able to recover his outlays for improvements plus normal interest on the latter *after* paying this tax. Wicksell was apparently unaware what a difficult problem this would pose at the level of tax administration.

"Unearned" incomes or gains in general should, in his opinion, be taxed more heavily than "earned" ones.[37] Apart from those which arise on land, many arise in the process of speculation in corporate shares and commodities. However, speculation as such is a useful economic activity. It tends to narrow the amplitude of temporary price fluctuations. Moreover, ordinarily—that is to say when the general level of prices is not changing decidedly in one direction or another —the gains of some speculators tend to cancel out against the losses of others. Consequently, he was not certain that there was any justification for special taxes on speculative gains "in ordinary times." [38]

Monopoly gains, particularly those which arise within large-scale corporate enterprises, he thought properly to be subject to a "super-tax," provided the law allowed full offset when losses occurred.[39] In an earlier connection, we have pointed out that he advocated that enterprises tending toward monopoly in various branches of production should be taken over by the state and operated as public enterprises. However, he realized that the "degree" of monopoly power large businesses possess is not easy to measure, hence only the most monopolistic ones would probably be taken over, leaving a remainder of other enterprises in possession of a lesser degree of monopoly power. As for loss offsets on the supertaxes to be placed on their monopoly gains, he once intimated that not only should full loss offsets be permitted against these taxes, but the yields of these taxes from enterprises with "gains" might properly be gathered in a fund from which they should be disbursed to *compensate* other enterprises for "un-

[37] Wicksell, *Våra Skatter—Hvilka betala dem och hvilka borde betala?* (Our Taxes: Who Pays Them and Who Ought To? Stockholm, 1894), pp. 50-51.

[38] *Finanztheoretische Untersuchungen*, p. 153.

[39] *Betänkande om Inkomst och Förmögenhetsskatt*, II (Report on Taxation of Income and Property-II) (1923), pp. 53-54, 59.

merited losses." [40] It is not clear how seriously he meant this to be taken, and it is even less clear whether he was aware of the difficulties which would be involved in determining what losses, or parts of losses, were "unmerited" and therefore entitled to compensation.

The final type of "unearned" and/or "unjust" wealth to which he reacted was what we may for short call "inflationary gains." These arise in periods of sustained inflation such as Sweden experienced during the first World War, approximately the period 1914-1920. Inflation gains tend to become permanent for large segments of the debtor interest in society in two ways. In the deflation which generally follows an inflation of several years' duration, the price level does not necessarily decline to its preinflation level. In Sweden in the 1920's it declined to a position about midway between its inflation peak and its prewar level in 1913 or 1914. Deflation reduces and wipes out some inflation gains, but it does not by any means wipe out all of them, even if the price level is returned to its preinflation level. The reason for this is that large segments of the creditor interest have been paid off in money of depreciated value during the inflation years. In effect part of creditor's wealth has been permanently expropriated in favor of the debtors, a phenomenon which Wicksell's colleague, David Davidson, aptly described as "capitalistic bolshevism," in one of his many wartime articles in *Ekonomisk Tidskrift*. Further, transfers in favor of the debtor-entrepreneur class occur in such a period because the money incomes of salaried personnel and wageworkers fail to keep pace with the rising level of prices. When the price level eventually declines, wageworkers and salaried workers receive no adequate compensation even if their money incomes decline with a lag behind the falling price level, because then they also face large-scale unemployment.

To be sure, some of the inflation gains were gathered into government coffers by application of the wartime excess-profits tax. To the extent that this was accomplished and the speculative fervor was dampened, Wicksell was in favor of it, but he considered it a totally inadequate measure. When the country's economy had returned to a more stable set of conditions in the 1920's he pointed out that the inflation-deflation sequence had left a legacy of a seriously distorted distribution of wealth. This had impoverished important elements of the community; namely, the middle class whose incomes had remained relatively fixed, particularly civil servants and certain professional groups. To redress this imbalance, he felt that something more fundamental than taxes was necessary. In fact, he urged that "restitution

---

[40] *Ibid.,* p. 70.

proceedings" be instituted to compensate persons who had suffered real hardship as a consequence of these transfers. Their losses were presumably to be compensated from the gains that mortgagees and others had made at their expense because of the inflation.[41] Wicksell was apparently alone among Sweden's leading economists in making this proposal. Neither did he elaborate it sufficiently to reveal how he thought it might have been carried out.

BENEFIT AND ABILITY TAXES

Given that "confiscatory" taxes of the types discussed above are needed to remove or reduce "injustices" in the distribution of income and wealth, all other taxes should be levied according to the benefit principle or the ability principle. The classic example of taxation according to the benefit of the public service supplied to the taxpayer is, of course, the payment of fees, sometimes also called tax prices. The amount of these fees is presumably determined to reflect the cost of government provision of these services. The fact that the taxpayer who uses the service pays the fee involved is also presumptive evidence that its value or marginal utility to him is at least equal to the amount paid. Moreover, fees have the advantage over general tax levies in that only users of the service in question are required to pay them, while nonusers escape them entirely.

Now it was Wicksell's view that under his proposal for "relative unanimity and voluntariness in taxation" the distinction between "fees" and general tax levies would largely disappear, and that, as a matter of fact, many services currently financed by fees would be likely to be transferred to general taxes for financial support.[42] However, the very existence of fees as a form of revenue brought up the intriguing question: According to what principles should the government charge for the services it "sells" in this manner to its citizens? This was by no means a simple question. Many of the services for which fees are charged, the use of a toll bridge, for instance, besides supplying benefits to users directly, also provide indirect and general benefits to nonusers.

But, said Wicksell, why should the fee per direct use be made equal to the average total unit cost per use of the bridge? Besides, what is this average unit cost? Once the bridge is built, does not the average

---

[41] 1920 Års Finanssakkunnige (The Finance Experts of 1920 [including Wicksell]), *Utlåtande angående Frågan Huruvida och I Vad Mån Ett Program För den Närmaste Framtiden För Svensk Finanspolitik Må Kunna Åstadkommas* (Report on the Question of How and to What Extent It Is Possible to Set Up a Program for the Near Future for Swedish Financial Policy, Stockholm, 1920), pp. 51, 61, 63.
[42] *Finanztheoretische Untersuchungen*, p. 126.

unit cost per use vary inversely with the number of uses in a given period? If so, the pricing problem involved here is analogous to that which arises under monopoly. But the government is not a profit-making organization as is a private monopoly. Would it not, therefore, be logical to charge additional users of the bridge only the additional or marginal cost of service that is involved?

This was the way the marginal-cost-pricing principle for public enterprises was born. It had two corollaries. Since most public enterprises operate under decreasing costs, charging the marginal-cost-price for the service necessarily results in a deficit on total costs. In Wicksell's opinion this deficit should be made up from general revenues. Why? Partly because the public enterprise, besides supplying services to direct users, provides indirect and general benefits to nonusers. But the primary reason was that regular users ought to be indifferent as to whether they pay substantially the same amount per annum for the service in one of two ways. Either they pay an average-cost-level fee for each use, or else they pay a much smaller marginal-cost-level fee for each use plus an annual tax equal to most of the difference between the former higher and the present lower fees toward the deficit. The cost per use, measured in marginal-cost fees plus taxes for the deficit, will decrease to all users because of decreasing cost economies which are realized as the demand for the service expands. And this is precisely the point—the rational and most economical way to use public enterprises and facilities is to use them to their full capacity.

The second corollary was that if the marginal cost of the public service could not be ascertained, or if it happened to be so small as to be outweighed by the cost of collecting the correspondingly small fees, then the service should be offered to the public on a "free" basis and all its costs should be met from general revenues.[43] The marginal-cost-pricing principle was stated as follows: "Reduction of fees should be carried on up to the point at which the revenue from the increase in the frequency of use at the price or fee last established just covers—neither more nor less—the additional or marginal costs to the enterprise which were caused by this increase in use-frequency."[44]

In the light of this principle, Wicksell thought it quite irrational on the part of the Prussian government to pride itself on operating its state-owned railways at passenger and freight rates which brought in a considerable annual profit.[45]

Apart from the services of government enterprises, other services of

[43] *Ibid.*, p. 130.
[44] *Ibid.*, p. 133.
[45] *Ibid.*, p. 134.

government supply a mixture of special and general benefits to the citizens. Local systems of police protection, sanitation, and street improvements benefit the locality served or the property owners adjacent to the improvement, although some benefits of a general nature also arise from the existence of these services. On the other hand, activities relating to the national defense, to diplomatic representation abroad, and the like provide primarily general benefits to all the citizens. Consistent with his orientation toward taxation, Wicksell held that wherever it is possible to ascertain that a *measurable, special benefit* accrues from some category of government service to particular citizens or localities, the corresponding portion of the total cost of the service should be met by benefit taxes, i.e., by taxes on the properties and/or incomes of the particular citizens or localities in proportion to the special benefit received.[46] He was, of course, willing to leave it to parliament operating under his procedure for "voluntariness and relative unanimity in tax decisions" to determine what types of benefit levies should be used for these purposes.

It follows by implication from his position as to measurable and special benefits, that that portion of the total cost of all government services which provide general benefits should be met by taxes levied according to ability to pay. Since the citizen as a member of the community has no practical choice of refusing to accept these general benefits, it is desirable that their cost be apportioned to the citizens on the basis of relative equality of sacrifice, that is to say in progressive relation to their incomes, the marginal utility of which decrease with an increase in their quantity.

Wicksell, however, was not very explicit about the principles on which the relations between benefit and ability taxes might be determined. Persons whose incomes afford them only a subsistence standard of living possess no real ability to pay taxes and ought to be exempt from having to do so.[47] The working class has a very legitimate reason for opposing taxes on commodities in wide consumption which can be regarded as necessities, but it may not have as good a reason to oppose taxes on relative luxuries such as alcoholic beverages, tobacco, etc.[48] Excises on these goods act after the manner of ability levies insofar as the yields of these taxes increase with a rise in the workers' wages and consumption of these goods, and decline with a decline in their wages. However, the emphasis in taxation must increasingly be

[46] *Ibid.*, p. 84.
[47] *Betänkande om Inkomst och Förmögenhetsskatt* (Report on Taxation of Income and Property), II (1923), p. 13.
[48] *Finanztheoretische Untersuchungen*, pp. 125-126.

on expanding the role of direct taxes and reducing the role of indirect ones in the revenue system.[49] Ultimately Wicksell hoped for the abolition of all commodity taxes, and urged that the workers would be better off to accept in their place a proportionate income tax on incomes above the subsistence level.[50]

TOWARD A THEORY OF PUBLIC FINANCE

Lindahl succeeded far better than Wicksell in bringing out the complementary nature of the relations between the benefit and ability principles of taxation, as is indicated in the following passages, which are quoted in rather free translation from *Die Gerechtigkeit der Besteuerung:*

To the extent that public activities provide subjective benefits to the citizens, their "interest" or stake in these activities, expressed in money, must vary in two respects: In part it must vary according to the size of the subjective tax-sacrifice which they are prepared to undergo for their share of the public services made available. In part it must also vary according to the size of the sum of money they would be able to forego without having to accept a tax-sacrifice of more than a given magnitude. The last of these two modes of variation is the most important one in practice.

In the first place, taxes must be distributed or levied directly according to ability to pay (*Leistungsfähigkeit*) *only if* the individuals (to be taxed) have an *equal interest* in the government activity in question. However, if certain legitimate differences in interest (in the activity) can be ascertained, then these differences must also be taken into consideration in administering the tax. Therefore, the content of the ability principle of taxation may be expressed in its most generalized form as follows, namely that the tax should stand in a relationship to the individual's ability to pay which corresponds to his "interest" or stake (normalized from a certain point of view) in the public activity in question.

In the second place, the ability principle must be invoked in all cases where it is a question of the distribution of public expenditures the marginal benefits of which are only of a subjective nature to the individuals involved.

Since the principle of objective benefits . . . is only usable to a limited extent in practice, it follows that, so far as the greatest part of taxation is concerned, the principle of ability-to-pay must be applied.[51]

By "principle of objective benefits" in the last passage, Lindahl means the same thing as we have discussed in terms of "measurable

---

[49] *Ibid.*, p. 125.

[50] *Betänkande om Inkomst och Förmögenhetsskatt* (Report on Taxation of Income and Property), II (1923), p. 57.

[51] E. Lindahl, *Die Gerechtigkeit der Besteuerung* (Lund, Sweden, 1919), pp. 181-183.

and special benefits." We have stated earlier that Lindahl elaborated a comprehensive theory of taxation largely on the basis of what he found in *Finanztheoretische Untersuchungen* and in the writings of those Italian, Austrian, and German authors Wicksell held up for admiration in that work. It would take us too far afield to sketch Lindahl's achievement here. Suffice it to say that he operated on more realistic assumptions than Wicksell had used, i.e., he did not presuppose a "just" distribution for his taxation scheme. Also he succeeded in clarifying the concepts of "benefits" and "ability to pay" more than Wicksell had, and finally, he placed less emphasis on the procedural devices of simultaneous expenditure-and-tax decisions approvable only by qualified majorities.

It seems worth mentioning here that these Wicksellian devices have received a limited amount of application at the level of local government finance in Sweden, where they have been incorporated into the constitutions of a few municipalities.[52]

TABLE 1

Schematic Presentation of Principles of Equity in Taxation

Ethical standpoint	Theoretical principles	Practical principles		Public revenues
		Exercise of power of taxation	Basis of taxation	
Existing property order regarded as partially unjust	Confiscation principle	Compulsory taxation	Unjust income or property	Capital gains taxes Inheritance taxes Capital levies Land-value increment taxes Revenues of government enterprises (public utilities) Fees
			Cost of benefits	
Existing property order regarded as just	Benefit principle	Voluntary taxation	Value of benefits	Real estate taxes Improvement or betterment taxes Business or corporation taxes
			Ability to pay	Taxes on personal income and property Taxes on consumption

SOURCE: E. Lindahl, *Die Gerechtigkeit der Besteuerung*, p. 18.

[52] *Betänkande om Inkomst och Förmögenhetsskatt* (Report on Taxation of Income and Property), II (1923), p. 45.

Because of its lucidity and because it sums up much of the foregoing discussion, a free translation of Lindahl's schematic representation of the relationship between principles of taxation and the forms of taxation is reproduced in table 1 (p. 189). This also indicates something about the scope of his theory of taxation.

CHAPTER IX

Wicksell's Static Synthesis— "The Theory of Exchange Value in Its Final Form"

Wicksell wrote two different syntheses for the static part of his analysis, the first in *Value, Capital and Rent*, and the second in *Lectures-I*.[1] Both express the nature of stationary general equilibrium for an economy producing more than one commodity without commodity prices being predetermined by assumption. Both models are masterpieces of compression, the first one proceeding on fourteen independent equations, and the last on the basis of six. The transition from the previous analysis of production and distribution for a one-commodity economy was made by considering the foreign trade relations which would arise between two separate one-commodity societies so situated that they trade finished products with each other, but neither labor nor capital is transferred between them.

Wicksell introduced this part of his analysis by stressing a criticism of J. S. Mill's doctrine that exchange equilibrium would be indeterminate between the two countries. His point was that several exchange equilibria are possible. Some of these will be stable, others will be unstable, but they will not be indeterminate.[2] What the equilibrium will be depends on the reaction in each country to a rise (or fall) in the exchange value of its product in terms of the other country's product. If the offer-component of one country's reciprocal demand

---

[1] Wicksell, *Value, Capital and Rent* (London, 1954), pp. 153 ff.; and *Lectures-I*, pp. 196 ff.

[2] Wicksell, *Lectures-I*, pp. 198-200.

function behaves like a back-sloping supply curve, multiple and unstable exchange equilibria are possible, just as there may be several market equilibrium prices for commodities which are readily substituted for one another.

To allow that commodity prices will be variable in a society which produces two or more commodities, and that factors of production may transfer freely between its two or more industries, two conditions were invoked. Now it was individual demand functions rather than commodity prices that were assumed to be given, or as Wicksell put it: ". . . the personal dispositions of all the individuals as regards consumption must be taken as given." [3]

This implied that the gross savings schedules of individuals were given, for there would be no net saving in a stationary economy. In the second place, owing to freedom of mobility of resources and freely competitive behavior on the part of their owners, in equilibrium the rates of wages, rent, and interest must be equal in the two (or more) industries.

For the production of the two commodities, P and P', the economy has available a total quantity of A current labor services and B current land services. These will be allocated to production in the two industries. Resources directly or indirectly engaged in production of P were designated by capital letters. Those engaged in production of P' were designated by primed capital letters.

The resources in each industry must further be divided into those engaged in "direct" production, and those in roundabout or "indirect" production. In a stationary economy the latter means resources engaged in producing replacement goods for the capital structure which each industry possesses. Resources engaged in "indirect" production were denoted by capital letters carrying subscripts indicating that the resource quantity in question is invested or "saved up" (while being replaced annually by similar replacement investments) in the maturation sequence of capital goods of different maturation terms.

Thus the first fundamental relation of Wicksell's general equilibrium system, the resource allocation equation, was:

$$\text{I} \quad \begin{cases} A_0 + A_1 + A_2 \ldots \ldots A_0', + A_1', + A_2' \ldots \ldots = A \\ B_0 + B_1 + B_2 \ldots \ldots B_0', + B_1', + B_2' \ldots \ldots = B \end{cases}$$

This states that in equilibrium all current labor and land services are engaged in either direct production or in indirect production of

[3] *Ibid.*, p. 198.

capital replacement investments, of commodities P and P'. By means of two production functions, which were explicitly assumed to be homogeneous and linear, three additional relations become determinate, if, for the moment we hold the exchange ratio of P to P' (relation II), or the relative prices of the two commodities, in abeyance.

The production functions were:

$$P = \phi(A_0, A_1, A_2, \ldots \ldots B_0, B_1, B_2, \ldots \ldots)$$

$$P' = \psi(A'_0, A'_1, A'_2, \ldots \ldots B'_0, B'_1, B'_2, \ldots \ldots)$$

The partial derivatives of these functions with respect to each factor quantity determine the marginal (value) productivity of the factors of production. If the conditions of factor supply are given or known, they also determine the proportions in which the different factors will be combined in each industry. Because of mobility of factors between the industries, the rates of wages, rent, and interest, indicated by w and w', r and r', i and i' in the two industries, will be equal in both industries. For familiar reasons, the marginal (value) productivity of invested resources is necessarily greater than that of uninvested resources engaged in "direct" production of consumption goods. As long as waiting has a supply price, the marginal productivity of resources invested for long maturation terms stands in a compound-rate relationship to that of resources invested for short terms. Thus the rates of factor remuneration in each industry expressed in terms of the product of that industry will be:

$$\frac{\partial \phi}{\partial A_0} = w; \qquad \frac{\partial \psi}{\partial A_0} = w'; \qquad \frac{\partial \phi}{\partial B_0} = r; \qquad \frac{\partial \psi}{\partial B_0} = r'$$

$$\frac{\partial \phi}{\partial A_1} = i; \qquad \frac{\partial \psi}{\partial A_1} = i'; \qquad \frac{\partial \phi}{\partial B_1} = i; \qquad \frac{\partial \psi}{\partial B_1} = i'$$

$$\frac{\partial \phi}{\partial A_2} = i(1+i); \quad \frac{\partial \psi}{\partial A_2} = i'(1+i'); \quad \frac{\partial \phi}{\partial B_2} = i(1+i); \quad \frac{\partial \psi}{\partial B_2} = i'(1+i')$$

$$\frac{\partial \phi}{\partial A_3} = i(1+i)^2; \quad \frac{\partial \psi}{\partial A_3} = i'(1+i')^2; \quad \frac{\partial \phi}{\partial B_3} = i(1+i)^2; \quad \frac{\partial \psi}{\partial B_3} = i'(1+i')^2$$

$$- - - - - - \quad - - - - - - \quad - - - - - - \quad - - - - - -$$
$$- - - - - - \quad - - - - - - \quad - - - - - - \quad - - - - - -$$
$$- - - - - - \quad - - - - - - \quad - - - - - - \quad - - - - - -$$

$$\frac{\partial \phi}{\partial A_n} = i(1+i)^{n-1}; \frac{\partial \psi}{\partial A_n} = i'(1+i')^{n-1};$$

$$\frac{\partial \phi}{\partial B_n} = i(1+i)^{n-1}; \frac{\partial \psi}{\partial B_n} = i'(1+i')^{n-1}$$

Once the exchange ratio of P to P', expressed here by a lower case letter p, i.e., $P = pP'$,[4] is determined, the rates of remuneration of the factors of production may be expressed in terms of P, as follows, whereby the three required relations are obtained:

$$\text{III:} \quad w = pw'$$
$$\text{IV:} \quad r = pr'$$
$$\text{V:} \quad i = i'$$

It is further clear that when respective factor quantities are multiplied by these rates of remuneration, the product is fully exhausted.

To express the circumstances which determine the exchange relations between P and P' requires a system of partial differential equations expressing the marginal utility of each commodity to individual consumers in the economy. Such systems were expressed in the earlier and more simplified discussions of value theory in *Lectures-I*.[5] Here the individual utility functions are more complex. They reflect not only the real income the individual receives by reason of his ownership of factor units engaged in one or both industries, but they also reflect the leisure alternative to work, and the savings alternative to full consumption of gross income if the individual is a capitalist.

However, ignoring the leisure alternative, the exchange ratio between P and P' may be derived in the following manner.

The initial real income of a person who owns factor units engaged only in industry P is some quantity, x units of P, which corresponds to the marginal product of the number of factor units he owns times their quantity. Another person is in the same position with respect to industry P', whence his factor-ownership yields him a real income of y units of P'. Each of these individuals can increase their total utility by exchanging some of their respective real incomes. The first person may be willing to trade some $(x - a)$ units of his supply of P for some (b) units of P'. The other person may be willing to give up some $(y - b)$ units of his supply of P' for some (a) units of P, and so forth. Thus each individual has essentially a reciprocal demand function for the products of the industry in which his factor units are *not* engaged. As for the capitalists, we can imagine that they receive a gross income at the end of the year consisting of the product equivalent of interest as well as repayment of the "advances" of real saving they made available at the beginning of the year. One can then visualize that the $(x - a)$ and $(y - b)$ units of P and P' respectively which they retain

---

[4] *Ibid.*, p. 204.
[5] *Ibid.*, pp. 49 ff., 66 ff., and especially pp. 79-80.

without trading for consumption purposes correspond, in the main, to the real savings they reinvest as advances for the coming year's production.

Each individual will then be willing to trade up to a point at which units of P (or P') remaining to him after the trade, and units of P' (or P) acquired by him by trade, have a marginal utility proportionate to the exchange ratio between P and P'. By adding the individual reciprocal demand functions for owners of factors of production in each industry, two aggregate reciprocal demand functions are obtained. Within limits determined by these functions by mutual bids and offers between persons in each ownership group, an equilibrium exchange ratio between P and P' will be established in the open market. That ratio must satisfy three conditions: (1) for each individual the marginal utility of units acquired and of units given up in trade must be proportionate to this exchange ratio; (2) the total value of goods in the possession of each person must be the same before and after exchange, and (3) the total supply of each commodity offered on the market must be equal to the quantity taken or demanded. In this manner relation II is established:

$$\text{II:} \quad P = pP'.$$

The sixth and last relation which is needed to make the general equilibrium determinate, is a relation expressing the value and the dimensions of society's structure of capital. Wicksell stressed the fact that neither the value nor the dimensions and composition of that structure would be determinate except in general equilibrium. As long as commodity prices are still varying, factors of production will shift between the industries, thus affecting the composition of labor- and land-capital in the structure. Accordingly on some investment placed in that process there will be losses, on others gains. This in turn will induce adjustments in the "dimensions" of the structure. Hence:

It can now be asserted that, so long as capital of this magnitude and composition, as well as a certain exchange value (expressed in terms of one of the commodities), is maintained and utilized from year to year, equilibrium cannot be disturbed, if from the beginning the other conditions of stability are fulfilled. But it would clearly be meaningless—if not altogether inconceivable—to maintain that the amount of capital is already fixed before equilibrium between production and consumption has been achieved.[6]

Wicksell did not write an equation expressing the value of the capital structure. To have done so would have been difficult because of

---

[6] *Ibid.,* p. 202.

the manner he used to account for the value and quantity of real capital, namely by "adding up" the number of annual replacement reinvestments which would be required to reproduce all the capital goods in full within the structure. Instead, he described a method for arriving at the reproduction costs of the structure, which equals its exchange value in general equilibrium as follows:

The quantities A_1, A_2 . . . B_1, B_2 . . . etc., are only those parts of capital which are annually consumed. Corresponding to them, under stationary conditions, there must exist other parts of the total social capital, whose amounts can be exactly determined. There must be *one* more element corresponding to A_2, *two* more elements corresponding to A_3, *three* to A_4, etc., and similarly as regards B_2, B_3, B_4, etc. In equilibrium the composition of the sum total of capital is thus definitely fixed. . . . If, for example, we now wish to impose the condition that in equilibrium the sum total of capital shall have a certain exchange value, measured in terms of one of the products, we need only calculate the exchange values of all the parts and add them. These exchange values are (in accordance with the above) the original exchange values of the portions of capital concerned, *plus accumulated interest.* Thus, for example, the present portion of capital indicated by A_3 has the exchange value of $A_3 w (1 + i)^3$. The two identical portions also represented quantitatively by A_3, since they represent equal quantities of saved-up labor, have, on the other hand, the values $A_3 w (1 + i)^2$ and $A_3 w (1 + i)$, respectively. The portion of capital represented by B_3 has the exchange value $B_3 w' p (1 + i)^3 = B_3 w (1 + i)^3$, etc.

If these values are summed and are put equal to a certain given quantity —the total exchange value of the capital employed *in the two industries together,* expressed in terms of the first commodity, we shall then obtain the necessary *sixth relation,* and the problem will at last be completely determinate.[7]

This concludes the formal exposition of Wicksell's general equilibrium synthesis except for two comments with which he intended to bring it closer to the real world.

He indicated first of all that more than one relative equilibrium price or exchange ratio between P and P' was possible if wages, rent, and interest as costs enter into the manufacture of the two commodities in different proportions. Then the production factor which dominates the total cost complex of the more valuable or the higher priced of the two commodities fares better than the rest; its relative product share will be the larger.

Secondly, in order to extend his two-commodity model into one suitable for a multiple-commodity system, he relaxed an assumption

---

[7] *Ibid.,* pp. 204-205. Italics in the original.

to the effect that the factor supply functions were of zero elasticity, i.e., an assumption of the total absence of factor reservation prices.

Under the designation of commodity we may also include the factors of production themselves when they are directly employed by their owners. We can therefore abandon the simplifying assumption . . . that all factors . . . are available in determinate quantities, which are offered in their totality . . . irrespective of the price they will fetch. This is very important, especially for labor, for we can now consider the case in which hours of labor are variable and determined by the workers themselves, on the basis of the equality of the indirect marginal utility of work and the direct marginal utility of leisure.[8]

As is evident, Wicksell's general equilibrium model is analogous to a large number drawn up since the days of Walras. Such models are not particularly significant per se, and their existence is justified primarily by the convenience in exposition they afford. If these summaries of relations were not employed, the preceding and more incisive analysis could not safely proceed by the method of successive approximation.

Nevertheless, Wicksell's synthesis is instructive from two standpoints, its delineation of a determinate structure of capital, and its extraordinary degree of compression. Like other models of its kind, besides focusing attention at the real level of analysis on the relations of the parts to the whole in a stationary economy, it also served as a point of departure to other and more vital economic inquiries. Foremost among these in Wicksell's time was the problem of money. What role does money play? How does it affect the relationships between all the major parts of the economy? It is to this inquiry of Wicksell's that we shall turn in the next two chapters.

---

[8] *Ibid.*, p. 206.

CHAPTER X

Theory of General Prices, Money and Credit

It would be convenient if there were only one version of Wick-sell's own monetary theory to deal with. The trouble is that there are at least two explicit versions of it, and even a third one which, however, was not fully developed by its author. Wicksell seems to have been forever revising his monetary analysis. What he published in *Interest and Prices* in 1898 is in several respects different from what he wrote in *Lectures-II*, second edition, 1915. Finally in 1925 he gave a famous lecture to the Swedish Economic Association and he also wrote a long article in *Ekonomisk Tidskrift* on the monetary problems of the Scandinavian countries. A close reading of these two documents shows that he was about to revise his monetary theory again in some important respects.

Ordinarily, when a writer revises at a later date what he has written earlier, he explains the reasons for his change of mind. Unfortunately, Wicksell left only some cryptic remarks in the prefaces to various editions of *Lectures-II* as to the changes he made in that work as compared with *Interest and Prices*. These remarks leave to the reader the task of inferring the reasons for change. As a consequence, we shall have to trace the "evolution" his monetary doctrine underwent over the years.

Finally, his monetary writings could have benefited from a different mode of organization, which we shall endeavor to impose here. Both in *Interest and Prices* and *Lectures-II*, his presentation of his own new ideas is "sandwiched in" between long sections on currency systems, earlier monetary theory, monetary history, history of price level fluctuations, and the like. This probably obscured and minimized the theoretical contribution he had made. There were historical reasons for this. As he explained in his preface to *Interest and Prices*,[1] he began that work with the intention of investigating the merits of bimetallism as compared with other monetary standards. Secondly, he wanted to make his theoretical contribution as an extension on, but within the framework of, the dominant version of the quantity theory of money. This may have been necessary in order for him to obtain a hearing for his own theory of price level fluctuations. But the novelty and explanatory power of his new approach would have been enhanced if he had given it a more complete exposition. It is also unfortunate that the models he relied on to illustrate his theory were defective in some crucial respects.

These matters will receive attention in due course, but first we shall trace the doctrinal antecedents of his monetary theory.

Doctrinal Antecedents of Wicksell's Monetary Theory

Certainly in the 1920's, when his works first began attracting attention outside Sweden, and even more in 1898 when his first writings in this field were published, Wicksell's monetary analysis must have impressed itself on discerning minds as something significant and distinctly new in a realm of economic thought which had for so long been dominated by the quantity theory. In fact, the latter had received its latest and thoroughly mechanistic interpretation in I. Fisher's *The Purchasing Power of Money* (1911). Yet most elements of Wicksell's monetary theory had been expressed by several writers in the earlier decades of the nineteenth century.

Wicksell's own writings reveal some of this background. Throughout *Interest and Prices* one encounters his comments on leading exponents on money and finance writing in the early and middle nineteenth century. But he never intended to deal with the development of monetary doctrines exhaustively and systematically. For that purpose some recent treatments are helpful in providing a certain perspective, since, *inter alia,* they have endeavored to accord Wicksell his place in the evolution of monetary doctrine which links Davanzatti with contemporary writers in this field. Two such accounts are of interest because they complement each other by reason of differences in viewpoint and scope of treatment. These are F. A. von Hayek's "Lecture I" in *Production and Prices* (1934), and Alvin Hansen's *Monetary Theory and Fiscal Policy* (1949), chapters 3 and 6, and Appendix A. For a more general survey of monetary doctrines, we

---

[1] Wicksell, *Interest and Prices* (London, 1936), p. xxiii.

refer to E. Whittaker, *History of Economic Ideas* (1940), chapters xiv and xv, and T. W. Hutchison, *A Review of Economic Doctrines 1870-1929* (1953), chapters 15, 22, 23, and 25.

The representation Wicksell's ideas has received by these writers is necessarily selective and incomplete. Yet it is the link they establish between his and past doctrines which is of interest here rather than their particular evaluation of his position. In passing it seems appropriate to mention that Hansen's and Hutchison's discussions are more representative and generous to Wicksell, while von Hayek does him less than justice in order to stake an excessive claim for his mentor, von Mises, and, finally, Whittaker treats him very superficially (and incorrectly) as simply a "rediscover" of Thornton's ideas.

THE FORERUNNERS—THORNTON, RICARDO, TOOKE

In retrospect it appears that Henry Thornton was in a greater measure than others a direct forebear of Wicksellian monetary theory. But one need not on that account accept Whittaker's statement: ". . . but the theoretical implications of Thornton's contributions had become somewhat neglected and it was left to Wicksell to rediscover and clarify the theory the English writer had expressed." [2]

This puts either too high an estimate on what Thornton said in *An Inquiry into the Nature and Effect of the Paper Credit of Great Britain* (1802), or too low an estimate on Wicksell's work. It is most unlikely that Wicksell ever read Thornton's work in his early monetary studies, because he never referred to it, while on the other hand he discussed the writings of Tooke and Ricardo on the currency debate at length. As it happened, his colleague Davidson was perhaps the first to "rediscover" Thornton. He wrote an article in 1916, "Thornton om penningränta och varupris" (Thornton on Interest and Prices) in *Economisk Tidskrift* (pp. 391-93), in which he quoted certain passages from Thornton's *Inquiry* (pp. 283-91) in Swedish translation. In these passages a theory of price movement due to divergence between the profit rate and the interest rate was succinctly expressed. On reading this, Wicksell said he was agreeably surprised at finding that ideas similar to his own were of such comparatively ancient origin as to antedate Ricardo.

At any rate, Thornton made clear that the depreciation of the paper pound in England was due to overissue of notes resulting from the circumstance that the legal maximum discount rate of the Bank of England was held to 5 per cent while the mercantile rate of profit was presumably much higher than this during the Napoleonic wars.

[2] E. Whittaker, *A History of Economic Ideas* (New York, 1940), p. 701.

In consequence he foresaw continued and cumulative inflation for as long as this condition persisted. The additional issue of bank notes could never become excessive as long as war scarcities and the 5 per cent discount continued, because by raising prices faster than costs the extra notes would not depress but rather increase or maintain the higher profit rate.

A similar position was taken by Ricardo a few years later in his tract, *The High Price of Bullion* (1811) and, in fact, an almost identical argument was presented in his *Principles of Political Economy and Taxation* (1817), chapter xxvii (Gonner edition). But Ricardo did not enter fully into its implications for price level stabilization. Neither, as Wicksell pointed out,[3] was Ricardo consistent in taking this position while at the same time he advocated the gold bullion standard in his *Proposals for an Economical and Secure Currency* (1816), as a means for achieving a currency of approximately stable value.

The essence of the antibullionist and the banking-school position was that variations in investment demand account for price level and money quantity variations. Thomas Tooke was the leading exponent of this point of view. This is the most general principle which emerges in his *Inquiry into the Currency Principle* (1846) as well as in some of the famous "summaries" contained in his and Newmarch's remarkable *History of Prices and the State of Circulation, 1792-1856*, published in six volumes over the period 1838-1857.

But this principle was overlaid by numerous observations concerning specific historical circumstances which contributed to particular price variations during the sixty years covered by that study. The general inference to which his work led was that the arts of banking are not to be interfered with as long as the banks serve the "legitimate" needs of the business community by lending only on good security and by varying the discount rate chiefly with an eye to eliminating disequilibria in the balance of payments. In such circumstances, he contended, note and/or credit issue could not become excessive. The reason was that borrowers must pledge as security, commodities and resources at least equivalent in value to the loans which they obtain. In addition they must pay interest on the loans. Because of this they would hardly be tempted to borrow more than they "need." On the other hand, if banks issued notes or extended credit to excess, this excess would subsequently revert to them for lack of sound and profitable opportunities for use in business investment.

But it was otherwise with governments who borrow without pledg-

---

[3] Wicksell, *Lectures-II*, pp. 175 ff.

ing security. In borrowing in times of full employment they withdraw from private consumption and/or investment an equivalent of goods and resources. The notes paid out for these tend to remain in circulation and to raise prices abnormally. Thus, the Napoleonic War inflation was traced chiefly to the increase in England's public debt. However, aside from the exigencies of public policy and their effects on the normal functioning of the monetary and banking system, the general rule, which Tooke thought was amply illustrated by his price data, was that periods of rising prices are periods of high investment activity and of rising discount and interest rates, and vice versa.

This observation of Tooke's caused consternation. On general quantity theory grounds, familiar since the days of Hume, periods of increasing gold production (i.e., increasing money quantity) were assumed, and over the long run were observed, to be periods of rising prices and falling interest rates.

This apparent contradiction was not resolved satisfactorily until Wicksell did so in *Geldzins und Güterpreise*.[4] There he reasoned that if there was equilibrium in the sense of the real rate of interest being equal to the loan rate prior to the discovery of new gold fields, this discovery need not, and would indeed not be likely to, induce banks in non-gold-producing countries to reduce the interest rate. Existing prices would begin to rise at the ruling rate, for the new gold fields would have to be equipped and supplied with general articles of consumption. Hence the gold discovery would increase the demand for exports from countries which do not produce gold, and this would raise commodity prices there. As a result the "real" rate of interest would rise, and with it the demand for investable funds. If the banks were "fully loaned up" before the gold discovery, the foregoing circumstances would increase the demand made on them for loans. Then they might find it necessary to raise loan rates of interest, especially during the interval which lapses between the news of gold discoveries and the delivery of significant quantities of bullion in return for exports bought on credit by gold producers.

Thus, first prices rise, then the interest rate rises, and subsequently a sustained gold inflow acts as a prop behind the price level and prevents it from receding to its earlier position. Apparently Tooke was right in claiming that the rise in prices generally precedes the increase in money quantity and that rising prices are accompanied (with a certain lag) by rising, not by falling, interest rates.

On the other hand, the classical quantity theorists were not wrong in observing that the "price revolution" which followed the discovery

[4] Cf. *Interest and Prices*, pp. 81 ff., and *Lectures-II*, pp. 197-198.

of the New World and its fabulous supplies of gold had been, and could be expected to be, accompanied by a secular decline in interest rates. However, this applied to long-run tendencies. It was mainly the result of a secular rate of increase of gold production which exceeded the increase in European commodity production. Tooke's observation, applicable to the short-run or transitional phase of such a situation, did not conflict with this apparently opposite long-run result. A substantial rise in the price level was attended by a considerable development of trade and industry in the course of which capital formation had been more rapid than the increase in other resources. As a consequence, in the new equilibrium at adjusted levels of prices, the marginal value productivity of capital, and with it the real rate and the long-term trend of the loan rate of interest, had declined relative to the levels they had held in the prediscovery era.

While the foregoing applied to the effect of increased gold production on prices and interest rates in countries with gold- or bimetallic-currency standards, as Wicksell pointed out in a later context, a similar argument could be made for a sustained increase of fiat money or of bank credit (related to large-scale government borrowing) in countries on free exchange or inconvertible paper standards. Then it was the indefinite duration and emergency nature of the object of increased government expenditures (armaments, warfare, etc.) that raised prices and the real rate on capital without an appropriate and timely adjustment in loan rates of interest. In the case of large-scale government borrowing there was the additional complication that the banks, even if they might otherwise have been willing to do so, could effectively be prevented by government policy from raising discount and interest rates sufficiently to curtail private demand for credit to the point where the increased government demand for resources might be met without inflation. The British experience during the Napoleonic Wars was only one of several cases of this type. It was to be repeated, with variations in detail, in many countries and on an even greater scale during World Wars I and II.

That variations in investment demand imply discrepancies between aggregate demand and supply and consequently repeal the applicability of Say's law of markets to short-run analysis; that the associated movement and changing distribution of money income affect both the magnitude and composition of real income (the cycle of forced saving, crisis, unintended investment, adjustment by partial capital consumption) were ideas deeply imbedded, if not always clearly expressed, in the thinking of the "unorthodox" section of the classical school. Apparently it was Sismondi and Malthus who were responsible for these insights, although others, notably Bentham and J. S. Mill, also contributed to them.[5] It was Sismondi who, earlier than Malthus, arrived at an underconsumption theory of "gluts," which he buttressed with his observations concerning technological displacement of labor.

It is peculiar that Wicksell, who built his monetary theory around the high probability and the frequently experienced occurrence of short-run discrepancies between aggregate supply and demand (as revealed by shifts between the real and the loan rates of interest) did not mention Sismondi or Malthus in this connection. He never once referred to the former in any of his writings, and he discussed Malthus only in connection with the population doctrine. One surmises that his silence concerning them was due to his implicit rejection of their underconsumption theory of "gluts." This was probably also the reason he insisted that his explanation of price fluctuations should not be taken as a monetary overinvestment theory of business cycles. He admitted that price level variations were not independent of the trade cycle, but he would not have concurred in the converse of this proposition.[6]

As a passage in *Interest and Prices* indicates, Wicksell seems to have derived his aggregate demand and supply approach from an undeveloped insight of Tooke's. This passage is immediately preceded by his discussion of some of Tooke's successful objections to the currency school and his criticism of Tooke's notions concerning the relation between discount rates and prices. Wicksell concluded that Tooke's theory of money—he labeled it a "credit theory" of money—amounted fundamentally to a negative criticism of the quantity theory. Then he asked himself the question whether Tooke had some positive monetary explanation to put in the place of the quantity theory, and he answered in the following vein:

. . . in fact almost all these conclusions of Tooke's are of the same negative character. . . . Only one of them, the thirteenth—(of 17 propositions of

[5] J. C. L. Simonde de Sismondi, *Nouveaux principes d'économie politique* (1819), Livre II, chaps. 3, 4, 6, Livre IV, chaps. 1, 3, 4, Livre V, chaps. 1, 4, 8, Livre VII, chaps. 2 and 8, and Eclarissements, chaps. 1, 2, and 3 (3d ed.; Geneva, 1951); T. R. Malthus, *Principles of Political Economy* (2d ed., 1830; reprinted London, 1936), Book I, chap. 4, Book II, chaps. 3, 5, 6, 8, 9, and 10; J. Bentham, "The True Alarm" (1801), Books II and III, in *Jeremy Bentham's Economic Writings*, III, ed. by W. Stark (London, 1954). For a concise appraisal of the development of Bentham's thinking on these subjects, see particularly T. W. Hutchison's article "Bentham as an Economist," *Economic Journal*, LXVI (June, 1956), 288-306. J. S. Mill, *Essays on Some Unsettled Questions of Political Economy* (2d ed.; London, 1874), pp. 111-119. For a brief history of the "forced savings" doctrine, cf. F. A. von Hayek, "The Development of the Doctrine of Forced Saving," *Quarterly Journal of Economics* (November, 1932).

[6] Cf. Wicksell's "Note on Trade Cycles," in *Lectures-II*.

Tooke's concerning the principle of currency)—attempts to provide a positive answer to the question at issue. It reads as follows: 'It is the quantity of money, constituting the revenue of the different orders of the State, under the head of rents, profits, salaries, and wages, destined for current expenditure, that alone forms the limiting principle of the aggregate of money prices. . . . As the cost of production is the limiting principle of supply, so the aggregate of money incomes devoted to expenditure for consumption is the determining and limiting principle of demand.' [7]

Now this would indeed be a piece of positive elucidation [of a monetary theory alternative or supplementary to the quantity theory, which he found Tooke to have treated only negatively] if the method of elucidation itself were not unfortunately almost as obscure and in need of elucidation as the phenomenon under discussion. Incomes determined prices; but we might just as well say—so at least it would appear—that the former are determined by the latter. . . . It might therefore appear that this method of elucidation is taking us quite hopelessly around a circle. . . . *For my part, I do not share this view. It is my belief that this observation of Tooke's, or more precisely its first half, does really provide a starting point from which a theory of the value of money and of prices can be developed. This I shall try to show later on.* But Tooke himself never elaborated his suggestion, which makes an appearance in other sections of his works.[8]

The foregoing when read in juxtaposition with the following, which appears in a later context in *Lectures-II,* reveals, we believe, the source and nature of Wicksell's approach to monetary theory: "Any theory of money worthy of the name must be able to show how and why the monetary or pecuniary demand for goods exceeds or falls short of the supply of goods in given conditions." [9]

Others, notably Walras, Edgeworth, Jevons, and Giffen, probably influenced Wicksell's concepts of credit, banking, and velocity of circulation of money by their research on these topics.[10] However, Wicksell's references to these writers were few and scattered, and he did not take up their positions for extended discussion.[11] Finally, we come to Alfred Marshall, who, though a contemporary of Wicksell's,

---

[7] Wicksell, *Interest and Prices,* p. 44.

[8] *Ibid.,* pp. 44-45. Italics supplied.

[9] Wicksell, *Lectures-II,* p. 160.

[10] Cf. Léon Walras, "Theorie Mathematique du Billet de Banque," *Bull. Soc. Vaud. Sci. Nat.,* XVI (1879), and *Theorie de la Monnaie* (1884); F. Y. Edgeworth, "Mathematical Theory of Banking," *Journal of the Royal Statistical Society* (1886); W. S. Jevons, *Money and the Mechanism of Exchange* (London, 1875), and *Investigations in Currency and Finance* (London, 1884); and R. Giffen, *Essays in Finance* (London, 1886).

[11] Wicksell's references to the foregoing writers are found in *Interest and Prices,* pp. 32, 46, 66, 109, 165, 169, 171, 172, 183.

must be treated as a forerunner of Wicksellian monetary theory from the standpoint of the history of monetary doctrines.

MARSHALL AND THE TRANSITION FROM THE MONEY QUANTITY TO THE
WICKSELLIAN SAVINGS-INVESTMENT APPROACH IN MONETARY THEORY

It seems rather unlikely that Marshall's early monetary writings "influenced" Wicksell to any appreciable extent. Some scattered references in *Interest and Prices* (pp. 46, 76, 158, 183) show that he was familiar with Marshall's *Evidence and Memoranda* before the Royal Commission on Depression of Trade and Industry (1886), and those before the Gold and Silver Commission (1887). Wicksell's comments on these were laudatory but brief, and revealed nothing of startling novelty in Marshall's position. At the same time Wicksell was probably not acquainted with Marshall's remarkable article "Remedies for Fluctuation of General Prices," *Contemporary Review* (March, 1887) (since then reprinted in *Memorials of Alfred Marshall*, 1925). This article presented in short space all the essential elements of Marshall's monetary analysis. In fact, what Marshall wrote about monetary problems later in life were essentially elaborations which record little advance beyond the position he stated first in this article. Undoubtedly Wicksell would have discussed this article in preference to the *Evidence and Memoranda* if he had been aware of its existence, for Marshall's explanation of price level fluctuations here exhibits some interesting similarities as well as contrasts to that of Wicksell in *Interest and Prices*.

On the other hand, Marshall ignored Wicksell's existence. There is no evidence that he read *Geldzins und Güterpreise*. Had he done so, he would certainly have commented on it in his work, *Money, Credit and Commerce* (1922). In 1906, on the one and only occasion when Wicksell made a professional appearance in England to read a paper before a meeting of the Royal Economic Society, Marshall was apparently not present. At least he was not heard from. Wicksell's paper, published as "The Influence of the Rate of Interest on Prices" in the *Economic Journal* (1907), elicited some brief comments only from Edgeworth and Palgrave. But, apart from this, Wicksell's monetary position received no further notice in England until J. M. Keynes discussed *Geldzins und Güterpreise* in his *Treatise on Money*, vol. I (1930).

Thus Wicksell and Marshall worked independently of one another. Although Marshall's positive restatement of his own monetary theory was published as late as 1922, I believe it is correct to treat his work as a forerunner to Wicksell's, chiefly because Marshall was never completely emancipated from the quantity theory. He remained halfway between the latter and the savings-investment approach to monetary problems. It was Keynes who was the first to sense that Marshall's monetary analysis as compared with that of Wicksell belongs to a different, an earlier and more primitive epoch in the development of monetary theory, as the following statements indicate:

> On the whole I am inclined to think that uppermost in Marshall's mind was the idea that what raises prices is the creation of additional purchasing power, but that in the modern economic world the organization of the credit system is such that 'speculators' are the people into whose hands new money is most likely to find its way in the first instance, bank-rate playing an obvious part in this causal train. This seems to me to be the doctrine on which I was brought up, and which certainly did *not* bring home to my mind any clear idea of the relationship between the volume of earnings at any time, the volume of savings, and the volume of goods coming forward available for consumption, or of the connection between these things with the equilibrium between savings and investment.[12]

> There remains, however, one outstanding attempt at systematic treatment (of the effect or '*modus vivendi*' of the bank-rate on investment and on changes in the level of prices), namely Knut Wicksell's *Geldzins und Güterpreise* . . . a book which deserves more attention than it has received from English speaking economists. In substance and intention, Wicksell's theory is closely akin to the theory of this Treatise.[13]

> At any rate, whether or not I have exaggerated the depth to which Wicksell's thought penetrated, he was the first writer to make it clear that the influence of the rate of interest on the price level operates by its effect on the rate of Investment, and that Investment in this context means *Investment* and not speculation.[14]

It was in view of this re-assessment that Keynes also made the following statement: "On this test I feel that what I am trying to say is the same at root as what Wicksell was trying to say. . . ."[15]

It will be convenient to consider Marshall's monetary doctrine and an element thereof elaborated by Irving Fisher, in relation to that of Wicksell. This affords us an opportunity to see Wicksell in the role of a would-be reformer of monetary institutions. In this field he also made a notable contribution, one which cannot readily be intruded on the discussion of more purely theoretical questions in the later phases of this treatment, and, moreover, one which cannot be altogether omitted.

---

[12] J. M. Keynes, *A Treatise on Money*, I (London, 1930), pp. 192-193.
[13] *Ibid.*, p. 186.
[14] *Ibid.*, p. 198.
[15] *Ibid.*, p. 198 n. 3.

Marshall himself seems to have been aware that the structure of his monetary doctrine remained unfinished in form with its several elements joined loosely together. As such it had more the character of a theory of currency than that of a general explanation of monetary phenomena. In a letter to Keynes in 1923, a few months before his death, Marshall referred to his own efforts in this field as those of an "amateur currency mediciner." [16] This self-assessment, we believe, evaluates the over-all impact of his monetary work fairly accurately, although it clearly understates his total contribution to monetary theory.

There were gaps in Marshall's doctrine. His advocacy of an international symmetallic standard was not harmoniously related to his recommendation of the use of a tabular standard for long-term contracts for the domestic economy, or within the separate national economies.[17] And if the purchasing power of long-term credit could be stabilized by that method, why should it not also be applied to short-term credit and to international monetary transactions? These questions Marshall left unresolved.

Marshall, Fisher, and Wicksell—Problems of Currency

THE PROBLEM OF EXTERNAL VALUE OF CURRENCY

Wicksell, who was also by necessity something of a currency reformer or "mediciner" succeeded in reaching a theoretical solution for the twin problems of stabilizing the internal purchasing power of money without sacrificing its external exchange rate stability, which latter was both the glory and the Achilles' heel of the gold standard. In so doing, he anticipated by almost fifty years the principles on which the International Monetary Fund has been developed. To this end he began his analysis of currency standards on the assumption of a closed economy, i.e., the international economy as a whole. By contrast, Marshall generally assumed an open national economy. Wicksell's problem was one of finding the conditions which would make money an invariant standard of value. He divided this problem into two parts, its value constancy "in time," by which he meant the internal value stability of money, and its value constancy "in space," or its external stability on the foreign exchanges.

At this juncture, let us *assume* that Wicksell had found the correct

---

[16] Cf. *Memorials of Alfred Marshall*, edited by A. C. Pigou (London, 1925), p. 33, n. 2.

[17] A. Marshall "Remedies for Fluctuation of General Prices," reprinted in *Memorials of Alfred Marshall* (London, 1925).

solution for the internal value constancy of money in his insistence that the aim of monetary policy should be to stabilize the general level of prices. This was the view he held until the last few years of his life, when he began changing his position on this point. The means to this end was for the Central Bank in each country to vary its discount or "loan" rate of interest in the same direction as the movement of the general price level (from some initial position measured by an index number), thus offsetting the movement of the latter and stabilizing it within a very narrow range of fluctuation.

That his solution for the internal value stability of money had its imperfections will be shown later on. But if we assume its correctness here, then there remained the dilemma that while price stabilization would be possible for each country if it adopted a free exchange standard, then the internal value constancy of its currency would have been obtained by sacrificing its external value stability. This was clearly not a complete nor a desirable solution in so far as the international gold standard provided a mechanism for guaranteeing external value stability of gold currencies (within gold import-export points), although often at the expense of the internal value stability of these currencies.

Wicksell's way out of this dilemma was first to show how international payments may be settled without gold shipments, and then to show how the value of money could effectively be divorced from that of gold. Finally, he outlined a method whereby exchange parity among various national currencies could be preserved by means of international agreements concerning certain common monetary policy standards. The latter were to be applied with sufficient flexibility so as not to infringe unduly on the economic and monetary sovereignty of individual nations.[18]

Drawing on the experience of the Scandinavian countries which had formed a monetary union in 1873, Wicksell pointed out that gold shipments would become unnecessary if the several central banks were to form an international clearings union and then agree to sell sight-drafts on each other at par to the public, and to redeem each others' currencies at par in their respective national currencies.[19] Further, the central banks must agree to follow a common discount policy with reference to an international price level index. This policy should be intent on stabilizing that index by means of the central banks in common raising their discount rates if the index shows a tendency to rise above, and reducing them if it tends to fall below, its normal

---

[18] Cf. Wicksell, *Lectures-II*, pp. 215-225, and *Interest and Prices*, pp. 189-194.
[19] Wicksell, *Lectures-II*, p. 121.

level. However, due to the vagaries of international trade and differences in economic development, some nations would from time to time develop persistent and increasing debit clearings balances with the majority of members of the international clearings union. Growing debit clearings would be indicative of disequilibrium in their balance of payments. This, then, would justify and permit central banks of such countries "to swim against the tide," i.e., to pursue discount policies of opposite impact to that pursued by the majority of countries, until the cause of their payments disequilibrium has been discovered and removed.

Once gold shipments have become redundant because of international clearings, gold reserves will be unnecessary. In due course they may be done away with by the same process of demonetization that had occurred with respect to silver during the last quarter of the nineteenth century. However, until that happens and because of the force of tradition, the international gold standard would probably be maintained at least until international clearings become a reality and a success. In the meantime there was the possibility of new discoveries giving rise to an overabundance of gold and thus causing inflation on a grand scale. To protect a national monetary system devoted to price stabilization against this danger without obliging it to adopt an inconvertible paper standard, Wicksell insisted that free coinage on private account be abolished and with it the obligation of the central bank to buy and sell gold in unlimited quantities at a fixed mint price. Let the currency be convertible into gold as long as gold is not a threat to the central bank's power to wage effective price stabilization policy. But if the gold inflow is so great as to jeopardize the latter, then the bank should be free to refuse additional coinage or purchases of gold. As a consequence, the value of its currency would appreciate above gold par. Then if the bank subsequently finds it necessary to reopen its gold purchases or to sell off part of its gold reserve after the currency has appreciated, it should not be forced to do so at the former fixed mint price, but at a new, lower price adjusted according to the degree of its currency's appreciation.

For the opposite case of a progressive gold shortage, which would tend to produce secular deflation in gold standard countries, the only solution compatible with price stabilization would be the abandonment of the gold standard and introduction of an inconvertible currency. Thus Wicksell concluded:

Indeed, our modern monetary system is afflicted by an imperfection, an inherent contradiction. The development of credit aims at rendering the holding of cash reserves unnecessary, though far from a sufficient, guarantee of the stability of money values. . . . Only by completely divorcing the value of money from metal, or at any rate from its commodity function, by abolishing all free minting, and by making the minted coin or banknotes proper, or more generally the unit employed in the accounts of the credit institutions, both the medium of exchange and the measure of value—only in this way can the contradiction be overcome and the imperfection removed.[20]

Marshall, like Wicksell, was also devoted to the aim of price stabilization. But he took an open economy as the basis for his analysis, and so failed to generalize several of the conclusions he derived. He preferred to treat international monetary questions in terms of the purchasing power parity doctrine. Internally, however, he came to the conclusion that avoidance of speculative excesses and crises, which accompany price fluctuations, required timely and aggressive discount policy with reference to short-term credit. To stabilize the purchasing power of long-term credit, which is less directly controlled by the discount, he advised the optional use of a tabular standard.

As it happened, Wicksell did not state his reaction to Marshall's proposed tabular standard directly. But he did engage in a controversy over the related compensated dollar proposal by Fisher. The conclusions he developed in regard to Fisher's proposal may be considered to be equally applicable to Marshall's suggestion.

CURRENCY REFORM AND INTERNAL VALUE OF MONEY,
FISHER'S "COMPENSATED DOLLAR PLAN"

Fisher's plan, although Irving Fisher himself was not a party to the debate, received a thorough airing in the pages of *Ekonomisk Tidskrift* (1913) by Davidson who reviewed *The Purchasing Power of Money*, by F. H-son Brock (who at the time was Wicksell's *docent* or assistant), who defended Fisher's proposal, and by Wicksell who joined in Davidson's critique, adducing, however, a different and more complete appraisal of the plan.

Fisher characterized his proposal as a combination of the tabular standard with the gold exchange standard.[21] It aimed at substituting a dollar of fixed purchasing power and varying gold weight for the familiar one of fixed weight and varying purchasing power. The gold weight of the noncirculating standard unit of money was to be changed in the same direction and proportion, 1 per cent at a time, as the fluctuation of the price level from some initial or normal value of 100. Only fully covered, representative money, i.e., gold certificates, were to be in circulation. The number of gold certificates would cor-

---

[20] *Ibid.*, p. 126.
[21] I. Fisher, *The Purchasing Power of Money* (2d ed.; New York, 1922), p. 337.

respond to the number of standard-unit weights of gold bullion contained in the country's gold reserve for note issue purposes. For best results Fisher visualized international adoption of his plan. It was to function as follows:

At the outset, when the index to be kept stable stands at 100, each mint or central bank has a particular purchase price (in gold certificates) for gold bullion, and also a selling price for bullion which is 1 per cent higher. This was intended to discourage private speculation on changes in the gold weight of the standard unit. The buying price would, consequently, be such that each certificate would correspond exactly to one standard-unit weight of bullion. If the general price index subsequently rose 1 per cent, the mint would announce a 1 per cent increase in the weight of the standard bullion unit. This comes to the same as saying that the mint would reduce its buying and selling price of bullion by 1 per cent in terms of certificates, always keeping its selling price 1 per cent above the purchasing price. If the price index at another time fell below its normal level of 100, the mint would reduce the weight of the standard unit or raise the buying price offered for bullion.

In the case of a 1 per cent weight increase in the money unit it was assumed that the public would be eager to convert certificates into bullion at a 1 per cent gain in gold weight. Since the certificates thus turned in would be canceled, the note issue or money quantity would be reduced. Because only certificates, not bullion, would be legal tender, it was expected that the price level would be forced down from the rise it had undergone prior to the weight increase. If by chance too many certificates were turned in as a result of this action, so that the price level would fall below normal, then the mint would reduce the weight of the money unit. Those who had recently bought bullion for certificates would then have good reason to turn in their gold and receive 1.01 times as many certificates for it. This, in turn, would augment the note issue and raise the price level toward 100. Thus, under ideal conditions the plan was intended to keep price fluctuations within the index range of 99 to 101. If the actual performance should be different, Fisher was in any case convinced the scheme would reduce price level fluctuations to a comfortably narrow range.

Fisher himself admitted that the success of his plan depended on whether changes in money quantity are independent of changes that occur in the circulation velocity of money and in the volume of transactions so that with the variations in quantity of money induced by his plan, one could expect a proportionate change in the price level, as the simple quantity theory required. At that time (1911) he thought there were good reasons for assuming this, especially at the short-run level of analysis. Given full employment, short-run changes in transactions volume would most likely be negligible. As for circuit velocity there was reason to believe and also some statistical evidence to support the belief that it varies slowly in response to changes in payment habits.[22]

Fisher also admitted that the motivation for the public to convert certificates into bullion or vice versa depended on whether the mints could vary their buying prices of gold without changing the world price of gold by an equal amount. He was of the opinion that while the world gold price would not in the long run be independent of prices offered by the major mints, there would remain a sufficient difference between changes in the latter and the level of the former for long enough to induce the reaction the plan anticipated.[23]

The main point which Davidson raised against Fisher's plan in his review was that variations in the circuit velocity of currency and deposits may readily nullify the anticipated effect of changing the quantity of money.

In one of his comments, Wicksell admitted that at first he had thought well of Fisher's proposal and had written to him to that effect. His erstwhile approval of it must have been due to the circumstance that Fisher's plan also involved an attempt to divorce the value of money from that of gold. To that extent it was akin to Wicksell's own preference for abolishing fixed mint prices for gold, and along with it, free coinage for private account. But now, in the light of some issues brought out between Davidson and Brock, he had come to a different assessment of it.

He concluded that, contrary to Fisher's intent, the plan's best chance for success would be if it were adopted in a single country rather than universally. If its mint or central bank had occasion to reduce its gold purchase price, new gold would not be offered it and its reduced buying price would not be likely to pull the world gold price down with it. Hence a differential would remain to motivate its citizens to act according to the plan. But if it were adopted by all countries, the world price would move with their changes of the weight of the standard money unit.

On an international basis Wicksell thought the proposal might be useful as a long-run preventive of a possible overabundance of gold. Successive 1 per cent reductions in mint buying prices of bullion might

---

[22] *Ibid.*, pp. 154-156.
[23] *Ibid.*, pp. 342-348, and Appendix, pp. 494-502.

reduce gold prices sufficiently so that, with costs of production given, eventually the world output of gold would be curtailed to an amount just large enough to accommodate the increase in commodity output, transactions volume, and population growth under a universal gold standard without secularly declining price levels.

But as a remedy for short-run fluctuations in the value of money he thought its efficacy would be infinitesimal. These fluctuations depend far more on changes in circuit velocity of money and the rate of turn-over of deposits than they do on changes in the quantity of money per se. Yet the plan made no provision for controlling these causes of short-run variations in the value of money. In fact, under a system of international clearings, the banks would be independent of the plan. Until such a system is developed, there is still considerable lee-way left for them to substitute the use of credit for any restriction in the supply or quantity of money. Moreover, in times of crisis the plan might actually be dangerous. Then a financial panic can only be avoided if a strong central bank is able to expand the note issue rapidly as it discounts and rediscounts the obligations of private banks and financial houses at increased discount rates. But under Fisher's proposal this expansion of cash must await the action of superior monetary authority and the reluctance of the public to turn in hoarded gold to permit an increase in the issue of gold certificates.

This entire episode only served to confirm a conviction Wicksell had formed back in the 1890's, namely that "mere currency reform," while often a necessary prerequisite for the rational development of a monetary system, is not sufficient to guarantee the rational function-ing of such a system. This is because currency reform is practically always limited to operating directly on only one dimension, on the "quantity" of money, as distinct from its second dimension, "a variable rate of turnover," which is subject to more frequent and subtle changes than the former.

Thus we believe it is fair to say that with Marshall and Fisher the problem of value constancy of money is reduced to finding ways and means to make investors reckon in real terms and to bar speculative as distinct from "sound" investment. But there was no direct path in their systems from the quantity and elasticity of currency to the forces which act upon individual income dispositions and production decisions.

On the other hand, Wicksell's apparatus for displaying the value instability of money did not require "speculation" to be set in motion. Normal entrepreneurial behavior was sufficient to produce cumulative fluctuations in the price level in the absence of deliberate policy action to prevent this. Nor did he seek the solution for his problem in terms of changing the mode of calculation from pecuniary to real terms. The problem was more fundamental than that. It entailed a search for the conditions under which monetary equilibrium is possible.

In that search Wicksell was fortunate in availing himself of an abstract schema and of assumptions which made it possible for him to transcend the limitations to thought which imposed themselves on his predecessors. For the most part the latter pursued their investigations with the image of some existing set of monetary institutions in mind, generally that of nineteenth-century Great Britain. One consequence of the method Wicksell adopted, in his attempt to study the "elasticity" of monetary systems and the causes of changes in the circuit velocity of money, was that he was able to raise monetary discussion to a purer level of theoretical discourse. As a result he endowed monetary theory with greater generality than had been possible on the narrower, institutionally determined premises on which it had been pursued up to his time. As Lionel Robbins has put it: "By means of his assumption of a pure credit economy, Wicksell successfully escaped from the tyranny which the concept 'quantity of money' has until recently exercised on monetary theory." [24]

Wicksell's Concept of Money

NATURE AND FUNCTIONS OF MONEY

For purposes of exposition in contexts where he wished to distinguish between money and its near substitutes, or between money and credit, Wicksell applied the following definition: ". . . we mean by money only metallic money." [25] But in the central part of his analysis, his treatment of equilibrium between the "money market" and the "market for commodities," he employed a more general and functional definition: ". . . economically speaking, money is a quantity in *two dimensions,* quantity of value on the one hand and velocity of circulation on the other. These two dimensions multiplied together give the efficiency (Helfferich) of money or its power to facilitate the turnover of goods during a given period of time." [26]

In order to distinguish money from ordinary commodities, Wicksell stressed its "conventional character" and held in substance that no hard and fast line can be drawn between "money" and "nonmoney." The history of currency shows that surprisingly diverse commodities

---

[24] L. Robbins, Introduction to the English edition of *Lectures-II,* p. xvii.
[25] Wicksell, *Lectures-II,* p. 3.
[26] *Ibid.,* p. 19.

have been chosen for use as media of exchange. For reasons of relative value constancy, malleability, portability, etc., one or another or both of the precious metals have been preferred for this use. But their use as "money" removes them effectively from the category of "commodities." "Money possesses in the highest degree—and this is one of its most important characteristics—the quality of a *res fungibilis.* . . . The characteristics of money as a commodity (its concrete qualities) are forced more and more into the background when it is used as a medium of exchange. They may emerge again, but only when it ceases to become money and becomes an ordinary commodity." [27]

The conventional character of money was best illustrated by inconvertible currencies, which were capable under effective monetary management, of maintaining their "value" independently of a metallic reserve. Within limits, this was also true of money substitutes—personal, bank, and state credit—by means of which almost anything possessed of the prospect of future value or income deemed sufficient to repay the principal of a loan with accrued interest could be "monetized."

If money is "a quantity of value multiplied by a variable rate of turnover," this explained why there could be no determinate relation between a stock of metallic money and the volume of trade that might be carried on by means of it, and why its quantity does not uniquely determine its value. Wicksell concluded that concepts such as "supply of" and "demand for" money, especially the supply concept, tend to be indeterminate in modern conditions, "a moot question of monetary theory." [28]

The distinction between money and ordinary commodities rests on the fact that money, unlike other goods, possesses no direct utility, only an indirect one, namely the utility of the real goods it may command. "Its [money's] subjective value depends entirely on its objective value" [i.e., on its purchasing power and its value stability as a storehouse of value].[29]

Further, unlike other goods, money is not consumed by being used, and therefore it remains in use constantly. It remains in circulation, and its quantity equals the aggregate of cash balances. As a "quantity of value," it is equal to the real value of aggregate cash balances. This also explains the paradox of hoarding, namely, that when everyone tries to add to his cash balance at the same time, in the aggregate

[27] *Ibid.*, pp. 18-19.

[28] Wicksell, "Den dunkla punkten i penningteorien" (The Moot Point in Monetary Theory), *Ekonomisk Tidskrift*, 5 (1903), 485 ff.; and *Lectures-II*, pp. 20-21.

[29] Wicksell, *Ekonomisk Tidskrift*, 5 (1903), 485.

no one succeeds, for the quantity of money being given, its rate of turnover declines while its value appreciates as prices fall.[30]

As for the "functions" of money, Wicksell distinguished three of an interrelated nature. Money serves as a medium of exchange, a measure of value, and a storehouse of value. Nothing can properly be considered money unless it serves as a medium of exchange, whereas it is possible both to measure and store value by other means than the exchange medium. As a medium of exchange, money performs the essential service of correlating exchange ratios of commodities with one another, thus facilitating the attainment of market equilibrium exchange ratios or prices.

Taken solely in its role of an exchange medium, the value of the commodity, or whatever else is used for money, is neutral with respect to (i.e., is determined independently of) the relative prices of commodities whose exchange ratios are correlated by means of it. In a perfect market relative prices are determined by the mutual interaction of consumers' preferences and costs of production. Clearly, the conditions which determine relative prices do *not* determine the value of money, for the relative price of the medium of exchange in terms of itself is by definition unity. Also from the standpoint of time discount or waiting (in the short run), the value of money as a medium of exchange must be neutral with respect to commodity values. Its exchange function is a service which is essentially applicable to "transactions near or simultaneous in time."

These were the main reasons, along with the indirect utility characteristic of money, why Wicksell made a categorical distinction between the "money market" and the "market for commodities," for the forces which determine "value" in these two spheres were *not* the same.[31]

Since no hard and fast line can be drawn in practice between transactions "simultaneous or near" and those which are "more remote in time," whatever serves satisfactorily as a medium of exchange also usually becomes the universal measure of value or the standard of value for deferred as well as current transactions. To serve as effectively as a value measure as it ordinarily does as an exchange medium, it would be necessary that money itself be of constant value through time with reference to commodities. In a sense Wicksell's entire monetary analysis was addressed to the problem of making money a more perfect measure of value.

But the very nature of money as a "value quantity multiplied by a variable rate of turnover" prevents it, in the absence of special pro-

---

[30] Wicksell, *Lectures-II*, pp. 8-9.
[31] Cf. Wicksell, *Interest and Prices*, pp. 23, 28, and *Lectures-II*, p. 20.

visions, from functioning as a completely satisfactory measure of value. This deficiency is most directly associated with its third function, to serve as a storehouse of value.[32]

VELOCITY OF CIRCULATION OF MONEY OR CASH BALANCES

Wicksell's treatment of the value storage function of money moves into his analysis of its velocity of circulation and the cash balance demand for money, where the development of credit and banking institutions hold the center of attention. Thence it proceeds to the terms on which credit becomes available, and on into the cumulative processes due to divergence between the natural and money or loan rates of interest. In fact, his entire monetary doctrine can be discussed from the value storage function as a point of departure.

In view of what follows later, we must bear in mind that in discussing the functions of money Wicksell assumed either an existing monetary system in "tranquil" conditions, or a "properly functioning one," i.e., a system in equilibrium in which savings find practically immediate placement in investment via the intermediation of banks.[33] Thus he assumed an economy in full employment equilibrium, presumably for the reason that the nature of the functions of money can best be understood in circumstances where they do not operate against unusual strains.

His concept of the velocity of circulation of money was expressed in the following manner: "The period during which any piece of money is on the average retained in the safe, between a sale and a subsequent purchase, may be called the average period of idleness; and the inverted value of this period of time, expressed as a unit (say a year) will be the average velocity of circulation. . . . Included in the circulation of money is of course the transfer of money from one person to another by means of loans or advances."[34]

Thus, if the quantity of money, M, is given, and the "average period of idleness" is t, then $1/t = V$, the circuit velocity, which, later on, received more elaboration in the hands of Irving Fisher. That this "V" was a concept with which Wicksell was not very happy is indicated by the following: "Theoretically, therefore, the concept of velocity of circulation is a very simple one. But in practice its investigation is one of the most difficult problems in economics, because, among other things, the velocity of circulation varies so enormously with each portion of the monetary stock of a country. . . ."[35]

[32] Wicksell, *Lectures-II*, p. 60.
[33] *Ibid.*, pp. 11-12.
[34] *Ibid.*, p. 60.
[35] *Ibid.*, p. 60.

Neither can it be said that his attempt to explain the actual (as distinct from the potential) behavior of V succeeded in resolving his doubts about it. If M, the aggregate of cash balances, is given, changes in its velocity, V, must be explained in terms of the forces which motivate changes in demand for money.

The demand for cash balances was viewed as composed of the following elements: (1) demand for till money, (2) for reserves for precautionary purposes, (3) for accumulating savings awaiting suitable investment opportunities, (4) to liquidate large blocks of capital, and (5) for hoards of hard money or bank notes.[36]

As for (1), the demand for till money, this he considered to be determined by an experience-tested ratio to business turnover, a ratio based on foreseen differences between receipts and disbursements. The precautionary demand for balances (2), is a demand for cash reserves for unforeseen discrepancies between disbursements and receipts. It is related to the degree of business risk, and while it cannot be determined accurately on an individual basis, it is capable of actuarial estimation for groups of enterprises or industries. These estimates, then, serve individuals as guides to their required safety margin.

In a properly ordered system, where savings are concurrently invested and financial panics do not occur, the cash balance demands for (3) accumulating savings awaiting investment opportunities, and for (5) hoards of hard money or bank notes, would be zero in net terms.

Finally, (4), the demand for balances to liquidate large blocks of capital, was viewed as an unpredictable but quantitatively unimportant composite of the total demand for cash balances. It arose chiefly in circumstances where the death of owners of large estates or enterprises forces the sale of securities to satisfy the claims of heirs, legatees, and of the state for inheritance taxes. As a case in point, he referred to the settlement of the Alfred Nobel estate which, because of its unusual size and the number of its foreign commitments, seems to have put a temporary strain on the Swedish money market.[37]

Having thus enumerated and commented on the constituents of the demand for cash balances, Wicksell skirted the problem of how the behavior of these demand elements are related to one another. His discussion of the relation of hoarding, saving, and investment to the demand for cash balances was not clear and tends to obscure the application he made of the velocity of cash balances in his analysis. By "hoarding" he meant the panic phenomenon of people hiding coins

---

[36] Cf. Wicksell, *Interest and Prices*, pp. 53-58, and the untranslated appendix of *Geldzins und Güterpreise*, "Anhang—Das Gesetz der Grossen Zahlen," pp. 180 ff.

[37] Cf. Wicksell, *Lectures-II*, p. 94.

and notes in strongboxes until the storm is over. The contemporary conception of hoards as "idle bank balances" held for speculative purposes hardly enters into his treatment at this stage.

Yet, the velocity of cash balances does play an important role in Wicksell's analysis, but this occurs *only* when their velocity is changing. That in turn takes place mainly when the net demand for balances from the savings-investment nexus is *not zero*, i.e., when savings and investment *ex ante* are *not* in equilibrium.

Having indicated that V is a function of several variables, he left to others the task of investigating its determination in detail while he devoted his attention to the potential range of variation of V as an integral magnitude relative to M. That brings us to his conception of the function of credit.

DEVELOPMENT OF CREDIT AS AN INCREASE
IN "VIRTUAL" VELOCITY OF CIRCULATION OF MONEY

In his analysis of credit, Wicksell made effective use of the commonplace observation that when payments are made by mutual cancellation of claims, use of currency is obviated. Currency that would otherwise have been used in the absence of credit is set free to do its money work elsewhere. Consequently, the use of credit amounts to a "virtual" transfer of currency or money; thus credit increases the virtual circuit velocity of a given stock of money. On the basis of this insight he began to see existing monetary systems in a new light and to classify them according to the degree of their development of credit.

In reality we find that every country's monetary system consists of a mixture in different proportions of the opposed extremes, the cash economy and the pure credit economy. If we are able to ascertain how the determination of prices takes place under first the one and then the other of these two assumptions, and if we succeed in finding a law common to both of them, then we may also claim that this law must be valid in the actual world with its different types of monetary systems.[38]

The "law" common to all monetary systems, except that of the pure cash system—and there it would fail to apply only by reason of the absence of credit—he formulated in the following statement:

. . . the influence of credit on currency may, *under all circumstances* be regarded as accelerating the circulation of money. . . . The occasions on which credit actually replaces money and thereby renders it superfluous may,

---
[38] *Ibid.*, pp. 10-11.

quite simply be regarded as special cases of the general acceleration of circulation; for instead of a purely physical transfer of money, we have a *virtual*, i.e., merely imaginary or possible transfer, but of the same effectiveness.[39]

At one extreme there is the pure cash economy in which no credit is given. Here the physical and actual velocity of money clearly depends on slowly changing payment habits. Here V is for practical purposes a constant. Consequently, any increase in the stock of money, dM, not finding a corresponding increase in the demand for cash balances at existing prices, enters the circulation or is used for purchases. If output is given in the short run, this raises the price level approximately in the proportion $(M + dM)/M$. At this higher level of prices, V being given by payments habits, $(M + dM)$ becomes equal to the normal demand for cash balances. In this situation, then, the simple quantity theory comes into its own. "The older quantity theory holds without modification if we assume a pure cash economy." [40] However, when person-to-person or "unorganized" credit develops in the former pure cash economy, V becomes slightly variable or elastic.[41]

From this point on the progressive substitution of credit for metallic currency in effecting an increasing proportion of payments (and finally practically all payments) was visualized in terms of an evolution of banking institutions. Commercial banks develop. They obviate the need for persons to keep cash balances in hoards of coin or notes by converting these into demand deposits. Then use of currency is limited to effecting small payments and to acting as a reserve for bridging temporary gaps between deposits and withdrawals at the banks. Banks form clearing house associations and thus become closely interdependent, forming a banking system between them. A central bank is created to centralize the reserves of private banks. This makes possible multiple expansion of deposits and bank notes. The central bank also acquires powers for exercising control over the expansion of credit, chiefly by its ability to vary its discount rate and by enforcing its credit policy on private banks via open-market operations. At this stage the evolution from an "organized" to a "pure" credit system may occur in several ways. But it would proceed most naturally through the formation of international clearings unions by central

---

[39] *Ibid.*, p. 67.

[40] Wicksell, "Penningräntans inflytande på varupriserna" (The Influence of the Money Rate of Interest on Commodity Prices), *Nationalekonomiska Föreningens Förhandlingar* (Proceedings of the Swedish Association of Economics), 1 (1898), 51.

[41] Wicksell, *Interest and Prices*, p. 62.

banks and the adopting of common standards of international price stabilization policy, as indicated above.

In discussing the pure credit system, Wicksell assumed a closed economy in which there is only one bank, the central bank. The latter, however, has branch offices in every hamlet. Almost all payments are effected by checks, and currency in the form of token coins is used only for small payments. In the pure credit system V would be infinitely elastic. Consequently the supply of money would be no obstacle to economic development. It would be indefinitely expansible, subject only to the terms on which the central bank is willing to make credit available. In these circumstances the powers of banking institutions would be commensurate with their responsibility for adopting a rational monetary policy, which he interpreted as a policy of keeping the value of money, the unit of account, constant.

VALUE OF MONEY AS AFFECTED BY CHANGES IN VELOCITY
OF CIRCULATION, AND THE DETERMINATION OF THE LATTER
IN WICKSELL'S ANALYSIS

At this point it may be worthwhile to raise the question of how the value of money is determined in Wicksell's approach to this problem via the value storage function of money. However, Wicksell himself did not attempt to demonstrate this explicitly. Instead he dealt with the money-value problem from an aggregate demand approach, leaving such matters as its velocity in the background.

As will be evident, the following "model" is somewhat awkward because all changes in the magnitude of cash balances must be expressed in variations of V, rather than in variations of both M and V, if they are to reflect Wicksell's assessment of the value storage function.

We assume a closed economy operating under free competition at full resource utilization. It is endowed with a pure credit system and is initially in monetary equilibrium, which, for short, may be taken to mean that the price level, P, of its current output, O, is constant. Here money is "a unit of account." In the aggregate it is "a quantity of value multiplied by a variable rate of turnover," i.e., MV. Here M, "the quantity of value," equals the sum of cash balances, the real value of which depends at any moment on P, or on what can be bought for the units of account at going prices if O and V are constant.

In consequence, V, "the variable rate of turnover," is $V = (PO)/M$ and depends on the community's disposition to value storage in the form of cash balances. The extent of value storage is $1/V = M/(PO)$. With M and O given, an increase in disposition to value storage in cash can only result in a reduction in V and a decline in P, and vice versa.

Since M, by definition, is at any moment equal to the demand and supply of cash balances, changes in the "value of money," i.e., in P, must be sought for among the forces which operate on the disposition to value storage in cash, i.e., operate on the demand for cash balances. As we have seen, the largest and most variable of these elements of demand for cash balances is the net demand by savers for balances in which to store the value of their savings while the latter await investment. But also in "a properly ordered system," this net demand was taken to be zero.

However, if the system is *not* in proper order, i.e., if it is in disequilibrium, then deposits may be created in favor of entrepreneurs faster than individuals are accumulating savings in balances. In that case V increases, and vice versa. Let us ignore the other elements of the cash-balance demand, chiefly the till-money and precautionary reserve elements, as being incapable of significant independent variation in a system which is in or near equilibrium.

Thus, in equilibrium $I = S$, both taken *ex ante,* and in the assumed circumstances P will be constant. But if I exceeds S *ex ante,* V must increase, since M is taken as constant at the outset. The contrary happens if I *ex ante* falls short of S *ex ante.* Let the variation in V be dV. Then if $I > S$, $[M(V + dV)]\,1/O = P'$; and P' must be greater than P. But if $I < S$, $[M(V + dV)] \cdot 1/O = P''$, P'' will be smaller than P.

However, V has a supply price, the discount or loan rate of interest, i, which is determined by the central bank. This rate also determines the flow of savings into balances. But if the banks are actively engaged in deposit creation, V may increase indefinitely from a supply standpoint independently of the flow of savings. Whether or not V shall increase at a given level of i, at which the flow of savings and the disposition to value storage in cash must also be taken as given, depends on investment demand. Investment demand, in turn, is a function of the net expected rate of return on newly created real capital, Wicksell's "real rate" of interest, r. With i given, investment attains to a magnitude for which $r = i$. If, due to inertia or to faulty policy, the central bank keeps i constant while r rises, I will exceed S and the consequence is a rise in P. The increase in P becomes cumulative since the initial rise in P increases r further. This cumulative process or rise in the price level continues until the central bank, or a crisis, stops it by a sufficient upward adjustment of i, or by a sufficient decline of r. But if instead of a pure credit system a gold coin standard is in use, at cumulatively rising prices an internal cash drain of coins demanded in circulation eventually depletes the central bank's gold reserves and forces it to brake the cumulative process by raising its discount rate.[42]

Enough has been said to reveal an interpretation of Wicksell's analysis of circuit velocity of money which is consistent with his main position. Relatively little of the customary quantity theory remained in this treatment.

In the pure credit system "an increase in the quantity of money" can only occur with the consent and coöperation of the powerful central bank. If such an increase occurs it must be due to an increase in the demand for money, say because of a rise in r relative to i. But then the "increase in quantity of money" takes the expression of net deposit creation, i.e., of an increase in V.

Thus Wicksell transformed the quantity theory into an income velocity theory of money.[43] That his formulation of the latter was not as explicit nor as complete as, for instance, that of D. H. Robertson in *Banking Policy and the Price Level* (1926), or that of J. M. Keynes in *A Treatise on Money* (1930) must be admitted. Nevertheless an income velocity theory of money was an integral part of Wicksell's monetary analysis.

However, now we must proceed to the center of gravity of Wicksell's monetary theory, his treatment of the conditions for and the inherent instability of monetary equilibrium. Following his usage, we shall initially refer to this as his theory of "the exchange value of money," although today it would more readily be recognized as a theory of monetary equilibrium.

Theory of Exchange Value of Money or of Monetary Equilibrium

THE MONEY MARKET VERSUS THE COMMODITY MARKET—"NATURAL-," "REAL-," AND "MONEY-," OR "LOAN-" RATES OF INTEREST

Wicksell defined the value of money and the means of measuring it as follows: ". . . we mean by value of money exactly the same thing as the exchange value of money, its purchasing power as against goods and services. To us, therefore, the value of money and the price level are synonymous, or more correctly, correlative ideas." [44]

With that definition plus his two-dimensional concept of money, it

---

[42] This sequence of an internal cash drain generated by the cumulative process itself in a gold standard economy and forcing the banks to restore equilibrium has recently been emphasized by D. Patinkin in "Wicksell's 'Cumulative Process,'" *Economic Journal*, LXII (Dec., 1952), 835 ff., and in "Supplementary Note E" of his *Money, Interest and Prices* (Evanston, Ill., 1956), pp. 420 ff.

[43] Cf. A. Hansen, *Monetary Theory and Fiscal Policy* (New York), p. 85.

[44] Wicksell, *Lectures-II*, p. 129.

almost follows of necessity that he would select an aggregate-demand-supply approach to the conditions which determine the exchange-value of money.

His constructive criticism of the received "simple" quantity theory became the starting point for his investigation into the conditions for monetary equilibrium. Among the "defects of the quantity theory," [45] he noted particularly its one-dimensional concept of money and the associated mechanistic view that in the short run changes in the quantity of money imply proportionate changes in the level of prices. This line of attack, however, afforded no direct insight into those changes in individuals' income dispositions and associated changes in entrepreneurial production decisions from which the variations in composition and magnitude of real output are derived, which inevitably accompany price level movements. Because of this, Wicksell suggested that a "rational theory" be attempted from the following point of departure:

> Every rise or fall in the price of a particular commodity presupposes a disturbance of the equilibrium between the supply and demand for the commodity, whether the disturbance has actually taken place or is merely prospective. What is true *in this respect* of each commodity taken separately must doubtless be true of all commodities collectively. A general rise in prices is therefore only conceivable on the supposition that the general demand has for some reason become, or is expected to become, greater than the supply. This may sound paradoxical, because we have so accustomed ourselves, with J. B. Say, to regard goods themselves as reciprocally constituting and limiting the demand for each other. And indeed, *ultimately* they do so; here, however, we are concerned precisely with what occurs *in the first place*, with the middle link in the final exchange of one good against another, which is formed by the demand of money for goods and the supply of goods against money. Any theory of money worthy of the name must be able to show how and why the monetary or pecuniary demand for goods exceeds or falls short of the supply of goods in given conditions.[46]

To come to grips with this problem—why "pecuniary demand may exceed or fall short of the supply of goods"—Wicksell made use of a categorical distinction between "the market for commodities" and "the money market." Later in his analysis, he indicated how these two markets relate to and interact upon one another by means of price level movements traceable to divergencies between the mobile "real" or "natural" interest rate and the more laggard "money" or "loan" rate of interest.

---

[45] *Ibid.*, pp. 159 ff.
[46] *Ibid.*, pp. 159-160.

His suggestion of the two markets was a fruitful analytical device. Keynes resorted to an analogous method when he distinguished between "the industrial" and the "financial circulation." [47] Its counterpart survives in contemporary theories of income and employment in the emphasis placed on the lack of any necessary coördination between income recipients' disposition to saving and entrepreneur-investors' decisions concerning the production of current output of capital and consumption goods.

In *Interest and Prices* Wicksell dealt with the "commodity market" in pure barter terms. This was the market for which the real national income was produced to become distributed in real income shares by a process of exchange in the course of which the relative prices of goods and services were also determined. One relationship in that market was of strategic importance for his theory; namely, the proportion in which current output is divided into "present" or consumption goods and "future" or capital goods. This proportion was determined by the "natural rate of interest." Given the time preferences of income recipients in allocating real income between consumption and real saving, the natural rate of interest reflected the physical marginal productivity of the corresponding real-investment or "roundabout process" of production. Consequently, the natural rate was defined as follows:

There is a certain rate of interest on loans which is *neutral* in respect to commodity prices, and tends neither to raise nor to lower them. This is necessarily *the same as the rate of interest* which would be *determined by supply and demand if no use were made of money* and all lending were effected in the form of real capital goods. It comes to much the same thing to describe it as the current value of *the natural rate of interest on capital.*[48]

The reason for this formulation was: "The exchange of commodities in itself, and the conditions of production and consumption on which it depends, affect only exchange values or *relative prices;* they can exert *no direct influence whatever on the absolute level of money prices.*" [49]

Now there is, of course, a meaningful sense in which the determination of relative prices can be separated in thought from that of the general price level itself, but for this purpose it was extravagant to construe the commodity market in barter terms. In conditions where several commodities are exchanged in the same market, the natural rate cannot be meaningfully conceived in barter terms. Even if entrepreneurs borrow, pay interest, and repay capital *in natura,* there is no

[47] J. M. Keynes, *A Treatise on Money,* I (London, 1930), chap. 15.
[48] Wicksell, *Interest and Prices,* p. 102. Italics supplied.
[49] *Ibid.,* p. 23; italics in the original. See also p. 39.

way of comparing the physical marginal productivity rate of, for instance, real capital in the form of wheat with other such capital in the form of cattle, *except* in exchange value terms, i.e., in monetary terms. Moreover, such comparisons would be equally necessary for entrepreneurs as for capitalists in order to determine which of several opportunities represent the better or best investment alternatives. Consequently, the marginal physical productivity rate had to be replaced by a marginal value productivity rate of real capital.

Once that was done, there was no reason to view the exchange processes of the commodity market in barter terms. Conceived of in exchange value terms, or in terms of money of constant purchasing power, it reveals the "real forces" at play as well, in fact more clearly, than on a barter basis.

Evidently for these reasons Wicksell changed the definition of "the natural rate" in *Lectures-II,* saying that he had introduced what he believed were "improvements" in developing his concepts of "normal" and "real interest rate . . . alongside the somewhat vague and abstract concept of the natural rate of interest on capital." [50] Hence, the "natural rate" was replaced by the "real rate" defined in exchange value terms as the marginal value productivity of real capital, or, in his own words, as ". . . the expected yield on newly created real capital." [51]

On the other hand, superimposed on the "commodity market," as it were, there was "the money market." Transactions in this market were viewed as mediated by the central bank and the dependent system of private banks. Although Wicksell recognized the existence of a stock market and of special investment banks, he did not differentiate their functions and behavior from those of commercial banks in his treatment of the money market.

The banks receive the money savings of income recipients, including firms, and lend them to entrepreneur-investors at a loan rate of interest which, in view of the existence of a structure of differentiated long and short rates, implies a standard combination of such rates. Other things equal, i.e., if the banks do not indulge in net deposit creation nor the public in net disinvestment (as in times of crisis or panic), the loan rate in the money market tends to be established by competition at a level such that gross investment equals the flow of gross saving.

Investment demand for funds in turn is determined by the real rate of interest. But owing to the elasticity of supply of money and credit (or owing to the variability of the rate of income velocity of cash

[50] Wicksell, *Lectures-II,* Preface, first Swedish edition, p. vi.
[51] Wicksell, *Lectures-II,* 3d ed., English translation, p. 192.

balances made possible by passive or deliberate net deposit creation by banks), the supply of investable funds need not in the short run be identical with the rate of saving. In a pure credit system, and within fairly wide limits in conditions short of that in a modern banking system, the supply of investable funds is highly elastic at any given level of the money rate of interest.

If the flow of saving is given at some prevailing loan rate of interest, a rise in the real rate increases investment demand for funds in excess of savings, and the difference is then made up by net credit expansion by the banks, and vice versa.

THE NATURE OF MONETARY EQUILIBRIUM—THE "NORMAL" LOAN RATE OF INTEREST AND THE INSCRUTABLE, MOVING REAL RATE

In Wicksell's own words, the condition for equilibrium on both the money and the commodities markets was expressed as follows:

> That loan rate which is a direct expression of the real rate, we call the normal rate. . . . *The rate of interest at which the demand for loan capital and the supply of savings exactly agree, and which* more or less *corresponds to the expected yield on the newly created real capital will then be the normal or natural real rate. It is essentially variable.* If the prospects of employment of capital become more promising, demand will increase and will at first exceed supply; interest rates will then rise as the demand from entrepreneurs contracts until a new equilibrium is reached at a slightly higher rate of interest. *At the same time equilibrium must ipso facto obtain . . . in the market for goods and services, so that wages and prices remain unchanged.* The sum of money income will then usually exceed the money value of consumption goods annually produced, but the excess of income—i.e., what is annually saved and invested in production—will not produce any demand for present goods but only for labor and land for future production.[52]

Thus equilibrium on the money market implied (1) real-income equilibrium on the commodity market. About this Wicksell was right. But for many years he also thought that (2) the "normal" or equilibrium loan rate on the money market would keep prices, i.e., the price level, stable on the commodity market. About this he was wrong, as he came to recognize later.

1. *Conditions for monetary equilibrium.* Wicksell assumed an economy operating under free competition and at full resource utilization for his monetary analysis. He also abstracted from the effects of government spending for goods and services and of taxation in the money and commodity markets, respectively. This comes to much the

---

[52] *Ibid.*, pp. 192-193. Italics supplied.

same as saying that he assumed a balanced budget of relatively small size compared with the national income.

Now, the equilibrium or "normal" loan rate of interest was, as has been shown, one at which investment demand (*ex ante*) for funds equals the flow of savings from persons and business enterprises. Hence both the level of national income and consumption demand are determinate. Because of free competition, consumer expenditures then pay for the supply of consumer goods and services in the commodity market at prices which, on the average, equal their costs of production. In the absence of changes in aggregate demand and in technology, the real rate of interest (or expected net rate of return) on capital goods to be produced must be equal to the real rate on "newly created real capital." With a given loan rate, investment is a function of the real rate so that investment will be expanded to all projects for which the real rate is greater than or at least equal to the loan rate. But in free competition, when the expected net rate of return on capital goods is discounted by the "normal" loan rate of interest, which reflects the real rate, the result is a set of capitalized values or prices for these goods which, on the average, equal their costs of production. Thus investors pay cost-prices for capital goods at the same time as consumers pay cost-prices for consumption goods and services.

Consequently money market equilibrium between investment and saving implied cost-price equilibrium in the commodity market. If this were not the case, equilibrium in the money market would be disrupted. For instance, if, in the absence of monopolistic restraints, net gains were obtainable either on consumption or on capital goods in significant branches of production, this would be an indication that the real rate on such goods is higher than on others, hence higher than the loan rate in these industries. If this were the case, it would give rise to an upward cumulative process. Production, hence investment demand for funds, would expand in industries having net gains. If savings are at all interest-elastic, and Wicksell assumed they were moderately so, they would not rise sufficiently to satisfy the increased investment demand, which would be financed by net credit expansion. Thus the only way monetary equilibrium (i.e., absence of net credit expansion in this case) could be preserved with net gains accruing in the commodity market under free competition, would be by the unlikely double coincidence that (*a*) the investment demand had expanded only by the amount of the gains, and (*b*) the gains were saved *in toto*.

However, cost-price equilibrium on the commodity market does not necessarily imply stable prices or an invariant general level of prices unless it is also assumed that production functions remain constant. If productivity increases, cost-price equilibrium is equally well preserved at prices varying inversely with the change in productivity, money incomes constant, as it is with stable prices, money incomes rising in proportion to the increase in productivity. In either case, if the necessary condition for preservation of monetary equilibrium is that cost-prices prevail on the commodity market when productivity changes, this, in itself, does not guarantee the maintenance of monetary equilibrium. The sufficient condition for the latter then is either (*a*), if the price level varies inversely with changes in productivity, that the increased real income of the community be allocated to consumption and to saving in the same proportion as the increased national product is made up of consumption goods and of investment goods, or (*b*), if the price level is held stable when productivity increases, that the increased money income of the community be allocated to saving and to consumption in the foregoing proportion. There was, of course, no reason to believe that this double adjustment would be performed automatically.

2. *Equilibrium in the money market as distinct from equilibrium of relative prices in the commodity market.* The categorical distinction Wicksell insisted on between the forces which determine values on the commodity market from those which determine value (i.e., the general level of prices) on the money market[53] was reinforced by a conception of a fundamental difference between the nature of equilibrium in these different markets. Commodity market equilibrium was described as inherently stable, like that of a freely suspended pendulum on which forces, which increase in proportion to its displacement from the position of equilibrium, are brought into play to restore it to its position of rest.

But monetary or price level equilibrium was by contrast described as "labile" or neutral in character. If any force, a divergence between the loan rate and real rate of interest, for instance, moved the system off its equilibrium position, it would react like a cylinder on a plane. The disturbing force would push the cylinder cumulatively further and further in a given direction on the plane. And when the propelling force had abated, the cylinder would remain at the point to which it had been rolled without any tendency to return to its former position.[54]

If a pure credit system prevails in the money market, the cylinder

[53] Wicksell, *Interest and Prices*, pp. 23 and 39.
[54] *Ibid.*, pp. 100-101; *Lectures-II*, pp. 196-197.

(i.e., the cumulative upward or downward movement of the price level) may be kept on rolling indefinitely in a given direction, upwards, if the banks keep the loan rate abnormally low relative to the real rate, and downwards if they keep the loan rate too high. Under more restrictive monetary conditions such as a gold standard system in which fractional reserve demand deposit banking is permitted, the cylinder will not keep rolling indefinitely but is eventually brought to a stop when the price level movement has reached a critical height or depth, as the case may be. As the price level approaches a critical height an internal cash drain sets in and depletes banks' reserves and forces them to raise their loan rates. On the other hand, if the price level declines to a critical depth the progressive accumulation of excess reserves among the banks, on which reserves Wicksell assumed they would pay a deposit rate of interest not much lower than their own loan rates, forces them, for lack of earnings, to reduce loan rates to the proper relation to the real rate and thus restore equilibrium.[55]

Moreover, the main (for several years Wicksell would have said "the only") connecting link between the forces of value determination in the commodity and money markets respectively are the cumulative price level movements engendered by discrepancies between loan rates and real rates of interest.[56]

From a microeconomic point of view, individuals and firms active in the commodity market have no direct concern about and even less influence over the course of the general level of prices. Only those institutions, chiefly the central banks and the system of commercial banks subject to their control, which are responsible for the provision of credit and the issuance of currency, are in a position to view the money market as a whole. Yet, even central banks have no direct control over and little knowledge or foreknowledge (which is even more important in this connection) of the demand side, i.e., the investment demand for funds, in the money market. This demand is a function of the real rate, and the latter frequently shifts to different levels and may remain at a new level for a considerable time before the banks become aware that its position has changed. The real rate cannot be known directly, for entrepreneurial expectations on which it is based, are not registered anywhere. The only evidence of its course are the price level movements it gives rise to some time after it has shifted away from the loan rate in one direction or another. Consequently, the banks can

---

[55] Wicksell, *Interest and Prices*, pp. 110-111, 113-117; *Lectures-II*, pp. 189, 200-201, 204, 207.

[56] Wicksell, *Interest and Prices*, pp. 109-110; *Lectures-II*, p. 206.

do no better than to adjust the level of their loan rates with a lag behind the movement of the real rate.[57] It is for this reason that their primary duty in an elastic monetary system, and particularly in a pure credit system, is to keep a sharp eye on the movement of prices, and to adjust their loan rates in the direction the price level tends to drift until its drift subsides.

In *Interest and Prices* Wicksell reasoned as if the banks' ability to stabilize the price level by interest-rate policy would be adequate no matter what the forces were which accounted for the vagaries of the real rate. In *Lectures-II* and later he qualified this position by recognizing that there are causes of price level movements which are autonomous of the banks or beyond their control by interest policy. Under gold standard conditions for the world as a whole one such force would be significant changes in gold production, and for any individual country considerable shifts in gold movements. For countries on inconvertible standards, fiat issues of paper currency by their governments or large-scale borrowing by them from their central banks would have inflationary consequences beyond the banks' powers of restraint.[58] After World War I, Wicksell also came to recognize another autonomous cause of price level change, namely considerable and rapid changes in productivity or in the availability of commodities (i.e., commodity shortages or surpluses), a matter which will be dealt with in the next chapter. In this manner he arrived at the conclusion that his real-versus-loan-rate theory of the behavior of the price level was at least an adequate "working hypothesis" for explaining those price level movements which were *not* directly attributable to the operation of the foregoing autonomous forces. In *Interest and Prices* (chap. 11), he attempted to test the validity of this hypothesis against the historical record of price level movements in the nineteenth century, and he concluded that:

It is, of course, to be understood that these considerations can claim to indicate only *very broad agreement between our theory and the facts.* . . . The theory must, therefore, be regarded for the moment as a mere *hypothesis.* . . . If it turns out eventually to be correct the practical consequences are of enormous importance. Banks and credit institutions have hitherto exerted only an *involuntary* influence on prices. . . . Now, however,

---

[57] Wicksell, *Interest and Prices,* p. 117; *Lectures-II,* pp. 204-205.

[58] Wicksell, *Lectures-II,* pp. 215 ff., and pp. 165 and 120 describes gold movements and changes in gold production as autonomous causes of price level changes. It was with these in mind he urged the monetary reforms discussed above. *Ibid.,* p. 166, deals with fiat issues and government borrowing from banks as inflationary forces beyond the control of the banks.

they will be able in full consciousness to pursue their objective, to the indisputable benefit of the world economy.[59]

However, his faith in his "working hypothesis" was further strengthened by what his analysis indicated about the potency of the cumulative process itself.

The Cumulative Process

The cumulative process or price level movement plays an ambiguous role in Wicksell's analysis. This has raised questions as to how it is to be interpreted. Wicksell himself was apparently content to show how it starts, by a divergence between real and loan rates of interest, and how it ends, by appropriate adjustments of loan to real rates of interest. What happens between its beginning and end was not made clear. The process may or may not terminate in a crisis of hyperinflation or deflation. It may be of long or short duration, and the maladjustments it may generate in production, in the capital structure, and with respect to employment and distribution of income were on the whole ignored.

Nonetheless, Wicksell was convinced that the cumulative process was one of great potency. Generally he discussed it as an upward movement of prices caused by the real rate having risen above the loan rate, as for instance because of an increase in productivity. He insisted that no matter how slight the excess of the real rate over the loan rate, the cumulative process which results increases progressively in proportion to the duration of the rate discrepancy and takes its expression particularly in rising values of durable capital goods.[60]

In fact, if the process is of long duration, it may accelerate in its later stages, or, as he put it, "create its own draft." This would happen if entrepreneurs (who are usually assumed to make decisions for the future on the expectation of the continuation of current prices), after having experienced some rounds of price increases, begin to make their decisions on the expectation of rising prices.[61] In such cases speculation is aroused and prices may reach great heights. The process itself may then terminate in a crisis as increasing production maladjustments, overextension of investment in various branches of the economy, etc., engender doubts concerning the continuation of further price increases.

But, as has been shown above, the price level movement is the primary connecting link between monetary equilibria separated in

[59] Wicksell, *Interest and Prices*, p. 176. Italics in the first sentence supplied.
[60] *Ibid.*, pp. 90-91, 120-121; and *Lectures-II*, pp. 195-196.
[61] Wicksell, *Interest and Prices*, pp. 96, 148.

time. Particularly in gold standard conditions, where the duration of the cumulative process is not likely to be very considerable, the process itself plays an equilibrating role. Ultimately an upward process generates an internal cash drain of gold into circulation, depleting the reserves of banks and forcing them to make appropriate upward adjustments of their loan rates. In the contrary case of a downward process, as excess reserves subject to a deposit rate of interest accumulate, banks are forced to make proper downward adjustments in their rates.[62] In these cases it is not clear how long the process will be nor whether it will end in a crisis.

However, in a pure credit system the process may be of indefinite duration, and it does not necessarily force the system to equilibrium. The rise (or fall) in prices may reach unprecedented heights (or depths). In this case restoration of equilibrium depends on whether the banks take appropriate action. Wicksell assumed tacitly that they would take such action promptly, for in such a system their power to arrest the cumulative process by interest policy[63] would be equal to what he conceived to be their manifest responsibility; namely, to stabilize the price level insofar as its movement is *not* due to the action of autonomous forces.

---

[62] *Ibid.*, pp. 107-110; *Lectures-II*, pp. 194-206. D. Patinkin, in "Wicksell's·'Cumulative Process,'" *Economic Journal*, LXII (Dec., 1952), 835 ff., and in "Supplementary Note E" of his *Money, Interest and Prices* (Evanston, Ill., 1956), pp. 420 ff., stresses the equilibrating role of the cumulative process in gold standard conditions and minimizes the fact that it cannot play that role in a pure credit economy. The latter, we believe, is contrary to Wicksell's trend of thought, for he strove for the realization of a pure credit economy in the monetary reforms he advocated.

[63] To make sure that central banks would have adequate power to enforce their interest policy on private banks and other credit institutions, Wicksell advocated that, in addition to their ability to vary their own discount rates and to engage in open-market operations, they be given the additional power of extending interest on deposits received and of varying this deposit interest rate. He recognized that this would put the central banks in direct competition with private banks (see *Lectures-II*, pp. 118-19), but he considered this to be of less importance than that the central bank should have the power requisite for its responsibility, and particularly a power which would force private banks to comply promptly with central bank policy. In 1917, and 1920, when Sweden was still on an inconvertible standard adopted at the outbreak of World War I, he reiterated this recommendation in the course of his services as monetary expert for some parliamentary commissions of inquiry. On this, see his "Yttrande angående ifrågasatt inlåningsrätt för Sveriges Riksbank" (Opinion Concerning the Question of Empowering the Bank of Sweden to Make Direct Loans), Stockholm, 1917, and his report, *Utlåtande angående frågan huruvida och i vad mån ett program för den närmaste framtiden for svensk finanspolitik må kunna kunna åstadkommas* (Report on the Question of How and to What Extent It Is Possible to Set Up a Program for the Near Future for Swedish Financial Policy), 1920 Ars Finanssakkunniga (by the Finance Experts Appointed for 1920), Stockholm, 1920. In this he was successful; the Bank of Sweden was in due course given this power. However, so far as the writer has been able to determine, the Bank has never made use of it.

The only model Wicksell constructed for his cumulative process is found in *Interest and Prices*.[64]

WICKSELL'S MODEL OF THE CUMULATIVE PROCESS

The model Wicksell developed of the cumulative process was constructed to fit his concept of "capital in the narrow sense." It would have been better if it had been set up to fit the "structural" concept of capital he developed in writing *Lectures-I* (1901), but this was not done. The assumptions he used were the following:[65]

1. The cumulative process is viewed as operating in a closed economy endowed with a pure credit system. This economy is initially in full resource-use equilibrium, and because free competition prevails on all its markets, remains in full resource-use operation while the process runs its upward and downward course.

2. The length of the production period and of the period of investment is the same in every industry and is equal to one year. Production begins at the same time everywhere, at the beginning of the year, and its proceeds are not available until the close of this period.

3. The annually renewable "liquid real capital" of this economy, i.e., its stock of consumption goods constituting its annual real wages and rent fund, is maintained in constant amount by the aggregate of capitalists.

4. Wages and rents are paid in advance by entrepreneurs at the beginning of the year, enabling workers and landowners to buy a sufficient stock of consumption goods from capitalists to make it possible for them to work during the year.

5. Entrepreneurs own no capital but work entirely with borrowed funds, obtained, not directly from the capitalists, but from the banks.

6. The capitalists are also traders in commodities (consumption goods), but owing to the force of competition, they earn no or at best negligible trading profits. How they, together with entrepreneurs, workers, and owners of natural resources, function in the model is described in the immediately following subsections. Production is limited to making a new stock of consumption goods.

7. The banks in this pure credit economy operate at no net profit. They make loans to entrepreneurs out of funds deposited with them by capitalists at the same rate of interest as the interest rate they pay the capitalists on their deposits.

8. During the first year the economy is entirely stationary, but after

---

[64] Wicksell, *Interest and Prices,* pp. 136-149.

[65] *Ibid.,* pp. 136-138.

that it undergoes a dynamic change by way of an increase in the productivity of the factors of production.

Wicksell's model operates through a ten-year sequence. Its main features can be seen in table 2. However, the following phases of this development bear further scrutiny.

Year I. Entrepreneurs borrow $\$K$ from the banks for wage and rent advances. Workers and owners of natural resources spend $\$K$ in the aggregate buying consumer goods from capitalist-traders, and obtain K units, the entire amount available, of "real liquid capital" as a result.

Capitalists in the aggregate deposit $\$K$ sales proceeds with the banks to earn interest at the loan and deposit rate, $i/100$, which equals the natural rate, and is concretely expressed as 5 per cent.

At the end of year I an output of consumption goods of $K(1 + i/100)$ units is available, having been produced from an input of K units of liquid real capital, which has a marginal physical productivity rate of i per cent. The money value of this output is consequently $\$K(1 + i/100) = \$1.05K$.

This output belongs to entrepreneurs who, owing $\$1.05K$ to the banks, sell it to capitalists at competitive equilibrium prices, i.e., prices equal to the cost of production, for $\$1.05K$, for just enough to pay the banks. But the banks owe this same amount to capitalists at accrued deposit interest, so now they clear their ledgers by clearing checks drawn by capitalists against loan repayments by entrepreneurs.

The output of consumption goods is now in the hands of capitalists, who set aside $(K)i/100$ physical units of it, at a value of $(\$K)i/100$. Thus they set aside the equivalent of their interest income for personal consumption for year II. The remainder, K units, at a value of $\$K$ at constant prices, they sell to workers and landowners.

Now entrepreneurs go to the banks and ask in the aggregate for loans for year II amounting to $\$K$, which they obtain at the same $i = 5$ per cent interest. These loans are now used to pay wage and rent advances, with which workers and owners of natural resources buy the K quantity of available consumption goods for an aggregate expenditure of $\$K$. Thus far the process may be viewed as an endless chain of annual exchanges with entrepreneurs earning a zero rate of net profit (while retaining, of course, competitive management wages out of aggregate annual advances), and the price level remaining constant at its base year index level of 100, as is shown in line one of the table.

Year II. Now the natural rate of interest rises from $i/100$ to

$(i + 1)100 = 6$ per cent because of an increase in the productivity of labor and natural resources. But the loan and deposit rate of interest remains constant at 5 per cent. Output now increases from $K(1 + i/100)$ to $K[1 + (i + 1)]/100 = 1.06K$. At constant prices, the value of this greater output is $1.06K$, and it belongs to entrepreneurs who, in the aggregate owe the banks $1.05K$. Entrepreneurs now have a windfall gain or net profit of $0.010K$, which Wicksell assumed they retain for themselves: "They have thus obtained a surplus profit of $K/100$ and they realize this profit by exchanging among themselves the corresponding quantity of goods and laying them on one side for the consumption of the coming year, while they offer the rest of their stocks to the capitalists at normal prices, that is to say for a sum of money $K(1 + i/100)$. In the first place, therefore, the level of prices remains constant." [66]

There is more to be said about the assumption that entrepreneurs retain their profit, but it is best to proceed with the remainder of the model.

Year III. The profit realized by entrepreneurs in year II now stimulates them to try to expand their activities in the hope of obtaining the same rate of net profit on an increased volume of business in year III. But with all resources in full use, no entrepreneur can expand except at the expense of some other entrepreneur. Thus their efforts to pirate labor and natural resources away from one another only leads to a bidding up of wages and rent to $1.01K$. But in return for this aggregate outlay they only obtain the same physical input of K as before; yet now they are forced to borrow $1.01K$ from the banks for wage and rent advances at the bid-up rates (see line 3 of table 2).

The "pure credit" banks now "accommodate" the increased demand by entrepreneurs for loans at the same rate as before. At the end of year III, entrepreneurs owe the banks $1.01K(1 + i/100) = $1.0605K$. Meanwhile workers and landowners use their $1.01K$ money income to buy the K quantity of consumer goods from capitalists, who now are able to charge $1.01 per unit, and hence deposit in the aggregate $1.01K$ in the banks to earn the 5 per cent deposit rate of interest.

Output of year III is, however, the same as in year II, $1.06K$, yet its money value increases. The value of input, at increased wages and rents, was $1.01K$. During the year its value increases in production at the rate of $(1 + i/100)$ to a total of $1.01K[1 + (i + 1)]/100 = $1.0706K$. Thus, higher wages and rent notwithstanding, entrepreneurs again have a net profit equal to the difference between $1.0706K$

---

[66] *Ibid.,* p. 142.

TABLE 2
The Cumulative Process Model

Col. 1	Col. 2	Col. 3	Col. 4	Col. 5	Col. 6
Investment period (annual)	Natural or "real" rate of interest (per cent)	Loan rate of interest by the banks (per cent)	Input of "liquid capital" in real or physical units	Money value of liquid real capital (input) = aggregate borrowing by entrepreneurs from banks at beginning of investment period	Output or product in real units
1	$i=5$	$i=5$	K	\$1.00000K	$K\left(1+\dfrac{i}{100}\right)=1.05K$
2	$(i+1)=6$	$i=5$	K	\$1.00000K	$K\left(1+\dfrac{i+1}{100}\right)=1.06K$
3	$(i+1)=6$	$i=5$	K	\$1.01000K	$K\left(1+\dfrac{i+1}{100}\right)=1.06K$
4	$(i+1)=6$	$i=5$	K	\$1.02010K	$K\left(1+\dfrac{i+1}{100}\right)=1.06K$
5	$(i+1)=6$	$i=5$	K	\$1.03030K	$K\left(1+\dfrac{i+1}{100}\right)=1.06K$
6	$(i+1)=6$	$(i+1)=6$	K	\$1.03030K	$K\left(1+\dfrac{i+1}{100}\right)=1.06K$
7	$(i+1)=6$	$(i+2)=7$	K	\$1.03030K	$K\left(1+\dfrac{i+1}{100}\right)=1.06K$
8	$(i+1)=6$	$(i+2)=7$	K	\$1.01990K	$K\left(1+\dfrac{i+1}{100}\right)=1.06K$
9	$(i+1)=6$	$(i+2)=7$	K	\$1.00980K	$K\left(1+\dfrac{i+1}{100}\right)=1.06K$
10	$(i+1)=6$	$(i+2)=7$	K	\$0.99970K	$K\left(1+\dfrac{i+1}{100}\right)=1.06K$

TABLE 2—Continued

Col. 7	Col. 8	Col. 9		Col. 10
Money value of output or product	Loans & accrued interest owed by entrepreneurs to banks & by banks to capitalists at the end of the investment period	Net profit or gain retained (+), or net loss sustained (−), by entrepreneurs		Average level of prices of output: {price level index number} Col. 7 divided by Col. 6 =
		In real terms	In money terms	
$K\left(1 + \frac{i}{100}\right) = \$1.05000K$	$\$K\left(1 + \frac{i}{100}\right) = \$1.0500K$	$\pm 0.0000K$	$\$\pm 0.0000K$	$\frac{\$1.05K}{1.05K} = 100.00$
$\$K\left(1 + \frac{i+1}{100}\right) = \$1.0600K$	$\$K\left(1 + \frac{i}{100}\right) = \$1.0500K$	$+0.0100K$	$\$+0.0100K$	$\frac{\$1.06K}{1.06K} = 100.00$
$\$1.01K\left(1 + \frac{i+1}{100}\right) = \$1.0706K$	$\$1.01K\left(1 + \frac{i}{100}\right) = \$1.0605K$	$+0.0100K$	$\$+0.0101K$	$\frac{\$1.0706K}{1.06K} = 101.00$
$\$1.0201K\left(1 + \frac{i+1}{100}\right) = \$1.081306K$	$\$1.0201K\left(1 + \frac{i}{100}\right) = \$1.071105K$	$+0.0100K$	$\$+0.010201K$	$\frac{\$1.081306K}{1.06K} = 102.01$
$\$1.0303K\left(1 + \frac{i+1}{100}\right) = \$1.092119K$	$\$1.0303K\left(1 + \frac{i}{100}\right) = \$1.081816K$	$+0.0100K$	$\$+0.010303K$	$\frac{\$1.092119K}{1.06K} = 103.03$
$\$1.0303K\left(1 + \frac{i+1}{100}\right) = \$1.092119K$	$\$1.0303K\left(1 + \frac{i+1}{100}\right) = \$1.092119K$	$\pm 0.0000K$	$\$\pm 0.0000K$	$\frac{\$1.092119K}{1.06K} = 103.03$
$\$1.0303K\left(1 + \frac{i+1}{100}\right) = \$1.092119K$	$\$1.0303K\left(1 + \frac{i+2}{100}\right) = \$1.102422K$	$-0.0100K$	$\$-0.010303K$	$\frac{\$1.092119K}{1.06K} = 103.03$
$\$1.0199K\left(1 + \frac{i+1}{100}\right) = \$1.08119K$	$\$1.0199K\left(1 + \frac{i+2}{100}\right) = \$1.091398K$	$-0.0100K$	$\$-0.010199K$	$\frac{\$1.081196K}{1.06K} = 101.99$
$\$1.0098K\left(1 + \frac{i+1}{100}\right) = \$1.07039K$	$\$1.0098K\left(1 + \frac{i+2}{100}\right) = \$1.080484K$	$-0.0100K$	$\$-0.010098K$	$\frac{\$1.070386K}{1.06K} = 100.98$
$\$.9997K\left(1 + \frac{i+1}{100}\right) = \$1.05968K$	$\$0.9997K\left(1 + \frac{i+1}{100}\right) = \$1.069679K$	$-0.0100K$	$\$-0.009997K$	$\frac{\$1.059692K}{1.06K} = 99.97$

value of output and $1.0605K they owe the banks, a net profit of $0.0101K. Moreover, the price level has now risen, for a total amount of $1.0706K has been spent for a physical output of 1.06K. Thus prices rise to an index level of 101.

Years IV and V. The profit of year III again encourages entrepreneurs to try to expand activities by bidding up wages and rent in year IV, this time to an aggregate amount of $1.0201K. This raises prices yet another per cent, so that the net profit becomes $0.01201K. The same process is repeated in year V, wages and rents being bid up to $1.030K. The resulting value of output is $1.092110K, with a net profit to entrepreneurs of $0.010303K, and a price level index of 103.03.

Year VI. Now the banks raise their loan and deposit rate of interest to 6 per cent, to equality with the natural rate at the level it had achieved because of the productivity increase which took place in year II. Despite the net profit of year V, entrepreneurs now no longer try to outbid each other for workers, but offer the same wages and rents as before, namely $1.030K in the aggregate. At the end of the year, the value of output is $1.092119K, exactly equal to what entrepreneurs owe banks, hence no net profit, but neither a decline in prices. As Wicksell put it: "The upward movement of prices now of course ceases, but prices do *not* return to their original level . . . everything is in equilibrium, at a higher level of money prices, wages, and rents." [67]

Years VII, VIII, IX, and X. During years VII-X a downward cumulative process sets in because the banks have raised their loan rate to 7 per cent in year VII, at which level this rate is 1 per cent higher than the concurrent natural rate of 6 per cent after the productivity increase. But from the end of year V and through year VII prices have been constant at an index of 103.03. Hence entrepreneurs have to borrow $1.0303K for wage and rent advances. At the end of year VII they owe this sum at 7 per cent interest, a total of $1.102422K, to the banks, while the value of their output remains at a total of $1.092119K (i.e., the input value of $1.0303K accruing in value at the natural rate of 6 per cent). Thus entrepreneurs have a net loss of ($0.010303K).

Further in year VIII the price level declines and continues to do so cumulatively. The losses suffered by entrepreneurs now prompt them to curtail production and offer lower wages and rents. Workers and landowners can consequently not buy the output from capitalists at $1.0303 per unit, but only at prices successively 1 per cent lower in each succeeding period.

---

[67] *Ibid.*, p. 148.

While losses induce entrepreneurs to restrict production, in fact, no output reduction occurs, for as Wicksell put it:

> But workers and landlords will respond by scaling down their claims for wages and rents, and on the whole activity will be maintained at its former level. . . . These diminished wages and rents have to be set against an unaltered amount of consumption goods (real capital). The result is a corresponding fall in the prices of commodities, and entrepreneurs are unable to avoid a loss which is expressed by the difference between the two rates of interest.[68]

This downward process might also go on indefinitely, particularly in a pure credit system. But it is more likely that after some cumulative decline in the price level, entrepreneurs, or the managers of the banks, or both, may persuade capitalists to accept a lower deposit rate of interest from the banks, a rate equal to the natural rate. In that event equilibrium will be restored after a run of one more year or investment period.

Concerning the foregoing cumulative process model, Wicksell made one reservation; namely, that the entire sequence was predicated on the assumption that entrepreneurs and others act and react only to prices current in their planning periods. For the contrary case, of their acting on anticipations of rising prices for the period ahead, he concluded: ". . . as soon, that is to say, as they start reckoning on a future rise in prices, the actual rise will become more and more rapid. In the extreme case in which the expected rise in prices is each time *fully* discounted, the annual rise in prices will be indefinitely great." [69]

DEFICIENCIES OF THE MODEL

It was unfortunate that Wicksell's process model suffered from certain internal inconsistencies. If it had been more realistic and more true to the character of the process he had in mind, it might have contributed to a clearer understanding of his monetary theory. As it was, it may have been more of a hindrance than a help, for it tended to raise unnecessary doubts about the "working hypothesis" it was intended to demonstrate.

First of all, Wicksell's statement that entrepreneurs retain the net profit that arises in years II through V contradicts one of his main assumptions; namely, that entrepreneurs act in free competition with one another. It would have been more natural to expect that, in the aggregate, they would offer the entire annual output of 1.06K to capi-

[68] *Ibid.*, pp. 149-150.
[69] *Ibid.*, p. 148.

talists at a 1 per cent reduction in price, since capitalists in the aggregate can spend only the $1.05K$ they have available at the end of year II in their bank accounts. But if entrepreneurs dispose of the increased output at a proportionate price reduction, then equilibrium is maintained, and the cumulative process fails to get started. In that case there will be no surplus profit left to motivate them to attempt to expand activity by bidding up wages and rent. As for the extra $0.01K$ of output capitalists then would have on hand, under free competition one would expect that they would dispose of most of all of it to workers and landowners at a 1 per cent drop in price. In that case, the price level would fall by 1 per cent and real wages and rent would increase *pro tanto*.

In effect, Wicksell admitted as much when he altered the situation in one part of his exposition to one where entrepreneurs sell the entire augmented output to capitalists, but now at *constant* prices. In order to buy it at these prices capitalists were assumed to borrow an extra amount of $0.01K$ at the banks in addition to drawing their full accounts of $1.05K$. But this is probably a more arbitrary assumption than the previous one, that entrepreneurs retain the output increment as profit. When he finally considered the possibility that the increased output may be sold at reduced prices, he concluded: "Even if it were desired to associate the increase in the quantity of goods with a tendency for a fall in prices, the fall that could on such grounds be expected would be a very small one. More important, it would, so far as I can see, occur only *once and for all,* and it would thus be put completely in the shade by the cumulative effect on prices that is to be ascribed to a difference between the two rates of interest." [70]

The last part of this conclusion was not well supported by further argumentation. If the natural rate rises above the loan rate in year II and output increases to $1.06K$ but is sold at 99 per cent of its former price, then all surplus profit is wiped out and no effort at expansion will be made. Moreover, this situation may repeat itself in years III, IV, V, etc. Hence the fall in prices, while it is a once-for-all event in year II, has become a permanently lower and stable level of prices for succeeding periods. There are, in fact, no cumulative forces acting to push the price level upwards, unless one assumes that either the capitalists or the workers and landowners, who between them have received a 1 per cent increase in real incomes as a result of the price decline, decide to invest all of their extra real income. But no such assumption was made. Instead equilibrium has been restored.

[70] *Ibid.*, p. 142.

When entrepreneurs sell $1.06K$ at \$0.99 *per* unit for $\$1.05K$ in the aggregate, then the net return over cost has in fact risen to 6 per cent, for their unit cost of production decreased by the 1 per cent increase in productivity. Moreover, the banks, by keeping the loan rate at 5 per cent have in fact made, not the nominal loan rate, but the effective real loan rate ("real" in the Irving Fisher sense), equal to the 6 per cent natural rate, for a 5 per cent loan rate accompanied by a 1 per cent decline in prices, equals a 6 per cent real rate, or equals a 6 per cent nominal loan rate at constant prices. This seems to have escaped Wicksell's attention.

Thus, unless we assume something less than free competition among entrepreneurs to enable them to retain the output increment as surplus profit, the upward cumulative process beginning in period III does not get started. It may, instead, be replaced by a one-period decline in prices which restores equilibrium at a lower level of prices. This was contrary to what Wicksell intended to show.

Even greater difficulties beset the downward process of the years VII through X inclusive. Entrepreneurs have losses because the loan rate exceeds the natural rate. How do they meet these losses? Wicksell held that they: ". . . will suffer losses, which they will cover in the first place out of their wages or out of income derived from their own fortunes." [71]

This nullified another of his initial assumptions, namely, that entrepreneurs have no capital and work entirely on borrowed funds. But even if they also have personal "fortunes," as the downward process continues these will be depleted, and will force entrepreneurs to seek refuge among the workers whose real wages seem to remain constant. In that event losses would be shifted to the banks. But since the banks operate at zero net profits, in one way or another they would have to shift the losses to capitalists. Then, if not before, the downward cumulative process would most likely be brought to a halt, perhaps by a crisis, or perhaps by an orderly readjustment of the loan and deposit rate of interest to the natural rate.

Wicksell also used another, an auxiliary sequence model, one where the natural rate falls because of continuous formation of real capital (here, a stock of consumption goods), but the loan rate remains constant, as do money wages and rents, while real wages and rents rise as the price level falls. Concerning this, he said: "This is precisely the phenomenon which characterizes the movement of prices in recent decades" [apparently the period, 1875-1896].[72]

[71] *Ibid.*, p. 149.
[72] *Ibid.*, pp. 150-151.

To make this sequence work, Wicksell used even more artificial assumptions. As capital accumulates, the ensuing increase in productivity is introduced with a one-year lag behind the incremental augmentation in capital in order to keep the natural rate from declining to zero. There is equilibrium in year I, but in year II capitalists decide to save $0.01K$ equal to $\$0.01K$ in value from their usual interest income to invest in further production. As a result of this investment the natural rate is assumed to fall from 5 to 4 per cent. Entrepreneurs now produce as usual at constant money wages and rents, but they suffer a nominal production loss. Their output is $1.04K + 0.01K + 0.01K = 1.06K$, but capitalists continue to save $0.01K$ or $\$0.01K$, so this output of $1.06K$ must be sold at a 1 per cent drop in price against a total expenditure of $\$1.05K$ by capitalists. Now it is the reduction in unit costs of production which saves entrepreneurs from actual losses: ". . . as a result of industrial progress, average productivity will have increased, and the output of the current year might be expected to increase by one per cent. It would thus appear as though entrepreneurs could carry on in the usual way and pay the usual wages and rents, for the expected increase in output compensates for the fall in prices that has already occurred." [73]

This process, which became a bone of contention between himself and Davidson, as we shall show in the next chapter, might, as Wicksell said, continue indefinitely. Moreover it might appear to be due to an increase in productivity pure and simple, because the quantity of bank loans has been constant while real capital and output continually increase at declining prices.

It might thus appear as though the downward movement of prices took its origin 'on the side of goods' to use the usual manner of speaking, rather than 'on the side of money.' The immediate cause, however, of the fall in prices is in this case just the same as in the case where the quantity of capital and of output *remain unaltered:* the immediate cause is the excess of the money rate of interest over the natural rate of interest.[74]

To arrest this downward process, the banks must reduce their loan rate of interest to equality with the natural rate. But since their loan rate equals the deposit rate, this would also reduce the income of capitalists who are counted on to keep on saving and investing $0.01K$, or $\$0.01K$ in value terms, which they annually deposit in the banks for reinvestment by entrepreneurs for the next period. As for the capitalists, Wicksell said: "Whether the capitalists, whose incomes

---

[73] *Ibid.,* pp. 151-152.
[74] *Ibid.,* p. 152.

have diminished as a result of the fall in the deposit rate of interest, will be able or willing to save the same amount as before is a separate question which need not concern us here." [75]

A SUGGESTED REMEDY

It is evident that Wicksell's models left much to be desired. The main difficulty with them was that they were too near-static in nature, and that the economy, confined to producing only consumption goods, left no room for introducing changes in the structure of capital or in the length of the period of investment.

The upward process, which is stalled if entrepreneurs sell the increased output at a reduction in price, can only get off dead center if the dimensions of capital structure or of the period of investment are variable. The increase in productivity that raises the natural rate above the loan rate may then become the occasion for introduction of longer production processes by shifting some resources from production of consumption goods to production of intermediate goods. Then the increment in output might take the form of intermediate goods, and as the process continues, the latter may become an increasing ratio of total output. In that case entrepreneurs, even under the freest of competition, would have no difficulty in retaining the output increment of intermediate goods as profits, or in selling the output of consumption goods to capitalists at rising prices. The capitalists in turn would be able to dispose of the consumption goods at similar prices to workers and owners of natural resources, whose money incomes have risen by the competitive actions of entrepreneurs.

It would then not be necessary for entrepreneurs to act uncompetitively and lay aside their profit as a hoard of consumption goods, in order to sell the normal output at constant prices, and then go out and bid up wages and rents prior to the rise in the level of output in year III. Neither would it be necessary to assume that entrepreneurs would have to sell both the consumption and the intermediate goods to capitalists at slightly reduced prices. This would again stall the upward process. Since the capitalists are traders in consumption goods only, which they sell to workers and landowners, they would most likely not want to buy the intermediate goods because they would have no market for them. Also as pure capitalists they would be unable to put these goods to productive use themselves.

One wonders why Wicksell did not use models with a variable investment period to illustrate his hypothesis in *Interest and Prices.* One contributing reason was, no doubt, the difficulty associated with

[75] *Ibid.,* p. 154.

the investment period concept. As he himself admitted when he abandoned this conception for the capital structure analysis in *Lectures-I,* the investment period is not independent of the rate of interest. It may well be that the reconstruction necessary to allow for this complication would have made his models too unwieldy for expository purposes.

At this point, before we take up the later development of Wicksell's monetary doctrine, we turn briefly to some implications of his analysis in the context of contemporary theories of income and employment.

Wicksellian Monetary Theory and Income-Employment Theory

CONTRASTS BETWEEN WICKSELLIAN AND CONTEMPORARY ANALYSIS

At least four interrelated contrasts are discernible between Wicksell's monetary theory and contemporary income-employment theory of the dominant post-Keynesian type.

1. Post-Keynesian theory has replaced the Wicksellian emphasis on price level movements via the interest rate nexus with a broader analysis of income-employment fluctuations in which price level changes play a subordinate role. Movements in general price levels are regarded as adaptive in nature and as symptomatic of changes in more fundamental variables, in the influences acting on entrepreneurial anticipations, which are strategic for the determination of income and employment in a private enterprise system. The comparison between this and the Wicksellian emphasis may become clearer if we recall that for Wicksell it was the quantity of money that was adaptive to and symptomatic of fluctuations in price levels. These fluctuations in turn were symptomatic of and limited by forces affecting the disposition of real income by factor owners and affecting also entrepreneurial production decisions.

2. A distinction is made between monetary or saving-investment equilibrium and employment equilibrium since it is realized that the former can arise at levels of activity far short of full employment. The theoretical gap between these two types of analysis is filled by a more complete theory of income determination than existed in Wicksell's system. This involves, *inter alia,* an explicit analysis of the consumption function as a diminishing function of income increments. Wicksell had little to say about the behavior of consumption, which enters his system more or less as a residual. Consumption is curtailed by "forced saving" when investment exceeds planned saving, despite the attendant rise in income. It expands by forced disinvestment when investment is less than saving while at the same

time income declines. Owing to this mode of treatment there is no suggestion of multiplier and acceleration effects in Wicksell's theory whereby to relate the behavior of consumption more closely to the other determinants of income.

3. Investment, and to some extent saving—although concerning the latter Wicksell was quite an agnostic—were construed as interest-elastic in his system. Current theory treats them as interest-inelastic and primarily as income-elastic, at least within a considerable range of income variation. This in turn necessitated a reconstruction of the traditional manner in which the determination of interest rates was described. On the demand side allowance had to be made for a potentially infinitely interest-elastic liquidity preference demand for money or cash balances along with the preëxisting, income-elastic transactions or investment demand. On the supply side the quantity of money (construed as currency and demand deposits), which appears as a very elastic quantity in Wicksell's pure credit system and plays an autonomous role only if monetary authority is subject to fiscal domination and/or subject to the restraints of the gold standard, has now been introduced as an autonomous, institutionally determined variable. Thus the supply of investable funds consists of the quantity of money plus saving, and the latter is deducible from income via the consumption function. The result is a more complete explanation of the determination of interest rates. It has permitted a synthesis between Wicksell's unresolved treatment of the value storage function of money and his interpretation of demand for money in terms of the income velocity of transactions balances.

4. Wicksell relied on monetary policy to restore and maintain equilibrium by loan-rate manipulation. Current theory attacks this problem differently. Countercyclical fiscal policy—which implies proper coördination with monetary policy as a helpful but less potent means—is expected to fill deflationary gaps by net increase in public expenditures and to eliminate inflationary bulges of aggregate demand by net increase in public revenues whenever gross private investment falls short of, or respectively exceeds, the difference between consumption expenditures and the full employment level of gross national product. But in order to lighten the burden of fiscal policy, and to raise the trend of real income closer to the widening limits afforded by secular expansion in productive capacity and secular rise in productivity, long-run measures are relied on to operate in the background in conjunction with short-run fiscal policy. These measures are chiefly concerned with resource development and with raising the propensity to consume by direct and indirect methods of income

redistribution so as to achieve greater relative income equality in the course of the secular growth of income. It is assumed that if the propensity to consume is raised in high-income economies, the problem of finding suitable investment offsets to their full employment rate of saving will be smaller. Consequently the amplitude and duration of employment fluctuations to be dealt with by countercyclical policy will also be smaller.

In this fashion a closer relation has been achieved between what were formerly regarded as the separate fields of monetary theory, public finance, and speculations concerning economic development. Wicksell also harbored ideas kindred to those we meet under the heading of fiscal policy and long-run "planning." However, these ideas, expressed in his theory of public finance, were not directly related to his monetary analysis. They proceeded on the assumption of a money of constant value as a necessary prerequisite for a rational calculus concerning social service benefits to be received in return for taxes imposed.

While the more important elements of current income-employment theory were accessible within the Wicksellian framework, yet the very fact that Wicksell failed to develop such a theory of his own raises a question of methodological import.

The strategic assumption which separates his work into two categories—first, his value-production, capital, and distribution theory in *Value, Capital and Rent* and in *Lectures-I* and, second, his monetary theory in *Interest and Prices* and in *Lectures-II*—is the employment of perfect foresight in the former and its omission in the latter. The economics of value and distribution may be reasoned under static or dynamic premises, but such determinate solutions as are derived owe their elegance to perfect foresight. There is no monetary problem until that assumption is discarded. But once it is abandoned, there arises a compound problem of economic stability in dynamic societies.

This is because the tempo of most economic activities is determined by entrepreneurial expectations and by factor owner's income dispositions. These two interdependent but uncoördinated forces not only react on one another but also react to exogenous impacts on the economic apparatus as a whole.

Wicksell's monetary analysis attempted only to solve one part of the problem of economic stability in a dynamic world. This was to be done by arranging the character and behavior of monetary institutions in a manner calculated to elicit responses from entrepreneurs and from other income-recipients (at the point when they "dispose" of or allocate their disposable incomes as between consumption spending and savings) which were on a priori grounds expected to approximate the design and conditions of monetary equilibrium. Rational monetary policy was expected to "slant" price and other relevant economic data on which, at the microeconomic level, members of these groups base their decisions, so as to bring out their "normal" responses. In the aggregate, at the macroeconomic level, these responses were thought capable of preserving dynamic equilibrium with narrow fluctuations around the economy's potential trend of growth. The benevolent "unseen hand," which proved unreliable after the abandonment of Say's law, was to be replaced by rational, hence also benevolent, economic policy—monetary as well as nonmonetary.

If the theory Wicksell fashioned to solve this problem had been entirely adequate to its task, that would not imply that it would also have been adequate for the larger problem of economic stability. Trade cycles, for instance, may still take place because of changes, independent of the monetary circumstances, which occur in real factors. But if monetary aberrations were removed, the stability problem would become smaller.

There was a wisdom, we seem in danger of losing sight of, about this manner of asking in effect: What are the measures requisite for maintenance of full employment *after* the monetary causes of instability have been removed or brought under control? Today we are prone to ask the employment question first and to find the answer largely in fiscal policy. Then the secondary question is asked: How shall the behavior of monetary institutions be arranged to assist in this task?

There is no intention to deny that this approach was necessary and was forced on economists and governments alike, their unpreparedness for it notwithstanding, by the exigencies of the Great Depression. But it may be worth noting that under this approach it is no longer the price data created by interaction of producers and consumers in the market which is being "slanted" by policy in order to influence their behavior in some desired direction. To an increasing extent it is the very data themselves that are created both as to quantity and quality by progressive reliance on the fiscal nexus.

One need not share the prophecies of the author of *The Road to Serfdom*[76] in order to recognize that there are dangers implicit in an almost exclusive reliance on fiscal methods to offset every downward business flurry, however slight. The great risk in such conditions is

---

[76] F. A. von Hayek (1944).

that the fiscal medicine suitable for depressions will still be administered in large doses in times of full recovery with the consequence
that the economic patient develops inflation fever after having been
relieved of the chills of deflation. Another difficulty is that fiscal
measures are not well adapted to deal with structural imbalances.
They sometimes augment the latter, since fiscal measures are often
subverted to strengthening and encouraging monopoly, as well as to
the erection of new market barriers, and the subsidizing of well-
entrenched producer groups. All this and more is generally condoned
in an atmosphere where corrective policies are decried as inimical to
recovery or to the maintenance of full employment.

It may well be that it is wiser not to ask the employment question
first and last, but to approach it by the less direct method which is
implicit in Wicksell's work. This would not mean that the resources
of fiscal policy would atrophy for lack of use. But it might mean less
frequent recourse to and more effective application of these resources.

The imperfectly competitive nature of industrial markets has
brought with it a nonoptimal allocation of resources, which in itself
aggravates the problem of full employment. Full employment, then,
is not at all times entitled to priority status over other economic difficulties. Monetary action, which is best adapted to deal with symptoms
of inflation, is on the whole no better equipped than is fiscal action
to cope with imbalances between industrial markets and with the
allocation of resources. But there is this difference; fiscal measures
are conceived outside the complex of market forces, and generally
place limits on the field of operation of the market mechanism, while
monetary action is designed for and operates through this mechanism.
Consequently, the opportunity to bring market forces to bear on matters relating to the economic structure and its development is greater
under an economic stabilization program pursued mainly by monetary means as a first, and by fiscal means as a last resort, than it is
when these conditions are reversed.

Although interest rate relations and price level movements held
the center of attention in Wicksell's work, behind these and accompanying their variations were movements or changes in aggregate
demand, in distribution of income, in the size and composition of
output. While little indeed was said concerning employment, it was
clearly implied that employment fluctuates with the cumulative movement of prices, however not necessarily in the same proportion.
Consequently the claim made by Keynes[77] and repeated by many of

[77] J. M. Keynes, *The General Theory of Employment, Interest and Money* (New
York, 1936), pp. 6-7, and appendix to chap. 19.

his followers, namely that neoclassical (or "classical," as Keynes calls them) economic theories, were incapable of dealing with unemployment except as a frictional problem, can at any rate *not* be sustained with reference to Wicksell.

NONFRICTIONAL UNEMPLOYMENT IN WICKSELL'S SYSTEM

From what Wicksell said concerning trade cycles,[78] it is clear that he did *not* argue that, given free competition and wage-rate flexibility and given also the absence of monetary aberrations, the problem of economic fluctuations and unemployment would be solved. In fact, for its alleviation, over and above what may be contributed thereto by price stabilization policy, he urged in substance a buffer-stock and credit subsidy plan. In his view, the trade cycle rested on "real causes independent of movements in commodity prices . . . although . . . the latter play a dominating part in the development of crises." [79] Since he also held that expansion of output was a function of aggregate demand, "when the demand for . . . goods begins to exceed . . . production capacity," [80] and that such expansion required "conversion on a large scale of liquid into fixed capital," [81] he did not fall into the error of regarding investment as independent of the wage level. Wages income represented too large a fraction of consumption expenditures to make it likely that waning investment demand in the downturn could be revived by means of general wage reductions.

Moreover, he treated savings as somewhat interest-elastic, at least sufficiently so that there could be shifts in the savings schedule with a given loan rate. In consequence, if an increase in thrift occurred in an initial equilibrium position with given loan and real rates standing in the proper relation to one another, there was no guarantee that the extra thrift would not disrupt the equilibrium and start a downward process. Even if investment were interest-elastic and the loan rate were reduced as a result of the extra saving, it did not follow that investment would expand sufficiently to absorb the new saving, for curtailment of consumption may have shifted the real rate downwards as much or more than the interest rate. If so, curtailment of output would follow and underemployment would develop, possibly only to be aggravated by substantial downward wage flexibility.

---

[78] See chap. vi, pp. 133 ff. above, and the writer's translation of Wicksell's article "The Enigma of Business Cycles," (1907) published in *International Economic Papers*, III (1953), 58 ff., and Wicksell's "Note on Trade Cycles and Crises," in *Lectures-II*, pp. 209 ff.

[79] Wicksell, "Note on Trade Cycles and Crises," *Lectures-II*, p. 209.

[80] *Ibid.*, p. 214.

[81] *Ibid.*, p. 212.

However, it was implied that if interest rates were adjusted sufficiently and rapidly to whatever level the real rate had taken, monetary equilibrium would be restored. But it was not implied that this would necessarily be a full employment equilibrium, as the following clearly shows:

> . . . if the banks at the beginning of a boom raised their interest rates sufficiently and on the other hand finally lowered them at the beginning of a depression . . . presumably the real element of the crisis would be eliminated and what remained would merely be *an even fluctuation* between periods in which the newly formed capital would assume, and, economically speaking, should assume other forms. . . . [This last phrase refers to Wicksell's idea that investment takes chiefly the form of fixed capital during booms. It becomes negligible during depressions except for the unintended investment in inventories which occurs at such times. This "form" of investment was one he thought might be expanded deliberately in the interest of greater economic stability, and it was to this end that he urged his buffer-stock and credit subsidy proposal.][82]

Contemporary theory has demoted interest rate manipulation by banks to secondary rank compared with other, mostly fiscal, measures for achieving an approximation to full employment equilibrium. The reason for this is that both on a priori grounds and in terms of experience, monetary policy per se (construed narrowly as central bank policy pursued by open market operations, changes in reserve requirements, direct central bank advances to nonbank institutions and industries, etc.) has been found relatively impotent in arresting the downward cumulative process. This brings us to the possibility of an impasse in Wicksell's system.

RISK AND THE REAL RATE—A NEGATIVE REAL RATE
AND AN IMPASSE IN WICKSELL'S THEORY

There is a limitation on central bank policy which Wicksell overlooked. This is connected with the probability that the real rate may decline further in a downturn than the loan rate can follow. In a severe downturn the real rate may, for a time, possibly become negative.

In a pure credit system with free competition, where investors have well-nigh perfect foresight, and where there is ample mobility of resources, there is little reason to suspect any such decline in the real rate. If, to the ideal Wicksellian conditions, we also add that population be stationary, then in such a society, maintenance of monetary equilibrium would be almost automatic, particularly if we also disregard technological change. To the extent that investment

---

[82] *Ibid.*, p. 212. Italics supplied.

occurs, the real rate would be subject to a secular rate of decline due to diminishing returns on the only increasing factor of production, real capital. In consequence, the capital structure would expand chiefly in the height dimension, and investments would tend to longer and longer maturation periods.

But if we disturb this society by exposing it to technological change and innovation, then the real rate becomes a more mobile and inscrutable variable. Technological change necessarily impairs foresight and introduces obsolescence risks. In consequence, real rates must be weighted by risk premia. Owing to the fact that technological change does not affect all industry uniformly nor at the same time, the real rate becomes a complex of differentiated rates. The corresponding loan rates, if they are to be capable of preserving equilibrium, must likewise become differentiated and weighted by risk. In these circumstances, interest-rate policy becomes operationally intricate, but thus far there is no reason in principle why it should be less effective on the downturn than on the upturn.

However, if technological change is frequent and obsolescence incidence high, the complex of differentiated real rates need no longer follow a secular trend of decline as capital formation continues, other factors constant. Technological change may stop their fall and may even reverse it. If so, long-maturity investment loses some of the urgency and advantage it possessed in the former situation. In fact, because of obsolescence, it may be that medium-term investment will replace an increasing number of investments of the long-maturity type, which are characteristic of the technologically stationary but economically progressive societies we discussed at the outset. Also when interest rates are changed they affect capital values of investments more than their net or gross returns. The latter are more directly affected by changes in demand and changes in prime costs. Interest rate changes have a more than proportionately greater effect (following an exponential law) on capital values of investments of long as compared with those of short maturity terms. So, it may come about that in a society subject to rapid technological change with investment predominantly of medium term, investment as a whole becomes relatively insensitive or inelastic to changes in interest rates. If so, the power of interest rates to effectuate adjustments in the volume of investment is immediately and considerably qualified.

If next, along Schumpeterian lines, we assume that innovations come in clusters, the consequence for the economy will be alternating periods of intensive capital formation and periods of little or no such activity—gestation period sequences. It may not be unreasonable to assume that at the end of an expansion phase the real rate may fall close to zero level and may remain in that position until pent-up replacement demand plus new innovation lay the basis for another period of expansion. In the interim, there is little the banks can do to relieve progressive contraction and stagnation by reducing their interest rates. For reasons of business risk they can hardly reduce rates on private business loans to zero levels. And even if it were possible for them to do so on riskless government loans, that may not help to revive private investment.

Moreover, at sharply reduced but yet positive interest rates another force exerts itself to prevent their further reduction, namely, liquidity preferences. These are said to become infinitely interest-elastic at reduced loan rates because of the risk of loss to asset values when and as rates are expected to be raised sometimes in the future, and also because at near-zero levels, the alternative cost of holding cash balances becomes negligible compared with the risk to the future value of low-yield securities.

If the real rate has fallen below the minimum practical level of loan rates, then the Wicksellian interest-rate adjustment is at an impasse. It may have been in recognition of this possibility that Wicksell suggested his buffer-stock and credit subsidy plan, which was to operate in the downturn.

Finally, if we imagine that clustered innovations also confer considerable economies of scale, then free competition will be replaced by imperfect competition of varying degrees of severity in the major markets and industries of the economy. In view of the frictions and rigidities as well as the nonoptimal resource allocation this introduces, such an economy may be one in which the only approach to equilibrium implies underemployment and excess capacity in the absence of government intervention in the dominant industries. Full employment may then only be attainable under inflationary conditions, and deflation would be attended by severe unemployment. It was with such an economy in mind that Wicksell urged the socialization of all industries showing unmistakable signs of monopoly and cartelization.

CHAPTER XI

Later Development of Wicksell's Monetary Doctrine

The link between Wicksell's monetary analysis and that of his followers in the Stockholm School emerges clearly in a review of criticisms of his theory, particularly those of his colleague Davidson, to which Wicksell responded. One may say that the Stockholm School was founded by Lindahl and was developed by him with the collaboration of Myrdal, Ohlin, Lundberg, and others. But it was built by them on the joint heritage of monetary doctrine which came to light in the protracted Wicksell-Davidson polemic over monetary policy norms and related matters.

The criticisms raised against Wicksell's theory in his lifetime reduce to six issues. First and foremost, there was Davidson's objection to his norm of price level stabilization as an inappropriate guide to monetary policy under conditions of changing productivity.

The other five issues were also raised by Davidson in one connection or another. Of these, the first three were brought up with more force, and independently of Davidson, by Ludwig von Mises; the fourth by G. Åkerman, and the fifth by B. Ohlin. These issues centered on (1) the interdependence of real and loan rates of interest; (2) the interdependence of the "money" market and the "commodity" market; (3) the problem of determining the absolute height of the price level; (4) some limitations on monetary controls by the central bank; and (5) the influence of entrepreneurial anticipations and of differences in market structures on the real rate and on the movement of the price level.

We shall examine these last five problems first, and refer to them as "minor issues," not because they are inherently less significant than the central issue between Wicksell and Davidson, but because they exerted a smaller influence on Wicksell's thinking than did his controversy with Davidson. Then we turn to the Wicksell-Davidson polemic, which calls first for a statement of the essential features of Davidson's monetary theory. This was not available in published form until 1922, although the debate with Wicksell began in 1899.

The chapter concludes with an account of the exegesis, reconstruction, and some of the further development the Wicksell-Davidson monetary theory underwent through the efforts of the leading members of the Stockholm School of Economics.

Five "Minor" Issues Raised by Wicksell's Monetary Theory

INTERDEPENDENCE OF REAL AND LOAN RATES OF INTEREST

Clearly, Wicksell's explanation of price level fluctuations depended fundamentally on the real rate of interest being able to move to, and to remain for a considerable time at, a level different from that of the loan rate. His "working hypothesis" would be refuted if the two rates are, in fact, so interdependent that a movement by one forces the other to adjust to the level of the former without any appreciable lag. If so, the cumulative process that the divergence between the rates would generate would either fail to occur or would be of short duration and narrow amplitude. In that case, this divergence could hardly serve as an explanation of those major price level movements which are *not* due to "autonomous causes."

Starting from different premises, both Davidson and von Mises stressed the interdependence of the two rates. But neither of them pressed their contentions to the point of denying that the rates could diverge for long enough to initiate a cumulative process. They inferred, rather, that this process might be of much shorter duration than Wicksell's writings seemed to imply.

This matter received no resolution for two reasons. First, Wicksell had never committed himself about the duration and amplitude of price level fluctuations. Secondly, his critics based their arguments on the assumption of a gold standard. Wicksell himself held that, other things equal, the cumulative process would be much shorter in such conditions than it would be likely to be in a pure credit system.

Ludwig von Mises, in his *Theorie des Geldes und der Umlaufsmittel,* Vienna (1912), translated into English as *The Theory of Money and Credit,* London (1934) held that the banks cannot for long maintain a loan rate lower than the real rate of interest. If they attempt to do so, either (*a*) the real rate is reduced to the level of the loan rate by real capital formation resulting from "forced saving," or (*b*) as the price level rises, nonbank creditors press for higher loan rates, and if the banks persist in maintaining the low rate against their wishes, the system spirals toward a crisis.[1] Wicksell replied to point (*b*), saying in substance that this is no issue since he had always contended that the crisis, if nothing else will, forces the banks to make the proper loan rate adjustment.[2] We shall confine ourselves to point (*a*).

As for capital formation based on forced saving, Wicksell interpreted von Mises as saying that entrepreneurs begin "lengthening the period of production" as soon as the loan rate becomes lower than the real rate whether the banks have reduced their rates, or because the real rate has risen. Wicksell objected by saying the process does not work exactly that way. If we assume that entrepreneurs used an optimum production period before the loan rate became low, then they will continue to produce for a while with the same length production period. Meanwhile they merely pocket their gain by being able to obtain credit at less expense than they had counted on. This gain induces them to extend their operations in the next period, in the sense of "widening" the capital structure. This attempt at widening forces them to bid up wages in competition with one another. Now, if prices remained constant, the increase in wages would reduce the real rate and would induce entrepreneurs to offset this tendency by lengthening the period in the sense of "deepening" or increasing its vertical dimension. But prices do not remain constant. Instead they rise, because real capital—the subsistence fund—has not increased appreciably in so short a time. In fact the subsistence fund may have decreased since the loan rate, as an inducement to saving, has been reduced. On the other hand, money wages and rents have risen. Thus as prices rise, entrepreneurs are again in a position to continue making gains, despite higher wages and rents. Consequently, they are not forced to extend the capital structure in the vertical dimension, and thus the real rate does not fall. But if they are ultimately forced to resort to "deepening," then: "In this case, the upward drift of prices would, of course, come to a stop. . . ."[3]

As is evident from this statement, Wicksell did not consider the sequence von Mises pointed to as an excluded possibility, especially

---

[1] L. von Mises, *The Theory of Money and Credit* (London, 1934), pp. 355-365.

[2] Wicksell, "Rezension: L. v. Mises: 'Theorie des Geldes und der Umlaufsmittel,'" *Zeitschrift für Volkswirtschaft, Sozialpolitik und Verwaltung*, 23 (1914), 148.

[3] *Ibid.*, p. 147.

in a protracted upward process. Incidentally, Cassel in 1918 repeated in substance von Mises' argument in his *Theoretische Sozialökonomie.*[4]

Davidson advanced three observations intended to prove the interdependence of real and loan rates of interest. First he pointed out that if productivity increases while loan rates are constant, the increase in output reduces prices of goods in proportion to the increase in productivity and thus adjusts the real rate to the level of the loan rate.[5] We shall defer comment on this point to the next section where it can more readily be dealt with as an element in the Wicksell-Davidson polemic. Secondly, Davidson insisted that the banks are neither isolated from nor independent of the nonbanking enterprises to which they extend credit, and that the effective alliance which exists between banks and industrial enterprises makes the real and the money rate of interest capable of simultaneous and parallel variation.[6] Finally, in periods of rising prices loan rates are in fact adjusted toward the level of the real rate, the banks notwithstanding, as nonbank creditors increasingly substitute a succession of short loans at increasing rates for long-term commitments to their clients at a fixed rate. Nonbank creditors then tend more and more to shift their investments from creditor to proprietary equities.[7]

Faced with these objections by Davidson and von Mises, in 1915 when the second Swedish edition of *Lectures-II* was published, Wicksell made the following "concession" to his "critics":

> I do not feel that it has been necessary for me to modify my general position, unless one considers as such a certain concession towards my critics concerning the mutual influence of the money rate and the natural rate of interest on one another.[8]

> The objection has been raised to the whole of the above reasoning, that a lowering of the loan rate must also depress the real rate so that the difference between them is more and more levelled out and thus the stimulus to a continued rise in prices eliminated. This possibility cannot be entirely rejected. *Ceteris paribus* a lowering of the real rate unconditionally demands new real capital, i.e., increased saving. But this would certainly occur, even if *involuntarily*, owing to the fact that higher prices would compel a restriction of consumption on the part of those who had fixed money incomes. . . .

---

[4] Our citations are to the first English edition of G. Cassel, *The Theory of Social Economy* (New York, 1924), paragraphs 48, 57, and 58.

[5] D. Davidson, "Om stabiliseringen af penningens värde" (Concerning Stabilization of the Value of Money), *Ekonomisk Tidskrift*, 11 (1909), 23.

[6] *Ibid.*, p. 11.

[7] *Ibid.*, pp. 16-17.

[8] From p. viii of E. Sommarin's Preface to the fourth Swedish edition of Wicksell's *Lectures-II*, in which Sommarin quotes the passage translated by the writer from Wicksell's original preface to the second Swedish edition.

Against this, however, would have to be set the decrease in voluntary saving which a lowering of interest rates tends to produce. But if the former influence prevails and if production is unable to absorb unlimited quantities of new capital without a reduction in net yield, then the incipient rise in prices, though it would certainly not recede, might yet be arrested, unless the banks reduced their rates still further.[9]

Despite the conditional language used as to whether "forced saving" would outweigh the reduction in voluntary saving caused by the decline in loan rates, there can be little doubt that it would. Wicksell did not consider voluntary saving to be highly interest-elastic. Assuming voluntary saving to have unit elasticity relative to interest rates, a reduction of a normal loan rate of 6 per cent to a subnormal one of 4 per cent would then reduce voluntary saving by about 33 per cent. If money wages and rents rise as a result of the rate reduction while output of consumption goods is reduced somewhat because of increased capital formation by entrepreneurs, then the normal consumption expenditure stream will now be swelled by the increase in money wages and rents as well as by the reduction in voluntary savings, with the result that prices of consumption goods rise relatively fast. Consequently "forced saving" becomes of significant magnitude almost from the outset and increases cumulatively with the upward process.

Moreover, in the event of a rise in the real rate with the loan rate held constant—and Wicksell considered such cases to be more likely starting points for upward processes than direct loan rate reductions taken on the initiative of banks—there would be no reduction in voluntary savings to act as an offset to the forced savings the process generates, and these savings would presumably be matched by an equivalent amount of net capital formation. Thus his "concession" was substantial. As for its bearing on Wicksell's monetary theory, a later interpretation of it by Lindahl shows clearly the modification it called for. Lindahl concluded that the result of a typical Wicksellian cumulative process may readily be a self-generated new equilibrium achieved via the effect on the real rate of capital formation from forced savings. But this would only be possible if entrepreneurs are *not* guided by anticipations of future price increases. On the other hand, if they act on such expectations, the cumulative process may continue indefinitely until it is brought to an end by a crisis, in the course of which the loan rate is adjusted to the level of the real rate.[10]

Wicksell's reply to Davidson's stress on the possibility of a parallel

[9] Wicksell, *Lectures-II*, pp. 198-199.
[10] E. Lindahl, *Studies in the Theory of Money and Capital* (New York, 1939), pp. 180-182.

and simultaneous movement of the real and the loan rate of interest was indirect. He was satisfied to point out that his real rate was defined as an expected rate of return on real capital, a rate which is essentially variable, and to add that its variations were sufficient to account for those price level fluctuations which were not due to "autonomous causes." [11] The point that was implicit in his position was made explicit some years later by Myrdal who said in substance that the sufficient condition for the cumulative process is that the real rate viewed *ex ante* should be capable of varying independently of the loan rate.[12] The necessary condition was, of course, that there be some lag in the adjustment of the two rates to each other. The length of the ensuing process would then depend on the duration of this lag.

INTERDEPENDENCE OF THE "MONEY MARKET"
AND THE "COMMODITY MARKET"—A METHODOLOGICAL QUESTION

Von Mises, writing in 1912, noted the celebrated passage in *Interest and Prices,* which states: "The exchange of commodities in itself, and the conditions of production and consumption on which it depends, affect only exchange values or *relative* prices: they can exert *no direct influence whatever on the absolute level of money prices.*" [13]

With respect to this von Mises made the following comment:

If the circumstances of the loan market can provide no explanation of the genesis of the exchange ratio subsisting between money and other economic goods, then neither can they help to explain why this ratio does not alter. The objective exchange value of money is determined in the market where money is exchanged for commodities and commodities for money. To explain this determination is the task of the theory of value of money.[14]

The problem von Mises posed—namely, the "determination of the objective exchange value of money"—comes to the same thing as the determination of the "absolute level of money prices" in Wicksell's terminology. This matter was left on an indeterminate basis in Wicksell's analysis. In developing his own position von Mises went on to say:

In the case of money subjective use value and subjective exchange value coincide. Both are derived from objective exchange value, for money has no

[11] Wicksell, *Lectures-II,* p. 200.
[12] G. Myrdal, *Monetary Equilibrium* (London, 1939), pp. 54 ff.
[13] Wicksell, *Interest and Prices,* p. 23. Italics in the original.
[14] L. von Mises, *The Theory of Money and Credit* (New Haven, 1934), p. 119.

other utility than that arising from the possibility of obtaining other goods in exchange for it.[15]

The subjective value of money must be measured by the marginal utility of the goods for which money can be exchanged.[16]

However, marginal utility calculations involve a principle of continuity, to which Wicksell sometimes referred as "the inertia of prices." In von Mises' treatment this continuity, which means that, emergencies excepted, today's prices are not expected to be very different from yesterday's or tomorrow's, was used to explain why people are apt to "overlook the variability in the value of money" [17] in times other than those of hyperinflation. The consequence of this oversight is that when prices rise because of excessive issue of "fiduciary media," which comes to the same as the net credit creation associated with an abnormally low loan rate in Wicksell's treatment, the marginal utility of money declines. Then those who first come to the market to buy goods make relatively the largest gains in a sequence where all holders of money incur real losses on an increasing scale the later they exercise the declining purchasing power of their money. Thus inflation redistributes real income and wealth in an arbitrary fashion. To account for this phenomenon on subjective value theory premises, and particularly for the role played in it by the banks, von Mises posed the following distinctions:

When the bank discounts a bill or grants a loan . . . it exchanges a present good for a future good. Since the issuer *creates* the present good that it surrenders in exchange—the fiduciary media—*practically out of nothing*, it would be possible to speak of a natural limitation of the quantity of fiduciary media if the quantity of future goods that are exchanged in the loan market against present goods was limited to a fixed amount [e.g., by the gold standard]. But this is by no means the case. The quantity of future goods is indeed limited by external circumstances, but *not* that of future goods that are offered on the market in the form of money. The issuers of fiduciary media are able to induce an extension of the demands for them by reducing the interest rate demanded below the natural rate of interest. . . .

The demand for money and money substitutes which determines the exchange ratio between money and other economic goods, achieves expression only in the behaviour of individuals. *Only when, say, money is being exchanged for bread is the position of the economic goods, money and commodity, in the value scales of the individual parties to the transaction worked out* and used as a basis for action; *and from this premise the arithmetical*

[15] *Ibid.,* p. 97.
[16] *Ibid.,* p. 109.
[17] *Ibid.,* p. 109.

262 *Later Development of Wicksell's Monetary Doctrine*

exchange ratio determined. But, when what is being demanded is a money loan that is to be paid back in money again then such considerations do not enter into the matter. Then only the difference in value between present and future goods is taken into account, and this alone has an influence on the determination of the exchange ratio, i.e., on the determination of the rate of interest.[18]

It seems peculiar, to say the least, to refer to a bank when granting a loan as *creating* present goods. If anything, all it does is to *create a claim to* present goods. It is hardly consistent to say that the subjective use value of money coincides with its subjective exchange value, which is measured by the marginal utility of the goods money will purchase, and then say that in loan transactions all such more or less concrete marginal utility considerations are absent. The borrower must carry on this calculus in pecuniary terms. As for the bank, this calculus, if any, must become considerably attenuated if, as von Mises puts it, it creates the loan "practically out of nothing." Seemingly, von Mises has set up a distinction without much meaning. The equilibrium by which the absolute level of prices is to be determined on the basis of subjective use valuations of "money versus commodity," is neither more nor less determined than in Wicksell's money market equilibrium. Then the equality of the loan rate with the real rate prevents any net credit expansion, or, in von Mises' terms, net issue of fiduciary media. If the absence of credit creation coincides with relatively stationary production conditions in the commodity market, then the exchange ratio, money versus commodities, is constant, but what its absolute level will be is indeterminate, a priori, as Wicksell stated in his reply to von Mises:

In my opinion, the problem is relatively simple. If we assume a pure cash economy, then, obviously, it is the need for cash balances which limits the demand for money and thus indirectly the height of the level of prices. . . . And, indeed, if we imagine an economy where all payments are effected by entries on the books of account of banks and that consequently the unit in which banks carry on their book-keeping alone functions as the measure of value, then equilibrium of general prices can occur at every possible height of the price level. Hence the problem which Mises alleges to have been 'the first' to solve simply does not exist. Then the only question that remains is concerned with the causes of a change, or respectively of the maintenance, of a given level of prices which has been attained, the height of which has only a conventional significance.[19]

[18] *Ibid.*, pp. 306-307. Italics supplied.
[19] Wicksell, *Zeitschrift für Volkswirtschaft, Socialpolitik und Verwaltung,* 22 (1914), p. 146.

Perhaps it was an overstatement to say that the problem of the absolute height of the price level does not exist. However, this is hardly the primary problem of monetary theory. In equilibrium, if the effective quantity of money is given, the price level is a simple quotient of this quantity divided by the transactions volume, which reflects the demand for cash balances, after the manner of the quantity theory. But in conditions of disequilibrium, even if the effective quantity of money is given, the level of prices varies and its height is not uniquely determined.

It is not surprising that Wicksell found von Mises' attempt to use subjective value theory directly for purposes of determining the "objective value" or purchasing power of money, "remains, despite his prolix discussion, very obscure." [20]

Davidson approached the problem of the relations between the money and commodity markets, hence of the exchange value of money, from his neo-Ricardian perspective on value theory. This was centered on "the objective value of commodities," essentially a real-cost interpretation of value. The "objective value" of reproducible commodities was expressed in relative terms; namely, that outputs which result from the same quantity of "productive power" (inputs of resource services) have as a rule the same objective value.[21] From this approach it seemed to Davidson that: ". . . the problem of controlling the value of money is restricted to controlling the value of the monetary unit. To keep the value of money constant means that the monetary system must be so managed that the prices of commodities will always be in the invariable and same proportion to the absolute magnitude of the objective but variable values of commodities." [22]

Because the "objective value" of commodities changes with variations in the supply of productive resources and with changes in the productivity of these resources, Davidson was never satisfied with Wicksell's definition of the value of money as the reciprocal of an index of the level of prices. At the same time he admitted he had no superior proposal for measuring the value of money. Further, he insisted that price level movements are not necessarily the result of changes in the value of money. Productivity was only one force acting on objective values of goods and services and on the level of prices.

[20] *Ibid.*, p. 149.
[21] D. Davidson, "Till frågan om penningvärdets reglering under kriget och därefter" (On the Problem of the Regulation of the Value of Money During and After the War), *Ekonomisk Tidskrift*, 24 (1922), 22. Davidson's objective value doctrine receives further attention in the third section of this chapter.
[22] *Ibid.*, p. 226.

There were also other influences such as price rigidities and the increasing degree of market imperfection, which affect these values. As a consequence, he urged that the conditions affecting the production and sale of commodities receive more explicit attention at the level of monetary theory. His position with respect to Wicksell's analysis is most clearly reflected in the following statements:

In saying this he (Wicksell) really admits that it is impossible to establish or demonstrate an unchanging or constant value of money, as if we were to say that the yard has its measure in the length of the objects that are measured by it and their lengths, in turn, are determined by the yard.[23]

Wicksell's standpoint implies . . . that the ultimate measure of value should be a stock of commodities of certain (arbitrarily chosen) size, composed of different commodities in the same manner as the country's entire supply of commodities. Is there any reason for regarding a quantity of commodities so composed as a measure of value? No convincing reason for this conception has ever been adduced.[24]

The solution of this problem of what changes in commodity prices do and do not represent a change in the value of money is difficult and I do not claim to be able to produce it. But I am inclined to believe that Ricardo was on the right track in holding that when it comes to a measure of value we must take changes in productivity into consideration, not only the productivity of labor, but changes in productivity as a whole.[25]

Now Wicksell says this is too subtle because productivity changes are too small and gradual and furnish no direct criteria for policy. . . . This depends on the method used. If we leave it to the banks, I grant it is impossible. According to my opinion there is no other really effective and practical way of regulating the value of money than for the governments to take this task upon themselves, eventually as a matter of mutual concern, as has happened in respect of measures and weights.[26]

Wicksell's reply was cryptic. He pointed out that all measures are relative, even those of weight and length, only they are less obviously relative than the price level measure he proposed for the value of money. Further, while not denying the usefulness of empirical and theoretical studies of the "conditions affecting the production and sale of commodities" that Davidson called for, he held that until further progress had been made along these lines, there was no

[23] Davidson, "Något om begreppet penningens värde" (Concerning the Concept Value of Money), *Ekonomisk Tidskrift*, 8 (1906), 460.

[24] Davidson, "Om stabiliseringen af penningens värde (Concerning Stabilization of the Value of Money), *Ekonomisk Tidskrift*, 11 (1909), 15.

[25] Davidson, *Ekonomisk Tidskrift*, 8 (1906), 467.

[26] Davidson, *Ekonomisk Tidskrift*, 11 (1909), 20-21.

alternative to his price level measurement, for there was no obvious and reliable way of proceeding from the conflicting variations in numerous relative commodity prices directly to a general ratio of exchange between money and commodities.[27]

Thus the issues which arose between Wicksell and his "critics" at this time concerning the relations between the money and the commodity markets brought no resolution, because his "critics" had no superior solution to offer.[28] Yet the line of inquiry they opened up turned out to be a fruitful one. The problem of the relationship between value theory in its broadest sense and monetary theory, obviously could not be left in the manner Wicksell left it, even after he modified his earlier position to make allowance for the fact that changes in productivity occurring in the commodity market have repercussions on the conditions of the money market.

One obstacle to a closer fusion at this time between value and monetary theory was that the analysis of value, by and large, was still carried on in barter terms. When this reasoning was bodily carried over into the money market, the result was confusion, as is evident from the last passage above quoted from von Mises.

Since then (the period 1909-1914), this impasse has been broken. In part this has occurred by the reconstruction value analysis underwent at the microeconomic level by R. G. D. Allen and J. R. Hicks in the early 1930's. The new concepts which they developed proved capable of aggregation and of application in that form at the macroeconomic and monetary levels of analysis.[29]

A fusion between the money market and the commodity market was also achieved in Sweden somewhat earlier than in Great Britain as a result of the joint efforts of Lindahl and Myrdal to reconstruct and expand the Wicksell-Davidson heritage of monetary doctrine, a subject we shall defer until later in this chapter (pp. 305 ff.).

The most recent contribution toward a closer integration of monetary and value theory has been attempted by D. Patinkin, whose treatment follows the paths laid out by Walras, Wicksell, and Hicks, to a higher synthesis in this field.[30]

---

[27] Wicksell, "Penningränta och varupris" (Money Interest and Commodity Prices), *Ekonomisk Tidskrift,* 11 (1909), 61-66.

[28] Just how inconclusive von Mises' solution was emerges clearly in the concluding section of his work, "The Basic Questions of Future Currency Policy," *The Theory of Money and Credit* (1934), pp. 406 ff.

[29] J. R. Hicks, *Value and Capital* (Oxford, 1939); see particularly chaps. 1, 5, 11-14, and 17-19.

[30] D. Patinkin, *Money, Interest and Prices* (Evanston, Ill., 1956).

LIMITATIONS ON CENTRAL BANK MONETARY CONTROLS

In 1922, Davidson had occasion to intercede in a controversy between Wicksell and one of his students, G. Åkerman, "in the role of an honest broker," as B. Thomas put it.[31]

Åkerman contested that Wicksell's analysis in *Interest and Prices,* according to which the banks could maintain stable prices as long as they applied a loan rate that was "normal" with respect to the real rate, was superior to the modifications he introduced in *Lectures-II* with qualifications concerning the banks' inability to do so if "autonomous" forces effect changes in the quantity of money.[32]

Åkerman posed a case of a community in initial monetary equilibrium in which the government suddenly finds it necessary to finance "unproductive expenditures" on armaments. To this end it issues fiat money in an amount equal to the people's annual savings, and thus it procures the resources which otherwise would have gone into private capital formation. The money savings of the community now increase by the amount of fiat money issued, but, if the banks keep the loan rate normal, these extra savings will, for lack of any other use, be deposited with them. While they are available to the community's entrepreneurs, the latter, assumed to be fully committed in their borrowing at "normal" loan rates, have no demand for the extra savings, which thus remain with the banks as idle balances. The extra savings might get out into circulation only if the banks make the interest rate subnormal, for then entrepreneurial demand will rise and a cumulative price rise ensues. The banks may, in fact, be forced to take this step if idle balances become large and are subject to a deposit rate of interest.

Then, Åkerman continues, as long as the fiat issue does not exceed the annual saving, and as long as the banks keep rates "normal," there will be no inflation, for the real rate will have become constant at its level prior to the fiat issue, because this issue prevents any

---

[31] B. Thomas, "The Monetary Doctrines of Professor D. Davidson," *Economic Journal,* XLV (March, 1935), 45.

[32] On this controversy see, G. Åkerman, "Inflation, penningmängd och penningränta" (Inflation, Quantity of Money, and Interest Rate), *Ekonomisk Tidskrift,* 23 (1921), 143-162; Wicksell, "Inflation, penningmängd och penningränta" (Inflation, Quantity of Money, and Interest Rate), *Ekonomisk Tidskrift,* 23 (1921), 167-171; G. Åkerman, "Inflation, penningmängd, och ränta" (Inflation, Money Quantity, and Interest), *Ekonomisk Tidskrift,* 24 (1922), 5-9; Wicksell, "Svar till Kand. Åkerman" (Reply to Mr. Åkerman, A. B.), *Ekonomisk Tidskrift,* 24 (1922), 10-12; D. Davidson, "Om begreppet normal penningränta" (On the Concept of Normal Interest Rate), *Ekonomisk Tidskrift,* 24 (1922) 13-30.

real capital formation. Annual savings are now being destroyed or consumed in unproductive state expenditure.

Wicksell replied that the new money, or new gold (for the same would apply to the latter), raises prices immediately, especially prices of consumer goods. New money competes in all markets with pre-existing money and thus cannot fail to raise prices. Neither will a problem of idle balances arise, for as the price level rises, the demand for cash balances increases. In these circumstances, it is arbitrary to assume that the fiat issue will only withdraw resources which other-wise would have gone into capital formation. The only way the "un-productive expenditures" may be confined in their impact to the amount of annual savings would be if they were financed by govern-ment loans from the public, loans of a character not admissible for use as collateral for bank credit. Thus normal loan rates are not adequate to prevent a rise in prices in these conditions. Finally, as for the destruction of potential real capital by diverting savings to unproduc-tive expenditure, this destruction is not likely to be complete. In place of voluntary savings, a new source of capital supply arises, namely "forced" saving, resulting from the price rise that occurs despite the banks keeping rates "normal" in these conditions.

Concerning this issue, Davidson made the following amusing com-ment:

The debate between Mssrs. Åkerman and Wicksell concerning the basic idea in the former's article 'Inflation, Money Quantity and Interest,' has several interesting aspects. First and foremost the peculiarity that the theories which are at issue both have Professor Wicksell as author. . . . This circum-stance may explain the mood in which the debate is carried on: however, Åkerman's article should only have aroused pleasant feelings in Wicksell inasmuch as, regardless of who is right, it will in any case be a Wicksellian theory that comes off with the victory.[33]

Observing that only bank credit is subject to the limitations of interest rates and that fiat money or new gold is not, Davidson re-marked that if the central bank is to offset the effect of fiat money, it must be able to reduce outstanding bank credit in proportion to the money issue. A given level of "normal" rates which enabled them to maintain a given supply of credit would not enable them to reduce this supply. Åkerman's case requires that when the government bor-rows from the central bank that the latter not only refrains from issuing notes or extending credit on the basis of the government

---

[33] Davidson, *op. cit.,* p. 13.

loans, but also that it raise the loan rate to a supernormal level so as to restrict the private use of credit. When the government later pays its debt to the central bank in fiat money, this money remains idle in the bank, for at supernormal rates entrepreneurs would not exert any demand for it.

To this resolution of the issue, Davidson added a further telling comment. He said that use of supernormal rates in cases of this kind raises an issue as to the appropriateness of price stabilization in the face of extraordinary government expenditures to be financed by other means than taxation. If the central bank succeeds in raising its rates high enough to prevent a rise in prices, then it is the country's new, potential real capital that is appropriated to pay for the armaments. On the other hand, if the bank simply keeps its loan rates "normal" and lets the price level rise as it will, then it is the community's consumption of goods and services rather than its potential real capital that pays for the armaments. For as the price level rises, the consumption of fixed income recipients is necessarily reduced. "This (raises an issue of) the influence of monetary policy on the formation of real capital. This influence is in certain cases such that it must be regarded as preferable for a country to submit to inflation rather than to resort to the means which are required to avoid inflation." [34]

Wicksell should have been impressed, but apparently was not at that time (1922), by how easily the phrase "increase in scarcity of commodities" or "decrease in productivity" could be substituted in the foregoing argument for "issues of fiat money" or "new gold" without altering the Davidsonian conclusion concerning the inappropriateness of price stabilization as a norm for monetary policy in such circumstances.

THE IMPACT OF ENTREPRENEURIAL EXPECTATIONS AND DIFFERENCES IN MARKET STRUCTURES ON THE REAL RATE OF INTEREST AND THE MOVEMENT OF THE PRICE LEVEL

As will be shown in the next section, in the course of World War I, Davidson developed a habit of distinguishing between types of inflation "it is preferable for a country to submit to" from other types which he regarded as "harmful and avoidable." Inflation that a country might prefer to submit to (rather than to resort to the measures which are required to suppress it) was inflation *not* connected with purely monetary causes such as "abnormally low" loan rates. "Harmful and avoidable" types of inflation rested on monetary causes. They

---

[34] *Ibid.*, p. 29.

were harmful in their impact on incomes and the distribution of wealth, and avoidable in the sense that an appropriate adjustment of the loan rate would prevent them. The adjustment Davidson had in mind was one of moving the loan rate into the proper relationship with the real rate (so that no net credit creation occurs), and then letting prices vary inversely with changes in productivity.

Ohlin attacked Davidson's distinctions between these two types of inflation and also his monetary policy norm.[35] To Ohlin, one type of price rise was just about as "harmful" or "not harmful" as the other. He averred that Davidson's analysis was only formally valid, and was saved only by the unrealistic assumptions he employed. As Ohlin put it, Davidson assumed that the "increase in scarcity of commodities" resulting from lack of raw materials, decline in labor efficiency, monopolistic tendencies in industry, etc., would (1) affect the production of all commodities uniformly, and (2) be neutral to or produce no significant changes in income shares.

To prove his point, Ohlin posed a case in which prices rise in manufacturing industry as this branch of the economy becomes progressively subject to monopoly, while agriculture remains purely competitive. Curtailment of output in manufacturing releases resources which are absorbed in agriculture. The resulting increase of agricultural output partially offsets the decline of output in manufacturing. But total output declines because the resources transferred to agriculture are working at a lower marginal productivity than in their previous employment in manufacture. The decline in total output tends to raise the price level proportionately if the banks keep the loan rate normal.

But, said Ohlin, the scarcity will not be uniform, and consequently the price rise will not affect the distribution of real income uniformly. Secondly, even if the banks keep loan rates normal, which means raising them to the level to which the real rate has risen because of the increase in scarcity, the price rise need not be a one-for-all affair, but may become cumulative. Whether it will or not depends on whether trustification in manufacturing is attended by unilateral and favorable forward price anticipations. If so, the real rate rises more than the increase in scarcity itself calls for, and a loan rate raised only by the estimated scarcity effect turns out to be subnormal to the real rate and initiates an upward cumulative process. Since the anticipations of manufacturers are not tagged or registered, there is no sure criterion of what the proper loan rate policy should be. On the other hand, if the

---

[35] B. Ohlin, "Något om prisstegring, inflation och valutapolitik" (Concerning Rising Prices, Inflation, and Monetary Policy), *Ekonomisk Tidskrift*, 23 (1921), 55-69.

scarcity-fostered tendency to rising prices is to be resisted by loan rate policy aimed at constant prices, then supernormal rates must be used, and these might initiate a downward process. On this basis Ohlin concluded:

We may conclude that in cases of increased commodity scarcity, it may *not* be appropriate to keep the national output at a constant monetary value, and that this will not be done if we are not to disturb equilibrium in the capital market. The result as to prices and the velocity of circulation of money will be that if the discount rate is to be kept at the level of the natural rate, the money value of national output will increase and so will the velocity and quantity of money. To keep the price level down to that level which would be required by a constant circulation by means of a supernormal discount rate, would in this case be just as unjustified as in the case of ordinary monopoly. Thus the ability of commodity scarcity to create temporary monopolies is a force which will generate an increase in the circulation if equilibrium in the capital market is to be maintained.[36]

Davidson made no direct reply to this analysis, but some references to it in his own long articles on monetary theory in 1922 and 1923 convey the impression that he accepted it in substance.

The Wicksell-Davidson Polemic—Monetary Policy Norms in Conditions of Changing Productivity

In order to make the Wicksell-Davidson polemic clear to present-day readers, we must first sketch the main features of Davidson's monetary theory.

MAIN FEATURES OF DAVIDSON'S MONETARY THEORY

Since Davidson, in contrast to Wicksell, did not limit the role of "value theory" to the explanation of relative prices but endeavored to extend its scope to include also general prices or the price level, his monetary theory must be approached from his perspective of "objective value" of commodities.

1. *The concept and measurement of "objective value."* Davidson distinguished between "objective" and subjective value or marginal utility as follows:

The tension [between a person's wants and means] is expressed in the utility that would be foregone if a minimal part of the supply of resources were . . . lost. This concrete utility . . . called marginal utility . . . indicates . . . how far a person's supply of resources suffices for satisfying his wants . . . marginal utility determines individual economic value . . . a person's individual economic valuation and the marginal utility of his supply are

---

[36] *Ibid.*, p. 65.

parallel phenomena of the same cause, scarcity, which influences this value as well as the marginal utility.

But scarcity also gives rise to another economic valuation different from the individual valuation in being concerned with different types of resources as such without attention to the fact that they enter as constituent parts of a person's average supply. If there were only one type of resource, then individual valuations would suffice. But the existence of different kinds of resources *necessitates a further valuation which has as its object to determine how much of one kind of resource corresponds to a certain quantity of another kind of resource,* a valuation which becomes *necessary* in order *to determine what changes in the composition of a person's supply* [of means or utilities] *are called for because of scarcity.* This holds whether these changes in composition take place by transforming a resource from one to another type by production or by means of exchange with other persons. *The result of this kind of valuation is appropriately called 'objective economic value.'*

The objective value of non-reproducibles is determined by their scarcity. . . . [That of reproducibles] is determined by their being supplied in such quantity that their value coincides with their cost of production. Thus the *degree of scarcity of every particular commodity is not a primary fact, but, to the contrary, is subject to a determination whereby the value of every commodity is such that it will coincide with the degree of scarcity of the primary resources which of necessity must be used up in its production.*[37]

Subjective value varies with the individual's income and wealth; yet the level of subjective values of individuals as a group is affected by changes in the population as a whole relative to the aggregate output of commodities. Objective value, on the other hand, is the same for rich and poor. It is expressed only in relative terms, i.e., as relative objective value in terms of commodity exchange ratios. By this Davidson definitely did *not* mean the same as relative prices. In his view, it is a problem of monetary analysis to determine under what circumstances and to what extent prices may be capable of expressing objective values.

Objective values are affected by (*a*) the productivity of economic resources, and (*b*) the supply or quantity of productive resources, or, as Davidson was in the habit of saying, by "the supply of productive power." The supply of "productive power" grows secularly in communities in which the population is increasing and in which net capital formation occurs. An increase in population means both an increase in the labor force and an increase in demand for commodities. Whether population growth augments or diminishes scarcity in net

---

[37] Davidson, "Några teoretiska frågor" (Some Theoretical Questions), *Ekonomisk Tidskrift,* 21 (1919), 233 235. Italics supplied.

terms depends on the productivity of labor and on concurrent changes in the quantity and productivity of other productive power or other resources. Net capital formation means a net increase in productive power. Land, on the other hand, is physically fixed in supply. Permanent improvements in land were reckoned as an increase in fixed real capital. Apart from these secular influences, productive power is also subject to short-run variations. These are of numerous types. Wars and catastrophes temporarily deplete or destroy productive power. Distortions in the allocation of resources due to tariff walls, which increase imperfection of competition, restrict the use of available productive power. But, assuming full resource utilization, all increases in productive power decrease scarcity and reduce objective values.

The "productivity" as distinct from the quantity of resources or of types of productive power was a force Davidson did not analyze, although he referred to it frequently in his treatment. He used this term in the sense of an increase of output per capita. "When productivity increases, a country's supply of goods rises *in relation to its population* and as a result the value (i.e., the objective value) of a unit of utility falls, and vice versa when productivity declines." [38]

Changes in "productivity" complicate the measurement of objective values. Since objective values are only known in terms of commodity exchange ratios, a *uniform* change in the productivity of all resources will not register on objective values as we know them, for such a change tends to affect all exchange ratios alike. This difficulty can only be remedied by arranging the circumstances of price formation, the monetary mechanism more particularly, in such a way that all changes in scarcity, absolute ones, due to uniform changes in productivity, as well as relative ones, are properly expressed in the prices of commodities. *"The price of a commodity unit should vary in the same proportion and direction as that quantity of productive power which has been required for its production."* [39]

But in addition to that "prices," i.e., the price level, should behave as follows: ". . . *prices* of commodities *ought to vary in the same direction and degree as the absolute magnitude of the objective value of commodities varies."* [40]

It was this last desideratum that moved Davidson to adopt as a norm for monetary policy that the price level should be left to vary inversely with changes in productivity or with changes in per-capita

---

[38] Davidson, "Till frågan om penningvärdets reglering under kriget och därefter" (On the Problem of the Regulation of the Value of Money During and After the War), *Ekonomisk Tidskrift*, 25 (1923), 226.

[39] Davidson, *Ekonomisk Tidskrift*, 24 (1922), 103. Italics supplied.

[40] Davidson, *Ekonomisk Tidskrift*, 25 (1923), p. 226. Italics supplied.

output. Incidentally, the foregoing and some subsequent passages show clearly that it was Davidson, rather than von Mises and Hayek, who was the inventor of the "neutral money" doctrine.

Now we are up against the relations of prices to objective values via the intermediation of money, and this requires a look at Davidson's concept of money and the circumstances under which objective values may properly be registered in prices.

Money differs from ordinary commodities in several respects. It stands, as it were, halfway between an economic good and a free good. Unlike ordinary commodities which have a limited service capacity in consumption or production, money has a potentially unlimited service capacity or productivity in terms of the amount of "money work" it can perform. In Davidson's words: *"The value of a commodity by the unit and by its entire supply* are related in this fashion: it is the value of the commodity by the unit which is the primary thing and from this, by summing, the value of the aggregate supply is derived."* [41]

But not so with money:

The principal difference between a commodity supply and a money supply inheres in the fact that *the commodity supply is a collectivum,* i.e., a whole consisting of a number of individual parts, *while the constituent parts of the supply of money are only fractions of the supply of money. The increase in the number of money units is nothing else than a further subdivision of the supply of money* into a larger number of fractions than before.[42]

Further:

The factors that determine the value of money are (1) the size of the supply of commodities which is turned over by money in a period, a year, (2) the quantity of money, and (3) the circulation velocity of money during the period. One should add (4) the time distribution of commodity turnover which is not a consequence of the circulation velocity of money, but rather the contrary. The more the turnover of commodities is divided and distributed over time, the greater is the number of transactions per year that the money unit will on the average perform and hence the greater the velocity of circulation of money. (Something similar to the concept of a coefficient of monetary transactions). But *the magnitude of the supply of commodities cannot be measured directly because of incommensurable units preventing a summation* of the grouped units as a whole. *Thus the problem of controlling the value of money is restricted to controlling the value of the monetary unit. To keep this value constant means that the monetary system must be so managed that the prices of commodities are in the invariable and same pro-*

---

[41] *Ibid.,* p. 214. Italics supplied.
[42] *Ibid.,* p. 222. Italics supplied.

portion to the absolute magnitude of the objective but variable values of commodities.[43]

Specifically this requires that: "*. . . when the value of the supply of money rises* in the course of social progress, *there ought to take place an increase in the number of quotients into which the supply of money is divided.*" [44]

This view of money was both related to and dissimilar to that of Wicksell, and in addition it was more quaintly expressed. Wicksell regarded an increase or decrease in credit media as an increase or decrease in the virtual velocity of money. Davidson described the same phenomenon as a further subdivision of, or as an increase in, the number of quotients into which the supply of money is divided. But Davidson also shared Wicksell's view that the limits within which velocity of circulation fluctuates is determined and susceptible of control by central banks through interest rate policy.

Now, however, if the task of monetary authority was to keep the objective value of money constant by managing the monetary system so that "prices of commodities will always be . . . in the same proportion to the absolute magnitude of objective but variable values of commodities," then it would first be necessary to ascertain what the absolute level of objective values is, for commodities in general. In addition, the relative objective values of commodities, or of a representative number of such, need to be determined. Moreover, this should be done not only for a given moment of time but rather on such a basis that one is able to trace changes in absolute and relative objective values back into time and develop methods for forecasting changes in these values into the future. This is necessary in order that the monetary authority may know how to adjust the money mechanism so as to prevent prices from giving us a distorted view of objective values. Davidson had no definitive solution for these problems but he indicated at least one of the prerequisites for their solution as follows:

In an earlier chapter of this article (*Ekonomisk Tidskrift,* 1922, pp. 104 ff.), *we set up as a principle that when a certain quantity of a commodity always is the result of the same quantity of productive power, it represents* as a rule *an objective value of unchanged magnitude.* But *one prerequisite for this is that the allocation of resources to the production of* various types of *commodities corresponds to the distribution of aggregate demand to these same commodities and to its manner of change.* Otherwise it is likely that the magnitude of the objective value of a certain commodity-quantity may change,

---

[43] *Ibid.,* p. 226. Italics supplied.
[44] *Ibid.,* p. 233. Italics supplied.

rise or fall, despite the fact that this commodity-quantity still requires the same quantity of productive power for its production as before.[45]

This, then, required the kind of long-run adjustment of production to demand that arises in general equilibrium under perfect competition. Then aggregate as well as particular supply and demand for commodities are in equilibrium at prices equal to optimum costs of production.

Why should this be necessary in order to ascertain the level and relative magnitude of objective values? The reason was that the various factors of production are not commensurable. They cannot be equated directly. Therefore the productive power required for a given commodity quantity must be measured indirectly, but under circumstances in which the various inputs of productive power are (a) not likely to change in quantity or in proportion to one another, and (b) when each factor quantity in the combination is used optimally. If this is not the case, there may be relative waste in some lines of production. If so the prices of nonoptimally produced goods increase relative to optimally produced ones which require the same quantity of productive power. Then prices of nonoptimally produced goods would be no safe guide to ascertaining their objective values.

This principle (that product quantities which result from the same quantity of productive power have as a rule the same objective value) proceeds on the basis of concepts which have not been fully analyzed. This is important *in view of the fact that there are different kinds of productive power, so that we need a reduction-norm or common denominator in order to arrive at a generalized concept of productive power.* Toward the end of his life Ricardo was much preoccupied with this problem. . . .[46]

We might add that this problem still awaits its solution. But let us proceed.

Another problem arises in reference to the effect that an increase of a country's productive power has on the objective value of those commodities which are produced by means of the country's supply of productive power. *This problem must be solved in such manner that the magnitude of objective value is independent of the increase in productive power. Only on the basis of such a solution will the principle we have referred to be correct,* namely that the products of the same productive power possess as a rule the same objective values.[47]

---

[45] *Ibid.,* pp. 228-229. Italics supplied.
[46] *Ibid.,* p. 222. Italics supplied.
[47] *Ibid.,* p 229. Italics supplied.

Although the real world never offers conditions which correspond to those of competitive general equilibrium, Davidson thought, nonetheless, that headway could be made toward making actual prices reflect objective values if the corollaries of his objective value analysis are applied. One such corollary was that if per-capita output or productivity increases uniformly, the absolute level of objective values decreases. This should be reflected in a decline in commodity prices in proportion to the increase in productivity. Further, in order to reflect relative objective values in prices as much as possible, it is necessary to render these values independent of changes in the country's productive power. This can be done approximately by adjusting the effective quantity of money in proportion to the change in productive power, for, unless this is done, the objective value of money does not remain constant. However, this poses a problem of applying Davidson's monetary policy norm.

2. *Application of Davidson's monetary policy norm—difficulties of the proper money quantity adjustment.*   Let us assume that a country's labor power increases while its effective quantity of money remains constant. One result of this is that commodities which require relatively more labor in their production than other forms of productive power decline in objective value relative to values of other commodities. This change in relative objective values is expressed in changed relative prices. But if the effective quantity of money has *not* been adjusted, then the prices that emerge will *not reflect the same quantity of productive power per money unit as before,* but rather a larger quantity. The value of money will have been permitted to increase relative to the supply of productive power. Consequently, when the quantity of productive power changes, the effective quantity of money should be changed in the same direction and by an equal proportion. Hence, Davidson's monetary policy norm: Let the money value of the annual output remain constant except for such changes in productive power, i.e., in labor force and real capital, as have occurred or are occurring. To make proper allowance for these changes adjust the effective quantity of money in the same direction and by the same proportion, primarily by operating on its velocity of circulation through the medium of central bank interest rate policy.[48]

One problem Davidson left unanalyzed with reference to his norm was that of the relationship of real capital to the labor force in adjusting the effective quantity of money. One reason for this was that he used mainly hypothetical examples in which population, real capital, and annual output increase in equal proportions. "If population, real

[48] Davidson, . . . , *Ekonomisk Tidskrift,* 4 (1922), 103-104.

capital and annual output increase in the same proportion . . . the degree of scarcity of utilities . . . remains, on the whole, constant . . . [but] when productivity increases, scarcity diminishes, and then prices ought to fall in proportion to the diminution in commodity scarcity." [49]

Yet it is clear that if real capital and population increase in equal proportions, this does not necessarily mean that annual output will increase in the same proportion. Whether it will depends on the nature of production functions. However, the problem which is of primary interest here is one concerning the relations between real capital and population in the money quantity adjustment. Concerning this, Davidson himself said: "One of the problems *not* taken up here is the question of the significance in this analysis of a change in the relation of real capital to population." [50]

On the basis of Davidson's general position, it is probable he thought this problem would be solved in the money market, for that was the logical place for money-quantity adjustments to be effected via the elasticity of credit media. Moreover, he accepted Wicksell's analysis at least this far that if the banks keep the loan rate equal to the real rate, he assumed that monetary equilibrium prevailed, or that money was "neutral" in the sense that the general economic situation was free from disturbances from "the side of money."

Now if real capital increases faster than the labor force, the effect will be a reduction in the marginal productivity of capital, an increase in total income and output, and a shift of income in favor of workers and landowners. The marginal value productivity or the real rate of interest on capital decreases. The banks, to maintain equilibrium, must reduce loan rates to the lower level of the real rate. In doing so, some credit creation occurs. At the reduced loan rate, savings recede to a level appropriate to the lower rate. Assume that savings are at that point smaller than necessary to provide for the increase in amortization quotas occasioned by the preceding net formation of capital. Since the loan rate has been reduced, entrepreneurs are now able to borrow enough from banks to maintain, but not to make net additions to, the existing enlarged capital structure. Thus credit, and indirectly velocity of circulation of money, have expanded by the increase in amortization quotas. Meanwhile output has increased at some reduction in commodity prices and with a tantamount increase in real income. In this manner, the capital or money market more or less automatically performs the requisite money quantity adjustment. The net increase in

---

[49] *Ibid.*, p. 111.
[50] *Ibid.*, p. 113.

real capital, while maintaining monetary equilibrium with the price level varying inversely with the increase in output, has been matched by an increase in the "virtual" velocity of money.

But this process does not work satisfactorily in the contrary case when the labor force increases while the quantity of real capital remains constant. Under Davidson's norm, the banks are now under obligation to increase the effective quantity of money in relation to the increase in the labor force. But now the marginal productivity of labor declines, and the distribution of income shifts in favor of capitalists. Total output increases absolutely, but probably not in relation to the labor force. Hence commodity prices tend to rise. What happens to the real rate? It cannot fall; to the contrary, it rises. With relatively more làbor and declining money wages the structure of production is shortened. If banks keep the loan rate equal to the rising real rate, as Davidson held they should, then there will be no net increase in credit, but rather a decrease. Hence the effective quantity of money decreases. Thus it appears that in this case the money market fails to perform the desired money quantity adjustment.

Precisely how the adjustment was to be made was not made clear by Davidson. However, in one of his rejoinders to Wicksell he admitted the impracticability of his norm from an operating standpoint. But he hoped that further analysis of pricing problems would yield a solution to this problem: "Possibly we may obtain some guidance for solving the problem of one and the same commodity's objective value at different points of time by investigating the causes of changes in price relations of different commodities and *by investigating the connection between causes and the conditions affecting production and sales of commodities.*" [51]

As has been shpwn above, Wicksell stated [52] that progress may be made on this problem if the government would take upon itself the task of investigating the causes and consequences and also the extent of productivity changes in the sphere of commodity production. However, we are left without a definite guide from Davidson's monetary norm to monetary policy.

It is evident that Davidson's neo-Ricardian perspective on value and monetary theory yielded a sophisticated analysis. In fact, the integration he attempted to achieve between the theory of relative prices and price level movements was superior to Wicksell's hypothetical separa-

---

[51] Davidson, . . . , *Ekonomisk Tidskrift,* 25 (1923), 233.

[52] Wicksell, "Penningränta och varupris" (Money Interest and Commodity Prices), *Ekonomisk Tidskrift,* 11 (1909), 61-66; see also n. 27, above; and Davidson, "Varu-värde och penningvärde" (Value of Commodities and Value of Money), *Ekonomisk Tidskrift,* 28 (1926), 3 n.

tion of these two areas of analysis, even if Davidson did not succeed in performing this integration for the case where the labor force increases while real capital remains constant. This brings us to the Wicksell-Davidson polemic about monetary policy norms.

THE EARLY STAGE OF THE WICKSELL-DAVIDSON POLEMIC, 1899-1909

The Wicksell-Davidson controversy opened in 1899 with Davidson's review of *Geldzins und Güterpreise* in the first volume of *Ekonomisk Tidskrift* (pp. 233-240), a journal which was launched under Davidson's ownership and editorship in that year. On the whole Davidson's review was complimentary but ended with the comment that price stabilization by interest-rate policy is appropriate only if no changes occur in per-capita productivity. Wicksell did not respond to this review. In fact nothing was heard in this matter until 1906 when Wicksell published the first edition of *Lectures-II*. This work, it seemed to Davidson, repeated in substance the analysis of the earlier book, and this moved Davidson to write a longer article attacking the norm of price stabilization. Then there ensued a series of exchanges between Wicksell and Davidson, in which the following points were brought up.[53] These points are more easily stated by a combination of paraphrase and direct quotation arranged in dialogue form:

(*a*) Davidson: To keep the price level constant by interest rate policy when per-capita productivity increases deprives recipients of fixed incomes of their pro rata share in the increase in real income. On the other hand, when productivity decreases, if prices are kept constant, recipients of fixed incomes receive a disproportionately large share of the decreasing real income at the expense of other classes. It is more equitable to let the price level vary inversely with changes in productivity, thus distributing real income gains or losses more or less uniformly over all income groups.

(*a'*) Wicksell: Davidson's norm of inverse price variation with changes in productivity is more just than a price stabilization norm in these circumstances. But his norm represents a transcendental standard of justice which, for lack of definite criteria for monetary policy, would fail of practical application. The banks cannot know the level and movement of the real rate directly. Because of this, they would be at a loss to decide how much of a

---

[53] In order to reduce documentation to a minimum, articles in which the Wicksell-Davidson polemic was carried on in its early active phase are listed in chronological order as follows: Davidson, "Något om begreppet penningens värde" (Concerning the Concept Value of Money), *Ekonomisk Tidskrift*, 8 (1906), 460-468; Wicksell, "Penningvärdets stadgande ett medel att förebygga kriser," (Stabilization of the Value of Money a Means for Preventing Crises), *ibid.*, 10 (1908), 207-214; Davidson, "Om stabiliseringen av penningens värde" (Concerning Stabilization of Value of Money), *ibid.*, 11 (1909), 1-25; Wicksell, "Penningränta och varupris" (Money Interest and Commodity Prices), *ibid.*, 11 (1909), 61-66; Davidson, "Replik" (Rejoinder), *ibid.*, 11 (1909), 67-68.

price decline corresponds to the increase in productivity, and how much of a decline is in excess thereof and should be counteracted by reducing loan rates. The practical alternatives lie between adopting price stabilization as a norm, or submitting to the violent price fluctuations which have characterized all crises in the past.

(*b*) Davidson: Among other things, Wicksell's norm implies a proportionate rise in money wages when productivity increases. Such wage increases have always been resisted by employers. In the reverse case of declining productivity, the wage reductions which would be necessary would be strongly resisted by organized labor. Consequently, Wicksell's norm conduces to industrial strife.

(*b'*) Wicksell made no direct response to the issue of industrial unrest but entered instead an argument on another point: Davidson's norm would be inappropriate if not impossible because of the international character of prices. If a mother country and one of its colonies are both engaged in international trade in similar commodities, and if, as can be expected, productivity increases in the colony with its virgin resources and declines in the mother country, then Davidson's norm cannot be applied. Similar goods cannot move in international trade at different prices.

(*c*) Davidson: Wicksell's norm is internally inconsistent. If it is applied when productivity increases, it disrupts equilibrium in the money market and gives rise to an upward cumulative process. The increase in productivity implies that the real rate has risen from its initial level. To keep the money mechanism neutral and maintain money market equilibrium, the banks should then raise the loan rate to the higher level achieved by the real rate. If they do this, then the increased output which arrives on the commodity market must be sold at declining prices. The level of money income has been kept constant by the increase in the loan rate, hence the greater output of goods must be sold against an aggregate expenditure which has not increased at prices lower than before by the cost saving implicit in the productivity increase. But, if the banks follow Wicksell, they would reduce the loan rate when productivity increases in order to keep the price level from falling. At its reduced level the loan rate would then be abnormally low relative to the real rate, which has risen. Then, on the basis of Wicksell's own analysis, a cumulative process would be set in motion.

(*c'*) To this Wicksell replied:

"He (Davidson) thinks I would urge reducing the loan rate, while he would let the price level fall. To the contrary, I too would let it fall, for it would only be a one-for-all reduction, soon overcome by the cumulative rise in prices that the increased rate would bring about. The improvement in productivity may well have raised it one or two percent above the loan rate. Hence I would raise the loan rate also in this case. . . .

"Now, however, Davidson holds that if the price level falls from the outset because of the increase in output, then the gains (anticipated on the basis of increased productivity) are wiped out and the real rate is brought back to equality with the bank rate. The result is that we would have a new equilibrium at lower prices. If this were right there would be a real gap in my argumentation. But it is not correct. Davidson implicitly assumes that at the same time *real capital* has increased as much as productivity. His case assumes that money wages remain constant. Now if the price level falls real wages will have risen. But how can they rise without additional real capital? . . .

"I work on the *ceteris paribus* assumption that real capital and real wages do not change. Then if the price level falls, money wages must also fall and entrepreneurs have the same return on their capital as at unchanged prices. Thus with the exception of the once-for-all decline in the price level, what I have said holds. The banks may reduce the bank rate for a short time in order to raise it all the more later to prevent an unlimited rise of prices. I do not quarrel with Davidson about the initial and temporary price·decline. But I disagree with him about his belief that the price decline will be definitive and that prices will then remain stable with unchanged bank rates despite the increase in productivity which has occurred. Increased productivity with unchanged real capital necessarily means an increased real rate of interest on capital, and equilibrium cannot prevail in the market if the money rate is not brought into agreement with this rate, i.e., in this case, increased." [54]

To this, Davidson replied in the following cryptic manner:

"He [Wicksell] seems definitely to deny that the development might be one in which when productivity increases commodity prices might fall while at the same time the worker's money wages remain unchanged. For if this is possible, then the case I have pointed to would arise, when the banks, according to Wicksell's proposal, ought to *reduce* their interest rates in order to force up the price level to its original level.

"I only wanted to establish this presupposition in Wicksell's theory and proposal, and will now refrain from further comments on it." [55]

This was the note on which this debate closed in its active stage. The issues it raised require further scrutiny since neither participant in this controversy expressed himself very clearly about them.

1. *The social equity issue.* Davidson rested his claim of "greater equity" of his norm on the grounds that the money mechanism should not be permitted to function as a device for arbitrarily redistributing real income and income shares in the community. When productivity changes, Wicksell's price stabilization norm could not help functioning in precisely such an undesirable and irrational fashion. So far as possible, the monetary mechanism should be kept "neutral" with respect to the level and structure of commodity prices. If this was impossible of immediate achievement, there was at least no reason to

---

[54] Wicksell, "Penningränta och varupris" (Money Interest and Commodity Prices), *Ekonomisk Tidskrift*, 11 (1909), 64-65.

[55] Davidson, "Replik" (Rejoinder), *Ekonomisk Tidskrift*, 11 (1909), 68.

make it unneutral with respect to relative income shares, since this was avoidable by letting prices vary inversely with productivity.

2. *Practicability of monetary policy norms.* As we have seen, Davidson admitted the "impracticability" of his own monetary norm in the then existing state of economic knowledge. Consequently, there was undeniable force in Wicksell's point that Davidson's counsel of perfection left monetary policy no alternatives to the vagaries of the gold standard. Thus, in spite of the distributive inequities it might work in the real income sphere, price stabilization was a superior practical alternative to the gold standard. This, taken in conjunction with Wicksell's eagerness to use the methods of public finance to mitigate distributive injustice strengthened his position considerably at the practical level as compared with Davidson's.

Concerning issue (*b*), the relation between the two monetary norms and industrial strife, it was Davidson's argument that his norm, which may not be capable of removing the causes of industrial conflict, would at least not constantly aggravate them. When prices decline with increasing productivity and real wages rise, an enlightened labor leadership may see the wisdom of concluding long-term nationwide collective bargains. But the same leadership will meticulously, and rightly, refrain from doing so if it becomes a matter of necessity to adjust money wages upwards at frequent intervals.

The difficulty Davidson's position encounters is that his norm presupposes a high degree of price flexibility. Yet in industries where trade union organization and parallel employer organizations have made the greatest advances, price flexibility is on the wane, being replaced by price rigidity in consequence of the imperfect market structures and the monopolistic tendencies which are characteristic of large-scale industry.

Although Wicksell did not respond directly to this issue, his position was indicated in a pamphlet he wrote at an earlier date (1902), *Allianser mellan arbetare och arbetsgifvare* (Alliances between Workers and Employers). There he expressed his reflections on collective bargaining in some British trades which had for years suffered the triple evils of weak and irresponsible union organization, sweated working conditions, and cutthroat competition among the employers. The strengthening of the union by employers on condition that the union effectively prevent its unemployed members from going to work for price-cutting firms resulted in greater employment and income stability for workers and employers alike, ultimately at the expense of consumers.

Evidently Wicksell was not as willing as Davidson to believe that organized workers and employers would be satisfied with rising real incomes and constant money incomes without indulging their propensity for making occasional joint assaults on the defenseless consumer, and for such a propensity neither his nor Davidson's norm would be an effective preventive.

Davidson thus succeeded in establishing a presumption against the price stabilization norm because of its tendency to increase industrial strife. However, another presumption urged against it at a later time by another authority also deserves attention here, since it belongs in the same universe of discourse. This is the charge made by F. von Hayek that price stabilization involves waste of economic resources.[56]

It will be made clear as we proceed that maintenance of constant prices subsequent to an increase in productivity which involves a gestation period of capital formation requires considerable interest-rate manipulation on the part of the banks. The reason for this is that the loan rate which may prevent a decline in prices is likely to initiate an upward cumulative process, and the increase in the loan rate which may stop the upward process is also likely to reverse it into a downward process, and this would call for a rate reduction before the downward process gathers momentum. Hence, price stabilization involves alternating oscillations around the original or "normal" level of prices, effected by timely shifts in interest-rate policy. With each upward movement production of capital goods expands. When the process is reversed, construction of real capital begun during the short upward process is abandoned. The same phenomenon recurs during the next upward movement, only then it is unlikely that the construction projects begun in the previous upward process will be resumed. Instead new ones would be started. Thus a succession of brief upward and downward oscillations of the price level might give rise to an increasing collection of unfinished and abandoned capital projects. This involves sheer waste in which the increase in productivity, for which considerable sacrifices may have been made during the gestation period, may be dissipated on unusable projects incapable of serving the purposes of production and/or of consumption. In that case, the increase in productivity becomes abortive, for the attempt to stabilize average prices introduces so much instability in the conditions of production as to prevent a rise in physical productivity from contributing to national welfare. We shall not try to decide how strong a case this represents, but it is on a sequence of this kind that von Hayek rests his charge of resource waste against the stable price norm.

3. *Monetary policy norms and international trade.* As to Wicksell's statement (*b'*) that Davidson's norm could not be applied be-

[56] F. A. von Hayek, *Prices and Production* (London, 1931), pp. 93-96.

cause of the international nature of prices, one çan only say that his treatment of it was too sketchy to be conclusive, but it probably established a presumption in favor of the stable price norm in circumstances where major changes are inevitable or are in progress. Assume that a mother country in which productivity is declining has half its resources allocated to production of commodity X. Its colony with increasing productivity has most of its resources devoted to production of X. Both countries produce X not for home consumption, nor for mutual exchange, but chiefly for export to the rest of the world. Both adopt the Davidsonian monetary norm, in consequence of which the price of X rises in the mother country and falls in the colony. The result will be that the colony takes over the mother country's share of their joint export market of X almost immediately.

The mother country suffers unemployment and deteriorating living standards unless and until it can rapidly move 50 per cent of its resources from production of X to some alternative use. To effect such a movement in the face of increasing decline of real income and deepening unemployment is, of course, a greater problem than if the same movement, which is inevitable in any case, were to occur under less severe pressure and over a longer period.

Now instead Wicksell's norm is adopted. Both the colony and the mother country continue their export trade of X, but money incomes and profits are rising in the colony and are gradually declining in the mother country. Production of X is consequently expanding in the colony and contracting in the mother country, perhaps by means of a gradual transfer of capital and manpower from the one into the other by the attraction of higher wages and profits. There can be no doubt that the inevitable production adjustment in store for the mother country will be much easier and equally complete under Wicksell's as compared with Davidson's norm.

4. *The norms and monetary equilibrium.*   As Lindahl has pointed out,[57] the price stabilization policy involves considerable manipulation of interest rates by the central bank, far more so than would be likely under Davidson's norm, and this holds true even if the latter lacks clear criteria for monetary intervention. This was a disadvantage of the price stabilization norm. When Davidson proceeded to show under (c) that price stabilization disrupts monetary equilibrium in conditions of changing productivity, Wicksell remained unconvinced until more than a decade later when World War I had, as it were, given empirical proof for Davidson's position.

---

[57] E. Lindahl, *Studies in the Theory of Money and Capital* (New York, 1939), pp. 210-222.

As it happened, this issue suffered from lack of precise formulation by both disputants. Wicksell's defense, as we have shown, turned on whether the increase in productivity was accompanied by an increase in capital formation. On the other hand, Davidson did not rise directly to this point made by Wicksell; instead he remained satisfied with "establishing a presupposition" in Wicksell's argument. In the end, there can be no doubt that Davidson had the better of this argument, but that can best be shown by means of two models developed for the purpose of clarifying this issue.

5. *Interest rate policy and increasing productivity—Two Models.* The issue between Wicksell and Davidson turns on whether the increase in productivity is attended by a gestation period of capital formation before the volume of output increases, or whether it is free from such a period so that the increase in output is immediate and does not require creation of additional capital.

To deal with this problem, we use two models of a closed economy initially in stationary equilibrium which is disturbed by an increase in productivity. Like Wicksell and Davidson, we treat the productivity increase as uniform in character and as equivalent to an increase in per capita output. In each of the two models we assume the community reverts to stationary conditions with an increased level of output after the productivity change has worked itself out. In the first model we assume that the increase in productivity requires a two-year gestation period for capital formation before its fruits become evident in terms of a significant increase in output. In the second model, it is assumed that the increase in productivity is immediate and involves mainly the application of a new division of labor for which no intervening period of capital formation is required.

Both models are admittedly unrealistic, the first because a definite gestation period and a uniform increase in production everywhere is not likely to occur. The second is unrealistic because it assumes the new division of labor does not require construction of new real capital. Yet it may not be so farfetched as it may seem at first. There are cases on record where so-called "backward" economies "discover" and adopt working methods which have long been in use in "advanced" economies. A case in point may be the Stakhanovite movement in the U.S.S.R., which apparently involves application of more effective routing of materials and manpower to mechanical tasks in mining on the basis of time and motion studies.[58]

5a. *The gestation period model and its implications for the Wicksell-*

---

[58] Cf. M. Dobb, *Soviet Economic Development Since 1917,* London (1947), pp. 429 ff.

Davidson polemic.   The primary features of the first model are as follows:

A stationary economy with a constant population is kept in equilibrium by the banks charging a loan rate of interest which, at the level of 5 per cent, equals the real rate or the marginal value productivity of real capital. No net saving occurs, but at this rate sufficient gross saving for reinvestment takes place to maintain the community's real capital. The price level is constant at an index of 100.

The annual output of goods and services in this society is 10,000 "commodity units," 33 per cent of which are used for replacing existing real capital and 67 per cent are consumption goods. The gross national income is $10,000, which the citizens in the aggregate divide into two streams, $6,700 for consumption expenditures, and $3,300 for savings. Hence each "commodity unit" has a price of $1.00 and a production cost of the same amount since we assume perfect competition. The capitalists, or savers, consume the proceeds of their 5 per cent interest income on their investments.

Now inventors come out with designs for new types of tools, which on their estimates will increase output 10 per cent on the average. But it requires two years and a net advance of capital for building shops in order to produce a sufficient quantity of the new tools to equip everybody properly for increased production.

To accomplish this, net savings for new investment of $1,700 a year for two years are necessary. The community responds with exactly that much of an increase in its savings as the loan rate is raised to 10 per cent, the real rate having risen to this level in the meantime because of favorable anticipations motivating entrepreneurs in view of the prospective production increase. Thus equilibrium is preserved during the gestation period, and the 1,700 commodity units per year required for construction of new real capital are provided.

However, if the community had not responded, for instance, because the banks failed to raise the loan rate, the needed savings would have been provided in any case by "forced saving." For an upward cumulative process would have set in, and rising prices, despite rising wages, would have reduced consumption sufficiently to provide the necessary commodity units for getting the new shops built and the new tools produced.

Now both Wicksell and Davidson agree that in this case—productivity increasing via a gestation period for net capital formation—the banks should raise the loan rate to the level to which the real rate has risen because of favorable anticipations. If this is done the transition to the increased productivity stage proceeds in an orderly manner on "voluntary" savings.

Their disagreement began at the point when the gestation period comes to a close and the annual output of goods increases. Precisely how the banks should react then was not made clear. Wicksell said in effect, reduce the loan rate. Davidson said, leave it alone. What matters is, on the one hand, how far it should be reduced, and, on the other, at what level it should be left alone. Neither of them were explicit on this. Wicksell had his eye on the decline in the price level which was bound to occur if the rate were not reduced, while Davidson had his mind focused on the fact that income recipients, capitalists in particular, would be prevented from sharing in the productivity increase if the price level was prevented from falling by a rate reduction. Both appear to have assumed that the real rate would recede to its pregestation period level of 5 per cent at this point.

Davidson may have meant one of three things: (a) keep the loan rate at the high level it has reached at the end of the gestation period; (b) that the loan rate should be kept constant after it has been reduced to its pregestation period level; or (c) that the loan rate should be kept constant only after it has been permitted to recede to a level which corresponds to the prospective real rate on capital in view of the increase in real capital which has occurred, and also in view of the attendant reduction in marginal value productivity of capital one has reason to expect in these circumstances. In 1909, Davidson's monetary theory was not sufficiently developed to enable us to tell which of these alternatives he had in mind. But in the light of his more fully developed theory of the 1920's, it seems likely that he may have meant alternative (c). Then this would permit that increase in effective quantity of money which corresponds to the permanent increase in "productive power" that has occurred by the formation of new capital.

Wicksell, on the other hand, may have meant (a') reduce the loan rate to its pregestation period level, or (b') reduce it to whatever level is necessary to keep the price level constant. Apparently he had alternative (b') in mind, for at this time, 1909, he had as yet made no "concession to his critics" concerning the possibility that the real rate may be adjusted to the level of the loan rate. That concession came later, in 1915.

But let us see what the model indicates concerning these different courses of action:

At the end of the gestation period in the third year, the annual output of the economy rises by 10 per cent to 11,000 commodity units. Meanwhile prices and money incomes have remained constant so that gross national product is $10,000. With the closing of the gestation period let us assume all "net" investment opportunities have been exploited so that the real rate has declined to its old level of 5 per cent.

Now if the loan rate is also reduced to 5 per cent we may expect the community's expenditure pattern to revert to its earlier composition. If so, consumption expenditures rise from $5,000 during the gestation period to $6,700, and savings decline from $5,000 to $3,300 again.

If the larger annual output now consists of 33 per cent replacement goods for capital maintenance and the remainder of consumption goods, then 7,370 units of the latter are now on the market, and 3,630 of the former. In view of the magnitude of money income and its expenditure pattern, this necessarily means that the price level must fall 9 per cent with a tantamount increase in real incomes for all classes.

Another possibility would be that the real rate, with an increased quantity of permanent real capital, in year three falls below its pregestation period normal level of 5 per cent. If so, the loan rate may also be reduced to this same level, and then we may imagine that the community reallocates its constant-size gross money income into $7,000 consumption expenditure and $3,000 savings. Then prices of the 7,370 units of consumption goods decline less, a little more than 5 per cent, while prices of capital-replacement goods fall all the more, by 21 per cent. But the weighted average decline in prices is still 9 per cent despite this shift in relative prices. If this situation continues for some years, one may imagine relative prices and relative output of capital-replacement goods and consumption goods will be adjusted until the stream of commodities matches the expenditure pattern. Then a new equilibrium will be attained with an output of 7,700 units of consumption goods being sold for a total consumption expenditure of $6,700 at $0.90 per unit. A similar adjustment will occur in capital-replacement goods, and so the general price level settles at 90.

Thus merely to reduce the loan rate to the level of the real rate subsequent to the increase in productivity at the end of the gestation period, will *not* keep the price level constant. On the other hand, if the loan rate is reduced sufficiently to keep the price level constant, it disrupts equilibrium and gives rise to an upward cumulative process. This becomes clear if we return to the case where the real rate has only fallen to its pregestation period normal level.

Suppose now the banks reduce the loan rate to 3 per cent, i.e., *below* the normal level of the real rate of 5 per cent, and suppose further that at this loan rate consumption spending rises to $7,370 out of a constant-size gross income of $10,000. Then prices of consumption goods will remain constant. But there are 3,630 units of capital-replacement goods and only $2,630 voluntary savings with which to purchase them. But the difference, $1,000, is made up by credit expansion at the lower loan rate. Hence nominal income rises to $11,000, and for the moment it looks as if the price level may remain constant.

But it will not stay constant very long. Entrepreneurs now make extra gains from the difference between the loan rate and the real rate. They are moved to expand activities and in doing so competition between them forces them to bid up wages of labor. At the same time, however, production is oriented more and more to production of capital goods. A typical upward cumulative process starts.

To arrest this process, banks may find it necessary to raise the loan rate above the real rate to 6 per cent. This stops the expansion, but it also reduces the demand for credit and increases the provision of savings, and thus gives consumption goods prices a deflationary twist. To block the latter the loan rate would again have to be reduced below the real rate, credit would have to be expanded, etc., to obtain the expenditure pattern which would keep prices from falling.

Thus to attempt to keep the price level from falling, and after that from rising, when productivity increases via a gestation period will alternately set off upward and downward cumulative processes. While an alert central bank management may conceivably be able to vary the loan rate fast enough and by proper amounts so as to keep the price level constant or within a narrow range of fluctuation, offhand, its task seems well-nigh impossible.

5b. *The nongestation period model and its bearing on the controversy.* Now let us turn to the second model of a productivity increase without a gestation period, a very simple model:

A new division of labor is rapidly adopted without involving additional capital investment. Within a negligible period of time, annual output increases uniformly 10 per cent to 7,370 units of consumption goods and 3,630 capital-replacement goods.

Now what happens to the real rate? Wicksell spoke as if it rose and stayed up while the loan rate remained unchanged. Yet he did not insist on this, for he recognized the price level would fall when additional output comes on the market while money incomes have remained constant.

If, as both he and Davidson admitted, in this case the price level falls 9 per cent, it is not likely that the real rate will stay at its high level. Davidson was not explicit about this. But let us assume that the real rate rises to 10 per cent for a short period while the new labor technique is being introduced. When the increase in output arrives on the market, the real rate will not have remained high long enough for entrepreneurs to take expansionary action before the decline in commodity prices drives it back to the level it had prior to the increase in productivity.

The result then will be that entrepreneurs produce and sell 110 per cent as much output as before at 9 per cent lower prices. They have neither gains nor losses, and equilibrium is preserved at a 10 per cent rise in real income to all classes.

Thus it seems the 9 per cent decline in the price level will be *permanent* unless another increase in productivity arrives to disturb this new equilibrium. This, at any rate, was Davidson's position; and it was on this basis he said that on Wicksell's principles the banks would have had to reduce their rates to keep prices from falling.

On this point Wicksell's answer was inept. The once-for-all increase in productivity, which occurred without a gestation period, has reduced prices. Still he seemed to hold that the real rate, which probably rose while the new production technique was being introduced, remains high, and in any case higher than the loan rate which has not been changed. This is very unlikely. Yet here he concluded that the drop in the price level, following the increase in productivity, would be a once-for-all affair, soon overwhelmed by upward-spiraling prices, since he thought the real rate would remain higher than the loan rate. Therefore, he said, when productivity increases the banks should raise their loan rates.

When pressed further on this point by Davidson, Wicksell referred to the condition of real capital. Of course, he said, the real rate has risen and is higher than the loan rate because real capital has *not* increased whereas productivity has, and that can only mean a rise in the real rate.

Here Wicksell was either wrong, or he used an implicit assumption not shared by Davidson. The increase in productivity required no increase in capital and was a once-for-all, permanent event, so that henceforth national output is at the level of 11,000 commodity units instead of 10,000. With money incomes constant, at the lower prices which result the real rate is not likely to rise.

In an attempt to make his position clearer, Wicksell said that when prices fall money wages must also fall, for otherwise real wages must have risen, and a rise in real wages is impossible unless there is a prior increase in real capital, i.e., an increase in the real-wages-and-rent fund. However, such an increase presupposes a gestation period and fits only the first model, not the one being discussed here.

So if Wicksell talked about a productivity increase that occurred only once and became permanent, the question of expansion of real capital would not arise. In order for the real rate to rise after prices have fallen a new increase in productivity would be necessary.

Here Davidson had the best of the argument, as can be seen if we ask what happens to the loan rate. If it was a once-for-all increase in productivity which reduced prices without an intervening gestation period, then Davidson was right in saying that to keep prices constant

Wicksell's theory demands that the loan rate be reduced. Furthermore, he was also right in saying that if this were done, the loan rate would become subnormal relative to the real rate and would initiate an upward cumulative process. Because of his mistake about the behavior of the real rate in this case, Wicksell insisted that the loan rate be raised. If that were done a downward process would start.

Conclusions. The conclusions we arrive at on the basis of this review of the polemic are:

1. If the increase in productivity requires a gestation period for capital formation before its fruition, then the loan rate should be raised during the gestation period in order to avoid an upward cumulative process and in order to accommodate the required expansion of capital on the basis of voluntary saving.

2. After the gestation period the loan rate must be reduced to the new level of the real rate, which may be lower than the level it had prior to the gestation period, in order to maintain equilibrium and avoid cumulative processes. But this lower and "normal" loan rate will prove incapable of preventing the price level from falling roughly in proportion to the increase in productivity.

3. If the loan rate is reduced sufficiently after the gestation period to prevent the price level from falling, then this lower rate will be subnormal and will set the stage for an upward, and alternatively for downward processes, as it is adjusted again. In these conditions the loan rate, which will for the time being keep prices stable, will disrupt equilibrium. Here the choice lies between price stabilization and sacrifice of equilibrium, unless a third possibility is present; namely, the maintenance of equilibrium by other means than those of interest-rate policy. Those means must then involve *either* a rise in real income proportionate to the increase in productivity, *or* a rise in money income of the same proportion, *and also* such a division or disposition of the real or money income between consumption and saving as corresponds to the composition of the increased output in the postgestation period into output of consumption goods and capital goods. It is not likely that the same means as may assure the requisite rise in income will also guarantee the appropriate disposition or expenditure pattern of the augmented income.

4. If the increase in productivity requires no gestation period but is an immediate productivity increase, then the real rate will not rise above its original level for long enough to permit expansion before it recedes again to that level. In this case the loan rate should not be disturbed if equilibrium is to be maintained. The new equilibrium

which will be established involves an adjustment from the preceding one by a reduction in the price level proportionate to the increase in productivity.

5. On balance, in either of the two foregoing cases, the loan rate which will maintain equilibrium and obviate cumulative processes when productivity changes, whether with or without attendant gestation periods, will *not* at the same time prevent a variation in the price level which will be approximately inversely proportionate to the change in productivity.

THE LATER STAGE OF THE POLEMIC, 1909-1925

The active phase of the Wicksell-Davidson polemic ended in 1909 with a cryptic rejoinder of Davidson's, who said he "would refrain from further comment" on Wicksell's monetary theory after having "established a presupposition" in it.[59] However, the controversy was carried on indirectly as both he and Wicksell became actively involved in interpreting the causes of the inflation Sweden experienced during World War I and in attempting to develop the basis for a monetary policy which would limit the inflationary spiral as far as possible and facilitate the economy's readjustment to postwar conditions.

According to leading contemporary observers, inflation in Sweden rested on at least three distinct causes, which tended to reinforce each other.[60]

First, there was the famous "gold invasion." This resulted from the fact that the growing Swedish export surplus was paid in gold by continental belligerents who progressively restricted their own exports of commodities to provide for the increasing requirements of their war effort. Secondly, associated with the first cause, there was "increasing commodity scarcity." With slender domestic resources, Sweden was dependent on raw materials imports to supplement the output of her own agriculture, and to keep her mechanical industries running. Lack of many of these imports during the war contributed seriously to a decline in man-hour productivity in some of the country's industries, and to the commodity scarcity in general. Thirdly, there was the effect of the "monetization" of large deficit budgets incurred for purposes

---

[59] Davidson, "Replik" (Rejoinder), *Ekonomisk Tidskrift*, 11 (1909), p. 68.

[60] The best brief account available in English of Sweden's inflation experience during World War I is found in B. Thomas, *Monetary Policy and Crises: A Study of Swedish Experience* (London, 1936); reference is also made to E. Heckscher's *Bidrag till Sveriges Ekonomiska och Sociala Historia under och efter Världskriget* (A Contribution to the Social and Economic History of Sweden During and After World War I, Stockholm, 1926).

of keeping Sweden's defense establishment ready and able to protect the country's neutrality. To this may be added a fourth cause, which was stressed with varying emphasis by Sweden's leading economists, namely the timid and at times inept monetary policies pursued by the Riksbank. But compared with the former three causes, this was probably a force of minor magnitude.

With so many causes to blame, there was, of course, no dearth of learnedly argued explanations of the country's inflation experiences. We shall, however, limit our discussion to the views expressed by Cassel, Davidson, and Wicksell.

Cassel's interpretation as stated in *Dyrtid och Sedelöverflod* (Inflation and Excessive Note Issue, 1917), in numerous articles in the press, and in his later work, *Money and the Foreign Exchanges after 1914* (1922), was that the inflation was due to excessive note issue. As to commodity scarcity, he recognized it as a contributory cause. But he held that this scarcity need not necessarily cause inflation, unless the banks aided the process by keeping interest rates artificially low. An increase in commodity scarcity ought only to raise the price level in proportion to the decline in output if the banks maintain the same effective quantity of money. But if they reduce this quantity in proportion to the decline in output no general price rise should occur. The effect of an increase in scarcity is not exerted directly on prices but rather on the supply of credit available for industry. Despite rising scarcity people endeavor to maintain their former consumption standard, and to do so they draw their bank balances at a greater rate than before, thus decreasing the supply of credit to industry.

Yet, this would not necessarily result in inflation, unless, as often happens, the banks make up for the deficiency of saving by making additional purchasing power available in the form of net credit expansion either at the same or at an inadequately increased rate of interest. Thus Cassel viewed the wartime price rise as a purely monetary phenomenon with the fault lying ultimately with the financial policy of the government, which directly or indirectly prevented the banks from pursuing a sufficiently vigorous credit control policy.

Wicksell shared some of Cassel's position. But, as has been shown, it was also Wicksell's view that central bank control over the price level by interest-rate policy is impaired when large "autonomous" changes occur in the quantity of money; he recognized that the banks were no longer in command of the situation under the twin obstacles of gold invasion and mounting government deficits. To counteract the gold inflow, he, along with Davidson and Cassel, recommended and prevailed on the authorities to adopt the "gold exclusion" policy in 1916.[61] Thereafter he endeavored to have that policy made more effective. When it was strengthened in 1917, he became increasingly critical of the desultory policy purused by the Riksbank, which had been put in possession of the means for exercising much stronger inflation control.

As for commodity scarcity, Wicksell did not share Cassel's facile analysis of its role, but neither did he emphasize it as much as did Davidson. It is clear he attributed a greater significance to commodity scarcity as an inflationary force than Cassel had done. To counteract the effect of commodity scarcity on the economy as far as possible he proposed an ingenious scheme of imposing high export duties in order to use the proceeds for subsidizing the procurement of strategically scarce imports. Such imports were to be sold on the domestic market at prices lower than acquisition cost by the amount of subsidy received from the export duties.[62] His scheme would have made the domestic price level in Sweden independent of price levels in nearby countries, and would have resulted in driving down the domestic price level. He hoped this process might be carried to the point where Sweden's price level might return to its 1914 height. However, from an immediate and practical standpoint, he wanted the export duties, particularly on Sweden's lumber and pulp, to be imposed at rates equal to the difference in their current high prices and their 1914

[61] Cassel, Davidson, and Wicksell were joint architects of the celebrated "gold exclusion" policy. It was adopted in 1916, perhaps to an appreciable extent as a result of the analysis Davidson published in an article, "Till frågan om penningens värde under kriget" (On the Problem of Value of Money During the War), *Ekonomisk Tidskrift*, 17 (1915), 415-423. In 1914 Sweden went off the gold standard. Exportation of gold was also prohibited; this was opposed by Wicksell in his article, "Riksbankens guldkassa" (The Gold Reserve of the Riksbank), *Ekonomisk Tidskrift*, 16 (1914), 263-270. He would rather have had Sweden get commodities for the gold outflow, and he was aware a large gold inflow would result in the course of the war. The gold exclusion policy he and the other economists recommended made it permissible for the Risbank to rescind free coinage of gold and to stop purchasing gold entirely, but if it did buy gold, it was further empowered to buy it at free-market prices, which at that time were lower than the prewar fixed mint prices. The gold exclusion policy was at first sabotaged by Denmark and Norway under the Scandinavian monetary agreement, which made the currencies of these three countries interchangeable at par. Hence Danes and Norwegians would buy gold in the open market, have it minted, and sell the minted coin in Sweden at a considerable profit since gold remained convertible into currency at the prewar mint price, which was higher than the market price. In 1917 an agreement was reached between the three countries to strengthen the gold exclusion policy by proscribing the importation from one country to the other of minted coin. The circumstances surrounding the adoption and application of this policy are discussed in an informative and entertaining manner in B. Thomas, *Monetary Policy and Crises* (London, 1936), pp. 1-61.

[62] Wicksell, "Medel mot dyrtiden" (Means for Counteracting the Inflation), *Ekonomisk Tidskrift*. 18 (1916), 304-308.

prices. The proceeds of this tax were to be used particularly for sub-sidizing the importation of coal, to relieve the fuel shortage.[63] Cassel opposed his proposal in principle. Davidson was fascinated by it but accepted it only with serious misgivings. He feared that foreign ex-porters, knowing the Swedish market price to be independent of the world price, would resort to price discrimination against Swedish im-porters.[64]

Wicksell's scheme is of interest as evidence of his recognition that "commodity scarcity," like "autonomous" changes in the quantity of money, must be treated as a condition qualifying the banks' ability as well as the appropriateness of maintaining stable prices by interest-rate manipulation. What makes this matter more emphatic is that he was moved to recognize this additional qualification to the price sta-bilization norm at a time when Sweden was on a free-exchange stand-ard with an inconvertible currency, conditions which approximated those of the "pure credit economy" in a greater measure than had been the case before the war. And it was precisely for such an economy that he had always considered price stabilization to be the only rational and practically achievable norm.

Two additional influences undoubtedly moved Wicksell to publish a final "concession" concerning his monetary policy norm in 1925 (see the following subsection). These were Davidson's analysis of Sweden's wartime inflation, and later (1923-1924) Lindahl's evaluation of the norm of price level stabilization versus that of price level variation inversely related to changes in productivity (or scarcity), which was published in his first work on monetary policy.[65]

Davidson, as we have seen, held that the task of the monetary authorities was to hold the effective quantity of money neutral with

---

[63] This more concrete proposal was expressed by Wicksell in two articles in Stock-holm's leading newspaper, *Dagens Nyheter* (The Daily News), Jan. 14 and 15, 1916.

[64] Davidson's additional objections involved questions about adjusting cost-price relations on exports. Where exports were being sold at little or no profit despite current high prices, how, he asked, would exporters get by after a tax is imposed on their goods, and how should the scheme be administered? These questions were raised in the articles, "Om exportavgifter och importpremier såsom medel mot dyrtiden" (On Export Duties and Import Premia as Measures Against Inflation), *Ekonomisk Tidskrift*, 18 (1916), 268-277, 347-350; and "Ännu några ord om Wick-sells botemedel mot dyrtiden" (A Few Words More About Wicksell's Measures Against Inflation), *Ekonomisk Tidskrift*, 18 (1916), 374-378. As to the main point, that producers of Swedish imports might practice price discrimination against Swedish buyers under the scheme, Wicksell thought competition between these producers would eliminate that difficulty; see Wicksell, "Strödda Reflexioner" (Ran-dom Reflections), *Ekonomisk Tidskrift*, 19 (1917), 81-90.

[65] E. Lindahl, *Penningpolitikens Mål* (The Aims of Monetary Policy), (Malmö, 1924).

respect to the market for commodities so as to preserve the "objective value" of money. This, in turn, he thought would be achieved if the money value of the annual national output were kept constant, subject only to such adjustments as would permit the quantity of money to change in proportion to such changes as occur with the passage of time in the nation's supply of productive resources.

Because of his adherence to this perspective, he thundered repeatedly against Cassel's interpretation of inflation as the equivalent of any general rise in prices. Davidson inferred from Cassel's analysis that all that would be necessary to prevent inflation, regardless of its causes, would be a sufficient rise in discount rates. In opposition to this, in 1918 Davidson developed the following analysis of the inflation problem.

Central bank control over the price level by interest-rate policy is only possible if: (1) free coinage of gold is abolished to block the effects of a gold invasion, against which discount policy is impotent; (2) no issue of fiat money by government takes place, or if the government refrains from large-scale borrowing from the central bank at artificially low interest rates, and if it borrows at all it does so in terms of bonds which are ineligible as security for bank credit and cover for bank reserves; (3) no change occurs in productivity or in the scarcity of commodities.[66]

Only if these causes are *not* operative would one be justified in concluding that the rise in the price level was due to overissue of notes or overextension of credit by reason of the banks charging a subnormal loan rate of interest. A year later, he adduced the following additional causes of a general rise in prices against which discount policy is impotent, except on pain of disrupting the monetary equilibrium which it is its function to preserve: (4) a rise in excise taxes if these are general in scope; (5) progressive monopolization in industry with a consequent curtailment in output; (6) decline in the efficiency of labor.[67]

Specifically with reference to cause (3), he held that the initial effect of an increase in scarcity of commodities is to raise the price level approximately in proportion to the decline in output. But its indirect effect over a period of time is to set the stage for a cumulative rise in prices, for, unless the loan rate has been raised in the meantime, the increase in scarcity has raised the real rate and made this loan rate subnormal. Faced with an increase in scarcity, the best the banks can do

[66] D. Davidson, "Spridda studier angående prisnivåstegringen" (Occasional Studies Concerning the Rise in the Price Level), *Ekonomisk Tidskrift*, 20 (1918), 119-33.

[67] Davidson, "Några teoretiska frågor" (Some Theoretical Problems), *Ekonomisk Tidskrift*, 21 (1919), 221-259.

is to accept the initial rise in prices it causes, and then to raise the loan rate to the higher level of the real rate in order to prevent the increase in prices from becoming cumulative. On the other hand, if they are also expected to prevent the initial rise in prices, they would have to raise the loan rate to supernormal levels, an action which is likely to precipitate a cumulative decline in prices.

To make his position in relation to Cassel, and indirectly also Wicksell, as clear as possible, Davidson also published an explanation of inflation in Sweden. In this he attempted to measure to what extent inflation was due either to commodity scarcity or to monetary causes. To this end he developed an index of "scarcity" of his own, the precise nature of which he did not describe in detail. He subtracted this index from the index of wholesale prices to obtain the residual of "monetary inflation." Then he divided this residual by the rise in wholesale index since 1914 for each subsequent year to show the cumulative effect of "monetary inflation." His findings are shown in table 3.[68]

TABLE 3

DAVIDSON'S ANALYSIS OF SWEDEN'S INFLATION
EXPERIENCE DURING WORLD WAR I

Year	Index of wholesale prices	Index of "commodity scarcity"	"Monetary inflation" (col. 1 minus col. 2)	Per cent of combined price rise since 1914 attributable to "monetary inflation"
1914	100	100	0	0
1917	244	162	82	50
1918	339	151	188	78
1919	330	132	198	86
1920	347	126	221	89
1921	211	106	105	94
1922	162	101	61	98

On this showing, it appears that commodity scarcity accounted for between one-half and one-third of the total price rise during the war years, while defects of monetary policy progressively accounted for the greater part of the total inflation in the postwar years.

Davidson concluded that "inflation" was too vague a term for general use, more like a "slogan" than a scientific concept, unless it be agreed that this term should be applied only to general price fluctuations which are directly traceable to the adoption of subnormal loan

---

[68] Adapted from p. 195 of Davidson's article "Till frågan om penningvärdets reglering under kriget och därefter" (On the Problem of the Regulation of the Value of Money during and after the War), *Ekonomisk Tidskrift*, 25 (1923), 191-234.

rates by the banks. But other causes of price level changes, which are numerous, originate in forces which are for the most part beyond the scope of monetary policy. If the price effects of these forces are to be counteracted, this must be done by other means than those of bank-directed discount policy.

Lindahl's treatise, which Wicksell read in manuscript prior to its publication in 1924, probably also exerted an influence on his thought.[69] Starting from the premise that the aim of monetary policy should be "to preserve the real value of economic contracts," [70] Lindahl systematized and extended Wicksell's and Davidson's monetary analyses. At the outset he decided that "the general price level," by which Wicksell measured changes in the value of money, was too vague a mode of measurement and had to be replaced by fluctuations in the price level of consumption goods. But even with this revision, its fluctuations would not reveal changes in the objective value of money unless production functions remained constant.

However, as long as productivity does not change, the policy aim he had defined would be realized by keeping the price level of consumption goods constant. This would be true regardless of what happened to the quantitative relations between economic resources. If these increase uniformly, the scope of production is extended without altering the relative marginal productivity of factors of production. Then equilibrium is maintained between the incomes and interest obligations of entrepreneurs as long as the consumption goods price level is constant, which requires that the effective quantity of money is expanded in proportion to the increase in resources. If labor decreases, capital being constant, or capital increases, labor being constant, the only change is that the loan rate must be adjusted to the new level of the real rate to keep consumption goods prices stable.

But if productivity changes, factor quantities being given, then the aim of monetary policy, preservation of the real value of contracts, or, as he reformulated it, "maintaining risks to creditors and debtors by a control of the price level such that the consequences of unforeseen events is neutralized by these controls," [71] required that the price level of consumption goods should vary in a manner inversely proportional to the change in productivity.

His reasoning on this point was that if the price level does vary in this manner, it protects entrepreneurs against losses to a desirable extent when productivity declines, and it also prevents them from realiz-

[69] E. Lindahl, *Penningpolitikens Mål* (Malmö, 1924), p. i.

[70] *Ibid.*, p. 10.

[71] *Ibid.*, p. 25.

ing extraordinary gains at the expense of creditors when productivity increases. Such gains would be economically undesirable.[72]

Suppose, for instance, a policy is adopted to let the price level of consumption goods rise in proportion to a decline in productivity and otherwise remain constant regardless of whether productivity remains the same or increases. Technological progress makes it more than likely that over the long run increases in productivity will more than offset decreases. Hence this policy implies a slow, secular increase in the price level and an equivalent decline in the value of money. Creditors would adjust to this condition by obtaining higher interest rates, partly by restricting the supply of capital for long-term loans in favor of short-term loans, and partly by reducing the supply of loan capital and expanding that of equity investments. Consequently, in the long run, entrepreneurs would not be able to benefit at the expense of creditors. But in the short run, entrepreneurs are likely to expect a certain minimum rise in the price level or a minimum decline in production costs which is not offset by an equivalent decline in prices, and, if so, they will take account of this in planning their investment programs. But net gains would accrue to them only if the price rise, or cost decline, were greater than they had anticipated. *Per contra,* losses would be unavoidable if their calculations had been too optimistic and had not taken sufficient account of the reaction of the creditor interest. Consequently, this type of policy widens the margin for losses and gains, while one of inverse variation of the consumption goods price level to changes in productivity minimizes this margin.

Further, the general entrepreneurial gains which would arise if the price level is kept constant except in times of declining productivity, when it would be permitted to rise in proportion to this decline, would serve no useful economic purpose. Entrepreneurs in general would have gains, although those of the innovators among them would be larger than for those of the laggards. But under a system of price level variation inverse to productivity changes, it is precisely the innovators who would have gains and the laggards who would suffer losses, and this would lead to a desirable reorientation of production. Thus in these latter circumstances alone would the gains serve a socially desirable purpose.

Then Lindahl went on to demonstrate that the Davidsonian monetary policy norm would operate best, not under an international gold standard to which Davidson seemed inclined, but under a Wicksellian free-exchange standard, provided that adequate indexes

---

[72] The argument of this and the following paragraphs is based on Lindahl's work. *Ibid.,* pp. 54-58.

for measuring changes both in productivity and in the price level of consumption goods were developed.[73] Further, he proved that Davidson's norm, as compared with that of Wicksell's of price level stabilization, had the virtue of minimizing risks of losses and gains to landowners and wageworkers alike.[74] Borrowing landowners could protect themselves against the contingency that their incomes may vary in the opposite direction to mortgage interest rates due to a temporary decline in the marginal productivity of land by negotiating mortgages for long term at the prevailing long-term bond rate of interest. However, wage earners, whose money incomes would remain constant while their real wages would vary directly with changes in productivity, would run the risk that their money wages would be reduced if the productivity of labor declined, productivity of other factors being constant, or if it failed to rise as much as that of other factors when general productivity increases. Then to keep wages from falling by allowing a rise in the price level would bring on consequences which would be worse for society as a whole than the decline of wages itself. Finally, the Davidsonian norm had the virtue of preserving the real value of cash balances, thus minimizing the need for varying the latter with the movement of the price level.

Thus Lindahl succeeded, to a greater extent than Davidson himself had done, in demonstrating both the applicability of his norm under a free-exchange standard and its value as a device for minimizing risks in contractual economic relations.

WICKSELL'S FINAL CONCESSION—THE NORM OF PRICE
STABILIZATION QUALIFIED FOR AUTONOMOUS CHANGES
IN PRODUCTIVITY OR IN "COMMODITY SCARCITY"

With Sweden's wartime experience and his own contributions to her economic policy still fresh in his mind, and with the foregoing analyses before him, Wicksell seized a unique occasion for introducing a last modification in his monetary doctrine, his "concession" to Davidson, as it has been construed by Wicksell's followers.

It was in 1925 that he received one of the greatest gratifications of his career. He, and not one of his critics, was invited to deliver the main lecture for opening the monetary discussions at the meeting of *Nationalekonomiska Föreningen* (National Economic Club). It was before this same body he had had his first word to say in monetary matters in the lecture of April, 1898, on "The Influence of the Interest Rate on Commodity Prices," shortly prior to the publication of

---

[73] *Ibid.*, chap. 6 and 7.
[74] *Ibid.*, chap. 5.

his treatise, *Interest and Prices*. And again it was here he was to
have his last word to say on monetary matters, in his lecture of
October 29, 1925, on "Det definitiva ordnandet av världens penningväsen" (The Definitive Organization of the World's Monetary System).[75] This lecture coincided in time with the publication of his last
article on monetary problems in *Ekonomisk Tidskrift* (1925), pp. 205-
222, an article now translated and appended to the English edition
of *Interest and Prices* with the title "The Monetary Problem of the
Scandinavian Countries." We shall state Wicksell's "concession" by
direct quotation of certain passages from the translated article, where
it was formulated more explicitly than in his lecture.

He opened his discussion by revealing doubts as to the adequacy of
received monetary theory to explain recent monetary experience satisfactorily. Businessmen generally claimed that wartime inflation was
due to commodity scarcity and the postwar deflation to its cessation,
while economists had in the main attributed these to aberrations of
monetary and fiscal policy. But, he said, while variations in scarcity
do by no means fully explain the monetary upheaval, he ". . . began
to wonder whether practical men of affairs, in spite of some obviously
wrong and illogical conclusions, have not in some directions advanced
further than we have towards an understanding of these phenomena"
[i.e., of changes in scarcity and their effects on the price level].[76]

Then turning to Cassel's conception of inflation as the result of
excessive creation of purchasing power, Wicksell said that in the event
of an increase in scarcity, it does not take an abnormally low loan
rate to account for the rise in purchasing power. People are loath to
suffer a reduction in their standard of living and draw their bank
balances more fully to maintain their consumption. This increases the
velocity of circulation of money and thus creates the purchasing
power needed to meet the rising prices of goods. "But it is this very
scarcity which causes the rise in prices; and the monetary purchasing
power so created is adequate to pay the sum actually demanded for
the available goods and services. . . . It therefore stands to reason
that a general rise in the market prices of both goods and services
itself creates the purchasing power required for meeting the higher
prices." [77]

If the banks attempt to counteract the scarcity-caused price rise,
which he considered unlikely, they will almost certainly fail in their

[75] See *Ekonomisk Tidskrift* 27 (1925), section on Nationalekonomiska Föreningens
Förhandlingar, pp. 85-100, where this lecture was printed.
[76] Wicksell, *Interest and Prices*, p. 199.
[77] *Ibid.*, p. 201.

endeavor to do so. If they refuse to extend additional credit, resort can be had to private credit and to an increase in note circulation. If they raise interest rates, this is not likely to be effective in reducing prices. Even if the increased rates may reduce producers' demand for credit, it will not noticeably reduce consumers' demand for credit, which is what matters most here, for this demand increases as consumers attempt to maintain their previous consumption standard. If scarcity becomes so great as to trench on the consumption of basic necessities, consumers will not be deterred from asking for additional credit by the fact that interest rates may have risen a few percentage points. It is for this reason that rationing of goods and services becomes necessary and is preferable to a free market in conditions of severe and general commodity shortages.

It is clear that this premise, namely the shortage of goods, regarded as the primary cause of the rise in prices, leads us to an entirely different presentation of the problem from the one on which monetary theory has hitherto been based. Under normal conditions . . . a rise in prices [apart from a rise due to an abnormal increase in production of gold] can actually be caused only by a too liberal credit policy on the part of the banks, making it possible for speculators to obtain an increase in money purchasing power which no longer corresponds to such increase as may be simultaneously brought about by voluntary saving. In this case the remedy is obviously to be found in a tightening of credit. . . . In the present case, however, it is not a question of additional purchasing power, for this is, as we have seen, provided automatically by the rise in prices.[78]

Now if the banks are to have any success in checking the rise in prices, "they must [act] at the very commencement of the rise in prices. Once prices have started to rise, it is too late for these factors [increased interest rates] to play any role."[79]

But if the banks are not able to prevent the rise in prices which follows an increase in scarcity, what are the consequences? Will the price rise be cumulative, or will the process end in a new equilibrium at higher prices? That depends on how the banks behave:

If new credit is entirely withheld, then prices will naturally become stable when the tension between the price level and the amount of available medium of exchange has become so great that it entirely counteracts the tendency towards a rise in prices. If, on the other hand, the banks offer credit, though at higher rates of interest, then theoretically at least the rise in prices might be expected to continue, for it cannot cease until a balance has been

---

[78] *Ibid.*, p. 203.
[79] *Ibid.*, p. 220.

attained between the supply and demand for goods, and this *never takes place so long as there is a general endeavor to maintain a degree of consumption which it is physically impossible to meet.* But such an attempt must eventually cease. *When scarcity is permanent, people will resign themselves to the inevitable and give up the attempt to maintain the normal standard of living.* . . . Thus demand and supply will again correspond to each other on a lower plane, and there will be no further cause for a rise in prices. If however the scarcity of goods extended to the necessities of life, this transition could not, under conditions of free competition, take place without entailing great suffering for the poorer classes, as the better situated classes would, despite the scarcity be able naturally to satisfy their needs for these goods. It follows, in my opinion, that rationing was a blessing, and that it should have been applied on an even larger scale. . . .[80]

But when scarcity has prevailed over a period of years and then production expands again toward its normal level, the foregoing changes repeat themselves in reverse. The public, inured to a lower consumption standard, does not immediately increase its consumption, hence the increased output must be sold at declining prices. This has a psychological effect evidenced by "buyers' strikes," namely a deferral of purchases in the expectation of a further decline in prices. This, in his opinion, accounted for the intensity of certain phases of Sweden's postwar deflation.[81]

Yet, for all that could be claimed by way of commodity scarcity, the wartime rise in prices was greater than could be explained in these terms alone. The remainder, that is to say the larger share, of that inflation was traceable to monetary causes. Moreover, the monetary aspect of inflation has a tendency to perpetuate itself even after commodity supplies return to normal levels.

Suppose, then . . . that the effect on prices of a shortage of goods is, so to speak, compensated by the subsequent restoration of normal output. There would still remain a very considerable residual rise in prices, and this would have to be looked upon as the cumulative result of *that* inflation which in the meanwhile would be caused 'on the side of money' through too liberal a granting of credit. It can scarcely be questioned that bank rates, both during the war and during the first years of the Armistice . . . were too low in relation to the real rate of interest, which must have been forced up by the lack of liquid capital caused by the war.[82]

Then, in view of the modification of monetary theory which was called for by the effect of changes in productivity or in the degree of scarcity, he concluded:

---

[80] *Ibid.*, pp. 204-205. Italics supplied.
[81] *Ibid.*, p. 213.
[82] *Ibid.*, pp. 214-215.

Looking upon the matter in this way, it seems to me that the lack of understanding between practical men of business and economists might dissolve into a higher unity; and since there is hardly any reason, short of another world war, to fear that a sudden shortage of goods will occur, a wise and foreseeing bank policy should, under normal conditions, be all that is needed to give all possible desirable stability to the level of prices and the purchasing power of money.[83]

This concludes our account of Wicksell's "concession" on the score of scarcity of commodities. He was still persuaded that price stabilization is the only practicable monetary policy norm under ordinary circumstances. But he was willing to make exceptions to this for three cases: (1) gold invasion, as long as gold is freely coined and the gold standard is in effect, but a remedy against this cause can be had by resorting to a free exchange standard; (2) the effect of fiscal deficit policy especially in wartime when the government either issues fiat money or borrows on large scale at artificially low interest rates; and (3) commodity shortages, which are apt to develop in times of national emergencies.

On the other hand, it is not clear that Wicksell was willing to modify his policy norm for an increase in productivity. Why? The chief reason was that increasing productivity is a secularly acting force. It is never so dramatic in its effect as the commodity shortage which results, for instance, from a tight blockade of a country's normal trade lanes. Increasing productivity spreads its effects gradually over economic life and involves no drastic changes in the output of commodities from one year to the next. In view of the elements of monopoly, immobility of resources, and economic frictions which affect the relations of particular prices and outputs of goods within the structure of prices, it seemed to Wicksell preferable to let the gradual increase in productivity be reflected in rising money incomes at stable prices, rather than in rising real incomes at falling prices.

In retrospect, one discerns a remarkable development of Wicksell's monetary doctrine after 1898 when he wrote *Interest and Prices*. This development was aided and complemented by Davidson's keen analysis. Yet there remained gaps in their joint doctrine, gaps which had to be bridged by more systematic analysis of the ground they covered as well as by analysis in new directions. That work was to a large extent performed by Lindahl and Myrdal, who may be regarded as the most gifted among their "students." [84] A sketch of the work by

---

[83] *Ibid.*, p. 215.

[84] In the formal sense it is not true to refer to Lindahl and Myrdal as "students" of Wicksell and Davidson. Lindahl's mentor was Professor Sommarin; see the preface

these two writers on the Wicksell-Davidson heritage of monetary doctrine is attempted in the next section. Meanwhile it may be appropriate to close this treatment by quoting the following judgment by Myrdal on that heritage:

It is just because Wicksell's formulation of monetary theory does not contain elements excluding from it the possibility of amendment and adaptation on every point, in correspondence with the facts to be observed, that it is scientifically so fruitful. It is obviously a very formal theory and is thus not based—as, to use only one example, the classical cost of production theory was based—on very rough approximations which are conceptually indispensable, cannot be dropped, and consequently block the way to a progressively more realistic analysis.[85]

Reconstruction of the Wicksell-Davidson Heritage of Monetary Doctrine by the Founders of the Stockholm School of Economics

Wicksell died in May, 1926, Davidson some fifteen years later. For more than a decade following the death of Wicksell, Davidson continued to publish lengthy articles at frequent intervals in *Ekonomisk Tidskrift*. Most of these were devoted to monetary questions, but they were more and more oriented to observations concerning the development of monetary institutions and to applications of monetary policy, rather than to monetary theory proper. He added little that was new to the monetary doctrine to which he had given expression during the years 1918-1923.

The exegesis, and extension that the Wicksell-Davidson heritage of economic theory was fated to undergo over a decade, began with Lindahl's study, *Penningpolitikens Mål* (Aims of Monetary Policy) in 1924. His second contribution to this labor is found in his work *Penningpolitikens Medel* (The Means of Monetary Policy, 1930), which is, in a way, a companion volume to his essay of 1924. Meanwhile Myrdal published his first work in monetary theory, *Prisbildningsproblemet och Föränderligheten* (The Pricing Problem under Conditions of Change, 1927). Although this work has not been available to the writer, we have Ohlin's testimony that: "This work . . . [has] vitally affected Swedish research in the field under discussion during

---

to his doctoral dissertation, *Die Gerechtigkeit der Besteuerung* (Lund, 1919). But it is also true that he studied Wicksell's and Davidson's writings assiduously and submitted both his dissertation and his first work in monetary theory, *Penningpolitikens Mål* (Malmö, 1924), to Wicksell for review prior to publication. As for Myrdal, he was probably Cassel's favorite student; see chaps. 10-13 in I. Gjöbel-Lilja, *Gustav Cassel—En Livsskildring* (Stockholm, 1948). Yet it is clear that Myrdal's thought and early works show how very much he was influenced by the writings of Wicksell and Davidson.

[85] G. Myrdal, *Monetary Equilibrium* (London, 1939), p. 207.

the last decade. Myrdal discusses the influence of the uncertain future on price formation. To what extent are economic actions influenced by anticipations of future events, i.e., by expectations?" [86]

Four years later Myrdal responded to Lindahl's works on the aims and means of monetary policy in a long article, "Kring den praktiska nationalekonomiska problematiken om penningteoretisk jämnvikt: En Studie över 'normala räntan' i Wicksells penninglära" (Concerning Practical Economic Problems and the Theory of Monetary Equilibrium: A Study of "Normal Rate of Interest" in Wicksell's Monetary Theory), *Ekonomisk Tidskrift* (1931). Accepting Lindahl's systematization of the Wicksell-Davidson doctrines, Myrdal pointed out that if monetary theory is to serve the ends of monetary policy, it needed reformulation of its basic concepts and of its criteria for monetary equilibrium. Then he suggested modifications of these concepts intended to eventuate in operational definitions. This article, the point of origin of the *ex ante ex post* analysis, was enlarged and rewritten the following year and published as "Der Gleichgewichtsbegriff als Instrument der Geldtheoretischen Analyse," in *Beiträge zur Geldtheorie* under the editorship of F. A. von Hayek (1933). A few years later, after undergoing some excision and revision, this treatise of Myrdal's was translated into English and published under the title *Monetary Equilibrium* (1939).

EXTENSION OF THE WICKSELL-DAVIDSON HERITAGE
OF MONETARY THEORY

Through the labors of Lindahl and Myrdal, post-Wicksellian economics in Sweden became endowed with methods which appear to be complementary. Lindahl's method of intertemporal equilibrium analysis, which he acknowledges as being due to von Hayek,[87] asks essentially how, in view of our knowledge of the behavior of savers and entrepreneurs, shall economic policy, and more particularly monetary policy, be fashioned so as to influence entrepreneurial anticipations in a direction which conduces to a stable performance of the economy at the level of full resource utilization? [88]

Myrdal's disequilibrium analysis, which has become generally ac-

---

[86] B. Ohlin, "Some Notes on the Stockholm Theory of Savings and Investment," *Economic Journal*, XLVII (March, 1937), pp. 53 ff., reprinted in *Readings in Business Cycle Theory* (Philadelphia, 1944); see p. 88 from which the quotation is taken.

[87] See F. A. von Hayek, "Das Intertemporale Gleichgewichtssystem der Preise und die Bewegung des 'Geldwertes,'" *Weltwirtschaftliches Archiv* (1928) , pp. 33 ff.

[88] E. Lindahl, *Studies in the Theory of Money and Capital*, pp. 232-235, 252, 267-268.

cepted in Sweden and has been adopted by Lindahl as well, asks a different kind of question concerned with the processes which connect divergent *ex ante* magnitudes of investment and saving with their *ex post* equality. Cognate economic variables are viewed from the two-way perspective of *ex ante* and *ex post*, and such terms as saving, investment, income, gains and losses are redefined in an effort to obtain insights from analysis of *ex post* results into whether equilibrium *ex ante* prevailed in the period studied. The aim is "to formulate the condition of monetary equilibrium in such a way as to obtain observable and measurable magnitudes." [89]

If we assume adequate development of the requisite "observable and measurable magnitudes" for the *ex post* calculus, and of criteria for interpreting the state of anticipations since the *ex ante* calculus cannot become "objective" in the registered sense, Myrdal's method asks: How shall monetary policy, properly coördinated with fiscal and other economic policies, be so arranged as to minimize the incidence of *ex post* losses and gains, which are indicative of disequilibrium, and thus contribute to economic stability by inducing greater stability in the state of expectations and a closer correspondence between expectations and objective economic realities? In working along these lines, Lindahl and Myrdal performed an exegesis and reconstruction of the Wicksell-Davidson monetary doctrine, which is outlined in the following subsections. [90]

LINDAHL'S RECONSTRUCTION BY INTERTEMPORAL EQUILIBRIUM ANALYSIS

Lindahl, as some of his colleagues have put it, "presented an elaboration" of the Wicksell-Davidson heritage. [91] Proceeding on the typical Wicksellian premises of a closed, competitive economy with a pure credit system, he set himself the task of investigating the causes of

---

[89] G. Myrdal, *Monetary Equilibrium*, pp. 46-47.

[90] In this and some of the subsequent discussion of Lindahl's and Myrdal's transformations of Wicksell's conditions for monetary equilibrium *no attempt has been made to evaluate the work of the Stockholm School.* Only the main lines of development the Wicksell-Davidson monetary doctrine underwent in the hands of these writers have been sketched.

That the Stockholm School's formulations are not always internally consistent and that they have not yielded many definitions leading to the desired "observable and measurable magnitudes" to be used in the *ex post* calculus emerges in the account given here of Lindahl's and Myrdal's positions. However, for an *evaluation* of their theories see T. Palander "On the Concepts and Methods of the Stockholm School," *International Economic Papers*, 3 (1953), 5-57, and a recent work by K. G. Landgren, *Economics in Modern Sweden*, Library of Congress, Reference Division, Washington, D. C., 1957.

[91] B. Ohlin, *op. cit.*, p. 88, and G. Myrdal, *Monetary Equilibrium* (London, 1939), pp. 7, 22, and 25.

fluctuations in the price level of consumption goods, which he defined more explicitly than Wicksell had done, as follows:

. . . In each period the portion of the total nominal income this is *not* saved is equal to the total quantities of goods and services consumed during the period multiplied by their prices. This may be expressed in the form

$$E(1 - s) = PQ$$

where E denotes total nominal income, s the portion of this income which is saved, P the price level of consumption goods, and Q the quantity of such goods in a certain period. P is then a price index number of goods and services consumed, the different prices having been weighted by the total consumption of each category of goods.[92]

To observe the interaction on one another of the elements of this equation, as one or more of them are affected by postulated primary changes, requires a method capable of following the resulting dynamic process in detail through its various stages. For lack of requisite criteria and data to do this by econometric methods, the process had to be sliced up, as it were, into a series of short intervals during which the analysis observes the equilibrium adjustment to the primary changes, which are introduced only at the transition points separating successive short intervals. For each type of primary change introduced, a separate short-period reaction model must be constructed. All variables are studied in their prospective or *ex ante* dimension, and the adjustments represent the most proximate consequences of primary changes on entrepreneurial expectations. This, the so-called method of intertemporal equilibrium analysis, permits considerable extension of the more rough and ready "successive approximations" used in the older literature. As such it is akin to Myrdal's *ex ante ex post* analysis, which, however, pursues similar dynamic changes as a procession of disequilibria. The object and aim of Lindahl's intertemporal analysis was: "If an average of these intertemporal price relations is worked out, an expression is found for the relative position of the price level in different periods. In this manner it should be possible to arrive at a theory of changes in the value of money." [93]

In his essay of 1930, Lindahl extended Wicksell's analysis considerably by dealing successively with five different problems: (1) the consequences of a bank initiated reduction (or rise) in the level of interest rates, (2) the possibility of augmenting the adjustment power of interest rate changes by differentiation of rates, adjustments of short and long rates at different times and sometimes in opposite

---

[92] E. Lindahl, *Studies in the Theory of Money and Capital* (London, 1939), p. 142.
[93] *Ibid.*, p. 142.

directions to deal more effectively with primary changes operating at different points of impact on the economy, (3) the possibility of keeping the consumption goods price level constant in the face of primary changes by means of interest policy, (4) the possibility of making it vary inversely with variations in productivity by interest policy, and (5) the meaning and consistency of Wicksell's triple conditions of monetary equilibrium. These matters were investigated successively under alternative assumptions of perfect foresight, imperfect foresight, full employment, unemployed resources, autonomous changes in consumers' demand, in saving, changes of productivity in capital goods industries, and in the consumption goods industries. In the course of this thorough analysis Lindahl uncovered some cases and conditions which are of interest for the transformation alluded to above.

(*a*) In a situation of full employment where society has a "rigid investment period," the banks reduce interest rates which previously were equilibrium rates, and the reduction is expected to be permanent. Entrepreneurs are benefited somewhat and endeavor to expand investment but succeed only in bidding up factor prices slightly, while in the consumption industries the lower interest costs are neutralized by the higher prices which must be paid for capital goods. Capitalists' incomes are reduced by the gains which are shared between workers and entrepreneurs. The consumption goods price level remains constant.

Artificial as this case was, it was aimed at Wicksell's demonstrations of the cumulative process in *Interest and Prices*. From this Lindahl reached the conclusion that: "A lowering of the interest rate does not necessarily occasion a price rise. . . . Such a rise will not set in unless there has been a reduction in the supply of consumption goods or an increase in the demand for them, caused by a larger total income, brought about through anticipations of high prices, or by a diminished degree of saving." [94]

(*b*) Society now has full employment and a "nonrigid" investment period, and the reduction of interest rates induces real capital formation on a larger scale than before. Saving, however, has not increased. The problem is one of the adjustment of saving to the increased investment, an adjustment which Wicksell generally thought of as effected by "forced saving." Lindahl interpreted this as a case of a rise in nominal income which provides for the extra saving on a voluntary basis.

The total nominal income will thus rise in about the same degree as the price level of consumption goods has increased. The increase in income will,

[94] *Ibid.*, p. 188.

however, not be evenly distributed but will be greatest for borrowing entrepreneurs who make an extra gain at the expense of capitalists [p. 171] . . .
entrepreneurs find their incomes increased and have a strong incentive to
apply it to further investment. . . . The shift in distribution of income thus
increases total saving [p. 174]. The required saving will then take place, voluntarily for the greater part, and the causal element will rather be an altera-
tion in the distribution of income due to a shift in the price level.

If we regard the dynamic process as consisting of a series of disequilibria,
[then] as a consequence of the lower rate of interest there will in some periods
be an excess of planned investment over planned saving . . . with the probable result that the incomes of entrepreneurs, as calculated *ex post,* will
exceed their anticipations. This additional income constitutes the 'uninten-
tional' saving for such a period [p. 175].[95]

(c) This case concerns the possibility of keeping the price level constant by interest-rate policy when the propensity to save increases.
There is full employment; production functions are constant, and
factors are freely transferable between industries, but the interest
rate, despite an increase in the propensity to save that is expected to
be permanent, is *not* adjusted downwards but is kept constant. The
first result is that prices of consumption goods fall. This has further
interesting consequences:

This drop in the prices of consumption goods which gradually leads also to a
fall in capital values, brings with it a shift in the distribution of real income
and property. As a result the original saving will be counteracted by reduced
saving or capital consumption elsewhere. It will therefore not give rise to
new real investment, but will be cancelled out by the decline in prices. . . .
If wage rates are rigid, unemployment and restriction of production are
inevitable. Total income will decline and this will lead to a new fall in saving or rise in dissaving. The effect of the original saving will then be, not a
formation of new capital, but a destruction of existing capital resources. Even
when wages and other current costs are flexible, the final result will thus . . .
be a changed distribution and a lower price level, without any resulting new
investment.[96]

This brings into view something analogous to Keynes' underemployment equilibrium. Its solution by means of interest-rate policy, stated
in the sequel to Lindahl's treatment, need not concern us here.

(d) As to the use of interest-rate policy for purposes of controlling
the behavior of the consumption goods price level, Lindahl concluded
in favor of Davidson's monetary policy norm on two grounds: It
minimizes business risk, and it involves less active and drastic intervention by monetary authority into economic life.

---

[95] *Ibid.,* pp. 171, 174, 175.
[96] *Ibid.,* pp. 206-207.

The point of view governing the author's treatment of the aims of monetary policy . . . was that the risks and disturbances in economic activity following from imperfectly foreseen events should be reduced as far as possible. The conclusion . . . reached was that the movement of the prices of consumers' goods in inverse proportion to productivity would be more effective in bringing about this result than an unchanged price level for these goods. The latter policy might on the whole imply a minimum of 'price risks' for entrepreneurs. But if the former policy is followed, their total risks will be smaller, in spite of the actual price risks being greater. For the risk of falling prices in this case, for all entrepreneurs taken together, is associated with a chance of improved conditions and opportunities, and conversely, so that the expected changes in the money value of output will then be minimized.[97] On the whole . . . it may be concluded that the maintenance of a constant price level presupposes relatively sharp movements in interest rates, adjusted on the basis of thorough knowledge of the character of the situation, whereas the regulation of the price level in inverse proportion to productivity can be carried out with a fairly moderate adjustment of interest rates. The disturbance to the business world will therefore be appreciably smaller under the second than under the first type of policy.[98]

As for the efficacy of interest rates in effecting substantial adjustments of economic activity or prices, the following comment, based on conclusions reached concerning the probable consequences of rate adjustments in conditions of price rigidity, relatively great factor immobility, and imperfect foresight, is of interest:

Public expenditure policy may be applied both where other monetary means are insufficiently effective, and where it is necessary to shift the price level in one direction or another. If a depression is not removed by low rates of interest, or, if the price level has to be raised with a minimum of friction, it is appropriate for the government to increase purchasing power directly. There is no difficulty in making the government increase expenditure, and therefore this means of raising the price level is always available.[99]

Thus already in this study of 1930, devoted to the causes and proper remedies for general price fluctuations, it was apparent that the prime mover is change in entrepreneurial anticipations, which implies a shift in investment demand. The latter initiates variation in money income and its distribution, and the consequent movement in the consumption goods price level represents an adaptation of real output and the allocation of resources to the foregoing changes. Further, with saving adapting itself to the movements in investment demand via variation in income, it was altogether possible that the real rate

[97] *Ibid.*, p. 199.
[98] *Ibid.*, p. 231.
[99] *Ibid.*, p. 234.

would adjust itself to the loan rate in the same process.[100] If so, the meaning of "normal loan rate of interest," and the nature of "monetary equilibrium" itself was no longer unambiguous. This led Lindahl to scrutinize Wicksell's "normal" rate concept and the equilibrium conditions more closely. In this process he rejected the "normal" for a "neutral" interest-rate concept, i.e., one which preserves monetary equilibrium, which he defined as follows:

In general the real rate cannot be determined independently but only as the rate which preserves equilibrium in the demand for and supply of saving.[101] When a 'normal' rate of interest is said to bring about equilibrium between demand and supply with respect to saving, it is implied that it does not set in motion any tendency toward a shift in the price level . . . (p. 249) . . . such as would alter the distribution of income and thence the supply of saving. . . . But fundamentally this is equivalent to the statement that the rate of interest is neutral with respect to the price level.[102]

A neutral rate of interest does not necessarily imply an unchanged price level, but rather *such a development of prices as is in accordance with the expectations of the public, as far as this is possible.*[103]

This was as far as Lindahl advanced the transformation of the "heritage" in 1930. His several contributions were noted and adopted by Myrdal. Yet, although Lindahl had made the relations between anticipations, investment, income, and the price level clearer than they were before, the processes connecting these variables with one another were only partially revealed by the intertemporal equilibrium analysis he had developed. Each short-interval equilibrium terminated with a set of price relations and anticipations. These apparently remain passive until they are changed by the shock effect of learning, at the transition points, that interest-rate policy, productivity, consumer demand, or·the propensity to save, will be different for the next interval ahead. All these changes impinge, as it were, on entrepreneurs from the outside. Was there not some principle on which to account for anticipation-changes as a means of self-adjustment by entrepreneurs to experience observable within their own enterprises?

There was. By going back to a fundamental postulate of epistemology, that man is capable of learning from experience, and that he does so mainly by comparing notions he has entertained about the near future with the actual course of events he can observe when that future has receded into the near past, Myrdal conceived of the idea

---

[100] *Ibid.*, pp. 248-249.
[101] *Ibid.*, p. 247.
[102] *Ibid.*, p. 251.
[103] *Ibid.*, p. 252.

of applying the same sort of two-way perspective to economic analysis, and thus the *ex ante ex post* "calculus" was born. Its use afforded greater insight into the processes at work in Lindahl's interval-equilibrium models, but at a price; namely, the obligation of viewing the dynamic process as a succession of disequilibria. This probably created a good deal of mental discomfort for a generation of economists who, apart from that perplexing matter of the Wicksellian cumulative process, were nurtured on equilibrium economics.

But if this new method of analysis was to be used with success in monetary theory, it would not do to construe monetary equilibrium as Lindahl had done, as "such a development of prices as is in accordance with the expectations of the public." The contents and drift of the public's expectations cannot be known in the sense of being observable either to theoretical intuition or to empirical investigation. Thus it seemed to Myrdal that Lindahl had effectively given up the concept of monetary equilibrium by this interpretation. Yet to Myrdal, a champion of disequilibrium analysis, surprising as it may seem, a concept of monetary equilibrium was, as he emphasized, all the more indispensable.

MYRDAL'S DISEQUILIBRIUM OR EX ANTE EX POST ANALYSIS

The reason for this was that in Myrdal's treatment a divergence of *ex ante* investment and savings would only be discernible in terms of *ex post* gains or losses (similar to the ones which propel the Wicksellian cumulative process) and corresponding "unintended" investment and saving.

The real problem to be solved in monetary theory is: How does this tendency to disparity in the saving-investment equation develop into an *ex post* balance? As we shall show, the route goes over purely dynamic elements of gains and losses which do not enter explicitly into the *ex ante* calculus—they are in fact caused by changes in anticipations—and which are also a very particular species of returns and costs in the *ex post* calculus.

Monetary analysis must use both these systems of definition if it is to make any progress. . . . It must be our endeavor to formulate the condition of monetary equilibrium in such a way as to obtain observable and measurable magnitudes.[104]

From this it follows that equilibrium must be a condition of equality of *ex ante* saving and investment. The existence of this condition would then register itself as the absence of gains or losses *ex post*. Since their absence implies "money market equilibrium" and since

---

[104] G. Myrdal, *Monetary Equilibrium*, pp. 46-47.

the existence of the latter implies "commodity" or consumption goods market equilibrium, monetary equilibrium was explicitly defined as ". . . the state where no tendency to cumulative deflation exists." [105]

The "instrumental" usefulness of this concept was described as follows:

The hypothesis of a monetary equilibrium does not afford a factual appraisal of reality. It is only an instrument by which observed facts can be analyzed in certain respects important from the monetary point of view. . . . It is a purely instrumental, auxiliary structure in *theoretical* analysis, while at the same time it indicates a definite programme of monetary *policy.* . . . the determination of monetary equilibrium is, however, also of indirect importance, since it formulates the problem of the *course taken by a change from one situation to another,* and it makes possible the analysis of this dynamic problem proper.[106]

But in order to serve these purposes, the conditions of equilibrium must be stated in terms of measurable, observable magnitudes. To that end an evaluation and reformulation of the Wicksellian conditions by the "method of immanent criticism" seemed preferable to Myrdal than a direct presentation of his own "positive ideas." Drawing on Lindahl's earlier treatment, which partly covered similar ground, Myrdal stated Wicksell's position as follows:

Wicksell, as is well known, defined the equilibrium position by specifying the level of the 'money rate of interest' which brings about monetary equilibrium. This equilibrium interest rate Wicksell calls the 'normal rate of interest' and determines it with reference to quantities in three different spheres of price formation:

(1) Productivity of the roundabout process of production;
(2) Conditions in the capital market;
(3) Conditions in the commodity market.

The 'normal rate of interest' must now, according to Wicksell, (1) equal the marginal technical productivity of real capital (i.e., the 'real' or 'natural' rate of interest); (2) equate the supply of and the demand for savings; and finally, (3) guarantee a stable price level, primarily of consumption goods.

Wicksell assumes that the three criteria for the normal rate of interest are equivalent—i.e., never mutually inconsistent; but he cannot prove it. . . . Only the first and the second of the equilibrium conditions are even consistent; they are interrelated in such a way that the first is conditioned by the second and otherwise not determined. They both correspond to the main argument which is implicit in the whole theory. . . . With respect to the commodity market, however, the fulfillment of these two monetary equilib-

---

[105] *Ibid.,* p. 40.
[106] *Ibid.,* pp. 40-41. Italics in the original.

rium relations means something quite different from an unchanged price level.[107]

In his investigation, Myrdal began with the first of these conditions. In that connection he rejected Wicksell's definition of the "natural rate" in physical productivity terms for a barter economy and replaced it with the marginal value productivity of real capital in a monetary economy. Whether this transformation was necessary in 1932 can be questioned. All he achieved by it was that he arrived at Wicksell's definition of the "real rate of interest" of *Lectures-II*, by which, since 1915, Wicksell had attempted to improve on the analysis he first published in *Interest and Prices* in 1898.

At any rate, it was clear that if we express Wicksell's "real" rate as he had done, namely as "the expected yield on newly created real capital," or as Myrdal did as the *ex ante* net yield on new real investment, and if we designate this rate as y_2, then Wicksell's first equilibrium condition can be expressed by the equation $y_2 = i$, where i stands for the current average level of loan rates of interest.

But y_2 and its position relative to i cannot be known directly because y_2 reflects a state of anticipations. So some criterion of its behavior must be found in cognate areas of observation, from the implications of *ex ante* net yield of existing real capital, y_1. The latter must equal the net expected return, e, on existing real capital stated as a ratio of the value, c_1, of this capital at the time of calculation. But the value of existing real capital is nothing else than its expected net return discounted by the applicable current rate of interest into a present sum: $c_1 = e/i$. Hence $y_1 = i$, for a change in e when i is constant is reflected by a proportionate change in the same direction of c_1.

As for e, there is a complication which makes its calculation by rational entrepreneurs difficult or problematic. For e, the net return, is the expected gross return, b, minus operating cost on real capital payable to "coöperating factors," m, but in addition another item must be deducted, namely, d, an allowance for "anticipated change in the value of real capital," (i.e., depreciation minus appreciation). Thus $e = b - (m + d)$. Conventional standards of business accounting and of asset valuation are inadequate for arriving at a reliable estimate of e. Only m is known with much certainty. As for the "expected value change," d, it must be estimated on a weighted basis according to entrepreneurs' evaluations of length of service life, intensity of utilization, and obsolescence risk on existing capital equipment, in ad-

---

[107] *Ibid.,* pp. 37-38.

dition to their anticipations of changes in sales and price data, all of which affect the magnitude of d.

But we must do as Myrdal, bypass these complications, for however crude estimates of e may be, they are reflected in entrepreneurs' end-estimates of c_1, and it is the latter which influences their conduct toward investment.

Now all existing capital goods have a reproduction cost, r_1, and the analogue of Wicksell's first equilibrium condition, $y_2 = i$, which is applicable only to newly created real capital or to capital to be created, is, for existing real capital, that $c_1 = r_1$. The cognate condition for newly created capital is that $c_2 = r_2$, where c_2 and r_2 respectively stand for the *ex ante* capitalized value and cost of production of such capital goods.

1. *The reconstructed equilibrium conditions.* Myrdal argues in effect that if $c_1 = r_1$ on existing real capital, then if we assume constant relative prices of factors used in construction of capital and unchanging technology, then c_2 must equal r_2 on planned new capital,[108] with the consequence that planned new capital will be of zero magnitude and society stationary.

If $c_1 = r_1$, then $i = y_1 = e/c_1$. Because of the first equality this comes to saying that $y_1 = r_1$. In order for $c_2 = r_2$, it is necessary that $i = y_2 = e_2/c_2 = e_2/r_2$. But whether $e_2/c_2 = e_2/r_2$ can be inferred from $c_1 = r_1$, so that c_1 and r_1 may be substituted for c_2 and r_2, as Myrdal prefers (because c_1 and r_1 are market values while c_2 and r_2 refer to anticipations), depends on what can be inferred about e_2 from e, and about r_2 from r_1.

In conditions of unchanging technology and factor prices, planned new capital will be similar to existing real capital, and on that basis it is reasonable to hold that $r_2 = r_1$. Will therefore $e_2 = e$? Of course, one can say that if e_2 is greater than e, then "new capital" of this higher yield may be substituted for a certain amount of reinvestment in preëxisting capital of e yield. Thus in order for c_1 to equal r_1 any difference between e_2 and e must have been eliminated by this substitution. Yet if one argues this way, and something of the kind is implied in Myrdal's treatment, then e and e_2 are not independent, but must be defined with reference to their mutual substitution relations.

Myrdal was, indeed, aware of this, for after dispensing with the assumptions of constant technology and factor prices, in attempting to use r_1 as an approximation to the production cost on planned new capital, so that its *ex ante* yield could be stated as $y_2 = e/r_1$, he found

---

[108] *Ibid.,* pp. 64-83.

it necessary to resort to the following dubious "corrective factor" to make this approximation viable:

In our approximate formula, r_1 should be adjusted by a corrective factor before c_1 and r_1 are compared. This factor should represent as exactly as possible the *difference in the expected net return* on a given sum if invested, on the one hand according to the old method of construction, and on the other hand according to the new optimal method. Account would have to be taken of a change in the optimum size of the unit of production.[109]

Later in his exposition, Myrdal uses the difference $(c_1 - r_1) = \pm q$, which he defines as the "net investment gain or loss," or as "the profit margin or profit rate" on investment, as the mainspring of the investment activity which may or may not preserve the more fundamental second Wicksellian condition of equilibrium (namely, that the "normal rate of interest" must equate the demand for and supply of savings). Concerning this, Lindahl made the following telling comment:

. . . it is impossible on the basis of this investment schedule alone to single out any definite real rate as having a decisive influence on the loan rate. . . . From this point of view Myrdal's exposition . . . is open to criticism. Myrdal treats the profit rate (*Ertragsquote des Kapitales*) as an independent factor determining the normal loan rate of interest, and even attempts to prove that agreement between the profit rate and the loan rate in certain circumstances means that saving and investment are equal. (An examination of the argument reveals that the latter equality arises through the assumptions introduced, and is thus independent of the former one.)[110]

Be this as it may, having made the substitution of e and r_1 for e_2 and r_2 in the first approximation, Myrdal interpreted the first equilibrium condition, $y_2 = i$ to mean: ". . . a condition of equality between the capital value and cost of reproduction of existing real capital." [111]

Since he concluded that this condition holds only in stationary societies, where monetary equilibrium offers no problems, he decided that the first equilibrium condition must be reformulated. In progressive, dynamic societies there is both net saving and net investment. Moreover, there is no uniform money rate of interest but instead a structure of such rates. Finally, y_2, the *ex ante* yield on planned investment, will not be uniform in all industries. For these reasons there arise "net investment gains or losses," and it is these gains, or the prospect of them, which motivate net investment: "Investment gains

---

[109] *Ibid.*, p. 73. Italics in the original.
[110] E. Lindahl, *Studies in the Theory of Money and Capital*, p. 262 and n.
[111] G. Myrdal, *Monetary Equilibrium*, p. 73.

and investment losses: These arise if capital goods *just being constructed* have, at the moment when they are ready for use, a capital value which is larger or smaller than the total cost of construction. The expectations of such investment gains or losses by the entrepreneurs form the profit motive in the course of Wicksell's dynamic process." [112]

Consequently, entrepreneurial demand for "loan capital," as Wicksell put it, is functionally related to these *ex ante* investment gains. Summing investment demand schedules for all the various firms, one obtains the gross investment demand *ex ante*, R_2, which can be stated as $R_2 = f(q', q'', q''', \ldots)$. But summation of prospective profit margins, or q's, presents a further difficulty because the elasticity of investment demand with respect to q will not be uniform among the firms because of differences in market structure.

At this level of the argument, Wicksell's assumption of universal free competition was not permitted to stand in the way of an analysis aiming at greater realism. Myrdal's resolution of this problem was that the q's of individual firms must, before being summed to obtain the gross investment demand, be weighted according to the investment-reaction they occasion. This was expressed in the equation $\Sigma_w(c_1 - r_1) = Q$, where the subscript w represents a weighted average index or coefficient of investment-reaction, and Q, consequently, represents the profit margin *ex ante* in the economy as a whole, which is functionally related to R_2. Thus $R_2 = f(Q)$. But gross investment must be related to the "supply of saving" or to the gross savings schedule *ex ante*. The gross savings *ex ante* consist of the sum of net savings of persons and firms out of nonconsumed income, S, plus the sum of the d-terms in firms' calculations of net capital yield, i.e., plus D, which reflects the "anticipated value change of capital" interpreted as (depreciation minus appreciation) for the economy as a whole.

Following Cassel's usage, Myrdal refers to the gross savings schedule *ex ante*, $(S + D)$, as "free capital disposal," so that $W = (S + D)$. Thus the equilibrium condition is one of $R_2 = W = (S + D)$.

At best one must interpret the requirement that the risk of changes in the 'real content' of contracts be minimized as underlying the general and also rather indefinite value premise that too large and uni-directional price movements should not be tolerated. If one combines this value premise with the premise that business cycle movements should be eliminated as far as possible, one comes to the conclusion . . . that one should attempt to achieve *the most complete fulfilment of the equation $R_2 = W$, compatible with the least possible movement of a price index weighted with regard to the sticki-*

---

[112] *Ibid.*, p. 70.

ness of various prices and their significance for profitability and real invest-ment.[113]

But in any other than a stationary society, this equilibrium does *not* imply a condition of Q = zero *ex ante* investment gains, which would be implicit if one construes the first condition, $y_2 = i$ as an identity. Instead it implies a relation between y_2 and i which fulfills the following condition with respect to a profit margin *not* equal to zero: "The profit margin which corresponds to monetary equilibrium is therefore, the *complex of profit margins in different firms which stimulates just the amount of total investment which can be taken care of by the available capital disposal."* [114]

Thus investigation of the first equilibrium condition led to the second one, equality between investment and savings *ex ante,* as the more fundamental of the two, as the condition which makes the first relation determinate. Yet the first relation was retained because it "gives the more intensive discussion of the causes—in terms of profitability—of the quantity of investment." Furthermore, it is only by operating on i with reference to y_2 and C_1, the latter standing for values of existing capital in the economy as a whole, that monetary policy may be able to restore equilibrium. If this is to be done, interest policy must adjust C_1 relative to R_1 (which is largely beyond its influence) so that the resulting profit margin evokes the anticipations which determine R_2 *ex ante* of a magnitude that will more nearly equal W *ex ante,* or that will at least prevent large and long-lasting divergencies between these two strategic *ex ante* magnitudes from occurring.

2. *Criteria for guidance of monetary policy.* However, if monetary policy is to adjust C_1 relative to R_1 in a manner such that R_2 becomes indirectly more nearly adjusted to W, those responsible for such policy must be in a position to know whether monetary equilibrium prevails, and, if not, in what direction away from equilibrium the economy is tending. Criteria for this are to be found in the accrual of *ex post* gains or losses, which result from preceding *ex ante* divergencies between R_2 and W, for in the *ex post* accounting, W always equals R_1. Myrdal's solution for this difficulty was as follows:

The method of solving the problem must obviously be to eliminate from the *ex post* balance those elements which actively compensate for the *ex ante* unbalance, and which have no equivalents in the *ex ante* calculation. These are (1) revenue and cost gains, or losses, and (2) the portion of investment

---

[113] *Ibid.,* pp. 198-199; italics in the original. Cf. also *ibid.,* pp. 133-136.
[114] *Ibid.,* pp. 82-83. Italics in the original.

gains and losses which consists in a difference between the anticipated production cost of real capital and the actually realized cost. When a downward Wicksellian process is going on, the net value of the first is negative, but of the second positive; the sum total is negative. In an upward movement the reverse is true. In a state of monetary equilibrium this aggregate of the indicated gains and losses for the economy as a whole should be zero. Its magnitude should be a measure of the intensity of the tendency to deviate from equilibrium in one or another direction.[115]

The effect of Myrdal's emphasis on the R_2 and W relation reinforced by his *ex ante ex post* analysis was to make clear, as Lindahl had done earlier, that W adapts itself via income variations to the movement of R_2, and also to show that while interest-rate policy may contribute toward stabilizing this relation, it operates under severe limitations in a society of imperfect competition.

This was achieved by discarding an assumption, traceable to Böhm-Bawerk and the Austrian School and also present in a more attenuated form in Wicksell's work; namely, that an increase in saving, *ceteris paribus* means a change-over to more capitalistic methods of production. The first effect is that an increase in saving means a reduction of consumption demand and probably of consumption goods prices. Their fall, in turn, causes a reduction in capital values, and in investment profit margins, for which reason R_2 becomes smaller; income declines, and the extra savings are destroyed or "absorbed" in *ex post* losses. For analogous reasons, an increase in thrift in a downward Wicksellian process simply intensifies that downturn.

By contrast, it was shown that income is affected by anticipations and that saving adapts itself to the consequent variation in investment. Anticipations take an optimistic turn; the banks raise interest rates to maintain monetary equilibrium. They succeed to the extent of keeping capital values constant. But now since both the net yield and interest rates on existing capital are higher, income rises. Since capital values have been constant relative to production and reproduction costs, R_2 has remained constant. Yet savings rise on the higher level of income, especially if we assume that consumption spending increases less than income. How is equilibrium maintained? One would expect that the rise in S or in W, R_2 constant, would result in a downward process. But instead the extra saving is offset by a decrease in D. One can therefore say that the extra savings have become "invested" in "increased appreciation and decreased depreciation." Thus equilibrium is maintained by $R_2 = S + dS + (D - dD)$

$= W$. But, if the banks had not raised interest rates, then the rise in anticipations might have initiated an upward process.[116]

These and other insights attainable by the disequilibrium method of analysis must have sounded startling in 1933. Yet some of Myrdal's most interesting work was focused on the third Wicksellian equilibrium condition; namely, that the configuration of loan rates relative to real rates which maintains equilibrium in the sense of $R_2 = W$ would also maintain a constant level of prices. Since the $R_2 = W$ equilibrium would not be disrupted by a uniform rise or fall in prices, Myrdal concluded that this third condition was "fundamentally false." Then he proceeded to consider the relation between the price structure and monetary equilibrium.

3. The reformulated monetary policy norm. Some prices are sticky, for instance, wage rates; others, especially values of capital goods, are flexible. Because of this a general movement of prices is never uniform. It affects wages less and later and values of capital goods more and earlier. One result of this is that price movements inevitably affect the distribution of income, and generally also the level of income. Thus price movements are quite likely to disrupt any preëxisting monetary equilibrium. Since capital values respond fairly readily to changes in interest rates, while wage rates and the products of monopolies and oligopolies respond only remotely and indirectly, a monetary policy intent on preserving equilibrium "must, therefore, adapt the flexible prices to the absolute level of the sticky ones," i.e., its aim should be one of "business stabilization." [117]

This norm or requirement seemed all the more necessary because the sticky factor and some raw materials prices were likely to be important in the production and reproduction cost, r_1, of real capital, while c_1 could be expected to vary inversely with changes in interest rates. To facilitate the adaptation of flexible prices, monetary authority should be guided by a requirement to stabilize, as far as possible, a weighted price index. In that index, particular prices would be weighted according to the degree of stickiness, and according to their relative importance in entrepreneurial calculations of profitability, i.e., according to the proportion in which they enter into the production and operating cost of real capital, and hence according to their importance for entrepreneurial investment-reactions.

But this, of course, means something entirely different from stabilizing a particular level of prices such as that of consumption goods. It

---

[116] *Ibid.*, pp. 90-95.
[117] *Ibid.*, pp. 136, 178-179, 191, 199.

was in terms of this compound index of stickiness and investment-reaction that Myrdal achieved an unusual resolution of the venerable Wicksell-Davidson polemic:

For if we can assume that the prices of the basic factors of production are the principal sticky prices which are important for the volume of real investment—practically this means an assumption that wages are relatively sticky prices and that they form an essential part of the cost in all kinds of production, and that the prices of finished commodities are, like capital values, highly flexible—then the implication of our third equilibrium condition is, that the money rate of interest is normal which maintains the equilibrium relations on the capital market while the prices of means of production are unchanged. With a general increase of productivity this equilibrium condition would require a corresponding downward adjustment of prices of finished products, exactly as Davidson always emphasized in opposition to Wicksell.

But this correspondence is only an accident from a more fundamental methodological standpoint; it is not based on any special character of the changes of productivity. It depends simply on the assumption that wages are sticky prices. If we, on the other hand, were to assume that wages are particularly flexible while prices for finished commodities are sticky, then, when the same primary changes in productivity occurred, the equilibrium condition would, instead, require an increase of wages with constant prices for finished commodities, as Wicksell maintained. In other words, Davidson was right as against Wicksell, not for the reasons he gave but because of certain institutional circumstances which determine the degree of resistance of different markets to external influences. But neither of the disputants brought forward this aspect of the question.[118]

With his monetary norm, Myrdal asked monetary authority in substance to do two things simultaneously. First, obtain "from *ex post* balances" data on *ex post* revenue-and-cost gains or losses, and on differences between planned and realized cost of real investment. If gains predominate, then R_2 is greater than W, and credit must be tightened, to reduce R_2 by reducing C_1 relative to R_1. At the same time that credit tightening reduces an excessive *ex ante* rate of R_2, it also adapts flexible C_1 prices more closely to the stickier R_1 prices. But there are complications involved here, among them lead-lag relations. It does not follow that these two requirements of Myrdal's norm would be consistent with one another, for instance, at the upper turning point of a cycle or cumulative process.

Further, in a prolonged downward process, the corresponding loosening of credit and reduction of interest rates may fail to restore $R_2 = W$ equilibrium. Depressive effects of gloomy anticipations as to sales

---

[118] *Ibid.*, pp. 139-140.

may swamp the tendency of reduced rates to raise existing and *ex ante* capital values relative to production costs. Myrdal was not unaware of this, but left it for further investigation while he stressed the limitations of monetary policy in a different manner.

By his emphasis on sticky prices, he did monetary theory a service in reducing the Wicksellian stress on the *labile* character of the practically attainable approximation to equilibrium. He was also very candid in pointing out that a monetary policy devoted to his aim of "business stabilization" would not remove underemployment and excess capacity in an economy with increasingly imperfect competition. To the contrary, not only would it not guarantee full employment, but rather the very equilibrium it would be striving to maintain must be predicated on a volume of underemployment of resources corresponding to the degree of imperfect competition prevailing in its product and factor markets.[119]

This clearly brought into view the possibility of underemployment equilibrium resting on market structure and on institutional premises, rather than on the narrower basis of infinitely elastic liquidity preferences at low interest rates and of an implied or explicit prognostication of secular stagnation to account for the failure of investment *ex ante* to revive sufficiently. These premises are characteristic of the related Keynesian analysis.

4. *Reappraisal of scope and role of monetary policy.* We have already seen that Wicksell's followers in the Stockholm School became increasingly cognizant of qualifications on monetary policy. First, there was the circumstance, (*a*) that the significant variable is investment *ex ante,* which responds to entrepreneurial anticipations and affects income, and via sticky factor prices, employment. Interest-rate manipulation by monetary policy is only one of several forces, and not always the major one at play here. (*b*) Variation in a general level of prices, such as that of consumption goods, as long as its variation is not cumulative and unidirectional, is not necessarily indicative of monetary equilibrium or disequilibrium; and with respect to price movements, interest-rate policy plays an adaptive rather than a determinative role. (*c*) If the proper aim of monetary policy was construed to be one of facilitating "business stabilization," this was a smaller and different aim than that of preserving full employment, which it cannot safeguard. In that connection the duty of monetary authority is to remove monetary causes of instability and to adapt the credit system to nonmonetary causes of economic change. As for the latter, the question of controlling them or mitigating their effects

---

[119] *Ibid.*, pp. 143-158, 195-196.

presents problems which must be dealt with by other types of economic policy.

In addition to these, the following qualifications were added in the closing phase of Myrdal's analysis. (*d*) The means of monetary policy must not be assumed to be limited to simple variation in the level of interest rates. Monetary equilibrium is subject to a wide indifference field resting on the different degree of investment-reaction to changes in capital values and in production cost of real investment in different industries. The existence of this indifference field makes it likely that changes in levels of interest rates will often have negligible investment effects. Further it leaves considerable room for the use of rate differentiation which Lindahl emphasized. Finally it indicated a wide range within which the terms of monetary policy may be modified in order to achieve more effective coördination with other economic policy.[120]

(*e*) To succeed within its more limited aim of business stabilization, monetary policy requires deliberate coördination with other economic measures, notably with fiscal policy. The consequences of monetary policy being perverted to even narrower purposes, such as maintenance of certain exchange rates, or removal of deficiencies in the balance of payments, while other policy is left in charge of "business stabilization" or "recovery"—conditions which were frequently encountered in the early years of the Great Depression—were poignantly described as follows:

Finally, I should like to emphasize once more what is really obvious, that, in brief, *all public intervention* directed against the social effects of the depressive process must impede the efficacy of credit policy, if the latter is concerned with intensifying the depression for some purpose or other . . . the purpose of credit policy in the example just treated is to intensify the depression (in consideration of the exchange position). If then other public bodies at the same time do everything they can to moderate the effects on income and consumption, we have the typical disintegration of political relations which generally characterizes most of the public activity of present capitalist societies. It is the 'planlessness' which is the bitter inheritance of the liberal automatism, after this automatism itself has everywhere been replaced by state and group control, which has not yet been centralized.[121]

Finally, (*f*) the relative impotency of monetary policy as a means to recovery from depression was stressed. During the depressive process consumption goods prices do not fall nearly as much as a downward cumulative Wicksellian process might lead one to believe. This is

[120] *Ibid.*, pp. 159-161, 167-168.
[121] *Ibid.*, p. 175.

because consumption habits are relatively inelastic. In modern communities reduction in consumption standards is resisted and retarded by private dissaving. Eventually it is arrested at some point short of its average level for the cycle by public expenditures for social security, public works, etc.

It is this tendency to maintain consumption, coupled with the negligible, possibly negative, character of net investment during the downturn, which puts a floor under the depression. Eventually this builds up sufficient pressure by way of deferred replacement and reinvestment demand to raise R_2 above the reduced level of W to initiate recovery. Consequently recovery depends far more on these forces than it does on the fact that interest rates have also been scaled down during the depression.[122]

The foregoing must suffice to show the modification the Wicksell-Davidson heritage underwent, and now we turn to some of its practical consequences.

SOME CONSEQUENCES OF THE "RECONSTRUCTION"

The conceptual apparatus developed by Lindahl and Myrdal called for new sources of data for *ex post* analysis from business accounts, government budgets, and general statistical information. One consequence of this was an early development of national income accounting in Sweden. The participants in this labor were Lindahl, Dahlgren, and Koch, who published the valuable study *National Income of Sweden, 1861-1930* (1933), translated into English in 1937.

But in addition to new concepts and data, application of the *ex ante ex post* analysis required an adaptation of it to a period analysis. Even if Myrdal did not use the latter in his treatment,[123] it is precisely at the applied level that an adequate period analysis is needed to interpret *ex post* results. For these results are not registered on a continuous basis, and, in addition, the consequences of primary changes involve reaction patterns of different duration. Some evidence of this, pointing to the necessity of adapting period concepts to the duration of reaction patterns, was provided by D. Hammarskjöld's study, *Konjunkturspridningen* (The Diffusion of Economic Fluctuations, 1933), which was issued as one of the many excellent studies rendered on behalf of the *Kommitten för Arbetslöshetsutredningen* (Commission of Inquiry into Unemployment), appointed by the Swedish government during the years 1931-1935.

A notable example of application of the *ex ante ex post* calculus

---

[122] *Ibid.*, pp. 175-176, 190-200.
[123] E. Lindahl, *Studies in the Theory of Money and Capital*, pp. 171, 174, 175.

to a period analysis deliberately adapted to the character of data likely to be available and to the known or estimated differences in reaction time, is found in Ohlin's study, *Penningpolitik, offentliga arbeten, subventioner och tullar som medel mot arbetslöshet* (Monetary Policy, Public Works, Subsidies and Tariffs as Measures to Counteract Unemployment, 1934), which was also published by the Unemployment Commission. Certain problems of method and of adaptation of the new tools of theoretical research to the contents of countercyclical fiscal policy and its implied requirements for budgetary reform were dealt with by Myrdal in his work, also for the Unemployment Commission, *Finanspolitikens ekonomiska verkningar* (Economic Effects of Public Financial Policy, 1934). This study was complemented by two shorter treatises by Lindahl, "The Dynamic Approach to Economic Theory," and its Appendix, "Algebraic Discussion of the Relations between Some Fundamental Concepts," both written in 1938 and later incorporated respectively as Part I and as the last Appendix into his *Studies in the Theory of Money and Capital*. At about this time *Konjunkturinstitutet* (The Economic Research Institute) was set up, under E. Lundberg's direction, to do continuous research on business cycle and related problems as they affect Sweden's economy.

On the basis of the foregoing, it is evident that a critical examination of the Wicksell-Davidson heritage led to the opening of new horizons for Swedish economics, and that in this process, the comfortable isolation premise under which it had previously been possible to cultivate monetary theory except in such unusual circumstances as wars, gold invasion, and the like, was broken. Monetary theory merged imperceptibly with that of public finance, and the latter with that of distribution. From this point it was but a short step to the theory of production and output under varying market conditions, and thence to the theory of price formation and demand, which closes the circuit by leading into the theory of income and employment.

The foregoing must suffice to indicate the several directions of growth in which the Wicksell-Davidson heritage of monetary theory was expanded. Wicksell's main contribution to this was to liberate monetary theory from the "tyranny of the quantity of money," from a preoccupation with the mechanism of payments, and to implant this theory firmly within the fields of price formation and income determination by centering it around an analysis of the investment-savings relation. The contribution of his followers was to systematize his analysis, supply it with new concepts and methods of investigation, and to widen its scope with respect to other branches of economics by removing the framework of restrictive assumptions within which he labored.

At this point there remains only one aspect of Wicksell's work and its relation to contemporary economics to be discussed—his ideas concerning economic progress. These will be dealt with briefly in the next chapter.

CHAPTER XII

Wicksell's Ideas
on Economic Progress

In the preceding chapters most of Wicksell's ideas on economic progress have already been discussed.[1] It remains only to gather them together here in a more systematic fashion than he was able to do so as to bring to light their inherent, logical relations to one another.

Wicksell's Appraisal of Western Europe's Economic and Political Tendencies

All of Wicksell's speculations concerning the economic future of Sweden and of Western Europe were based on an assumption he made explicit in several places, namely that the rapid population increase of the closing decades of the nineteenth century must be brought to a stop before any significant rise in the mass standard of welfare would be attainable.[2] In his view the ideal relationship between population and economic resources was a population of optimum size, which he defined simply as "a population of such size that any further increase in it must mean a decrease of welfare." [3] He concluded that Western Europe had long since passed this stage in its development because its

---

[1] See the preceding discussion in chapter i, pp. 10 ff., chapter ii, pp. 26-27, chapter iii, pp. 52 ff., chapter iv, pp. 74 ff., chapter vii, pp. 154 ff., and chapter viii in its entirety. In order to keep documentation to a minimum, we also refer here to the various works cited in the foregoing list of chapters and sections.

[2] Wicksell, *Läran om Befolkingen, dess sammansättning och förändringar* (The Theory of Population, Its Composition and Changes), Stockholm (1910); *Allianser mellan Arbetare och Arbetsgifvare* (Alliances Between Workers and Employers), Stockholm (1902), pp. 26-28; *Socialiststaten och Nutidssamhället* (The Socialist State and Contemporary Society), Stockholm (1905), pp. 33-35.

[3] Wicksell, *Läran om Befolkningen* . . . , p. 42.

food import requirements were rising, having already at that time (about 1910) reached the rate of 20 to 30 per cent of its total consumption. At the same time he observed that Europe's granaries—Russia, the U. S., Canada, Argentina, Australia—had rapidly growing populations of their own. Also several of these countries were building up urban populations centered around their fast-growing manufacturing industries. This was particularly true of the U. S. and the British Dominions.

Although he thought that the great inventions of the nineteenth century would not readily be exceeded in the future, he recognized that rapid technological progress is likely to continue in manufacturing. But he was certain, and this point was strategic for his argument, that a similar rate of progress was impossible in agriculture where production is not notably subject to economies of scale. Thus he concluded that the days of huge crop surpluses available for export to Europe from these "granaries" would be coming to an end within a matter of decades.

On this analysis he held that the first requirement for Western Europe was to attain a stationary population, and the sooner the better. As the only rational means to that end he urged adoption of the neo-Malthusian principles of voluntary population control by means of early marriages, by limiting the number of children to two or at any rate not more than three per family, and thereafter, by voluntary sterility via the application of contraceptive techniques.[4]

While this goal of a stationary population was being approached, he looked for political and organizational developments in society as a prelude to certain economic transformations he believed would be their inevitable consequences. He noted with sympathy the growing political strength of Social Democratic and labor parties and the spread of trade unionism. He was certain that with the gradual achievement of universal suffrage, the day would not be far off when labor would take over political power. But he also observed that as the labor parties were gaining in strength their revolutionary fervor and attachment to various doctrinaire Marxist positions was abating. In fact, at the practical level, the Social Democrats were more and more embracing a broad program of social reform with the aim of attaining at any rate some features of the socialist state by peaceful, gradual tactics rather than by revolution.

Meanwhile other parties, separated both from the working class and from the conservatives among the ruling class, namely the liberal-bourgeois parties, were also changing their orientation. At one time

---

[4] *Ibid.,* p. 49.

they had followed a strict laissez-faire or Manchester School program
in matters of social reform. As such they had been hostile to the rise
of the labor movement and to other forms of collective organizations
within the social structure, including business cartels and trusts. Yet
these parties had vigorously supported parliamentary reform, the expansion of the franchise, and also such non-Manchesterian developments as compulsory "free" public elementary education and the introduction of progressive taxes on corporate profits, personal incomes, and
inheritances.

Gradually the liberal-bourgeois had come to recognize the need for
group organization both in the production and marketing of commodities and in the labor market in order to restrain destructive competition or to mitigate its consequences. More and more, these parties
were also embracing a broad program of social reform and were learning to live with, and on occasion to aid and encourage, the rising labor
movement.

In view of these tendencies, it seemed to Wicksell it would be a
natural development for Social Democrats, no longer devoted to a
revolutionary program, and for liberal-bourgeois, now no longer committed to the Manchester School doctrines, to make common cause
politically around a workable program of social reform, which would
gradually usher in the "welfare state." [5]

In the economic sphere Wicksell foresaw as inevitable the progressive decline of "free competition" in favor of other forms of market
structure imposed for the most part by and in the interest of producer
groups whose preference was for "regulated" competition. Farmers
were forming marketing coöperatives. Labor was organizing on an
increasing scale. Small- and medium-size manufacturers were forming
employer associations, sales cartels, and the like. All of these forms of
combination had for their primary purpose restriction of price competition. Meanwhile large business enterprise was growing to giant size,
extending its production and market controls often across entire con-
tinents. In all this group organization the least protected party was
the ultimate consumer, but even he was awakening to the benefits of
collective action in his own interest by developing consumer coöperatives.

Wicksell realized that certain general economic gains were likely to
result from all these combination tendencies. Small business in particular, ground between the upper millstone of big business competition and the nether one of increasing wage demands by unions, prob-

---

[5] Wicksell, *Socialiststaten och Nutidssamhället* (The Socialist State and Contemporary Society), pp. 1-12.

ably stood to benefit most by forming industry-wide organizations, which could obtain some of the economies otherwise only available to big business. Improved management, adoption of more efficient marketing, purchasing, and production techniques, and better record keeping were some of the benefits which were becoming available to small business through its associations. Moreover, these gains would also benefit society at large insofar as they amounted to cost-saving techniques in production. In addition there was, of course, the more palpable advantage to small business from agreements to maintain prices and to hold cutthroat competition at bay, made possible only by means of associations and which constituted the primary incentive for forming business organizations.[6]

In Wicksell's view, the benefits to the workers deriving from the trade-union movement were a mixture of economic and noneconomic gains. Collective bargaining raised the individual laborer from his inferior role in individual bargaining; it protected him against wage discrimination and against arbitrary dismissal. These were great advantages not only from an economic point of view but also in terms of personal security and dignity for the worker. In addition Wicksell regarded the workers' participation in the labor movement as an edifying influence which strengthened their status in society and made them more capable of pressing their claims for equality with other classes and for an effective voice in society's public affairs.

As for the future prospects of real wages under a more fully developed labor movement, this, thought Wicksell, depended less on collective bargaining than on the supply of labor coming into the market under a general policy of voluntary population control on the one hand, and on improvements in the productivity of industry on the other. His reasoning on this, although he was not explicit on this point, seems to have been that in its growth from weakness and instability to strength, the labor movement will have obtained for itself the real-wage gains attainable at the collective-bargaining table. However, additional gains, though probably not spectacular ones, would likely accrue from the increase in tranquility of industrial relations and the attendant production improvements which could be expected if unions enter into alliances with organized employers. Some evidence of this had come to Wicksell's attention from the success of such alliances in some industries in England, Switzerland, and Germany.[7]

Prior to the forming of a series of alliances, some small manufactur-

---

[6] Wicksell, *Allianser mellan Arbetare och Arbetsgifvare* (Alliances Between Workers and Employers), p. 10.

[7] *Ibid.*, Preface, and pp. 15 ff.

ing industries in England had suffered from weakness on the part of both the employers' and the workers' organizations. Despite many attempts by the manufacturers to form organizations to make a common front against labor and to achieve a profitable price maintenance agreement among themselves, they had never succeeded in enforcing such agreements. Particularly in times of slow business several firms reneged on their commitments and resorted to "cutthroat" competition. Likewise the union, which had been able to secure wage increases for the workers in good times, proved unable to control the labor market in poor times. Then, as the manufacturers cut back production, its unemployed members sooner or later were forced to seek hire at wages below the union scale among firms which had broken the agreement and among unorganized shops.

However, about 1900 a Mr. E. J. Smith, a Birmingham manufacturer of iron beds, conceived the idea of inviting the union into an alliance with the employer organization. The conditions he proposed were (a) that the union agree that its members would work only for firms in good standing with the employer federation, and (b) that this federation agree to hire only union members. Further, (c) the federation offered an immediate 10 per cent wage increase to the workers, and (d) a predetermined share in the increased profits the employers expected to earn after the alliance was formed. To protect the federated firms against price-cutting tactics and also to protect the union men against downgrading of piece-work rates and other sources of grievances, the alliance set up a board consisting of an equal number of representatives from the federation and from the union jointly to administer the alliance agreement, with provision for settling tied cases by calling in an independent umpire.

The alliance was a success for some years and other alliances were formed as a consequence. For the first time the manufacturers were able to exclude ruthless competition from the weaker firms among them whose workers would strike if they broke the alliance agreement. At the same time those who upheld the agreement were ensured against work stoppages. This released energies and funds for concentrating on cost-saving production improvements, an effort which succeeded so well that the alliance prospered without raising the prices of its products. The workers, on the other hand, were able peacefully to negotiate for further wage increases in addition to sharing in the profits realized from cost savings.

Wicksell's interest in alliances of this type was stimulated not only because of the benefits they conferred on workers and employers alike, but even more because of the prospect of peaceful industrial relations they offered. In effect, in these circumstances, each organization strengthened the other, and with increasing common interests to protect, this promoted industrial peace, with beneficial consequences for society as a whole.

But he also pointed out that if alliances of this character were to spread throughout industry, two consequences would follow. The direct gains they would be able to obtain for their members would become less spectacular than when such combinations are novel and few in number. The alliances he had studied had usually refrained from raising prices on their products, relying instead on cost savings and increased sales volume to increase profits and wages. But in due course these savings might become smaller, and then the temptation to raise prices might become irresistible, particularly among the stronger alliances. But to raise prices would be generally self-defeating if the time should come when most industries had formed worker-employer alliances. As he put it, "when everyone is out to skin everyone else the general result will necessarily be equal to zero." [8]

If such alliances were to become general, their pricing, marketing, and production behavior would, consequently, have to be regulated by public authority. This would protect the consumer. It would also serve to break deadlocks which might develop in negotiations between alliances in different stages of production (for instance, as between alliances which produce final output and appear as buyers to raw materials producing alliances).

Given, then, that in Wicksell's view Western European society would, in the not too distant future have achieved a stationary population, a more advanced level of industrial development, a greater development of its democratic institutions with political power for the most part in the hands of a reform-minded coalition of Social Democrats with liberal-bourgeois parties, in what fundamental economic respects would this society be different from the one in which he lived?

Wicksell's Vision of the Future Economy—the Welfare State

Wicksell did not think that the future society would be very different from the present one in its economic production arrangements. There would still be freedom of consumer choice, of choice of occupation, and freedom and incentives to save and invest. To be sure, natural monopolies such as public utilities would most likely be in public ownership and operation to a greater extent than during his time. Also some basic industries and resources outside this field might come under public operation in order to obviate the waste of oligopolistic

[8] *Ibid.,* p. 25.

competition between very large enterprises and in order to conserve resources against competitive depletion in private enterprise production.

But all such publicly owned enterprises would be subject to his marginal-cost-pricing rule in the public management of their operations. Yet probably the greater part of the national output would still be produced by private enterprise under more or less restricted, therefore more or less publicly regulated, forms of competition because little or nothing would be gained by socializing these enterprises. Most private firms would tend to, or be directed to, produce the output for which marginal cost equals price. Agriculture, in particular, he thought would remain much as it was, with a vast number of small farms and a few large ones acting in free competition with one another.[9]

In its distributive aspects, however, the future society would exhibit considerable differences from the economy of Wicksell's time.

The first duty of the emerging new society, he thought, would be to expand those social services which tend to develop human resources and widen economic opportunities as well as to equalize them as between qualified individuals regardless of their income status.

First among these services was greater provision for education, from elementary levels through high schools, vocational schools, technical institutes, the universities, and professional schools. He wanted this education not only to be provided free of tuition to all applicants who qualified on competitive examinations, but also with provision for their maintenance. This was the keystone in his program for reducing to the minimum, as he put it, "the waste of society's intellectual capital," [10] which occurs in communities where only relatively well off families can afford to provide their children with higher education.

In line with his emphasis on developing the abilities of youth, he also visualized that the future society would have the wisdom of protecting its citizens, so far as possible, against the hazards of illness, accident, involuntary unemployment, and unemployability in advanced age. Where protection might not be possible, it seemed to him that it was society's duty to mitigate the impacts of these hazards on the individual by proper compensation under a comprehensive social security and health insurance system.

He reasoned that the net cost of extending these services would at

---

[9] Wicksell, *Socialiststaten och Nutidssamhället* (The Socialist State and Contemporary Society), pp. 19-23.

[10] *Ibid.;* the quoted passage occurs on page 18; the proposal for free education and maintenance on pp. 29-30.

most be negligible, even negative if account is taken of the economic gains which would result for society as a whole from the increased level of education, the improvement in health and efficiency of the people, and the reduction of economic insecurity implicit in this program. In the absence of such a program these costs must in any case be met by private individuals with much less desirable consequences for society as a whole.[11]

However, over and beyond this he also wanted a distribution of a social dividend or a "social inheritance" each year to those in the population who reach the age of 25 during that year. This was intended to implement two of his aims. First, according to his neo-Malthusian convictions, early marriages are desirable because they contribute to happiness, make for healthier families, and reduce extra-marital promiscuity and vice. A social inheritance of about 8,000 crowns (roughly the equivalent of $6,000 per couple in current purchasing power) as he calculated it in 1905[12] might become available to young couples 25 years of age. This would facilitate their establishing a home, or acquiring a skilled trade, or setting themselves up in some small business. Secondly, he had for many years contended that "labor should not live from wages alone." By this he meant that in a well-ordered society the laborer should be able to look forward in his maturity to some secondary social distribution or dividend over and above what he might be capable of earning on the basis of the marginal value productivity of his labor in primary distribution in industry.[13] Moreover, in his old age, when he might long since have exhausted his "social inheritance," he should be able to look forward to a pension sufficient to keep him and his wife in comfort without having to depend for support on his children in his declining years.

Whence would come the wherewithal for this social inheritance for young couples of age 25 or thereabouts? Wicksell had in mind, as was explained in chapter viii, that it would largely come from "confiscatory" sources of revenue, levied on incomes and wealth deemed to be "unjust" or at any rate "unearned." As has also been pointed out in chapter viii, it was Wicksell's view that progressive "confiscatory" taxes would act in part as a capital levy, and for the remainder would appropriate for the treasury portions of incomes which, were it not for the tax, would have been saved and as such would have been available for investment in private capital formation.

---

[11] *Ibid.*, p. 31.

[12] *Ibid.*, pp. 33-34; Wicksell, *Allianser mellan Arbetsgifvare och Arbetare* (Alliances Between Employers and Workers), p. 14.

[13] Wicksell, *Socialiststaten och Nutidssamhället* (The Socialist State and Contemporary Society), pp. 20-21, 32.

Since he was ever anxious to stimulate the process of capital forma-tion in the interest of increasing social welfare, he took the postion that revenues of the foregoing types should *not* be used for current govern-ment expenses. This would amount to consumption by public spend-ing of funds which otherwise would have been invested privately. Hence he held that the proper thing for government to do with these revenues was to invest them productively, presumably in public enter-prises. The interest earned on revenues thus invested, plus possible profits earned on enterprises and resources owned by the government, he estimated would be sufficient to pay the social dividend he talked about if the population of Sweden (about 5.4 million in Wicksell's day) were to become stationary without major changes in its age com-position.

Obviously, taxes additional to those on "unearned" income and "unjust" wealth would be required; namely, taxes on "earned" in-comes and property values. Even commodity excises would be needed to support the customary government services and the expanded edu-cation and social security program. What taxes these would be and at what rates he never took the trouble to investigate. All one can gather from his views on nonconfiscatory taxation in general is that he wanted to reduce the proportion of excises and tariffs to a minimum within the revenue structure because of the regressive nature of these taxes and because of their uncertain incidence.

Perhaps he did not concern himself in detail about how the welfare state he envisioned would be financed on the assumption that when the public really wants to have government services expanded or wants government to assume new functions, the means for financing will be found. It is more probable, however, that he did not trouble much about this problem because he hoped that the future society would find the means of abolishing war and the attendant necessity for large armament expenditures.[14] Already in his time a substantial portion of Sweden's budget, and the budgets of most countries in Europe, was devoted to maintaining elaborate defense establishments, including compulsory military training of male citizens for a year or more. This represented a considerable tax burden which, if it could safely be abolished or reduced considerably, would make correspondingly large revenues available for the welfare purposes he had in mind without increasing the net tax burden.

This, then, was Wicksell's view of the future development of Swe-den's and the West European community's economy. If a recent work

---

[14] *Ibid.*, pp. 37-39 and 39 n.

of Fleisher's, *Sweden, the Welfare State*,[15] is accepted as a fairly accurate description of Sweden's recent economic growth, then it is clear that this country has made considerable strides toward the goals Wicksell foresaw. According to Fleisher, Sweden at present enjoys the highest standard of living in Europe with greatly expanded educational opportunities for all citizens and vastly expanded welfare services, as contrasted with Wicksell's time. Moreover, most of this development has occurred in the surprisingly short span of thirty years since Wicksell's death, despite disruptions in domestic development resulting from World War II. Hence Wicksell may be regarded as a successful prophet of things to come, but this is subject to two qualifications.

First, Sweden's economy has grown and the welfare of its people has risen notably during this period without its population (now about 7.5 million) becoming stationary, as Wicksell insisted it had to before the standard of living could rise appreciably. Still it must be admitted that Sweden's net rate of population growth is smaller than that of most European countries.

Second, this economic advance has occurred despite the necessity for Sweden to increase the size and cost of its defense establishment far beyond what was known or thought of in Wicksell's time.

Therefore, his remarkable foresight and analytic powers notwithstanding, Wicksell underestimated some of his own country's growth potentials, chiefly in the technological realm as it affects productivity and industrial diversification. In this he shares the fate of many who have attempted to peer into the distant future. It is clear that while he was not an infallible prophet, he was far more foresighted about the shape of things to come, and much less wrong, than some of his distinguished contemporaries, notably, Walras, Pareto, and Alfred Marshall.

---

[15] W. Fleisher, *Sweden, the Welfare State* (New York, 1956).

BIBLIOGRAPHY

The first part of this bibliography is a selected list of Wicksell's economic writings in chronological order. It does not pretend to be an exhaustive bibliography, partly because he wrote on other than economic subjects, and partly because some of his minor economic writings, which were not important for developing the trend of his thought, have been omitted. A somewhat more extensive bibliography of his economic writings by Arne Amundsen has appeared and has been translated and added to S. Frowein's translation of Wicksell's first theoretical treatise, *Value, Capital and Rent* (London, 1954), pp. 168-175.

Many of Wicksell's articles, and responses to them by his Swedish colleagues, appeared in the Swedish economic journal, *Ekonomisk Tidskrift*. To save space the title of this journal has been abbreviated as *ET*.

Lists of books and articles by various authors who have commented significantly on Wicksell's works, or who have been referred to in the text, make up the remainder of the bibliography.

Selected List of Wicksell's Economic Writings

Några ord om samhällsolyckornas viktigaste orsak och botemedel med särskilt afseende på dryckenskapen (Some Words about the Most Important Cause of Social Misfortune with Special Emphasis on Drunkenness). Uppsala, 1880, 95 pp. (A published lecture.)

Om utvandringen, dess betydelse och orsaker (On Emigration, Its Meaning and Causes). Stockholm, 1882, 111 pp. (A lecture with a technical appendix.)

"Überproduktion oder Überbevölkerung," *Zeitschrift für die gesammten Staatswissenschaften*, 46 (1890), 1-12.

"Tomme maver—og fulde magisiner" (Empty Stomachs—and Full Warehouses), *Samtiden* (Contemporary Times), 1 (1890), 245-247, 293-304. (A Norwegian periodical.)

"Kapitalzins und Arbeitslohn," *Jahrbücher für Nationalökonomie,* 59 (1892), 852-874.

Über Wert, Kapital und Rente nach den neueren nationalökonomischen Theorien. Jena, 1893, 143 pp. An English translation: *Value, Capital and Rent,* by S. Frowein. London, 1954.

Våra skatter: Hvilka betala dem, och hvilka borde betala? Synpunkter och föreslag af Sven Trygg (Our Taxes: Who Pays Them and Who Ought To? Views and Proposals by Sven Trygg). Stockholm, 1894, 96 pp. Written under the pseudonym of S. Trygg.

Zur Lehre von der Steuerincidenz. Uppsala, 1895, 75 pp. This was Wicksell's doctoral dissertation, later incorporated as Part One of his *Finanztheoretische Untersuchungen.*

Progressiv beskattning af inkomst och förmögenhet (Progressive Taxation of Income and Property), *Verdandis Småskrifter,* No. 56 (Verdandi Series, published by faculty and students at the University of Uppsala). Stockholm, 1895, 39 pp.

Finanztheoretische Untersuchungen nebst Darstellung und Kritik des Steuersystems Schwedens. Jena, 1896, 352 pp.

"V. Pareto, 'Cours d'économie politique,' " a review in *Zeitschrift für Volkswirtschaft,* 6 (1897), 159-166.

"Der Bankzins als Regulator de Warenpreise," *Jahrbücher für Nationalökonomie,* 68 (1897), 228-243.

"Penningräntans inflytande på varuprisen" (The Influence of the Money Rate of Interest on Commodity Prices), *Nationalekonomiska Föreningens Förhandlingar* (Proceedings of the Swedish Association of Economics), 1 (1898), 47-70.

Geldzins und Güterpreise: Eine Studie über den Tauschwert des Geldes bestimmenden Ursachen. Jena, 1898, 189 pp. An English translation by R. F. Kahn as *Interest and Prices.* London, 1936.

Den Politiska rösträtten och skatterna (The Political Franchise and Taxation). Stockholm, 1898, 16 pp.

"V. Pareto, 'Cours d'économie politique,' " a second review on the appearance of this work in its second edition, in *Zeitschrift für Volkswirtschaft,* 8 (1899), 95-100.

"Om överflyttning av skatt" (On Shifting of Taxes), *ET,* 1 (1899), 211-232.

"Ytterligare om överflyttning af skatt: ett genmäle till Dr. Cassel" (More About Shifting of Taxes: Reply to Dr. Cassel), *ET,* 1 (1899), 383-387.

"Om gränsproduktiviteten såsom grundval för den nationalekonomiska fördelningen" (Concerning Marginal Productivity as the Basis of Economic Distribution), *ET,* 2 (1900), 305-337.

"Zur Verteidigung der Greznutzenlehre," *Zeitschrift für die gesammten Staatswissenschaften,* 56 (1900) 577-591.

Föreläsningar i Nationalekonomi: Första delen: Teoretisk Nationalekonomi (Lectures on Political Economy: Volume One: Economic Theory). Lund, 1901, 219 pp.

"Om arfsskatten" (Concerning the Inheritance Tax), *ET,* 3 (1901), 75-119.

"Till fördelningsproblemet" (Concerning the Problem of Distribution), *ET*, 4 (1902), 424-433.

"J. B. Clark 'Distribution of Wealth' och J. A. Hobson 'Economics of Distribution,'" Reviews, *ET*, 4 (1902), 560-562.

Allianser mellan arbetare och arbetsgifvare: En ny företeelse på det socialpolitiska området (Alliances Between Workers and Employers: A New Phenomenon in the Field of Social Policy), No. 109, *Verdandis Småskrifter* (Verdandi Tracts). Stockholm, 1902, 33 pp.

"Om begreppen produktivitet, räntabilitet, och relativ afkastning inom jordbruket" (The Concepts of Productivity, Profitability, and Relative Yield in Agriculture), *ET*, 5 (1903), 169-174.

"Jordbrukets produktionskostnader" (Costs of Production in Agriculture), *ET*, 5 (1903), 340-347.

"Den dunkla punkten i penningteorien" (The Moot Point in Monetary Theory), *ET*, 5 (1903), 485-507.

"Framtidens myntproblem" (Currency Problems of the Future), *ET*, 6 (1904), 82-106.

"Mål och medel i nationalekonomien" (Aims and Methods in Economics), *ET*, 6 (1904), 457-474. This article reproduces Wicksell's inaugural lecture on the occasion of his appointment as full professor at University of Lund.

Socialiststaten och nutidssamhället: Några socialekonomiska betraktelser (The Socialist State and Contemporary Society: Some Observations on Social Economy). Stockholm, 1905, 40 pp.

Föreläsningar i Nationalekonomi: Andra delen: Om penningar och kredit (Lectures on Political Economy: Volume Two: On Money and Credit). Stockholm, 1906, 208 pp. An English translation from the third Swedish edition: *Lectures on Political Economy*, II. London, 1935.

"Knapps penningteori" (Knapp's Monetary Theory), *ET*, 9 (1907), 41-52.

"Några felkällor vid försök till verifikation af lagen för jordens aftagande afkastning" (Certain Sources of Error in Attempts at Verifying the Law of Diminishing Returns), *ET*, 9 (1907), 277-285.

"Über einige Fehlerquellen bei Verifikation des Bodengesetzes," *Thünen Archiv*, 2 (1907-08), 347-355.

"Noch einiges über die Verifikation des Bodengesetzes," *Thünen Archiv* (1908), 568-577.

"The Influence of the Rate of Interest on Prices," *Economic Journal*, XVII (1907), 213-220.

"Krisernas gåta" (The Enigma of Crises), *Statsøkonomisk Tidskrift*, 21 (1907), 255-275. This article has now been translated by C. G. Uhr and published as "The Enigma of Business Cycles," *International Economic Papers*, 3 (1953), 58-75.

"En lektion i banklagstiftning" (A Lesson in Banking Legislation), *ET*, 10 (1908), 41-54. This contains Wicksell's comments on the American panic of 1907.

"Penningvärdets stadgande, ett medel att förebygga kriser" (Stabilization of the Value of Money, A Means for Preventing Crises), *ET*, 10 (1908), 207-214.

"Hvarför inskränkes fabriksdriften?" (Why are the Factories Cutting Back?), *ET*, 10 (1908), 373-382.

"Penningränta och varupris" (Money Interest and Commodity Prices), *ET*, 11 (1909), 61-66.

Tronen, altaret, svärdet, och penningpåsen: Föredrag (The Throne, the Altar, the Sword, and the Bag of Money). Stockholm, 1909, 48 pp. This was the celebrated lecture in which Wicksell's areligious and anticlerical expressions led to a near-riot and resulted in his being adjudged guilty of breach of the religious peace and being sent to prison for two months.

Läran om befolkningen, dess sammansättning och förändringar (The Theory of Population, Its Composition and Changes), Stockholm, 1910, 52 pp., No. 170 in *Verdandis Småskrifter* (Verdandi Tract). This essay was written by Wicksell during his short prison service for disturbing the religious peace by the lecture noted above.

"F. H-son Brock, 'Ekonomiska fördelningsproblemet och kriser' " (F. H-son Brock, The Economic Problem of Distribution and Crises), a review, *ET*, 12 (1910), 190-201.

"Sveriges utvandringsfråga" (Sweden's Emigration Problem), supplement to *Emigrationsutredningen* (Report on the Investigation of Emigration— a Swedish government report), supplement no. 18, pp. 99-131. Stockholm, 1910.

"Böhm-Bawerks kapitalteori och kritiken däraf" (Böhm-Bawerk's Theory of Capital and Its Critics), *ET*, 13 (1911), 39-49.

"Varuprisens stegring" (The Increase in Commodity Prices), in *Tiden*, (The Times, a serial), 3 (1911), 239-246.

"Tullar och arbetslöner" (Protective Tariffs and Wage Rates), *ET*, 14 (1912), 43-48.

"Kapital und Kein Ende: Svar till Brisman" (Capital, and No End of It: Reply to Brisman), *ET*, 14 (1912), 309-322.

"Monopolvinsten och dess beskattning, jämte något om gross och detalj-handelspris" (The Taxation of Monopoly Gains Together With Some Reflections concerning Prices at Wholesale and Retail Levels of Trade), *ET*, 14 (1912), 432-433.

"Ålderdömsforsäkringskommittens betänkande" (Deliberations and Report of the Committee on Old Age Insurance), *ET*, 14 (1912), 443-468. This article expresses Wicksell's criticism of the proposed old age insurance legislation as altogether inadequate for its intended purposes.

"Penningvärdets Reglerande" (Regulation of the Value of Money), *ET*, 15 (1913), 134-142.

"Resultatet (av pensionsförslaget)" (The Result [Of the Pension Proposal]), *ET*, 15 (1913), 211-217. A further comment on the old age insurance proposal.

"Det föreliggande pensionsförsäkringsförslaget från nationalekonomisk syn-punkt" (The Present Proposal for Social Insurance Pensions from an Economic Point of View), *Svenska Fattigvårdsförbundets Tidskrift* (The Journal of the Swedish Association for the Care of the Poor), 7 (1913), 3-13.

"Villfredo Pareto 'Manuel d'économie politique,' " a review, *Zeitschrift für Volkswirtschaft, Sozialpolitik und Verwaltung*, 22 (1913), 132-151.

"Dyrtid, tullar och arbetslöner" (Boom-periods, Protective Tariffs, and Wages), *ET*, 16 (1914), 75-84, 126-127.

"Kan ett land få för litet folk?" (Can a Country Become Underpopulated?), *ET*, 16 (1914), 195-208.

"Riksbankens guldkassa" (The Gold Reserve of the Riksbank), *ET*, 16 (1914), 263-267.

"Lexis och Böhm-Bawerk" (Lexis and Böhm-Bawerk), *ET*, 16 (1914), 294-300, 322-334. Two memorials to these well-known economists who died earlier that year.

"Mises, L. v., 'Theorie des Geldes und der Umlaufsmittel', (Rezension)," *Zeitschrift für Volkswirtschaft, Sozialpolitik und Verwaltung*, 23 (1914), 144-149.

"Ekonomiska gåtor (Än en gång om riksbankens guldkassa)" (Economic Enigmas [Once More, The Gold Reserve of the Riksbank]), *ET*, 17 (1915), 30-38.

"Marknadsprisets inverkan på utbudet" (The Effect of Market Price on Supply), *ET*, 17 (1915), 39-42.

"Växelkurs och bankränta" (The Foreign Exchanges and the Rate of Interest), *ET*, 17 (1915), 159-171.

" 'Financiellkrigsberedskap' i Tyskland" ('Financial War-Preparedness' in Germany), *ET*, 17 (1915), 230-233.

"Frivilliga besparningar eller tvungna" (Voluntary or Forced Savings), *ET*, 17 (1915), 364-368.

"Den 'kritiska punkten' i lagen för jordbrukets aftagande produktivitet" (The 'Critical Point' in the Law of Diminishing Returns in Agriculture), *ET*, 18 (1916), 285-292.

"Medel mot dyrtiden" (Means for Counteracting the Inflation), *ET*, 18 (1916), 304-308.

"S. Brisman: 'De Moderna affärsbankerna': (Recension)" (Brisman: Modern Commercial Banks: [A Review]), *ET*, 19 (1917), 19-29.

"Strödda Reflexioner" (Random Reflections), *ET*, 19 (1917), 81-90.

"Varupris och fraktsatser" (Commodity Prices and Freight Rates), *ET*, 19 (1917), 280-284.

"Penningränta och varupris" (The Rate of Interest and Commodity Prices), *ET*, 19 (1917), 309-311.

"Goschen och växelkurserna: (en rättelse)" (Goschen and the Foreign Exchanges: [A correction]), *ET*, 19 (1917), 320-321.

"Småanmärkningar" (Minor Observations), *ET*, 19 (1917), 381-386.

"Gold after the War in Relation to Inflation and the Foreign Exchanges," *Economic Journal*, 28 (1918), 409-412.

"International Freights and Prices," *Quarterly Journal of Economics,* 32 (1918), 404-410.

"Ett angrepp på kvantitetsteorien" (An Attack on the Quantity Theory), *ET,* 21 (1919), 57-63.

"Växelkursernas gåta" (The Riddle of the Foreign Exchanges), *ET,* 21 (1919), 87-103.

"Professor Cassel's Ekonomiska system" (The Economic System of Professor Cassel), *ET,* 21 (1919), 195-226. This article has been translated into English and appears as Appendix I, vol. 1, of the English edition of *Lectures on Political Economy,* under the title "Professor Cassel's System of Economics," pp. 219-257, of that volume.

"Riksbanken och privatbankerna: (Förslag till reform af det svenska kredit och penningväsendet)" (The Riksbank and Private Banks: [A Proposal for Reforming the Swedish System of Money and Credit]), *ET,* 21 II-s (1919), 177-188.

Yttrande ångaende ifrågasatt inlåningsrätt för Sveriges Riksbank (Opinion Concerning the Question of Empowering the Bank of Sweden (the Riksbank) to Make Direct Loans). Stockholm, 1920, 16 pp.

This was a separately published statement of *1917 års bankkommittee:* betänkande no. 2 (Report no. 2 of the Banking Committee of 1917).

Utlåtande angående frågan huruvida och i vad mån ett program för den närmaste framtiden för svensk finanspolitik må kunna åstadkommas: 1920 års finanssakkunniga (Report on the Question of How and to What Extent It Is Possible to Set Up a Program for the Near Future for Swedish Financial Policy: By the Financial Experts Appointed for the Year 1920). Stockholm, 1920, 63 pp.

This contains the substance of Wicksell's proposals for monetary policy and anti-inflation program, propounded in the course of his service in the 1920 Committee on Finance.

"Carl Menger," *ET,* 23 (1921), 113-118.

"Inflation, penningmängd, och penningränta" (Inflation, Quantity of Money, and Interest Rate), *ET,* 23 (1921), 167-171.

"Svar till Kand. G. Åkerman" (Reply to G. Åkerman, A. B.), *ET,* 24 (1922), 10-12.

"Inkomstbegreppet i skattehänseende och därmed sammanhangande skattefrågor" (The Income Concept in Taxation and Tax Problems Connected With This Concept), *ET,* 24 (1922), 127-154. (This article was later separately printed and incorporated among some of the Swedish government's taxation reports, see below.)

"Särskilt Yttrande" (Separate Statement) in *Betänkande om Inkomst och Förmögenhetsskatt, I* (Report on Income and Property Taxes, part I), Stockholm, pp. 131-133, 1923.

"Inkomstbegreppets historiska utveckling" (The Historical Development of the Concept of Income), in *Betänkande om Inkomst och Förmögenhetsskatt, II* (Swedish Government Report on Income and Property

Taxes, part II separate statements by experts). Stockholm, pp. 3-39, 1923. "Inkomstbegreppet i skattehänseende och därmed sammanhängande skattefrågor" (The Income Concept in Taxation and Tax Problems Connected with This Concept). This article was included in the government tax reports, in *Betänkande om Inkomst och Förmögenhetsskatt, II*, pp. 40-62, Stockholm, 1923. These *Betänkanden* are published as *Statens Offentliga Utredningar* (Official State Reports).

"Några Erinringar" (Some Recollections) in *Betänkande om Inkomst och Förmögenhetsskatt II*, pp. 63-70, Official Government Reports, 70; 1923. This same article first appeared in *Ekonomisk Tidskrift*, 25 (1923), 77-86, from which source it was reprinted and incorporated in the official statements of the government tax experts' report.

"Realkapital och kapitalränta" (Real Capital and Interest), *ET*, 25 (1923), 145-180. This article, a review and a mathematical elucidation of the analysis in G. Åkerman's *Realkapital und Kapitalzins* (Lund), 1923-24), has also been translated into English as Appendix II to Vol. 1 of *Lectures on Political Economy*, pp. 258-299.

"Tullskydd och frihandel" (Protective Tariffs and Free Trade), *ET*, 26 (1924), 149-164.

"Ett skolexempel i tullfrågan" (A Class-Room Case on The Tariff Question), *ET*, 27 (1925), 23-42.

"Det definitiva ordnanet av världens penningväsen" (The Definitive Regulation of the World's Monetary System), *Nationalekonomisk Föreningens Förhandlinger* (Proceedings of National Economic Association), *ET*, 27 (1925), 85-100.

"Matematisk nationalekonomi" (Mathematical Economics), *ET*, 27 (1925), 103-125. This article, a searching review of Bowley's *The Mathematical Groundwork of Economics* (1924) was translated into German and published as "Mathematische Nationalökonomie" in *Archiv für Sozialwissenschaft*, 58 (1927), 252-281, with an introduction by J. A. Schumpeter.

"Valutaspörsmålet i de skandinaviska länderna" (The Monetary Problems of the Scandinavian Countries), *ET*, 27 (1925), 205-222. This article has been translated into English as Appendix I to the English edition of *Interest and Prices*, under the title "The Monetary Problem of the Scandinavian Countries," pp. 199-219.

"Zur Zinstheorie (Böhm-Bawerks Dritter Grund)," in *Wirtschaftstheorie der Gegenwart*, edited by Hans Mayer, vol. 3, pp. 199-209. Vienna, 1928.

Selected Papers in Economic Theory, edited by E. Lindahl, London, 1958.

General Works

Åkerman, G. *Realkapital und Kapitalzins*. Stockholm, 1923-1924. 2 vols.

Böhm-Bawerk, E. von. *Geschichte und Kritik der Kapitalzinstheorien*. Vienna, 1880.

——. *Positive Theorie des Kapitalzinses*. Vienna, 1888. 2 vols. References in the text are to the 4th edition, Jena, 1921.

————. "Einige strittige Fragen der Kapitalstheorie," *Kleinere Abhändlungen.* Vienna, 1922. Pp. 123 ff.

Bowley, A. *Mathematical Groundwork of Economics.* Oxford, 1924.

Cassel, G. *Nature and Necessity of Interest.* London, 1903.

————. *Dyrtid och sedelöverflöd* (Inflation and Excessive Note Issue). Stockholm, 1917.

————. *Theoretische Sozialökonomie.* 1918. An English translation: *Theory of Social Economy.* London, 1923.

————. *Money and the Foreign Exchanges since 1914.* London, 1922.

Clark, J. B. *The Distribution of Wealth.* New York, 1899.

Cournot, A. *Researches into the Mathematical Principles of the Theory of Wealth.* 1838, N. Bacon translation, 1897; New York, 1929.

Davidson, D. *Bidrag till Läran för Kapitalbildningen* (Contribution to the Theory of Capital Formation). Stockholm, 1879.

Dobb, M. *Soviet Development Since 1917.* London, 1947.

Fellner, W. J. *Competition Among the Few.* New York, 1949.

Fisher, I. *Interest and Appreciation.* New York, 1896.

————. *The Rate of Interest.* New York, 1907.

————. *The Purchasing Power of Money.* New York, 1911.

Fleisher, W. *Sweden, The Welfare State.* New York, 1956.

Giffen, R. *Essays in Finance.* London, 1886.

Giöbel-Lilja, I. *Gustav Cassell—En Livsskildring* (Gustav Cassel—A Biography). Stockholm, 1948.

Gårdlund, T. *The Life of Knut Wicksell.* Stockholm, 1958.

Hammarskjöld, D. *Konjunkturspridningen* (The Diffusion of Business Fluctuations). Stockholm, 1933.

Hansen, A. *Monetary Theory and Fiscal Policy.* New York, 1949.

Harrod, R. G. *The Trade Cycle.* London, 1936.

Hayek, F. A. von, ed. *Beiträge zur Geldtheorie.* Vienna, 1933.

————. *Prices and Production.* London, 1934.

————. *Profits Interest and Investment.* London, 1939.

————. *The Pure Theory of Capital.* London, 1940.

————. *The Road to Serfdom.* London, 1944.

Heckscher, E. *Bidrag till Sveriges Sociala Historia Under och efter Världskriget* (A Contribution to the Social History of Sweden during and after the World War). Stockholm, 1926. 2 vols. Later translated and incorporated in *Sweden, Norway, Denmark and Iceland during the World War,* Yale University, 1930.

Hicks, J. R. *Theory of Wages.* London, 1932.

————. *Value and Capital.* Oxford, 1939.

————. *A Contribution to the Theory of the Trade Cycle.* Oxford, 1950.

Hutchison, T. W. *A Review of Economic Doctrines 1870-1929.* Oxford, 1953.

Keynes, J. M., ed. *Official Papers of Alfred Marshall.* Cambridge, 1926.

————. *A Treatise on Money.* London, 1930-1931.

————. *The General Theory of Employment, Interest and Money.* London, 1936.

Landgren, K. G., *Economics in Modern Sweden*. Library of Congress, Reference Division, Washington, D. C., 1957.

Lindahl, E. *Die Gerechtigkeit der Besteuerung*. Lund, 1919.

——. *Penningpolitikens Mål* (The Aims of Monetary Policy). Malmö, 1929.

——. *Penningpolitikens Medel* (The Means of Monetary Policy). Malmö, 1929.

——. *Studies in the Theory of Money and Capital*. New York, 1939.

Lindahl, E., Dahlgren, and Kock, *National Income of Sweden, 1861-1930*. London, 1937.

Malthus, R. T. *The Principle of Population* (1803), 7th ed., London, 1872.

——. *Principles of Political Economy* (1826). Reprinted, London, 1936.

Marshall, A. *Economics of Industry*. London, 1879.

——. *Principles of Economics* (1890). 8th ed., London, 1920.

——. *Money, Credit, and Commerce*. London, 1922.

Menger, Carl. *Grundsätze der Volkswirtschaftslehre* (1871). London, 1934. An English translation: *Principles of Economics*. Glencoe, Ill., 1950.

——. *Principles of Political Economy*. 7th ed., 1872, edited by W. J. Ashley.

Mises, L. von. *Theorie des Geldes und der Umlaufsmittel*. Vienna, 1912. An English translation: *The Theory of Money and Credit*. London, 1934.

Myrdal, G. *Monetary Equilibrium*. London, 1939.

——. *Finanspolitikens Ekonomiska Verkningar* (Economic Effects of Fiscal Policy). Stockholm, 1934.

——. *Prisbildningproblemet och Föränderligheten* (The Problem of Price Formation in Conditions of Change). Stockholm, 1927.

Ohlin, B. *Penningpolitik, Offentliga Arbeten, Subventioner och Tullar som Medel mot Arbetslöshet* (Monetary Policy, Public Works, Subsidies, and Tariffs as Means against Unemployment). Stockholm, 1934.

Pareto, V. *Cours d'économie politique*. Lausanne, 1896.

——. *Manuel d'économie politique*, Paris, 1906.

Patinkin, D. *Money, Interest, and Prices*. Evanston, Illinois, 1956.

Ricardo, D. "High Price of Bullion" (1811), "Proposals for an Economical and Secure Currency" (1816), in *Ricardo's Economic Essays*, edited by E. C. K. Gonner, London, 1926.

——. *Principles of Political Economy and Taxation* (1817), E. C. K. Gonner edition, London, 1891.

Robertson, D. H. *Banking Policy and the Price Level*. Cambridge, 1926.

Smith, Adam. *The Wealth of Nations* (1776), Modern Library (Cannan) edition, New York, 1937.

Stigler, G. J. *Production and Distribution Theories*. New York, 1941.

Thomas, B. *Monetary Policy and Crises—A Study of Swedish Experience*. London, 1936.

Tooke, T. *Inquiry into the Currency Principle*, London, 1846.

Tooke, T., and W. Newmarch. *History of Prices and the State of Circulation 1792-1856*. London, 1838-1857. 4 vols.

Walras, L. *Élements d'économie politique pure*. Paris, 1874.

——. *Theorie de la monnaie*. Paris, 1884.

Whittaker, E. *History of Economic Ideas.* New York, 1940.

Wicksteed, P. *Coordination of the Laws of Distribution.* 1894, London, 1934.

Wieser, F. von. *Der Natürliche Wert.* Vienna, 1889. An English translation: *Natural Value.* New York, 1893.

———. *Theorie der Gesellschaftlichen Wirtschaft.* Tübingen, 1914.

Articles

Åkerman, G. "Inflation, penningmängd och penningränta" (Inflation, Money Quantity, and Interest Rates), *ET*, 23 (1921), 143-162.

———. "Inflation, penningmängd och ränta," (Inflation, Money Quantity, and Interest), *ET*, 24 (1922), 5-9.

Black, D. "Wicksell's Principle in the Distribution of Taxation," in *Economic Essays in Commemoration of the Dundee School of Economics 1931-1955*, J. K. Eastman (editor), Dundee, Scotland (1955), pp. 7-23.

Böhm-Bawerk, E. von. "Grundzüge der Theorie des wirtschaftlichen Güterwertes," *Conrads Jahrbücher.* Jena, 1886.

Bowley, A. "Note on Bilateral Monopoly" *Economic Journal*, XXXVIII (1928), 651-665.

Brisman, S. "Kapitalet och kapitalräntan" (Capital and Interest), *ET*, 14 (1912), 89-121.

———. "Professor Wicksell's framställning av kapitalet och kapitalräntan" (Professor Wicksell's Treatment of Capital and Interest), *ET*, 14 (1912), 157-170.

———. "Ännu några ord om kapitalet och kaptalräntan" (Once More Concerning Capital and Interest), *ET*, 14 (1912), 399-416.

Brock, F. H-son. "Till frågan om fördelningen och kriserna" (The Problem of Distribution and Crises), *ET*, 12 (1910), 190-200.

———. "Om möjligheten för a 'Compensated Dollar' " (Concerning the Possibility of 'A Compensated Dollar'), *ET*, 15 (1913), 218-226.

———. "Ännu något om möjligheten för 'A Compensated Dollar' " (Once More on the Possibility of 'A Compensated Dollar'), *ET*, 15 (1913), 264-271.

Cassell, G. "Om skatteincidens" (Concerning Incidence of Taxation), *ET*, 1 (1899), 316-328.

———. "Ytterligare om överflyttning av skatt" (More About the Shifting of Taxation), *ET*, 1 (1899), 383-387.

———. "Kriser och Dåliga tider" (Crises and Bad Times), *ET*, 6 (1904), 80-111; 311-331.

———."Riksbanken och dyrtiden" (The Riksbank and Inflation), *ET*, 19 (1917), 291-294.

Davidson, D. "Thornton om penningränta och varupris" (Thornton on Interest and Prices), *ET*, 18 (1916), 391-393.

———. "K. Wicksell 'Geldzins und Güterpreise,' " a review, *ET*, 1 (1899), 233-240.

———. "Något om begreppet penningens värde" (Concerning the Concept Value of Money), *ET*, 8 (1906), 460-468.

———. "Om stabiliseringen af penningens värde" (Concerning Stabilization of Value of Money), *ET*, 11 (1909), 1-25.

———. "Replik (till Wicksell)" (Reply [to Wicksell]), *ET*, 11 (1909), 67-68.

———. "I Fishers förslag att reglera penningens köpkraft" (I. Fisher's Proposal to Regulate the Purchasing Power of Money), *ET*, 15 (1913), 87-107.

———. "Anmärkningar till Doc Brocks uppsats" (Comments on Brock's Article), *ET*, 15 (1913), 227-228.

———. "Penningfonder och penningens värde" (Money-Funds and the Value of Money), *ET*, 16 (1914), 128-133.

———. "Till frågan om penningens värde under kriget" (On the Problem of Value of Money during the War), *ET*, 17 (1915), 415-423.

———. "Om exportavgifter och importpremier såsom medel mot dyrtiden" (On Export Duties and Import Premia as Measures Against Inflation), *ET*, 18 (1916), 268-277, 347-350.

———. "Ännu några ord om Wicksells botemedel mot dyrtiden" (A Few Words More About Wicksell's Measures against Inflation), *ET*, 18 (1916), 374-378.

———. "Den Pågående starka sedelstegringen i Sverige" (The Continued Increase in Note Issue in Sweden), *ET*, 20 (1918), 87-106.

———. "Spridda studier angående prisnivåstegringen" (Occasional Studies Concerning the Rise in the Price Level), *ET*, 20 (1918), 119-133.

———. "Riksbankens sedelutgivning" (Riksbank's Issuance of Notes), *ET*, 20 (1918), 87-106.

———. "Frågan om penningvärdets reglering" (The Problem of Controlling the Value of Money), *ET*, 20 (1918), 283-288.

———. "Ransonering av kapital än en gång" (Capital Rationing Once More), *ET*, 20 (1918), 289-298.

———. "Några teoretiska frågor" (Some Theoretical Questions), *ET*, 21 (1919), 221-259.

———. "Valutaproblemets teoretiska innebörd" (Theoretical Implications of the Problem of Value of Money), *ET*, 22 (1920), 71-123.

———. "Om begreppet normal penningränta" (On the Concept of Normal Interest Rate), *ET*, 24 (1922), 13-30.

———. "Till frågan om penningvärdets reglering under kriget och därefter" (On the Problem of the Regulation of the Value of Money during and after the War,) *ET*, 24 (1922), 89-114. Another article of the same title in *ET*, 25 (1923), 191-234.

———. "Riksbanken och penningens värde under kristiden" (The Riksbank and the Value of Money during the Crisis-period), *ET*, 27 (1925), 1-22.

———. "Varuvärde och penningvärde" (Value of Commodities and Value of Money), *ET*, 28 (1926), 1-18.

———. "Knut Wicksell och varuvärdet" (Knut Wicksell and the Value of Commodities), *ET*, 36 (1934), 21-25.

Fellner, W. J. "Wages and Prices under Bilateral Monopoly," *Quarterly Journal of Economics*, LXI (August, 1947), 503-532.

Hayek, F. A. von, "Das Intertemporale Gleichgewichtssystem der Preise und die Bewegung des 'Geldwertes,' " *Weltwirtschaftliches Archiv,* 1928, pp. 33 ff.

―――. "The Development of the Doctrine of Forced Saving," *Quarterly Journal of Economics,* XLVI (November, 1932).

―――. "The Nature and History of the Problem," chap. i, p. 1-41, and "The Present State of the Debate," chap. v, pp. 201-241, in *Collectivistic Economic Planning,* edited by Hayek, F. H. von, *et al.* London, 1935.

―――. "The Mythology of Capital," *Quarterly Journal of Economics,* L (February, 1936). Reprinted in *Readings in the Theory of Income Distribution,* American Economic Association, 1946.

Keynes, J. M. "Alfred Marshall 1842-1924," pp. 1-66, in *Memorials of Alfred Marshall,* editor, A. C. Pigou, London, 1925.

Knight, F. H. "Professor Hayek and the Theory of Investment" *Economic Journal,* XLV (1935), 77 ff.

―――. "The Quantity of Capital and the Interest Rate," *Journal of Political Economy,* August, 1936, reprinted in *Readings in the Theory of Income Distribution,* American Economic Association, 1946.

―――. "On the Theory of Capital—Reply to Mr. Kaldor" *Econometrica,* 6 (1938), 82 ff.

―――. "The Quantity of Capital and the Interest Rate," *Journal of Political Economy,* August, 1936, pp. 484 ff.

Knight, F. H. "Capital and Interest," reprinted in *Readings in the Theory of Income Distribution,* American Economic Association, 1946.

Lexis, W. "K. Wicksell—'Über Wert, Kapital und Rente,' " a review, *Schmollers Jahrbuch,* XIX (1895), 332 ff.

Marshall, A. "Remedies for Fluctuation of General Prices," *Contemporary Review,* March, 1887, reprinted in *Memorials of Alfred Marshall,* edited by A. C. Pigou, pp. 188-211, London, 1925.

Myrdal, G. "Der Gleichegewichtsbegriff als Instrument der Geldtheoretischen Analyse," *Beiträge zur Zinstheorie,* Vienna, 1933.

―――. "Kring den praktiska nationalekonomiska problematiken om penningtheoretisk jämnvikt: En studie över 'Normala räntan' i Wicksells penninglära" (Concerning the Practical Problem of Monetary Equilibrium: A Study of 'Normal Interest' in Wicksell's Doctrine of Money), *ET,* 33 (1931), 191-302.

Ohlin, B. "Något om prisstegring, inflation och valutapolitik," (Concerning Rising Prices, Inflation, and Monetary Policy), *ET,* 23 (1921), 55-69.

―――. "Some Notes on the Stockholm Theory of Saving and Investment," *Economic Journal,* XLVII (March, 1937), 53 ff., reprinted in *Readings in Business Cycle Theory,* American Economic Association, 1944.

Palander, T. "On the Concepts and Methods of the Stockholm School," *International Economic Papers,* 3 (1953), 5-57.

Uhr, C. G. "Knut Wicksell—A Centennial Evaluation," *American Economic Review,* XLI: 5 (Dec. 1951), 829-860.

Walras, L. "Theorie Mathematique du Billet de Banque," *Bull. Soc. Vaud. Scient,* XVI (1879).

INDEX